Conrad Carlberg's Microsoft Series

STATISTICAL ANALYSIS:
Microsoft® Excel 2013

MORE PREDICTIVE ANALYTICS:
Microsoft® Excel®

REGRESSION ANALYSIS
Microsoft® Excel®

R FOR MICROSOFT® EXCEL USERS
Making the Transition for Statistical Analysis

Visit **informit.com/carlberg** for a complete list of available publications.

Conrad Carlberg, a nationally recognized expert on quantitative analysis and data analysis applications, shows you how to use Excel to perform a wide variety of analyses to solve real-world business problems. Employing a step-by-step tutorial approach, Carlberg delivers clear explanations of proven Excel techniques that can help you increase revenue, reduce costs, and improve productivity. With each book comes an extensive collection of Excel workbooks you can adapt to your own projects. Conrad's books will show you how to:

- Build powerful, credible, and reliable forecasts
- Use smoothing techniques to build accurate predictions from trended and seasonal baselines
- Employ Excel's regression-related worksheet functions to model and analyze dependent and independent variables—and benchmark the results against R
- Use decision analytics to evaluate relevant information critical to the business decision-making process

Written using clear language in a straightforward, no-nonsense style, Carlberg makes data analytics easy to learn and incorporate into your business.

Pearson

informIT.com
the trusted technology learning source

O'REILLY®
Safari

Predictive Analytics: Microsoft® Excel

Conrad Carlberg

800 East 96th Street,
Indianapolis, Indiana 46240 USA

Contents at a Glance

Predictive Analytics: Microsoft® Excel

ISBN-13: 978-0-7897-5835-4
ISBN-10: 0-7897-5835-0

Library of Congress Control Number: 2017941428

Printed in the United States of America

1   17

Trademarks

All terms mentioned in this book that are known to be trademarks or service marks have been appropriately capitalized. Que Publishing cannot attest to the accuracy of this information. Use of a term in this book should not be regarded as affecting the validity of any trademark or service mark.

Microsoft is a registered trademark of Microsoft Corporation.

Warning and Disclaimer

Special Sales

For information about buying this title in bulk quantities, or for special sales opportunities (which may include electronic versions; custom cover designs; and content particular to your business, training goals, marketing focus, or branding interests), please contact our corporate sales department at corpsales@pearsoned.com or (800) 382-3419.

For government sales inquiries, please contact governmentsales@pearsoned.com.

For questions about sales outside the U.S., please contact intlcs@pearson.com.

Editor-in-Chief
Greg Wiegand

Acquisitions Editor
Trina MacDonald

Development Editor
Charlotte Kughen

Managing Editor
Sandra Schroeder

Project Editor
Mandie Frank

Indexer
Cheryl Lenser

Proofreader
Abigail Manheim

Technical Editor
Michael Turner

Publishing Coordinator
Courtney Martin

Designer
Chuti Prasertsith

Compositor
codeMantra

Contents

About the Author

Conrad Carlberg (www.conradcarlberg.com) is a nationally recognized expert on quantitative analysis and on data analysis and management applications such as Microsoft Excel, SAS, and Oracle. He holds a Ph.D. in statistics from the University of Colorado and is a many-time recipient of Microsoft's Excel MVP designation.

Carlberg is a Southern California native. After college he moved to Colorado, where he worked for a succession of startups and attended graduate school. He spent two years in the Middle East, teaching computer science and dodging surly camels. After finishing graduate school, Carlberg worked at US West (a Baby Bell) in product management and at Motorola.

In 1995, he started a small consulting business that provides design and analysis services to companies that want to guide their business decisions by means of quantitative analysis—approaches that today we group under the term "analytics." He enjoys writing about those techniques and, in particular, how to carry them out using the world's most popular numeric analysis application, Microsoft Excel.

Acknowledgments

My particular thanks go to Charlotte Kughen and Michael Turner. Charlotte has guided the development of my books in the past, and Michael has provided technical suggestions that simplify and clarify. I was delighted to learn that they would be working on this book. And my thanks as well to Trina MacDonald for pulling it all together.

We Want to Hear from You!

We welcome your comments. You can email or write to let us know what you did or didn't like about this book—as well as what we can do to make our books better.

Please note that we cannot help you with technical problems related to the topic of this book.

When you write, please be sure to include this book's title and author as well as your name and email address. We will carefully review your comments and share them with the author and editors who worked on the book.

Email: feedback@quepublishing.com

Mail: Que Publishing
         ATTN: Reader Feedback
         800 East 96th Street
         Indianapolis, IN 46240 USA

Reader Services

Register your copy of Predictive Analytics: Microsoft® Excel at quepublishing.com for convenient access to downloads, updates, and corrections as they become available. To start the registration process, go to informit.com/register and log in or create an account*. Enter the product ISBN, 9780789758354, and click Submit. Once the process is complete, you will find any available bonus content under Registered Products.

*Be sure to check the box that you would like to hear from us in order to receive exclusive discounts on future editions of this product.

INTRODUCTION TO THE 2013 EDITION

A few years ago, a new word started to show up on my personal reading lists: *analytics*. It threw me for a while because I couldn't quite figure out what it really meant.

In some contexts, it seemed to mean the sort of numeric analysis that for years my compatriots and I had referred to as *stats* or *quants*. Ours is a living language and neologisms are often welcome. McJob. Brexit. Yadda yadda yadda.

Welcome or not, *analytics* has elbowed its way into our jargon. It does seem to connote quantitative analysis, including both descriptive and inferential statistics, with the implication that what is being analyzed is likely to be web traffic: hits, conversions, bounce rates, click paths, and so on. (That implication seems due to Google's Analytics software, which collects statistics on website traffic.)

Furthermore, there are at least two broad, identifiable branches to analytics: *decision* and *predictive*:

■ *Decision analytics* has to do with classifying (mainly) people into segments of interest to the analyst. This branch of analytics depends heavily on multivariate statistical analyses, such as cluster analysis and multidimensional scaling. Decision analytics also uses a method called *logistic regression* to deal with the special problems created by dependent variables that are binary or nominal, such as buys versus doesn't buy and survives versus doesn't survive.

■ *Predictive analytics* deals with forecasting, and often employs techniques that have been used for decades. Exponential smoothing (also termed exponentially weighted moving averages or EWMA) is one such technique, as is autoregression. Box-Jenkins analysis dates to the middle of the twentieth century and comprises the moving average and regression approaches to forecasting.

Of course, these two broad branches aren't mutually exclusive. There's no clear dividing line between situations in which you would use one and not the other, although that's often the case. But you can certainly find yourself asking questions such as these:

- I've classified my current database of prospects into likely buyers and likely non-buyers, according to demographics such as age, income, ZIP Code, and education level. Can I create a credible quarterly forecast of purchase volume if I apply the same classification criteria to a data set consisting of *past* prospects?

- I've extracted two principal components from a set of variables that measure the weekly performance of several product lines over the past two years. How do I forecast the performance of the products for the next quarter using the principal components as the outcome measures?

So, there can be overlap between decision analytics and predictive analytics. But not always—sometimes all you want to do is forecast, say, product revenue without first doing any classification or multivariate analysis. Still, at times you believe there's a need to forecast the behavior of segments or of components that aren't directly measurable. It's in that sort of situation that the two broad branches, decision and predictive analytics, nourish one another.

You, Analytics, and Excel

Can you do analytics—either kind—using Excel? Sure. Excel has a large array of tools that bear directly on analytics, including various mathematical and statistical functions that calculate logarithms, regression statistics, matrix multiplication and inversion, and many of the other tools needed for different kinds of analytics.

But not all the tools are native to Excel. For example, some situations call for you to use logistic regression: a technique that can work much better than ordinary least-squares regression when you have an outcome variable that takes on a very limited range of values, perhaps only two. The odds ratio is the workhorse of logistic regression, but although Excel offers a generous supply of least-squares functions, it doesn't offer a maximum likelihood odds ratio function.

Nevertheless, the tools are there. Using native Excel worksheet functions and formulas, you can build the basic model needed to do logistic regression. And if you apply Excel's Solver add-in to that model, you can turn out logistic regression analyses that match anything you can get from SAS, R, or any similar application designed specifically for statistical analysis. Furthermore, when you build the analysis yourself you can arrange for all the results that you might find of interest. There's no need to rely on someone else's sense of what matters. Most important, you maintain control over what's going on in the analysis.

Similarly, if you're trying to make sense of the relationships between the individual variables in a 20-by-20 correlation matrix, principal components analysis is a good place to start, and often represents the first step in more complex analyses, such as factor analysis with different kinds of axis rotation. Simple matrix algebra makes it a snap to get factor loadings and factor coefficients, and Excel has native worksheet functions that transpose, multiply, and invert matrices—and get their determinants with a simple formula.

This branch of analytics is often called *data reduction*, and it makes it feasible to forecast from an undifferentiated mass of individual variables. You do need some specialized software in the form of an Excel add-in to extract the components in the first place, and that software is supplied via download with this book.

Now, if you're already an analytics maven, you might have little need for a book like this one. You probably have access to specialized software that returns the results of logistic regression, that detects and accounts for seasonality in a time series, that determines how many principal components to retain by testing residual matrices, and so on.

But that specialized software sometimes tends to be singularly uninformative regarding the analysis. Figure I.1 shows a typical example.

Figure I.1

A logistic regression analysis prepared using the freeware statistical analysis application R.

```
> summary(mlogit.model)

Call:
mlogit(formula = Purchase ~ 1 | Income + Age + Zip, data = Pchsdata,
    reflevel = "1")

Frequencies of alternatives:
      1       0
0.38889 0.61111

Newton-Raphson maximisation
gradient close to zero. May be a solution
6 iterations, 0h:0m:0s
g'(-H)^-1g = 6.89E-27

Coefficients :
                Estimate Std. Error t-value Pr(>|t|)
alt0          20.000501  8.595602  2.3268 0.019974 *
alt0:Income   -0.091115  0.032594 -2.7955 0.005182 **
alt0:Age      -0.126686  0.120781 -1.0489 0.294228
alt0:Zip      -2.584307  1.057398 -2.4440 0.014524 *
---
Signif. codes:  0 '***' 0.001 '**' 0.01 '*' 0.05 '.' 0.1 ' ' 1

Log-Likelihood: -14.16
McFadden R^2:  0.71627
Likelihood ratio test : chisq = 19.794 (p.value=0.00018731)
> |
```

R is a fairly popular statistics application that, like all applications, has its fair share of detractors. (I use it, but mostly for confirmation and benchmarking purposes, and that's how I use it in a couple of chapters in this book.) Its documentation is terse and dense. It can take much more work than it should to determine what a particular number in the output represents and how it was calculated. If you're an experienced R user, you've probably tracked down all that information and feel perfectly comfortable with it.

If you're like many of the rest of us, you want to see intermediate results. You want to see the individual odds ratios that come together in an overall likelihood ratio. You want to know if the Newton-Raphson algorithm used a "multistart" option. In short, you want to know more about the analysis than R (or SAS or Stata or SPSS, for that matter) provides.

Excel as a Platform

And that's one major reason I wrote this book. For years I have believed that so-called "advanced" statistical analysis does not require a greater degree of intelligence or imagination for understanding. That understanding tends to require more work, though, because there are more steps involved in getting from the raw data to the end product.

That makes Excel an ideal platform for working your way through a problem in analytics. Excel does not offer a tool that automatically and credibly determines the best method to forecast from a given baseline of data and then applies that method on your behalf. It does give you the tools to make that determination yourself and use its results to build your own forecasts.

On your way to the forecast, you can view the results of the intermediate steps. And more often than not, you can alter the inputs to see the effects of your edits: Is the outcome robust with respect to minor changes in the inputs? Or can a single small change make a major difference in the model that you're building? That's the sort of insight that you can create very easily in Excel but that comes only with much more effort in an application that is focused primarily on statistical analysis.

I would argue that if you're responsible for making a forecast, if you're directly involved in a predictive analytics project, you should also be directly involved at each step of the process. Because Excel gives you the tools but in general not the end result, it's an excellent way to familiarize yourself not only with how an analytic method works generally but also how it works with a particular data set.

What's in This Book

Because the term "analytics" is so wide-ranging, a single book on the topic necessarily has to do some picking and choosing. I wanted to include material that would enable you to acquire data from websites that engage in consumer commerce. But if you're going to deploy Google Analytics, or one of its more costly derivatives, on Amazon.com, then you have to own Amazon.com.

Of course, there are ways to use Excel and its data acquisition capabilities to get your hands on data from sites you don't own. I've been doing so for years to track the sales of my own books on sites such as Amazon. I have tens of thousands of data points to use as a predictive baseline and much more often than not I can forecast with great accuracy the number of copies of a given book that will be sold next month. I start this book showing you the way I use Excel to gather this information for me 24 × 7.

It seemed to me that the most valuable tools in the analytics arsenal are logistic regression, data reduction techniques, and Box-Jenkins forecasting. Logistic regression underlies everything from studies of predictive survival curves used by oncologists to the marketing programs designed to sell distressed resort properties. The singular aspect of that sort of work is that the outcome variable has two, or at most a few, nominal values. In this book, I discuss both the binomial analysis traditionally employed to assess that sort of data and the benefits—and drawbacks—of using logistic regression instead. You also see how to perform a logistic regression directly on an Excel worksheet, assisted by Excel's Solver (which does tell you whether or not you're using a multistart option).

As introduction to the more involved techniques of factor analysis, I discuss the rationale and methods for principal components analysis. Again, you can manage the analysis directly on the Excel worksheet, but you're assisted by VBA code that takes care of the initial extraction of the components from the raw data or, if you prefer, from a correlation matrix.

And this book addresses the techniques of forecasting in several chapters. Regression and autoregression get their own treatments, as do moving averages and the extension of that technique to exponential smoothing. Finally, I introduce ARIMA, which brings together autoregression and moving averages under one umbrella. The most exacting part of ARIMA analysis, the derivation of the autocorrelation and the partial autocorrelation coefficients from a baseline of data, is handled for you in open source VBA code that accompanies this book—so you can see for yourself exactly how it's done.

INTRODUCTION TO THIS EDITION

Back in 2012 when I was writing the first edition of this book, I really had no good clue as to how it would perform in the marketplace. As things turned out, the book was welcomed by its intended audience.

Oh, some people didn't get what they thought they were buying when they purchased the book. And they let me know about it. So I'd like to stress a few points right off the bat:

■ The book's 2013 edition came with at least one Excel workbook for each chapter, so that the reader could more easily follow the discussion of each analytic technique. The workbooks could be downloaded from the publisher's website. The same is true of this edition.

■ As before, we're putting the publisher's URL on the book's back cover, but we're using a larger typeface. It's repeated here anyway: www.que-publishing.com/title/9780789758354.

■ Also as before, this is not a book about acquiring statistics on Internet traffic and customer behavior during visits to websites. It continues to be about what you can do with that data—and various other types of information—*after* you have acquired it.

■ Like General Sternwood's butler in *The Big Sleep*, I make many mistakes. I do try to correct them. So, *not* as before, we have included the automated data collection function described in Chapter 1 as a standalone workbook. The first edition of the book showed a couple of the workbook's sheets and some of its VBA code. Quite a few people thought that we should have included the entire workbook.

In this edition I have added material that extends the reach of the analytic procedures. For example, I have expanded the material on forecasting by means of exponential smoothing, such as material on Holt-Winters methods, which analyze baselines that are trended *and* that have seasonal components. Microsoft has chosen to include a Forecast Sheet in Excel 2016, so you might want to compare its results with those returned by Holt-Winters and by different time series packages in R. In fact, I urge you to do so. (I have included some R commands to replicate these analyses in Chapter 5, "More Advanced Smoothing Models.")

Speaking of R, I like to use it to confirm analyses I've prepared in Excel. Chapter 8, "Logistic Regression: Further Issues," and Chapter 9, "Multinomial Logistic Regression," now discuss how to carry out logistic regression using R's functions. Those functions include one that is fairly easy to use but is limited to binomial outcomes, and one whose syntax is more arcane but can handle multinomial outcomes.

Why would you not use R for all your statistical analysis? Why use Excel at all? I think there are some very sound reasons. Here are two:

Inside the Black Box

If you are using this book as a means of learning how certain analytic procedures take place—why they work, what the internal calculations are all about—then an application such as Excel is an ideal platform.

Take logistic regression, for example. That sort of analysis stands on three legs: odds ratios, logarithms and maximum likelihood estimation. If you carry out a logistic regression analysis in Excel using formulas and functions on the worksheet, you can see for yourself how the tools get you from a raw data set to an equation that enables you to predict outcomes that are measured on a nominal scale.

Because you're forced to construct the analysis in the worksheet, you can't help but see how odds ratios protect you from probabilities that exceed 100%, how logarithms protect you against probabilities that fall below 0%, and how Excel's Solver uses the logs of the odds to arrive at the logistic regression equation.

If you're a student of analytics, you'll learn about these techniques much more thoroughly if you assemble them yourself than if you simply read about them—or if you depend on the results of a function that tells you little more than the equation's intercept and coefficients.

Helping Out Your Colleagues

Unless you work or study in a statistical lab, very few of your colleagues are apt to have R or some other specifically statistical application such as SAS or SPSS. But most of them probably have Excel running on their computers. Their comfort level with Excel is probably relatively high, and with SAS, relatively low.

You might work with someone who needs to understand what's going on with an analytic procedure but doesn't have the background to decode the often mysterious labels and numbers that characterize the output of most specifically statistical analysis. Suppose that you could use Excel to show that person how SAS (or an external consultant who uses SAS) got from the raw data to the prediction equation and its confidence intervals. If you could do so, that person will usually come much closer to understanding what the analysis has to say about customers, about patients, about future revenues—in short, anything that your business or institution wants or needs to subject to analytic processes.

And I promise you that the colleagues who are well versed in Excel will appreciate seeing the analyses in a platform they feel comfortable with, rather than in one that seems designed to make them feel as though they're not up to the task.

Perhaps, like me, you have run a smoothing analysis in R and you get back results that you can't reconcile with what you know about the data. In that case it's good to check the results against what you can get back from Excel. An application such as R or SPSS returns static results, so if you need to experiment with the baseline to determine how an unexpected result might have come about, you have to rerun the analysis with revised data.

But if you're working with Excel, you can alter an observation or two to see how that might affect the outcome of the analysis. This is one of Excel's great strengths as compared to strictly statistical packages: the ability to use the volatile nature of its formulas to produce immediate recalculation (and re-charting, for that matter).

In sum, an application such as Excel and one such as R can be made to produce identical results, but their architectures require that they get to the results via different routes. If you're running analytics in support of decisions that are even remotely mission-critical, you owe it to yourself to understand how those results come about. And the best way I know of to do that is to analyze it in Excel. Analyze it in R as well, by all means, if only to confirm the outcome. But there's nothing like seeing it there, in formulas on the worksheet.

Building a Collector

The word *analytics* connotes, among other notions, the idea that the raw data that gets analyzed includes quantitative measures of online browsing behavior. Data collection instruments such as Adobe Analytics and Google Analytics are useful in part because they track a variety of behavior—hits, views, downloads, buys, and so on—along with information about the source of the visit. However, there are times that you want to measure product performance but can't access the traffic data.

Suppose you supply a product that another company or companies resell on their own websites. Although those companies might share their web traffic information with you, it's more likely that they regard it as proprietary. In that case, if you want to analyze end users' purchasing behavior, you might be limited to any data that the resellers' websites make generally available.

That's the position that I'm in when it comes to sales of my books by web resellers such as Amazon. Although I hear rumors from time to time that Amazon shares data about actual sales with book authors, suppliers of music, and manufacturers of tangible products, it hasn't reached me in any particularly useful form. Maybe I'm too far down the food chain. Whatever the reason, I have to roll my own.

Fortunately, one of the sales and marketing devices that Amazon employs is product rankings. As to books, there are a couple of different rankings: overall sales, and sales within categories such as Books > Computers & Technology > Software > Microsoft > Microsoft Excel. Although as an author

I hope that my books achieve a high sales ranking in a category—that gives them greater visibility—I really hope that they achieve a nice, high overall sales ranking, which I believe to bear a closer relationship to actual sales.

So what I want to do is create a means of accessing information about books' sales rankings (including titles that compete with mine), save the data in a form that I can use for analysis, and make inferences about the results of the analysis.

In this chapter, I show you how to do just that: get analytics without the active cooperation of the website. The techniques don't require that you be interested in book sales. They can be used for anything from product sales to stock prices to yards gained per pass attempt.

Planning an Approach

Before you undertake something like the project I'm about to describe, there are a few issues you should keep in mind. If you can't think of a satisfactory way to deal with them, you might want to consider taking a completely different approach than the one I describe here.

A Meaningful Variable

The most important issue is the availability of one or more variables on a website that bear on what you're interested in, even if only indirectly.

For example, Amazon does not publish on a publicly accessible web page the number of copies of a book it has sold, whether actual, physical books or downloaded electronic copies. But as I mentioned in the prior section, Amazon does publish sales rankings. For the project described here, I decided that I could live with the sales rankings as an indicator of sales figures.

I also learned that although Amazon usually updates the sales ranking every hour, sometimes the updates don't take place. Sometimes they're a little late. Sometimes several hours pass without any update occurring. Sometimes days go by when the updates come every two hours instead of hourly. And sometimes the rankings don't entirely make sense; particularly in the wee hours, a ranking can drift from, say, 20,000 at 4:00 a.m. to 19,995 at 5:00 a.m. to 19,990 at 6:00 a.m. and so on. That kind of movement can't reflect sales, and the deltas are much smaller and more regular than at other times of day. But I found that most of the time the updates take place hourly—give or take a couple of minutes—and correspond either to no sales (the rankings get larger) or to a presumed sale (the rankings get smaller, often by a generous amount).

I have also found that on occasion the Amazon site does not recognize a query made by software other than a browser such as Google Chrome, Firefox or Internet Explorer. This sort of "outage" can last for several hours, and can come and go over a period lasting several days. During these time spans it appears that the only option is to arrive at an Amazon page manually, via one of those browsers. Otherwise I get no useful results.

Identifying Sales

I decided that I could live with changes in rankings as a stand-in for actual sales. I also decided that I could make an assumption about an increase in ranking, such as from 25,000 to 20,000. That's a big enough jump that I can assume a sale took place. I can't tell for sure how many units were sold. But these books don't sell like an adventure novel. Amazon sells four or five copies of one of my books each day. So when I see an improvement in ranking of a few thousand ranks, it almost certainly indicates the sale of a single unit.

Given that information (or, maybe more accurately, educated guesses), it's possible to get a handle on what you need to include in a workbook to access, analyze, and synthesize the data sensibly.

Planning the Workbook Structure

Your workbook needs three types of worksheets: one type to collect the data from your web queries, one type to bring the query data together in a single place, and one type to run whatever analyses you decide are needed. (You also need a VBA module to hold your code, but that is covered in a later section of this chapter.)

Those three types of worksheet are discussed in the next three sections.

Query Sheets

If you haven't used Excel to retrieve data from the Web, you might be surprised at how easy it is. I'm not speaking here of using your browser to get to a web page, selecting and copying some or part of its contents, and then pasting back into the workbook. I'm speaking of queries that can execute automatically and on a predetermined schedule, thus enabling you to walk away and let the computer gather data without you micromanaging it.

Suppose that you want to retrieve data from Amazon about a book entitled *Statistical Analysis with Excel*. You open a new workbook and rename an unused worksheet to something such as "Stats."

Next, start your browser if necessary and navigate to Amazon's page for that book. When you're there, copy the page's full address from the browser's address box—drag across the address to highlight it and either press Ctrl + C or use the browser's Edit menu to choose the Copy command.

Switch back to Excel and click the Ribbon's Data tab. Click the From Web button in the Get External Data group. The New Web Query window displays as shown in Figure 1.1.

Figure 1.1
What you see at first depends on your browser's home page.

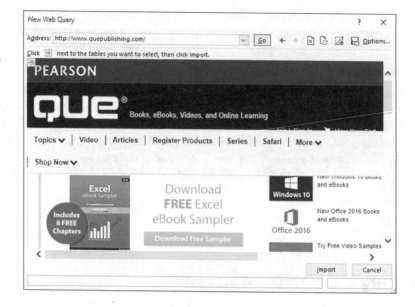

Drag through the address that appears in the Address box and press Ctrl + V to paste the address you copied. When you click the Go button, the query window opens the Amazon page (see Figure 1.2).

Figure 1.2
Web pages sometimes consist of several tables, rectangular areas that divide the page into different segments.

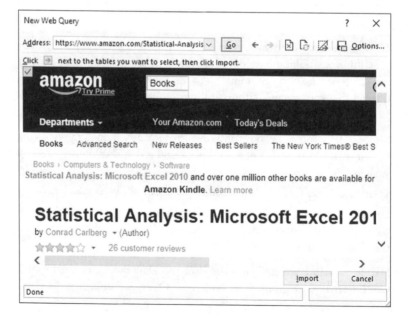

Typically you see one, and sometimes more than one, square icon (a red arrow on a yellow background) that identifies the location of part of the web page, called a *table*. You can select a table by clicking its icon. When you click one of these icons to select it, the icon turns blue to indicate that you want to download the data in that table.

I recommend that you select the entire page by clicking the icon in the upper-left corner of the window. If you select only a table or tables that contain the data you're interested in, it could easily happen that a day, week, or month from now the page might be changed, so that the data you want appears on the same page but in a different table. Then your query will miss the data.

But if you select the entire web page instead of just a table or tables, the page's owner would have to remove the data you're interested in completely for you to miss it, and in that case it wouldn't matter how much of the page you selected to download.

The individual table icons are useful mainly when you want to do a one-time-only download from a web page. Then you might want to avoid downloading a lot of extraneous stuff that would just make it harder to find the data you're after. In the type of case I'm describing here, though, you'll let Excel do the finding for you.

Furthermore, you don't save much time or bandwidth by selecting just a subset of the web page. In most cases you're picking up a couple of megabytes of text at most in an entire page.

Speed of Execution

Nevertheless, you should be aware of a speed versus version tradeoff. I have learned that using Excel 2007 and more recent versions, web queries can take significantly more time to complete than in earlier versions of Excel. Among the changes made to Excel 2007 was the addition of much more thorough checks of the data returned from web pages for malicious content.

I've found that when using an earlier version, it takes about 30 seconds to execute eight web queries in the way I'm describing here. Using Excel 2016, it takes about three times as long.

The basic intent of the project I'm describing here is to automatically and regularly update your downloaded data, so it probably seems unimportant to worry about whether the process takes half a minute or a minute and a half. Occasionally, though, for one reason or another I want to get an immediate update of the information and so I force the process to run manually. On those occasions I'd rather not wait.

> **NOTE** Microsoft has distributed a Power Query add-in for use with Excel 2013 and later. The add-in is intended to provide and extend the functionality offered by Excel 2010's Get External Data feature (discussed in this chapter section). In turn, Excel 2016's Data tab has supplanted Power Query by the tools in the Get and Transform group. I don't suggest that these changes constitute feature creep. But for the purposes of automatically importing web data into an Excel workbook, I find that both the add-in and the Get and Transform tools have much more scope than I need and are much slower than I want. Perhaps your experience will be different than mine, or perhaps Microsoft will improve them in subsequent releases.

Bringing the Data Back

After you have clicked a red-and-yellow icon to turn it blue (using, I hope, the icon in the upper-left corner of the New Web Query window so that you get the entire page), click the Import button at the bottom of the New Web Query window. After a few seconds, the Import Data window appears as shown in Figure 1.3.

Figure 1.3
You can import immediately, but it's a good idea to check the property settings first.

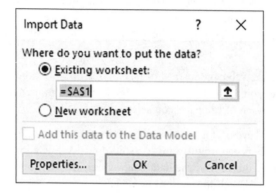

Accept the default destination of cell A1 and click OK. (The reason to use cell A1 becomes apparent when it's time to refresh the query using VBA, later in this chapter.) There are some useful properties to set, so I recommend that you click the Properties button before you complete the import. The Properties window that displays is shown in Figure 1.4.

Be sure that the Save Query Definition box is checked. That way you can repeatedly and automatically run the query without having to define it all over again.

The Enable Background Refresh checkbox requires a little explanation. If it is filled, any VBA procedure that is running continues running as the query executes, and other direct actions by the user can proceed normally. Sometimes that can cause problems if a procedure depends on the results of the query: If the procedure expects to find data that isn't available yet, you might get a runtime error or a meaningless result. Therefore, I usually clear the Enable Background Refresh checkbox.

The various options in the Properties dialog box listed under Data Formatting and Layout are subtly different but can be important. I spend three pages detailing the differences in another Que book, *Managing Data with Excel*, and I don't propose to do it again here. For present purposes, you might just as well accept the default values.

Click OK when you have made any changes you want and then click OK in the Import Data window. Excel completes the query, usually within a few seconds, and writes the results to the worksheet (see Figure 1.5).

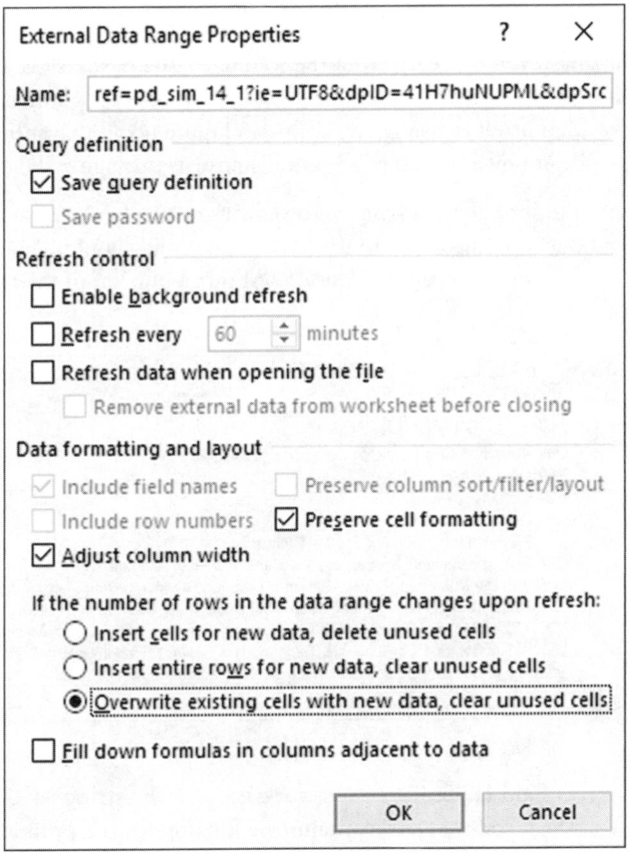

Figure 1.4
By default the Save Query Definition checkbox is filled, but you should verify the setting when you create the query.

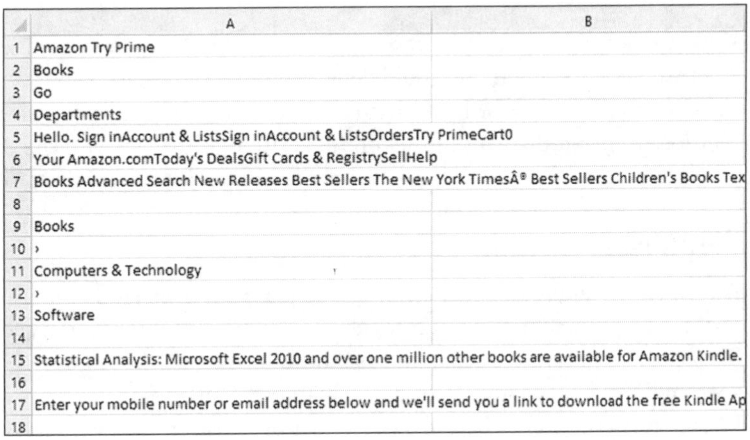

External Data Range Properties ? ✕

Name: ref=pd_sim_14_1?ie=UTF8&dpID=41H7huNUPML&dpSrc

Query definition
☑ Save query definition
☐ Save password

Refresh control
☐ Enable background refresh
☐ Refresh every 60 ⟳ minutes
☐ Refresh data when opening the file
☐ Remove external data from worksheet before closing

Data formatting and layout
☑ Include field names   ☐ Preserve column sort/filter/layout
☐ Include row numbers   ☑ Preserve cell formatting
☑ Adjust column width

If the number of rows in the data range changes upon refresh:
○ Insert cells for new data, delete unused cells
○ Insert entire rows for new data, clear unused cells
◉ Overwrite existing cells with new data, clear unused cells

☐ Fill down formulas in columns adjacent to data

OK   Cancel

Figure 1.5
When the query has finished executing, you wind up with a haystack of text and numbers. The next step is to find the needle.

	A	B
1	Amazon Try Prime	
2	Books	
3	Go	
4	Departments	
5	Hello. Sign inAccount & ListsSign inAccount & ListsOrdersTry PrimeCart0	
6	Your Amazon.comToday's DealsGift Cards & RegistrySellHelp	
7	Books Advanced Search New Releases Best Sellers The New York Times® Best Sellers Children's Books Tex	
8		
9	Books	
10	›	
11	Computers & Technology	
12	›	
13	Software	
14		
15	Statistical Analysis: Microsoft Excel 2010 and over one million other books are available for Amazon Kindle.	
16		
17	Enter your mobile number or email address below and we'll send you a link to download the free Kindle Ap	
18		

Finding the Data

After the data has been retrieved from the web page, the next task is to locate the piece or pieces of information you're looking for. I want to stress, though, that you need do this once only for each product you're tracking—and quite possibly just once for all the products. It depends on how the web page administrator is managing the data.

What you need to look for is a string of text that's normally a constant: one that doesn't change from hour to hour or day to day. That text string should be near—ideally, adjacent to—the data you want to retrieve. Figure 1.6 shows a portion of the results of a query.

Figure 1.6

In this case, the string `Sellers Rank:` in cell A296 uniquely locates the product ranking.

	A
286	Series: Statistical Analysis: Microsoft Excel 2010
287	
288	Paperback: 464 pages
289	Publisher: Que Publishing; 1 edition (May 2, 2011)
290	Language: English
291	ISBN-10: 0789747200
292	ISBN-13: 978-0789747204
293	Product Dimensions: 6.9 x 1 x 9 inches
294	Shipping Weight: 1.5 pounds (View shipping rates and policies)
295	Average Customer Review: 4.1 out of 5 stars See all reviews (26 customer reviews)
296	Amazon Best Sellers Rank: #20,881 in Books (See Top 100 in Books)
297	#18 in Books > Computers & Technology > Software > Microsoft > Microsoft Excel
298	#23 in Books > Computers & Technology > Business Technology > Software > Spreadsheets
299	#28 in Books > Business & Money > Accounting > Financial
300	
301	

If you use Excel's Find feature to scan a worksheet for the string `Sellers Rank:`, you can locate the worksheet cell that also contains the ranking for the product. With just a little more work, which you can easily automate and which I describe in the next section about VBA code, you can isolate the actual ranking from the surrounding text; it's that ranking that you're after.

Why not just note the cell address where the ranking is found after the query is finished? That would work fine if you could depend on the web page's layout remaining static. But the website administrator has only to add an extra line, or remove one, above the data's current location, and that will throw off the location of the cell with the data you're after. No, you have to look for it each time, and the Find operation takes place very quickly anyway.

Summary Sheets

After you've acquired the data from a web page and isolated the figure you're looking for, you need a place to put that figure, plus other relevant information such as date and time. That place is normally a separate worksheet. You expect to be querying the same web page repeatedly, as hours and days elapse. Therefore, you'll want to store information that you've already retrieved somewhere that won't get overwritten the next time the query runs.

So, establish an unused worksheet and name it something appropriate such as *Summary* or *Synthesis* or *All Products*. There are a few structural rules covered in the next section that you'll find helpful to follow. But you can include some other useful analyses on the summary sheet, as long as they don't interfere with the basic structure.

Structuring the Summary Sheet

Figure 1.7 shows some of the structures that I put on my summary sheet.

Figure 1.7
You can put snapshot analyses supported by worksheet functions on the summary sheet.

	A	B	C	D	E	F	G	H	I
		Repeat		Don't repeat					
1									
2									
3	When	Stats 2010 Rank	Decide Rank	Stats 2010 K Rank	Decide K Rank	Pred Rank	Pred K Rank	Stats 2013 Rank	Stats 2013 K Rank
4	10/7/14 23:15								
5	10/8/14 0:15	86,497	158,712	70,417	238,072	38,668	65,174	627,019	71,515
6	10/8/14 1:18	96,163	177,020	83,505	243,875	43,381	43,186	632,599	82,764
7	10/8/14 2:21	96,163	177,020	83,505	243,875	43,381	43,186	632,599	82,764
8	10/8/14 3:23	102,100	186,747	95,491	248,386	46,084	48,475	634,587	92,644
9	10/8/14 4:26	103,988	187,971	102,300	250,592	46,811	51,667	632,420	97,541
10	10/8/14 5:29	103,988	187,971	102,300	250,593	46,811	51,667	632,420	97,541
11	10/8/14 6:32	103,988	187,971	102,300	250,593	46,811	51,667	632,420	97,541
12	10/8/14 7:09	104,316	186,126	105,512	251,060	46,617	53,206	628,549	98,922
13	10/8/14 7:34	104,316	186,126	105,512	251,060	46,617	53,206	628,549	98,922
14	10/8/14 8:37	105,047	183,914	110,190	252,658	46,357	55,723	625,010	102,031
15	10/8/14 9:40	105,047	183,914	110,190	252,658	46,357	55,723	625,010	102,031
16	10/8/14 9:53	110,017	185,614	115,649	254,346	28,338	58,869	623,036	106,047
17	10/8/14 10:43	110,017	185,614	115,649	254,346	28,338	58,869	623,036	106,047
18	10/8/14 11:46	49,904	63,411	122,558	256,917	21,639	63,481	100,119	111,762
19	10/8/14 12:48	49,904	63,411	122,598	256,057	21,639	63,484	100,123	111,803

In Figure 1.7, the first few columns are reserved for the rankings of several books that I have obtained via web queries from the appropriate Amazon pages. I also store the date and time the queries finished executing in column A. That time data provides my basis for longitudinal summaries: a baseline for the forecasting analyses that I discuss in Chapters 3 through 6 and 11.

It's at this point that you have a decision to make. It's nice to be able to retrieve data about sales rankings for products such as books. If you've written a good one, it's gratifying to see the rankings drop as time goes by. (Remember, numerically lower rankings are better: A rank of 1 is a best seller.) But you likely never got paid a royalty or a commission, or had to fill a re-order, strictly on the basis of a sales ranking. It's the sales themselves that you're ultimately seeking: Granted that intermediate objectives such as clicks and conversions and rankings are key performance indicators, they don't directly represent revenue.

From Rankings to Sales

So how do you translate sales rankings into a count of sales? I started by tracking sales rankings on Amazon for about a week and noticed some points of interest.

Telling a Sale from No Sale A jump from a poorer ranking to a better ranking probably means the sale of at least one item. If the product has no sales during a given period, its ranking declines as other products do sell and move up. (It is of course possible that a book might experience sales even as its ranking declines, if its competition experiences greater sales.)

Ranking Sales How do you rank sales? You can't do it strictly on the number sold. A book, for example, might have sold 200 copies over a two-year period. Another book might have sold 100 copies since it was published last week. The second book is clearly performing better than the first, so you somehow have to combine elapsed time with number sold. Amazon doesn't say, but my guess would be that the rankings are based in part on the ratio of sales to days elapsed since publication—in other words, sales per day.

Improved Rankings Without Sales There are periods when an item's ranking improves very gradually over a period of hours. There's no reason to believe that an improvement from a ranking of, say, 20,000 to 19,999 indicates a sale. More likely it is a result of another day passing and the rankings recalculating accordingly. That means that before you conclude a sale took place, you need a credible minimum criterion.

Deciding on a Criterion The criterion should be a rate, not a constant number. If a book jumps from a ranking of 200,101 to 200,001, that 100-place increase is considerably different from a book that jumps from a ranking of 101 to 1. I decided to conclude that a sale had taken place if an increase in rankings equaled or exceeded ten percent of the prior ranking. So, if a book ranked 15,000 at 3:00 p.m. and 13,000 at 4:00 p.m.:

$$(15000 - 13000)/15000 = 0.13 \text{ or } 13\%$$

I conclude that a sale took place.

Structuring the Formula Suppose that I have two rankings for a given product, one taken at 3:00 p.m. in cell C18 and one taken at 4:00 p.m. in cell C19. If I want to test whether a sale took place between 3:00 p.m. and 4:00 p.m., I can enter this formula in, say, L19:

    =IF((C18-C19)/C18>0.1,1,0)

The formula returns a 1 if the difference between the two rankings is positive (for example, an increase from a ranking of 1,000 to 900 is positive) and exceeds 10% of the earlier ranking. The formula returns a zero otherwise. After the formula is established on the worksheet, I use the same VBA code that re-executes the queries to copy the formula to the next available row.

Snapshot Formulas

I also like to watch one statistic that doesn't depend on an ordered baseline of data the way that sales estimates do. That is the minimum (that is, the highest) sales ranking attained by each book since I started tracking the rankings.

I use Excel's MIN() function to get that analysis for each book (in hard copy format). I put the functions at the top of the columns so that they won't interfere with the results that come back from the web pages as the queries execute over time.

Figure 1.8 shows what those analyses look like. To get the minimum, best sales ranking for the same book, I use this formula in cell M2:

= MIN(OFFSET(B4,0,0,COUNTA($A:$A),1))

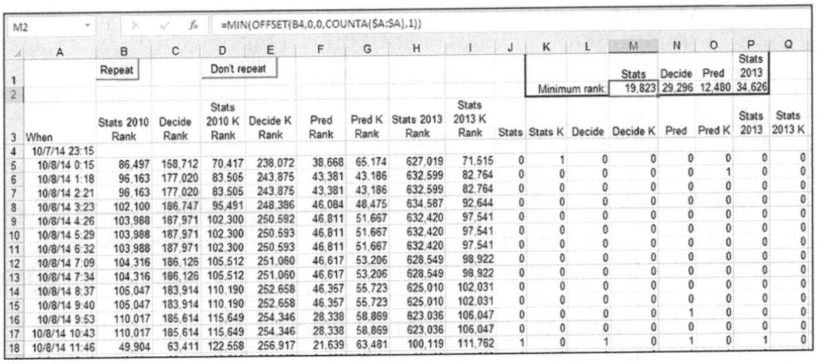

	A	B	C	D	E	F	G	H	I	J	K	L	M	N	O	P	Q
1		Repeat		Don't repeat									Stats	Decide	Pred	Stats 2013	
2											Minimum rank		19,823	29,296	12,480	34,626	
3	When	Stats 2010 Rank	Decide Rank	Stats 2010 K Rank	Decide K Rank	Pred Rank	Pred K Rank	Stats 2013 Rank	Stats 2013 K Rank	Stats	Stats K	Decide	Decide K	Pred	Pred K	Stats 2013	Stats 2013 K
4	10/7/14 23:15																
5	10/8/14 0:15	86,497	158,712	70,417	238,072	38,668	65,174	627,019	71,515	0	1	0	0	0	0	0	0
6	10/8/14 1:18	96,163	177,020	83,505	243,875	43,381	43,186	632,599	82,764	0	0	0	0	0	1	0	0
7	10/8/14 2:21	96,163	177,020	83,505	243,875	43,381	43,186	632,599	82,764	0	0	0	0	0	0	0	0
8	10/8/14 3:23	102,100	186,747	95,491	248,386	46,084	48,475	634,587	92,644	0	0	0	0	0	0	0	0
9	10/8/14 4:26	103,988	187,971	102,300	250,592	46,811	51,667	632,420	97,541	0	0	0	0	0	0	0	0
10	10/8/14 5:29	103,988	187,971	102,300	250,593	46,811	51,667	632,420	97,541	0	0	0	0	0	0	0	0
11	10/8/14 6:32	103,988	187,971	102,300	250,593	46,811	51,667	632,420	97,541	0	0	0	0	0	0	0	0
12	10/8/14 7:09	104,316	186,126	105,512	251,060	46,617	53,206	628,549	98,922	0	0	0	0	0	0	0	0
13	10/8/14 7:34	104,316	186,126	105,512	251,060	46,617	53,206	628,549	98,922	0	0	0	0	0	0	0	0
14	10/8/14 8:37	105,047	183,914	110,190	252,658	46,357	55,723	625,010	102,031	0	0	0	0	0	0	0	0
15	10/8/14 9:40	105,047	183,914	110,190	252,658	46,357	55,723	625,010	102,031	0	0	0	0	0	0	0	0
16	10/8/14 9:53	110,017	185,614	115,649	254,346	28,338	58,869	623,036	106,047	0	0	0	0	1	0	0	0
17	10/8/14 10:43	110,017	185,614	115,649	254,346	28,338	58,869	623,036	106,047	0	0	0	0	0	0	0	0
18	10/8/14 11:46	49,904	63,411	122,558	256,917	21,639	63,481	100,119	111,762	1	0	1	0	1	0	1	0

Figure 1.8
You can put snapshot analyses supported by worksheet functions on the summary sheet.

The formula returns the smallest numeric value for the fourth to the final populated row in column B.

Customizing Your Formulas

As shown in the final section of this chapter, I keep a monthly total of sales by book title in a pivot table that immediately follows the final and most current row of downloaded data. But because I often find it useful to know the total sales on the current day, I make a special provision for that. I keep it next to the pivot table that records monthly sales. It totals the number of books sold on the current day, regardless of the book title.

The formula that returns the current day's total uses two named ranges, ranges that relocate themselves as each hour passes. The ranges are named RecentDays and RecentSales. Both range names take advantage of Excel's mixed addressing feature.

For the formula to work properly, it needs to locate the rows that contain the data that was downloaded on the current day. Suppose that I select cell N2500 and define the range name RecentDays as referring to this range on the worksheet named Summary:

Summary!$A2468:$A2497

The name I have defined exists 14 columns to the left of cell N2500, and it occupies the rows from 33 to 4 rows above cell N2500—that is, the range encompasses 30 rows.

But the range name involves a *mixed* reference: a combination of a fixed and a relative reference. In this case, the column is fixed (by the dollar signs) to column A. We could enter a formula that uses the defined name in, say, Column B, and then copy and paste the that formula into column C. The formula would still refer to cells in column A because the dollar signs fix it there.

But if we copied and pasted the formula into cell N2501—that is, one row below where it was originally entered—the relative portion of the range's address would increment by one row. As used in cell N2501, the mixed reference in RecentDays would point to $A2469:$A2498. The reference is *relative* to the location of whatever cell uses it.

I use the same approach with the range name RecentSales, which also uses a mixed reference but captures more than just one column. Here's what RecentSales refers to, again assuming that cell N2500 is active when I define the name:

=Summary!$J2469:$Q2498

On the Summary sheet of the Collector workbook, column A contains the date and time when the rankings in columns B through I were downloaded. Columns J through Q contain a 1 (if the change in rankings indicate that a particular book was sold) or a 0 (otherwise).

Suppose that the most recent download wrote the ranking in row 2241. Suppose further that we *array* enter this formula in cell N2244:

=SUM(IF(DAY(RecentDays)=DAY(NOW()),RecentSales,0))

When the range names RecentDays and RecentSales are used in a cell in row 2244, the relative portions of the mixed references cause the names to refer to values in rows 2212 through 2241. So the array formula does the following:

- It checks to see if the value that identifies the current day (returned by the function DAY) equals the days in the range RecentDays (that's the range A2212:A2241 as the name is used in row 2244). If the values are equal, then the record was downloaded today.

- If a record in rows 2212 through 2241 was downloaded today, the array formula includes it in the sum of the values in the range named RecentSales. As used in the array formula, that is the range of 1s and 0s in J2212 through Q2241.

And that results in the number of inferred sales made today. Because the named ranges include 30 rows, the formula does not have to look all the way back to the beginning of the data in row 5. Because the named ranges include 30 rows, the formula is pretty sure to include all the hourly downloads that took place on the current day. The IF function ensures that the SUM function will ignore records downloaded on any prior day.

As you'll see in this chapter's section on VBA, when a new record is captured from a website and written to the worksheet, a new row is inserted at the bottom of the existing set of records. So doing pushes the cell with the array formula one row further down the worksheet, and the defined names now refer to ranges one row further down than before the insertion took place. So the array formula always points to a range of cells from 33 to 4 rows above the array formula itself.

You will doubtless have many questions that you'd like to ask of your data. The little summary formula that this section has described is idiosyncratic and of limited value beyond the specific data set that the Collector project downloads. I've spent this much time on it principally to demonstrate that Excel's worksheet tools, formulas, functions and names are powerful enough to accommodate very specialized requirements.

It's time to look closely at the VBA code needed to automate the project.

The VBA Code

This section walks you through the VBA code that I use to update my data collector hourly. It runs itself, so I can get it going, walk away, and not come back for hours or days. Meantime, the code runs hourly and obtains data from websites during each run. You can view the code by using the Visual Basic command on the Ribbon's Developer tab.

> **NOTE** If you don't see the Developer tab on the Ribbon, you have several choices. One is to customize the Ribbon: Click the File menu and choose Options, and then click Customize Ribbon. Fill the checkbox for the Developer tab and return to the Excel worksheet. This gives you access to all the important commands for developing a VBA project. If all you need to do is get at the Visual Basic Editor from time to time, use the Alt+F11 keyboard combination.

You arrange for a fresh module by choosing Insert, Module. The code that's shown in this chapter, or your own VBA code, goes into the new module.

I have provided all the code needed for the example given in this chapter. You'll find it in a workbook named Collector.xlsm, which you can download from the publisher's website. After opening the workbook, open the Visual Basic Editor as the prior Note describes. You see a Project window, usually at the left side of the screen. There's an entry in that window that's headed VBAProject(Collector.xlsm). If necessary, click the Expand button (with the plus sign) to the left of that project—this displays the objects stored in the project. The final object in the project's list is named Module1. Double click it to display the VBA code that's stored in that module. I describe that code in subsequent sections of this chapter.

The figures in this chapter show that I'm obtaining data on eight books. You can extend it to more products (or restrict it to fewer) if you want.

I should also note that I've revised the code somewhat to make clearer what's going on. A number of modifications would structure the code a bit more tightly and run a little faster. But they tend to obscure the general flow of the task.

```
Option Explicit
```

I always specify Option Explicit at the top of my VBA modules. Doing so forces me to declare variables explicitly, often with Dim statements. For example:

```
Dim NextRow as Integer
```

Dim, short for *dimension*, informs VBA that a variable named NextRow is intended to exist in the module's code: The variable is *declared* to exist. Later on, if I mistype the name of the variable in the code

```
NextRoe = NextRow + 1
```

for example, VBA complains that I'm trying to use a variable that I haven't declared. If I don't have Option Explicit at the top of the module, VBA assumes that I meant to *implicitly* declare a new variable, NextRoe, and assigns to it the current value of NextRow + 1. The implicit, on-the-fly declaration of variables was common programming practice 50 years ago. VBA still tolerates it unless you protect yourself with Option Explicit.

NOTE Another helpful option, used in the same spot as Option Explicit, is Option Base 1. If you declare a memory array along these lines:

```
Dim MyArray(5,5)
```

then MyArray has five rows and five columns, but by default the lowest element in the array is numbered zero. So the cell in the array's first row and first column is, by default, MyArray(0,0). There are times when this behavior is convenient, but at other times you would prefer to use 1 instead of 0 as the first element in an array's dimensions. If that's your preference, use Option Base 1 at the start of a module where you declare arrays. Then, the cell in an array's first row and first column is identified as, for example, MyArray(1,1) and there is no zero-th row or zero-th column. I don't use arrays in the code described here so I don't bother with Option Base 1.

The DoItAgain Subroutine

This very short, three-statement subroutine causes the main GetNewData subroutine to run an hour from now:

```
Private Sub DoItAgain( )

GetNewData True
End Sub
```

The DoItAgain subroutine runs in two cases:

- The user has clicked the button labeled Repeat on the Summary worksheet.
- Excel's timer has run to the point when Excel has been instructed to run the GetNewData subroutine again.

In either case. The `DoItAgain` subroutine calls the `GetNewData` subroutine with the argument `True`. I explain the effect of that argument in the section on `GetNewData`.

You normally initiate the code in the Collector workbook by clicking the Repeat button on the Summary worksheet, right after opening the workbook. Doing so gets things going and tells Excel to repeat the process an hour later without any further prompting from you.

The DontRepeat Subroutine

This is another very short subroutine, and it's used at times when you want to query the online data source and record the query's results, without initiating a sequence of repeating subroutines.

Suppose that you open the workbook at 8:00 p.m. and click the Repeat button. That causes the queries to execute, the results to be saved, and that sequence to repeat at 9:00 p.m. (or a little later). Fifteen minutes later, at 9:15 p.m., you decide that you want a fresh set of results. If you get that fresh set by clicking the *Repeat* button again, you initiate a new set of repeating subroutines. The first set will repeat at 10:00 p.m., 11:00 p.m. and so on, and the second set will repeat at 10:15 p.m., 11:15 p.m., and so on. You wind up with twice as many sets of query results as you wanted.

That's the point of the `DontRepeat` subroutine:

```
Sub DontRepeat( )
GetNewData False
End Sub
```

Just like the `DoItAgain` subroutine, the `DontRepeat` subroutine calls `GetNewData`, but it does so with a `False` argument instead of `True`. As you'll see, the `False` argument prevents `DoItAgain` from initiating a new set of queries one hour hence.

The PrepForAgain Subroutine

Yet another very brief subroutine. Its code is

```
Sub PrepForAgain( )
Application.OnTime Now + TimeValue("01:01:00"), "DoItAgain"
End Sub
```

As you'll see in the next section, `PrepForAgain` runs only if the `GetNewData` subroutine has been called with its `Again` argument set to `True`. This True/False distinction enables the user to choose to initiate a new sequence of hourly queries, or to run the queries once only.

The `PrepForAgain` subroutine uses VBA's `OnTime` method to schedule the time when a procedure is to run next. The time is specified first, using the fragment `Now + TimeValue("01:01:00")`. VBA has a function named `Now` that returns the current system date and time. VBA has another function named `TimeValue` that converts a string to a time value.

So, `Now + TimeValue("01:01:00")` gets the time as of right now and adds to it one hour, one minute, and zero seconds.

The second argument to OnTime as used here is DoItAgain, which calls the project's main procedure, GetNewData. (The name of the subroutine DoItAgain must be enclosed in quotes when it's used as an argument.) So, if it's run, the PrepForAgain subroutine instructs VBA to run the procedure named DoItAgain, 61 minutes after the OnTime method is invoked.

I settled on an hour and a minute after some experimenting. Amazon states that it updates the rankings hourly, and that seems to be nearly correct. During and around national holidays the website seems to update sales figures every two hours instead of each hour. Sometimes the update doesn't happen exactly when it should, and sometimes several hours pass before the next update takes place. These events are mildly atypical, though, and something close to an hour is normal.

However, it takes a bit of time for my code to run: to acquire new data by way of the queries and to test the changes in rankings for evidence of a sale. So I add a minute to the one hour in order to sync back up with Amazon's schedule.

The GetNewData Subroutine

Here's the project's main procedure: GetNewData. It executes web queries, obtains sales rankings, and copies and pastes formulas that convert rankings to assumed sales figures.

```
Sub GetNewData(Again As Boolean)
```

The first statement in GetNewData, the Sub statement, informs VBA that the statement that calls GetNewData also passes a Boolean, True/False value to GetNewData. That Boolean value, which is to be referred to by the variable name Again, later determines whether GetNewData is to run again automatically, 61 minutes later.

```
Dim NextRow As Integer, NextRank As Long
```

I begin by declaring the variables I need in this procedure:

- NextRow is the worksheet row where I write the next set of query data.
- NextRank contains the next sales ranking for a given book.

> **NOTE**
>
> A variable such as NextRow, if declared as type Integer, can take on only integer values with a maximum positive value of 32767. I don't expect to use more than that number of rows in my application. A variable such as NextRank can easily have a value greater than 32767, and so I declare it as Long.
>
> *Long* is a "long integer," takes integer values only, and has a maximum positive value of more than two billion.

```
Application.ScreenUpdating = False
Application.Calculation = xlCalculationManual
```

I don't like to be distracted by the screen if I happen to be looking at it when the code changes the active worksheet. So I turn off screen updating and the Excel window stays put until the code has finished running, or until a statement turning screen updating back on is executed (you set its value to True instead of False). As a side benefit, the code executes a trifle quicker with ScreenUpdating turned off.

Also, I don't want formulas recalculating as the queries write new data to the worksheets; I let them recalculate after the queries have finished running. That can have a substantial effect on the project's speed of execution. So, I set Excel's calculation property to manual—later on I reset it to automatic.

```
Application.StatusBar = "Read 1"
RefreshSheets ("Decide")
Application.StatusBar = "Read 2"
RefreshSheets ("Decide Kindle")
```

The next 16 statements consist of 8 pairs of commands. The first command updates Excel's Status Bar, so that the user can check the code's progress. (The Status Bar's value is independent of the ScreenUpdating property's value.) The pairs of commands are redundant, so I'm showing only four of the 16 commands here.

The second of each pair of commands calls the RefreshSheets subroutine with the name of the query sheet (in quotes) as the argument. It calls RefreshSheets once for each query sheet. As noted earlier, Collector's code actually calls this subroutine eight times but I don't want to subject you to all eight calls here—what happens is largely the same in each call. The RefreshSheets subroutine is shown and described following this description of the main GetNewData subroutine.

```
NextRow = ThisWorkbook.Sheets("Summary").Cells(Rows.Count, 1).End(xlUp).Row + 1
```

After the query for the eighth query sheet is complete, the code needs to find the next available row on the Summary sheet so that it can write the new data from the queries to that sheet without overwriting existing records. Here's how it does that.

If you're using an Excel worksheet directly, one of the ways to move around is with Ctrl + *arrow*, where *arrow* means up or down arrow, right or left arrow. If the active cell is in a column of data, for example, you can find the last contiguous non-empty cell with Ctrl + Down Arrow. If you're at the bottom of a column, something such as A1048576, and that cell is empty, you can find the lowermost non-blank cell with Ctrl + Up Arrow.

Using VBA, the way to emulate that keyboard action is with the End property that belongs to a cell object (really a range object because a cell is a special instance of a range). So, Cells(Rows.Count, 1).End(xlUp) tells VBA to go to the final row (Rows.Count) in Column A (1) and act as though you had pressed Ctrl + Up Arrow. That takes VBA to the lowermost non-empty cell in Column A, assuming as I do that the cell defined by the final row of Column A is itself empty. In the Collector project, I also assume that there are no extraneous values in column A between the final legitimate date and the last row of the worksheet.

Then all I have to do is get the row where the non-empty cell is found, add 1 to the row number, and I have the row number that I need to write into next. The result is assigned to the variable NextRow.

I do have to tell VBA which cell to regard as the active cell, and I do that by citing the Summary worksheet, and directing VBA's attention to that worksheet's final row, first column. I start things out with `ThisWorkbook` just in case I have more than one workbook open and some other workbook is active at the time that the code starts to run. The `ThisWorkbook` object specifies the workbook that contains the code that is running.

```
ThisWorkbook.Sheets("Summary").Cells(NextRow, 1) = Now
```

Having found the next row to write in, I put the current date and time into the Summary worksheet, in the first column of that row.

```
With ThisWorkbook.Sheets("Summary")
```

The `With` statement initiates a block of code in which objects that are preceded by a dot, such as `.Cells(NextRow,2)`, are deemed by VBA to belong to the object named in the `With` block—here, that's the worksheet named Summary. This convention in VBA relieves you of having to repeat the containing object over and over in a block of statements such as this one, whose end is indicated by the `End With` statement.

```
Application.StatusBar = "Write 1"
.Cells(NextRow, 2) = GetRank("Stats", " in")
Application.StatusBar = "Write 2"
.Cells(NextRow, 3) = GetRank("Decide", " in")
```

The four statements just shown are repeated for the next six books, making for eight pairs of statements. The first of each pair again informs the user of the code's progress in the status bar. The second statement in a pair tells Excel which cell to write a book's current ranking to (for example, `NextRow, 2` and `NextRow, 3`). The second statement also tells Excel which query sheet contains the ranking of interest (`"Stats"` and `"Decide"`) as well as a pointer (`"in"`) to help Excel find the ranking in that sheet. More on that pointer shortly.

The `GetRank` procedure, which is actually a function written in VBA, is discussed later in this section. The value returned by that function, which is the current sales rank of the book in question, is written to the appropriate row and column. (Column 2 is specific to and reserved for sales rankings of the book identified in the worksheet tabs as *Stats*. When queries on other books are run later in the code, the value assigned at that point to `NextRank` is written to a different column.) Because of the earlier `With` statement, the cell in the `NextRow`-th row and the second column is taken to belong to the worksheet named Summary in the workbook that contains the running code.

Continuing with the code, the next two statements—like the prior four—show the progress, get the sales rank for the book whose query sheet is named "Stats Kindle," and write the sales rank to the `NextRow`-th row, fourth column on the Summary sheet:

```
Application.StatusBar = "Write 3"
.Cells(NextRow, 4) = GetRank("Stats Kindle", " Paid in")
```

Notice that the second argument to the `GetRank` function is now `"Paid in"` instead of `"in"`. The reason is that this is a Kindle book, and its Amazon web page follows the sales rank with `"Paid in"` rather than simply `"in"`. The string passed to the `GetRank` function is used to help strip out the actual ranking from its surrounding verbiage; you find out how when we get to that function.

In the prior section titled "Identifying Sales," I discussed how some worksheet formulas can be used to decide if a sale of a book occurred by comparing two consecutive rankings of the same book. Now the VBA code selects, copies, and pastes those formulas into the next row down. The newly pasted formulas then recalculate based on the differences between the most recent and the now-current rankings. Begin by activating the Summary worksheet, which belongs to the ThisWorkbook object:

```
.Activate
```

Select the cells that contain the formulas to copy. They are found in the prior row—that is, in the row that precedes NextRow, where we have just written the current query data. Select the cells in that row from the tenth column to the seventeenth:

```
.Range(.Cells(NextRow - 1, 10), .Cells(NextRow - 1, 17)).Select
```

Autofill the selection one row down. The addresses used by the formulas automatically adjust so that they point to the newly current row:

```
Selection.AutoFill Destination:=.Range(.Cells(NextRow - 1, 10), _
    .Cells(NextRow, 17)), Type:=xlFillDefault
```

Notice that the destination of the autofill includes the row NextRow - 1 as well as NextRow. It's a minor peculiarity of the Autofill method that the destination range must include the source range. In this case, the source range is the row NextRow - 1 (columns 10 through 17) and that range is to be autofilled into the row NextRow (columns 10 through 17). But that destination range as specified in the VBA statement must include the source range.

```
.Rows(NextRow + 1).Select
Selection.Insert Shift:=xlDown
.Cells(NextRow, 1).Select
```

The prior three statements insert a blank row following the NextRow row—that is, the row that the code has just populated with sales rankings and sales formulas. The reason is that there is a pivot table (discussed later in this chapter) that is found a few rows below the rankings. It's helpful to push that table down a row when a new row has been populated with rankings.

```
End With
```

Terminate the With block that deems any object beginning with a dot (such as .Cells) to belong to the Summary worksheet in ThisWorkbook.

```
Application.Calculation = xlCalculationAutomatic
```

Turn automatic calculation back on.

```
Application.StatusBar = False
```

Remove the most recent progress message from the status bar.

```
ThisWorkbook.Save
```

Save the workbook.

```
Application.ScreenUpdating = True
```

Turn screen updates back on.

```
If Again Then
    PrepForAgain
End If
```

The value of the Boolean variable Again was passed to the GetNewData procedure by either DoItAgain, which passed the value True, or by DontRepeat, which passed the value False. If Again is True, then PrepForAgain is run, informing Excel to run GetNewData another time, one hour hence. If Again is False, Excel is not so informed and processing will cease until the next time the user clicks one of the buttons on the Summary sheet.

```
End Sub
```

End the GetNewData subroutine.

The GetRank Function

Here's the function named GetRank. Notice that it has two arguments, SheetName and TrailingString. The values are passed to the function by the statement that calls it. For example:

```
.Cells(NextRow, 2) = GetRank("Stats", " in")
```

where "Stats" is the worksheet name and "in" is a string of characters that can be found on the web page for the Stats book. The string follows—that is, trails—the actual ranking.

```
Function GetRank(SheetName As String, TrailingString As String) As Long
```

The function returns a value to the statement that called it. That value is often of a certain type: integer, a text string, a decimal number, and so on. To accommodate that, the function itself is declared to be of a certain type. Here, that type is Long. In VBA, Long means an integer value that might be much larger than the maximum value for a regular integer, which tops out at 32,767. There are many more books than that in Amazon's inventory, and this function is intended to return a book's ranking. Therefore, to accommodate the possibility that the rank is greater than 32,767, I declare the function as type Long, which can return a value greater than 2 billion—more than large enough.

```
Dim FoundString As String
Dim StartPos As Integer, StopPos As Integer
```

Three variables are declared. FoundString holds the value of the sales rank. It's declared as a string because when the code strips it out of the surrounding text from its web page, it's a string. Later it's converted to a Long integer.

StartPos and StopPos determine the starting and stopping positions of the sales rank within the string. For example, this string:

```
Amazon Best Sellers Rank: #64,788 in Books
```

has its first numeric representation in character number 28 of the string, so StartPos is assigned the value 28.

```
On Error GoTo EarlyOut
```

This code is designed to run 24/7, so I can't expect myself to nurse it along if it runs into an error that it can't recover from. The On Error statement tells VBA that if it encounters an error such as a letter right in the middle of what is supposed to be a numeric sales ranking, it shouldn't terminate processing. Instead, transfer control to a point named `EarlyOut`. That way, processing can continue. Even if it happens at 2:00 a.m., I can check it out at 9:00 a.m. and fix whatever happened, and I won't necessarily have missed data from the intervening seven hours.

The next five statements are responsible for finding the cell in the worksheet that contains the sales ranking, stripping the numeric ranking out of that cell, and assigning the result to the `GetRank` function.

First, find the cell that contains the string `"sellers Rank:"`. The rank we're looking for comes directly after that string.

```
Cells.Find(What:="sellers Rank:", After:=ActiveCell, LookIn:= _
    xlFormulas, LookAt:=xlPart, SearchOrder:=xlByRows, SearchDirection:= _
    xlNext, MatchCase:=False).Activate
```

The `Find` method is used to locate the string—in this case, the string is `"sellers Rank:"`. Most of the arguments, such as `LookIn` and `LookAt`, are there to keep the settings in place for the Find dialog box in Excel's user interface. I don't much care about forcing a Case match, so long as I get the string I'm looking for. Note that if the string is not found, an error occurs and the earlier `On Error` statement transfers control to the subroutine's `EarlyOut` label.

```
FoundString = ActiveCell
```

For convenience in subsequent handling, I set the string variable `FoundString` to the contents of the newly active cell, where `"sellers Rank:"` is found.

```
StartPos = InStr(FoundString, " #") + 2
```

I use VBA's `InStr` function to locate the space and the pound sign (#) in the contents of the active cell. I want to start the string that contains the sales rank numbers immediately after the space and pound sign, so I add 2 to the position where that substring is found. The result is stored in `StartPos`.

```
StopPos = InStr(FoundString, TrailingString)
```

Then I look inside `FoundString` again, this time to find the trailing string—the characters that Amazon supplies right after the sales ranking. In the case of tangible books, the ranking is followed by `"in"`. In the case of Kindle books, the ranking is followed by `"Paid in"`—or at least that's the case in June 2017. So the value of `TrailingString` is passed to the `GetRank` function, along with the name of the query sheet. If I'm querying for a tangible book, I pass `"in"` and if I'm querying for a Kindle book, I pass `"Paid in"`.

```
GetRank = 1 * Mid(FoundString, StartPos, StopPos - StartPos)
```

Finally, the code gets the value of the sales ranking using VBA's `Mid` function, which returns a string that is inside another string. In this case, `Mid` is instructed to look in `FoundString`, beginning at `StartPos`, and to return (`StopPos - StartPos`) characters. Those characters are the ranking, but because they came from a string they are still a string. Therefore I multiply the result by 1 to coerce the string to a numeric value, and assign it to the function `GetRank`, which returns the numeric value to the calling procedure.

> **NOTE** One thing you should always do in a function that you write yourself is to assign a value to the function before the function terminates. This is not an absolute requirement—you won't get a compile error if you fail to do so—but it's important nevertheless and particularly so if you're writing a function that the user can enter on the worksheet.

The prior statement assigns the value of the sales rank to the function `GetRank` itself. When the function terminates and control returns to the statement that called the function, `GetRank` itself equals the value that it calculated. And in the statement that called the function, which is

```
.Cells(NextRow, 2) = GetRank("Stats", " in")
```

the value of the `GetRank` function is written to the specified cell.

```
On Error GoTo 0
```

This second `On Error` statement returns Excel's behavior if it encounters a runtime error to its default status. Telling VBA to "go to 0" in the event of an error causes VBA to terminate with a runtime error if it hits another error. When this function cedes control back to the calling statement, the prior `On Error` statement is no longer in effect and so this `On Error GoTo 0` statement could be omitted, but I wanted you to know about it.

```
Exit Function
```

In the normal course of events, the function terminates at the `Exit Function` statement and control returns to the statement that called the function. But if something goes wrong, the `Exit Function` statement is bypassed (when the first `On Error` statement transfers control to the `EarlyOut` label) and some minor housekeeping takes place before the function terminates.

Here's the label I mentioned earlier. Control transfers here if something goes wrong in the portion of the function that locates the sales ranking and converts it to a `Long` integer:

```
EarlyOut:
GetRank = 0
```

The value returned by the function is set to zero. That's the value that is written to the Summary sheet as the sales rank. When I see that, I know that something went wrong. Perhaps Amazon's code had removed the old ranking from its page and was getting ready to put the new ranking in place at the moment that this code executed its query.

```
End Function
```

After a value, even an illogical one such as a sales ranking of zero, is assigned to the function, its task is completed and control returns to the calling statement in `GetNewData`.

The `RefreshSheets` Subroutine

This subroutine runs once for each query sheet. It's called by the main `GetNewData` subroutine.

```
Sub RefreshSheets(SheetName As String)
```

The name of the query sheet is passed as an argument.

```
With ThisWorkbook.Sheets(SheetName)
```

A `With` block is initiated so that subsequent objects, properties, and methods that begin with a dot are taken to belong to the sheet named `SheetName` in `ThisWorkbook`.

```
.Activate
```

The current query sheet is activated so that its query can be run.

```
.Cells(1, 1).Select
```

Select cell A1. Earlier I recommended that you cause the queries to return their results beginning in cell A1. If you adopt that recommendation, you know that the query results include that cell A1 and that if you select it you're able to refresh the query. (It's necessary that a cell in the query results range be active for the refresh to take place.)

```
Selection.QueryTable.Refresh BackgroundQuery:=False
```

Refresh the query. Set `BackgroundQuery` to `False` so that the code does not continue while the refresh is taking place.

```
End With
End Sub
```

Terminate the `With` block and end the subroutine.

The Analysis Sheets

I use several worksheets and chart sheets to analyze what's going on with the sales of my books. For an analysis that looks at the data over time, a pivot table (and pivot chart) is a nearly perfect solution. It collapses the hourly figures that I get from my web queries into more manageable time slices—I find that summarizing by month strikes a good balance between the overwhelming amount of data in an hourly analysis and the lack of detail in an annual or even quarterly analysis. Of course, when your baseline extends over several hundred days, it's time to start thinking about quarters or years as your unit of analysis.

Figure 1.9 shows one of the pivot tables that I rely on to synthesize the data on sales rankings.

Figure 1.9
When you connect this pivot table to a pivot chart, you can start making real sense of the data.

		Data			
Years ▼	When ▼	Stats 2010	Predictive	Decision	Stats 2013
2014	Oct	52	111	55	37
	Nov	46	134	49	39
	Dec	73	157	71	55
Grand Total		171	402	175	131

As powerful as pivot tables are—and I believe that pivot tables are the most powerful and flexible tool for data synthesis and analysis available in Excel—they can't tell when you have changed the underlying data, and (without help) they can't tell that their underlying data range has added another row.

In contrast, something as simple as the SUM() function can update itself when the underlying values change. If you have entered this formula

    =SUM(A1:A5)

in some cell, the value it returns changes immediately if you change any of the values in A1:A5. That's not true of a pivot table that's based on those cells or any other cell. You have to do something special to refresh the table when the underlying data changes.

But even SUM() won't change its own argument. If you now put a new value in A6, SUM() doesn't change itself from SUM(A1:A5) to SUM(A1:A6).

The way I prefer to handle that is by means of *dynamic range names*. You might already know that you can assign a name to a worksheet range and use that name instead of a range address. If you have given A1:A5 the name *Addends*, you can use this instead of SUM(A1:A5):

    =SUM(Addends)

I show you how to name a range shortly. First, you should know that if you define a range properly, you can get it to change its own dimensions when you add a new row or column to it. (Tables, which were new in Excel 2007 and have therefore been around for a while now, do that automatically. If you're not familiar with them you should probably investigate their capabilities. I still prefer dynamic range names because of a possibly irrational belief that I can control them better. And I don't care for the *structured formulas* that, optionally, come along with tables.)

Defining a Dynamic Range Name

Begin by selecting the worksheet that contains the range that you want to name. This step is not strictly necessary, but I usually find it helpful. Then follow these steps:

1. Click the Ribbon's Formulas tab.
2. Click the Define Name button in the Defined Names group. The New Name dialog box shown in Figure 1.10 appears.

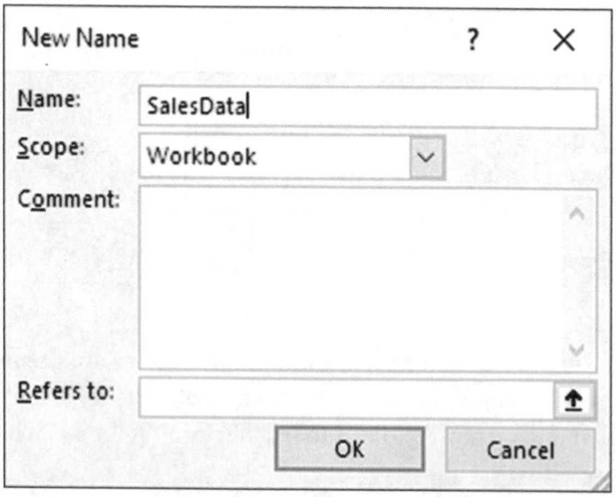

Figure 1.10
You can use a formula instead of an address in the Refers To box.

3. Enter the name you want to establish in the Name box. I use SalesData as the name of the dynamic range in the Collector workbook.

4. In this case, leave the Scope with the default value of Workbook.

5. I base the pivot table on the data in my Summary sheet, shown in Figure 1.8. With the Summary sheet's layout as shown there, type the following formula in the Refers To box:

```
=OFFSET(Summary!$A$3,0,0,COUNTA(Summary!$A:$A),17)
```

6. Click OK.

Here's a quick explanation of the Refers To formula. The OFFSET() function returns a range of cells that are offset from an anchor cell. Here, the anchor cell is defined as $A$3 on the Summary sheet, and the dollar signs make it a fixed reference. Notice in Figure 1.7 that cell A3 is where the label When is entered, and more labels follow it in row 3, columns B through Q. I want to include those labels in the defined range name because they're needed for the pivot table.

The two zeros that follow $A$3 in the OFFSET() function tell Excel how many rows and how many columns away from A3 the resulting range should begin. In this case, because both values are zero, the resulting range is offset by zero rows and zero columns: that is, the range begins at cell A3.

The fourth argument to the OFFSET() function, COUNTA(Summary!$A:$A), tells Excel how many rows to include in the offset range. The COUNTA() function tells Excel to count the number of values in (here) column A on the Summary worksheet. So when the VBA code runs and adds a new value in column A, the COUNTA function counts an additional value and redefines the number of rows in the range. That's how adding a new row at the bottom of the range causes the definition of the range to automatically increase by one row.

> **NOTE** I use COUNTA() instead of COUNT() because I want to include the text value in cell A3. Using COUNT() would ignore that text value; COUNTA() pays attention to both numeric and alphanumeric values.

The final argument to the OFFSET() function tells Excel how many columns to include in the result range. Here I want to include seventeen columns: one for the date, eight for the book rankings in columns B through I, and eight for the presumed book sales in columns J through Q.

It's called a *dynamic* range name because the dimensions of the range can automatically change depending on the number of records that are added to or removed from the range.

Using the Dynamic Range Name

With the dynamic range name defined, you can use it when you create a pivot table. Here's how to do that:

1. Begin by activating a blank worksheet and then click the Ribbon's Insert tab.
2. Click Pivot Table in the Tables group. The dialog box shown in Figure 1.11 appears.

Figure 1.11
Use the dynamic range name you defined in the Table/Range box.

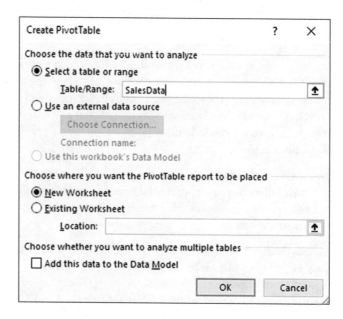

3. Type the name you supplied in Step 3 of the prior numbered list into the Table/Range box. This causes Excel to use that range as the data source for the pivot table.
4. Click OK. The PivotTable Fields pane appears.
5. Drag the When field into the Rows box.
6. Drag the Stats field into the Σ Values box.
7. Drag the Stats K field into the Σ Values box. Continue adding to the Σ Values box each sales estimate field that you want to appear in the pivot table.
8. Dismiss the PivotTable Field List by clicking its Close box. The pivot table now appears as shown in Figure 1.12.
9. Right-click in the date column of the pivot table and choose Group from the shortcut menu.
10. Grouping by Months is the default selection. Click OK.
11. The pivot table might seem to disappear from the visible worksheet. That can happen when the grouping operation causes the pivot table to occupy many fewer rows. Just scroll up to it.

Figure 1.12
You still need to group on date.

	A	B	C
1			
2			
3	Row Labels ▾	Sum of Stats	Sum of Stats K
4	10/7/14 23:15		
5	10/8/14 0:15	0	1
6	10/8/14 1:18	0	0
7	10/8/14 2:21	0	0
8	10/8/14 3:23	0	0
9	10/8/14 4:26	0	0
10	10/8/14 5:29	0	0
11	10/8/14 6:32	0	0
12	10/8/14 7:09	0	0
13	10/8/14 7:34	0	0
14	10/8/14 8:37	0	0
15	10/8/14 9:40	0	0
16	10/8/14 9:53	0	0
17	10/8/14 10:43	0	0
18	10/8/14 11:46	1	0

The pivot table should now appear as shown in Figure 1.13. (It differs from the pivot table shown in Figure 1.9 because that figure shows the total of the paperbound and the electronic editions.)

Figure 1.13
You can also use the Value Field Settings to select a display format for the summary values in the pivot table.

	A	B	C
1			
2			
3	Row Labels ▾	Sum of Stats	Sum of Stats K
4	Oct	39	13
5	Nov	35	11
6	Dec	58	15
7	Grand Total	132	39

A pivot table such as the one in Figure 1.13 isn't very informative by itself. Fortunately, it's easy to create a pivot chart from a pivot table. Just select any cell in the pivot table, click the Ribbon's Insert tab, and choose (say) a Line chart from the Charts group.

You get a chart embedded in the active worksheet, and you can usually tell more about your data, at least on a macro level, from the chart than directly from the pivot table (see Figure 1.14).

One of the useful aspects of pivot charts is that they don't need any special handling to keep up with the underlying pivot table. When the pivot table's data changes, or gets more rows, the pivot chart updates automatically.

1

Figure 1.14
You usually need to do some tinkering with the pivot chart before it starts to show you what you need to know.

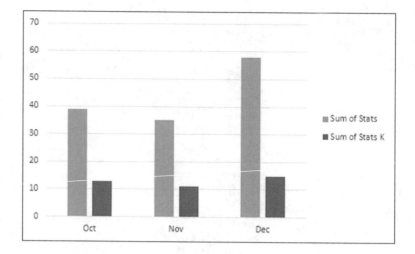

You do need a way to force a refresh of the pivot table. There are many ways to handle that. Some are mildly complicated, such as writing a special Worksheet Activate event handler using VBA. That event handler would force a refresh any time you activate the worksheet that contains the pivot table. Probably the simplest way is to right-click any cell in the pivot table and to choose Refresh from the shortcut menu.

Among the tweaks I like to apply to a newly created pivot chart are the following:

- Right-click an embedded chart, click Move in the shortcut menu, and choose to move the chart to a new sheet.

- Right-click a data series in the chart and choose to format it. Reduce the width of the lines and change any obnoxious color to a more acceptable one—black, for example.

- Add a trendline. Right-click a data series and choose Add Trendline from the shortcut menu. In line charts, linear trendlines and moving average trendlines are often very informative. Tinker with the length of a moving average trendline until you get something that smooths out the rough in the series but preserves its basic movement. Chapter 3, "Forecasting with Moving Averages," and Chapter 4, "Forecasting a Time Series: Smoothing," provide guidance on selecting the length of a moving average.

Linear Regression

When two variables are quantitatively related to one another, they are said to be correlated. Weight and height are correlated: Taller people tend to weigh more. Personal income and tax liabilities are correlated: People who make more money tend to pay more income taxes. Unit price and units sold are correlated: Other things being equal, the more that a product costs, the fewer units that you tend to sell.

Correlation and Regression

There are some important points hidden in the prior paragraph. One of them is the word *tend*. Most interesting pairs of variables do not move together in lockstep. It's not true that all men whose height is 72 inches weigh two pounds more than all men whose height is 71 inches. Some six footers weigh 160 pounds, others weigh 220, still others weigh anywhere between 150 or less and 250 or more. The relationship, although real and measurable, is imperfect.

Some pairs of variables don't just tend to move together, but really do move in lockstep: Your age in days, for example, and your age in weeks. Perfectly correlated variables such as these have relationships that are trivial or otherwise uninteresting. Degrees Fahrenheit and degrees Celsius are perfectly correlated, but who cares?

So when we speak of correlations, we are normally speaking of *tendencies*. We are also speaking of positive and negative relationships. Weight and height vary together—or *covary*—positively: Greater weight is associated with greater height. Price and volume vary together, but negatively: Higher price is associated with lower volume. Just because the direction of the relationship is negative doesn't mean there isn't a strong relationship.

If you can quantify the strength and direction of the relationship, that puts you in a position to predict one variable using your knowledge of the other variable. If you know John's height, you can make a reasonable estimate of his weight. If you know that Mary makes $60,000 a year, you can estimate her income tax liability.

For reasons that have more to do with the history of statistics than anything else, the process you use to estimate the strength of a relationship is called *correlation analysis*, but the closely related process you use to predict one variable from another is called *regression analysis*.

The field generally referred to as *analytics* makes frequent use of techniques that are based on regression and correlation. As it happens, traditional regression techniques aren't well suited to the types of analysis that you often want to explore when it comes to variables of interest to analytics.

For example, one of the variables you often want to look carefully at is a dichotomy: *bought* versus *didn't buy*, for example, or some other variation on conversion. Traditional regression doesn't do a good job of analyzing variables like that. In fact, traditional regression analysis makes some assumptions about the nature of the outcome variable that are clearly not met by a dichotomy such as purchasing behavior.

So, analytics often abandons the traditional regression approach and instead uses something called *logistic regression*, which does handle that sort of variable much more accurately than traditional regression does. I want to show you how logistic regression works, but to understand the nuances of that kind of analysis, it's important that you understand traditional regression techniques. In particular, you need to see why traditional regression makes the assumptions it does, why those assumptions are violated when you apply regression to dichotomous variables, and how logistic regression helps you work around those problems.

Furthermore, one very standard technique used in forecasting—another arm of analytics— uses something called *autoregression* to make certain forecasts. Autoregression is not as far removed from traditional regression as is logistic regression, but it's much easier to understand with a grounding in traditional techniques.

This chapter is designed to give you that grounding. I expect that you'll find subsequent chapters on logistic regression and autoregression much easier to follow with the current chapter under your belt.

Charting the Relationship

Suppose that you have obtained data on two variables that interest you—for example, revenue generated daily from a web page and number of hits on that page. You could enter the data in an Excel worksheet, as shown in columns A and B of Figure 2.1.

When you're evaluating a relationship between two variables, it's critically important to look at a chart that shows the relationship visually. Statisticians have been counseling this practice since the late 19th century, but it is only since personal computers and applications such as Lotus 1-2-3 and Excel came into widespread use that most people have been acting on the advice.

Figure 2.1
With the data entered as shown in columns A and B, it takes three mouse clicks to get the chart.

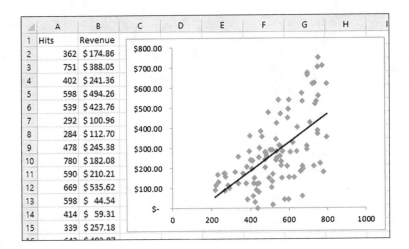

To get the chart shown in Figure 2.1, click in some data cell in column A or B, and then do the following:

1. Click the Insert tab.
2. Click the arrow next to the Scatter chart icon in the Charts group.
3. Click the Scatter chart icon that shows the markers only.

With such an easy way to get a look at the relationship, there's really no excuse not to. (You're also likely to get a chart title, which I've deleted from Figure 2.1 for clarity.)

The data you see charted in Figure 2.1 describe a positive, moderate relationship between the two variables. It's positive because the larger the number of hits, the greater the revenue on any given day. The markers generally run from the lower left of the chart to the upper right.

It's moderate because there's a fair amount of spread in the values for revenue for any given number of hits. Contrast the appearance of the markers in Figure 2.1 with those in Figure 2.2.

Notice that the markers in Figure 2.2 cling more closely to the heavy straight line than they do in Figure 2.1. That's typical of a strong relationship between the variables, the sort that you're seeing in Figure 2.2. Figure 2.3 shows what things might look like if there were no relationship between hits and revenues.

NOTE The heavy straight lines shown in Figures 2.1 through 2.3 are typically termed *regression lines*. Excel uses the term *trendlines* instead.

Figure 2.2
The relationship between the two variables is stronger than that shown in Figure 2.1.

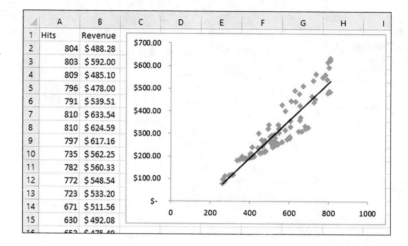

	A	B
1	Hits	Revenue
2	804	$488.28
3	803	$592.00
4	809	$485.10
5	796	$478.00
6	791	$539.51
7	810	$633.54
8	810	$624.59
9	797	$617.16
10	735	$562.25
11	782	$560.33
12	772	$548.54
13	723	$533.20
14	671	$511.56
15	630	$492.08

Figure 2.3
When there's no relationship between the variables, the trendline is very close to horizontal.

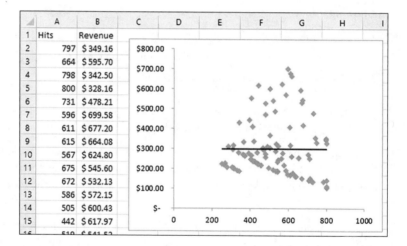

	A	B
1	Hits	Revenue
2	797	$349.16
3	664	$595.70
4	798	$342.50
5	800	$328.16
6	731	$478.21
7	596	$699.58
8	611	$677.20
9	615	$664.08
10	567	$624.80
11	675	$545.60
12	672	$532.13
13	586	$572.15
14	505	$600.43
15	442	$617.97

Taking the brief time needed to chart the relationship can pay off for you. It could be that the relationship is not best described by a straight line, as it is in Figures 2.1 and 2.2. The relationship between some variables is best described by a curve. Sales of a new product over time is an example. The sales of some widely anticipated products really take off at first and subsequently quiet down. Other new products start out with flat sales figures that then increase exponentially as they catch on in the marketplace.

NOTE It's possible to model this sort of curvilinear relationship using standard regression techniques by raising the predictor variable to some power.

Of course, the words I've used to describe relationships—moderate and strong—are subjective. The standard way to quantify the relationship and to express its strength objectively is by means of the *Pearson correlation coefficient*, denoted by the symbol r. Excel has a worksheet function, PEARSON(), that calculates the value of the correlation coefficient for two variables. The function is named for Karl Pearson, who developed the method. (The CORREL() function does the same thing.)

The possible values of r range from –1.0 (a perfect, negative relationship) to +1.0 (a perfect, positive relationship). The midscale value of 0.0 indicates no relationship between the variables.

Calculating Pearson's Correlation Coefficient

The math that underlies the Pearson correlation is actually informative; it helps you understand what's going on in the data. But while it's enlightening, I'm not going to get into it here because it's also lengthy—too lengthy for a book that isn't a statistical primer. If you're interested, another book that I wrote, *Statistical Analysis: Microsoft Excel 2013*, goes into the matter in some detail.

Excel, of course, does the heavy lifting for you when it actually calculates the correlation. All you need to do is provide the data in the right way. Figure 2.4 repeats the data from Figure 2.1 with additional data in columns A and E that identifies when the measures were taken.

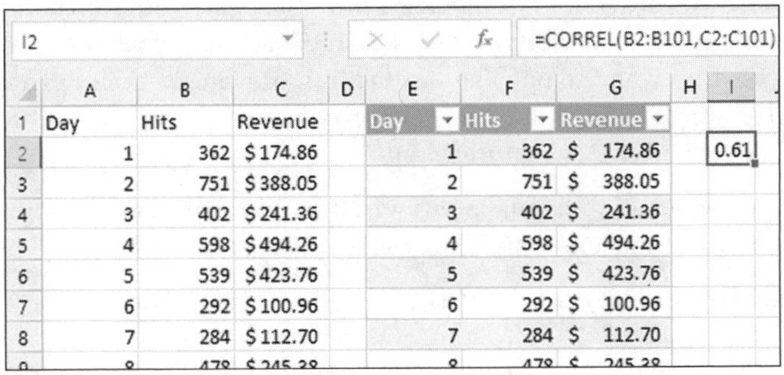

	A	B	C	D	E	F	G	H	I
1	Day	Hits	Revenue		Day	Hits	Revenue		
2	1	362	$174.86		1	362	$ 174.86		0.61
3	2	751	$388.05		2	751	$ 388.05		
4	3	402	$241.36		3	402	$ 241.36		
5	4	598	$494.26		4	598	$ 494.26		
6	5	539	$423.76		5	539	$ 423.76		
7	6	292	$100.96		6	292	$ 100.96		
8	7	284	$112.70		7	284	$ 112.70		

Figure 2.4
The layout in columns A through C is called a list. The layout in columns E through G is called a table.

The values in columns A through C constitute what Excel calls a *list*. It is not a formal structure in Excel—just a standard way to lay out data in a worksheet. Different records go in different rows, so all the values for Day 2 show up in the same row—row 3 in this instance. Different variables go in different columns, and each column is headed by the name of the variable it contains. Meet these requirements—records in rows, variables in columns, names of variables at the tops of columns—and you have a list.

The values in columns E through G are the same as in A through C, and the rules regarding rows and columns, records, and variables are the same as for a list. But what you see in columns E through G is what Excel calls a table. It differs from a list in some subtle ways, as well as some that are not so subtle:

■ It's a formal structure in Excel, like a chart or a named range of cells.

■ The fact that it's a formal structure means that it can carry certain attributes with it, such as the full worksheet address that it occupies. For example, a table has certain built-in formats, such as alternating the shading of adjacent rows.

■ Another example of a table's attributes: If you add another record, or delete an existing one, the address of the full table updates itself accordingly.

■ An automatically updating address is extremely handy when you chart the data in a table: When you add data to the table, the chart automatically updates itself in response. You can do the same sort of thing with a list, but because a list is not a formal structure, you have to manage its attributes yourself.

What does all this have to do with correlation coefficients? Recall that I described a positive correlation as one where the higher values on one variable are associated with higher values on the other variable. Lower values on one are associated with lower values on the other.

With a negative correlation, higher values on one variable are associated with lower values on the other. For example, in a golf tournament you find that the lower your score—the fewer strokes you take—the more competitors you beat. If you take 64 strokes to complete 18 holes, you might beat 50 other golfers, but if you take 94 strokes, you might beat only 1.

That means that the correlation coefficient—or more precisely, Excel, which calculates the coefficient—needs a way of telling which value goes with which. It needs to know how to pair up the number of hits on Day 1 with the amount of revenue on Day 1, and that goes for Day 2, Day 3, and so on. The way that you pair those values in Excel is by using a list or a table, where all the values in a given row belong to the same record. In this instance, all the values in row 2 belong to Day 1.

When you've set up your data in this way, it's easy to calculate the correlation. Just enter the following formula in some blank cell:

=CORREL(B2:B101,C2:C101)

(The formula assumes that your observations extend from row 2 to row 101.) With this set of data, Excel returns 0.61. You can pick your own subjective adjective, but most would regard that as a moderately strong correlation. It confirms what you would like to expect if you owned the website in question: More hits are associated with greater revenue. (That's not a guarantee that you'll create more revenue if you create more hits, but it's consistent with that notion. See the next section, "Correlation Is Not Causation," for more on the issue.)

You could use this formula instead:

=PEARSON(B2:B101,C2:C101)

I mentioned earlier in this chapter that Excel has a PEARSON() function that calculates the correlation, and there it is. It is identical to the CORREL() function with regard to both its arguments and results. Excel doesn't have much redundancy of that sort, but those two functions are duplicates and they have been since 1995. Use whichever you prefer.

Why worry about the table in Figure 2.4? Suppose that another day passes and you enter another number of hits and another revenue figure in row 102. If you use the PEARSON() or CORREL() function on the list values in columns B and C, your formula would not update to capture the new values. That is, the formula would not automatically adjust to read as follows:

=CORREL(B2:B102,C2:C102)

But suppose you built the formula by dragging through the ranges F2:F101 and G2:G101, instead of typing the addresses. Then the formula would read as follows:

=CORREL(Table1 [Hits], Table1 [Revenue])

The result is that Excel presents not a specific 100 records to the CORREL() function but however many records there are in Table1's Hits column and Revenue column. That means you can add records as needed, and CORREL() responds by recalculating itself to show the current value of the correlation coefficient. (Of course, this feature is not specific to CORREL() itself. It works with any worksheet function that takes a column of values as an argument.)

If you're not familiar with correlation coefficients, it's likely to take a while to develop a sense for the strength of a relationship indicated by a correlation such as 0.35 or 0.68. In the meantime, I go into that matter in more detail in Chapter 6, "Forecasting a Time Series: Regression," where the issue of the relationship between correlation and shared variance is explored.

For now, it's important to visit the issue of correlation and causation, after which I move on to regression and prediction.

Correlation Is Not Causation

I've mentioned a few examples of related variables in this chapter: height and weight, page hits and revenues, income and taxes. It's pretty clear that causation is present in each of these three pairs of variables. When you get taller, it's because your bones get longer and therefore heavier. When more people reach a web page that sells products, more people are positioned to buy those products, and in the absence of contrary evidence it makes good sense to conclude that more hits cause more revenue. And when you make more money, you cause yourself to pay more taxes.

Of course there are counterexamples to each of these. A radical change in diet can keep a child's weight near a particular value even while the height increases. It's conceivable that one person could buy 100 units from a website, thereby increasing revenue, whereas another 100 users visit the site and buy nothing. And certain deductions and methods of tax avoidance tend to be available only to upper-bracket taxpayers.

Still, it's straining at gnats to claim that each of these examples does not represent a causal relationship between the variables. And correlation often does indicate the presence of causation. But not always.

Suppose there is a correlation of, say, 0.7 between the number of gun permits issued in 100 communities and the incidence of violent crime in those same communities. That's a solid correlation and might indicate causation is present. Do you conclude that people who live in high-violence communities buy more guns to protect themselves? Or do you conclude that the presence of more guns increases the likelihood that the guns are used in crimes?

The problem here is the directionality of cause. A correlation coefficient by itself cannot tell you which variable is the cause and which is the effect—if either.

And there's the problem of the third variable, or the fourth or the fifth. A classic example is the incidence of births in Oldenburg, Germany during the 1930s. As the number of births increased over a seven-year period, so did the number of observations of storks in the city. The correlation was 0.95—a very strong correlation. Apparently storks do deliver babies.

Of course the third variable in this case was the increase in the population of the city during the years in question: that increase brought about both more births and more birdwatchers.

So, using analytic procedures, be careful of committing resources to activities that assume there's a causal relationship between two variables. Because of the directionality of the relationship, or the presence of a third variable that causes the two that you're interested in, you might find yourself investing in a causal relationship that isn't really there.

Simple Regression

How do you get from a correlation coefficient to a prediction? Given a correlation of 0.6 between the number of page hits and the revenue generated, how do you forecast the amount of revenue that will result if you can drive some number of users to a page?

In simple regression you forecast one variable from another, and getting from the correlation to the forecast is pretty straightforward. The equation is as follows:

$$b = r_{xy} \left(s_y / s_x \right)$$

The *regression coefficient*, which is b in the preceding equation, is obtained as follows:

1. Find r_{xy}, the correlation between the predictor variable x and the forecast variable y.
2. Multiply r_{xy} by the standard deviation of the forecast variable y (s_y).
3. Divide the result by the standard deviation of the predictor variable x (s_x).

Besides the regression coefficient you need the *intercept*, denoted as a, which you can calculate as follows:

$$a = \bar{y} - b\bar{x}$$

In words:

1. Multiply the regression coefficient, b, by the mean of x.

2. Subtract the result of step 1 from the mean of y.

Figure 2.5 shows how this comes together in a worksheet.

It turns out that r, the correlation coefficient, is actually the regression coefficient *when both variables have a mean of zero and a standard deviation of 1*. (If you're familiar with z-scores you'll recognize this characteristic.) So the first step is to calculate the regression coefficient by taking into account the actual standard deviations.

As noted earlier in this section:

$$b = r \left(s_y / s_x \right)$$

Figure 2.5
This is just to show you how the correlation coefficient is related to the regression equation. Figure 2.6 shows how one simple formula does it all at once.

	A	B	C	D	E	F	G
F1					f_x =CORREL(B2:B101,C2:C101)		
1	Day	Hits	Revenue		Correlation, Hits with Revenue	0.61	=CORREL(B2:B101,C2:C101)
2	1	362	$174.86				
3	2	751	$388.05		Standard deviation, revenue	178.24	=STDEV.S(C2:C101)
4	3	402	$241.36		Standard deviation, hits	152.17	=STDEV.S(B2:B101)
5	4	598	$494.26				
6	5	539	$423.76		Mean revenue	279.21	=AVERAGE(C2:C101)
7	6	292	$100.96		Mean hits	530.7	=AVERAGE(B2:B101)
8	7	284	$112.70				
9	8	478	$245.38		Regression coefficient	0.71	=F1*F3/F4
10	9	780	$182.08		Intercept	-98.52	=F6-F9*F7
11	10	590	$210.21				
12	11	669	$535.62		Forecast revenue given 300 hits	115.02	=F9*300+F10

In Figure 2.5, the standard deviations are calculated in cells F3 and F4. They are combined with the correlation (in cell F1) to get the regression coefficient b in cell F9.

The correlation coefficient has now been adjusted for the standard deviations. We still need to take into account that the predictor and the forecast values can't be counted on to have a mean of zero. This is managed by taking the actual mean of the forecast values (the revenue) and subtracting the product of the regression coefficient and the mean of the predictor values (the hits).

So the equation for the intercept a is as follows:

$$a = \bar{y} - b\bar{x}$$

The mean of the y values is in cell F6, and the mean of the x values is in cell F7. The intercept is calculated in cell F10.

We can now use the regression coefficient and the intercept to forecast a value for revenue from a new value of hits. For example:

$$y = bx + a$$

If x, the number of hits, is 300, we forecast the revenue as follows:

$$= F9 * 300 + F10$$

This returns 115.02. Given the observed relationship between hits and revenue in columns B and C, we forecast that 300 hits would return 115.02 in revenue. This sort of analysis helps to show how the correlation is related to the regression formula, but it's a waste of time for everyday work. For that, you would use a different worksheet function, LINEST(). Figure 2.6 shows how you might use it on this data set.

Figure 2.6 shows how to use the LINEST() function to bypass all the intermediate calculations shown in Figure 2.5. The LINEST() function calculates the regression coefficient and the intercept directly. They appear in cells E2:F2 of Figure 2.6. Notice that they are identical to the values shown in cells F9:F10 in Figure 2.5.

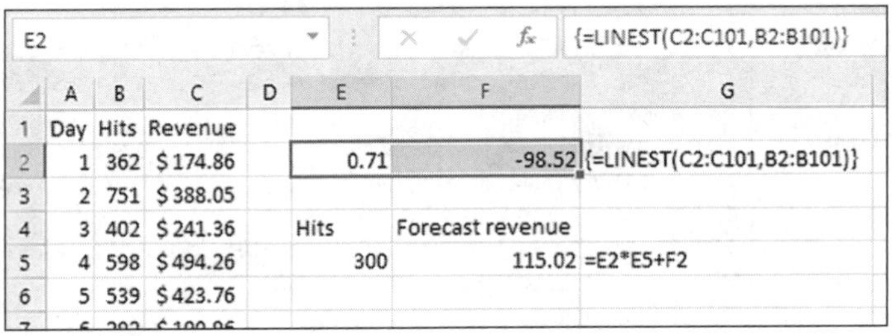

Figure 2.6
An example of using the LINEST() worksheet function to create a forecast.

Array-Entering Formulas

The LINEST() function is one of the subset of Excel worksheet functions that must be *array-entered* to function properly. Array-entering a formula in Excel is just like normal formula entry, but instead of typing the formula and pressing Enter, you type the formula and hold down the Ctrl and the Shift keys as you press Enter.

There are several reasons that you would need to array-enter a formula in Excel. The reason that applies to LINEST() is that you want to obtain several results from the same function. LINEST() calculates the regression coefficient and intercept (and several other values that are discussed in detail in Chapter 6). To see those on the worksheet, you must begin by selecting the cells where you want them to appear—not just a single cell as you do with many other worksheet functions such as SUM().

Array-Entering LINEST( )

So, in the case shown in Figure 2.6, the sequence of events is as follows:

1. Select cells E2:F2.
2. Type the formula =LINEST(C2:C101,B2:B101)
3. Hold down Ctrl and Shift, and while holding them down, press Enter.

You now see the regression coefficient appear in cell E2 and the intercept in cell F2.

If you look in the formula box, you see that what you typed is surrounded by curly brackets: { and }. Excel supplies them—don't type them yourself or Excel will treat what you type as text, not as a formula—and when you see them you know that Excel has interpreted what you entered as an array formula.

> **NOTE** If you're a long-time user of Excel you might wonder about the worksheet functions SLOPE( ) and INTERCEPT( ). They return the regression coefficient and the intercept, respectively. You could use them in the situation shown in Figures 2.5 and 2.6. However, they are seriously underpowered (they've been around since one-dot-zero) and there's no point in learning about two functions that work in limited situations instead of one function that works in many different situations.

Just as in Figure 2.6, you can use the regression coefficient and the intercept returned by LINEST( ) to calculate a forecast value based on a new predictor value. The formula to return forecast revenue for 300 hits, given the relationship between hits and revenue in columns B and C, is in cell F5. The formula that's entered in F5 is shown as text in cell G5.

Actually, Excel makes it even easier to get a forecast. The TREND( ) function wraps up everything in Figure 2.6 into one step. It calculates the regression coefficient and intercept and applies them to one or more new predictor values (here, hits). Then it displays the result of the forecast on the worksheet. I cover TREND( ) in detail in Chapter 6.

Why would you want the equation—specifically, the regression coefficient and the intercept—via LINEST( ) when you can get the forecast value directly with TREND( )? By looking at the equation and some of the other results that pertain to the equation, you can do a better job of evaluating whether and how you want to use it. More on that matter in the next section.

Multiple Regression

It turns out that you can often improve the accuracy of forecasts by running an analysis that's called *multiple regression* instead of the simple regression I discussed in the prior section. There, you saw how to use one predictor variable, page hits, to forecast another variable, revenues. Using multiple regression, you combine two or more predictor variables to forecast a variable such as revenues.

You can do this using LINEST(), just as you saw with one predictor variable in the prior section. And if you want to use TREND() to obtain the forecasts (instead of or in addition to using LINEST() to get the equation), you can do that too. I cover much of the functionality in the TREND() function in Chapter 6, but there the discussion is limited to a single predictor in *autoregression* (in autoregression, you use earlier observations of one variable to predict the values of later observations). There's an example of using TREND() in place of LINEST() in the next section of this chapter.

Creating the Composite Variable

You sometimes see the term "best combination" in statistics books that deal with multiple regression. Here's what that means:

In multiple regression, just as in simple regression, you analyze the relationship between one predictor variable and one forecast variable. But multiple regression creates a composite predictor variable on your behalf. Suppose that you want to forecast revenues from both page hits and another variable such as fiscal quarter. You suspect that the revenues are driven not only by number of page hits but also by a seasonal component, and you would like to account for both.

You can use LINEST() to calculate a combination of fiscal quarter (measured, say, by the numbers 1 through 4) and number of hits. This combination creates a new, composite variable that LINEST() then uses as the predictor variable.

After it creates that composite variable, LINEST() calculates the correlation coefficient between the composite and the forecast variable. That correlation is usually called the multiple R. It's capitalized to distinguish it from the standard Pearson correlation coefficient that is covered in the first section of this chapter. It's still a Pearson correlation, but it differs in that one of the variables is a composite of two or more other variables.

Here's where the phrase *best combination* comes in. The composite variable that multiple regression creates has a stronger correlation with the forecast variable than any other possible linear combination of the predictor variables. Figure 2.7 shows an example of this aspect of multiple regression analysis.

Figure 2.7
You can create the composite variable yourself by using the regression coefficients from LINEST().

	A	B	C	D	E	F	G	H	I	J	K	L
					Coefficients		**Intercept**				**Correlations**	
1												
2	Days	Hits	Revenue		Hits	Days			Composite			Revenue
3	1	362	$138.97		0.67	1.79	-171.71		74.01	Days		0.30
4	2	751	$279.63						337.93	Hits		0.60
5	3	402	$175.55						104.55	Composite		0.67

E3 • : × ✓ *fx* {=LINEST(C3:C102,A3:B102,,TRUE)}

In Figure 2.7, the results of the LINEST() function are in cells E3:G3. In Figure 2.6, the LINEST() results occupy two cells only: one for the regression coefficient and one for the intercept. In Figure 2.7, it takes three cells. Two predictor variables, not just one, are being analyzed, so there are two regression coefficients—but there's still just one intercept.

Entering LINEST( ) with Multiple Predictors

The procedure to get the LINEST() analysis in Figure 2.7 is as follows:

1. Select three adjacent cells in one row, such as E3:G3 as shown.
2. Type the LINEST() formula:

   =LINEST(C3:C102,A3:B102)

   Notice that the second argument specifies the two variables in columns A and B as the predictors.

3. Enter the formula with Ctrl+Shift+Enter instead of simply Enter. You should see the formula in the formula box, surrounded by curly brackets, and the results in the three cells that you began by selecting.

> **NOTE** Notice that the regression coefficient for Hits is in column E, before the regression coefficient for Days in column F. This is the reverse of what you might expect, given that the data for Day in column A precedes the data for Hits in column B. For information about this anomaly, see a rant titled "Reverse English" in Chapter 6.

Merging the Predictors

Column I in Figure 2.7, labeled Composite, contains that best combination of Day and Hits to forecast revenue. To get it, you need to apply the regression equation that LINEST() supplies to the predictor variables; the result is the forecast of Revenue. Cell I3 in Figure 2.7 uses this formula:

   =($F$3*A3)+($E$3*B3)+$G$3

where

- Cell F3 contains the regression coefficient for Day, and A3 contains a value for Days.
- Cell E3 contains the regression coefficient for Hits, and B3 contains a value for Hits.
- Cell G3 contains the intercept.

The addresses for cells F3, E3, and G3 are made absolute by the dollar signs. That means that you can copy and paste the formula in I3 down into I4:I102 without changing the addresses for the coefficients and the intercept. All that change are the relative addresses for Days and Hits, so the final formula in cell I102 is as follows:

   =($F$3*A102)+($E$3*B102)+$G$3

Another way to get the forecast values is by way of the TREND() function. Figure 2.8 shows an example, using the same data set as used in Figure 2.7.

Figure 2.8
Use TREND() to bypass LINEST() and get the forecast values directly.

	A	B	C	D	E	F	G
	E2			fx	{=TREND(C2:C101,A2:B101)}		
1	Days	Hits	Revenue		Composite		
2	1	362	$138.97		74.01		
3	2	751	$279.63		337.93		
4	3	402	$175.55		104.55		
5	4	598	$258.58		238.41		
6	5	539	$243.66		200.45		
7	6	292	$100.00		35.79		
8	7	284	$100.00		32.19		
9	8	478	$190.56		164.71		
10	9	780	$170.66		370.00		

In Figure 2.8, you see the same forecast values—that is, the composite variable—as you see in Figure 2.7. The difference is that Figure 2.8 shows the use of the TREND() function to return the forecasts directly, without having to go to the trouble of picking up the regression coefficients and the intercept from LINEST(), and then applying them to the observed values for Day and Hits.

The formula and function arguments are very similar to the LINEST() usage. Begin by selecting a range one column wide and with as many rows as you have observations. In Figure 2.8, that means E2:E101. Then type the following formula and array-enter it using Ctrl+Shift+Enter instead of simply Enter:

=TREND(C2:C101,A2:B101)

In this case, the only two differences in how you enter TREND() instead of LINEST() are the size and dimensions of the range you select to display the results, and the use of the function name TREND instead of LINEST.

The TREND() function is a handy one when you want to get a quick peek at the results of a regression forecast. But I lean strongly toward grinding things out with LINEST(), particularly while I'm developing a new model. LINEST() provides you with some diagnostic tools that we haven't yet looked at, and won't until Chapter 6. Those tools help you assess the quality of the model you're applying when you use regression analysis, whether simple or multiple.

Just keep in mind that LINEST() gives you the nuts and bolts of a regression analysis along with some diagnostic data. TREND(), on the other hand, is a quick way to get the results of the regression.

Analyzing the Composite Variable

Refer to Figure 2.7, where three correlation coefficients appear in cells L3:L5. Each is a simple correlation. Cell L3 shows that the correlation between Day and Revenue is 0.30. The correlation between Hits and Revenue, 0.60, is in cell L4. Cell L5 shows the correlation of 0.67 between the composite of Day and Hits, in column I, with Revenue.

The composite variable has a somewhat stronger correlation with Revenue than does either Day or Hits by itself. Therefore we expect the composite variable to do a somewhat better job of forecasting Revenue than either Day or Hits by itself. Combining Day with Hits, by using their regression coefficients and the intercept, leads to more accurate forecasts.

And in fact it's the best possible linear forecast, given the data in columns A through C. Suppose you make the slightest adjustment to either regression coefficient, or to the intercept, and calculate a new composite variable using that change. It is guaranteed that the new composite variable will correlate lower with Revenue than the one you get from using the exact LINEST() results.

Why should the composite predict more accurately than either variable by itself? Both Days and Hits appear to bear a relationship to Revenue, but in different ways (see Figure 2.9).

Both Days and Hits, individually, correlate with Revenue—you can tell that from the correlations reported in Figure 2.7 and from the charts in Figure 2.9. In each case, the lower the Days (or the Hits), the lower the Revenue; the higher the Days (or the Hits), the higher the Revenue.

And Hits has a stronger correlation with Revenue than does Days. But Days adds something to our knowledge of Revenue that Hits doesn't. It is clear that over time, as Days changes from 1 to 100, Revenue increases.

So, we multiply each Days value by Days' regression coefficient, and multiply each Hits value by Hits' regression coefficient. We add the results and also add the intercept. The result is a composite variable that correlates higher with Revenue than either predictor variable does by itself.

There's no reason, intrinsic to multiple regression, that limits you to two, three, or more predictor variables. But things start to get flaky when the ratio of the number of observations to the number of predictors starts to get too small.

Suppose that you had 10 observations and four predictor variables. The ratio of observations to predictors is far too small. A multiple regression equation would still return the best combination of your predictors given the forecast variable. But it is extremely unlikely that you'd get the same, or even similar, results if you took a different 10 observations and ran the multiple regression analysis on them.

That's not a good outcome. You want the results of your analysis to be replicable. That is, you want to be able to depend on your forecast equation when the inputs change—for example, when you get beyond Day 100. If your initial sample is too small for the number of predictors, your results will bounce around when you replicate the analysis with different records.

Figure 2.9
You can create the composite variable by using the regression coefficients from LINEST().

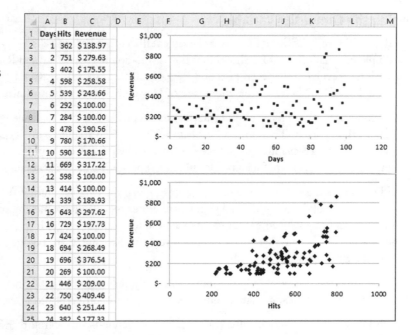

	Days	Hits	Revenue
1	**Days**	**Hits**	**Revenue**
2	1	362	$138.97
3	2	751	$279.63
4	3	402	$175.55
5	4	598	$258.58
6	5	539	$243.66
7	6	292	$100.00
8	7	284	$100.00
9	8	478	$190.56
10	9	780	$170.66
11	10	590	$181.18
12	11	669	$317.22
13	12	598	$100.00
14	13	414	$100.00
15	14	339	$189.93
16	15	643	$297.62
17	16	729	$197.73
18	17	424	$100.00
19	18	694	$268.49
20	19	696	$376.54
21	20	269	$100.00
22	21	446	$209.00
23	22	750	$409.46
24	23	640	$251.44
25	24	382	$177.33

To avoid this problem, you should be sure that you have plenty of observations in the data set that you use to benchmark your regression equation. Of course that begs the question of how many is plenty? That's difficult to answer. If you look hard enough, you'll find some authors who recommend a sample size of 30 for each predictor variable—so, a total sample of at least 60 in this chapter's example regarding Days and Hits. Others recommend at least 400 (!) observations for each predictor variable. That's quite a stretch, from 30 to 400 for each predictor, so you can see that it's difficult to come up with a rule of thumb that has much consensus behind it.

Still, the more observations the better, until your returns start diminishing and you're getting less and less additional information to justify the cost of acquiring and manipulating additional data. There is a shrinkage formula (which has nothing to do with *Seinfeld* episodes) that can help you estimate what the multiple correlation, R, would be for a given number of predictor variables and a varying number of observations. I discuss that formula in the "Using Excel's Regression Tool" section later in this chapter.

Assumptions Made in Regression Analysis

Three assumptions concerning the nature of your data are important in regression analysis. If any one of the assumptions is violated to a serious degree, you'll have problems making good use of the regression analysis. In nearly all cases, you'll be able to get an analysis. The problems occur when you apply the results, either to your original data set or to different sets of observations.

These assumptions, and the effects of their violation, are of intrinsic interest to statisticians. In the broader area of analytics, they are also important because in many situations they force us to resort to logistic regression. Before taking up that topic in Chapter 7, it's helpful to get a handle on assumptions made by the sort of regression analysis discussed in this chapter.

The assumptions have to do with the following three issues:

- The variability of the forecast errors
- The means of the forecast errors
- The distribution of the forecast variable

Variability

Let's have the tooth out right away. The property we're concerned about here is called *homoscedasticity*. That's an ugly word, so much so that it doesn't make the *New Shorter Oxford English Dictionary*. It means *equal spread* and implies that the variance of the residuals of the forecast variable should be the same at all values of the predictor variable.

The residuals are the values you get when you subtract the forecast values from the actually observed values.

When you run a regression analysis, you assume that homoscedasticity exists in the forecast variable. (Another term that you often see for this property is *homogeneity of variance*.)

Figure 2.10 shows something of this concept.

According to the assumption, the variance of the residual values at each level of the predictor should be the same. The levels of the predictor in Figure 2.10 are 1 through 9. Looking at the scatterplot, it appears that there's less variability in the residuals of the forecast variable at the tails of the plot than in the center. Does that mean that this data set violates the assumption?

You can't tell yet. The assumption pertains to the variance, and what you perceive just looking at the scatterplot is not the variance but the range: the largest value minus the smallest value. Figure 2.11 shows the variance of the forecast residuals at each level of the predictor, along with a statistical test of the variances.

In columns A and B of Figure 2.11, the data shown in the scatter chart in Figure 2.10 is shown. (There are actually 70 observations, so most don't show up in Figure 2.11.)

The additional information in Figure 2.11 shows how to test homogeneity of variance, which is described in the next section.

Figure 2.10
The tails of the scatterplot pinch in.

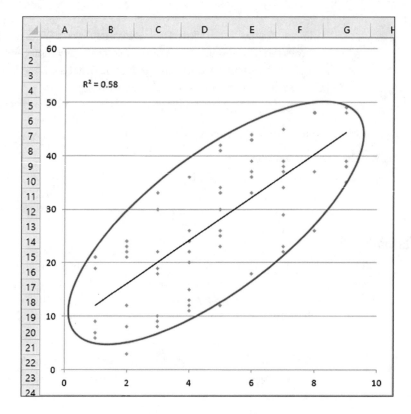

Figure 2.11
The variances tell a different story than the ranges do.

I15 f_x =H13*LN(I13/H13)-K13

	A	B	C	D	E	F	G	H	I	J	K
1	Predic-tor	Residual		Predictor Value	Variance of Residual	Range of Residual		Count of Records, less 1 (v)	Sum of Squared Deviations	Natural Log of Variance	v Times Log
2	1	6		1	52.2	15		5	260.8	4.0	19.8
3	1	7		2	70.5	21		6	422.9	4.3	25.5
4	1	9		3	89.7	25		7	627.9	4.5	31.5
5	1	19		4	66.4	25		8	530.9	4.2	33.6
6	1	21		5	79.2	30		9	712.9	4.4	39.3
7	1	21		6	67.3	26		8	538.0	4.2	33.7
8	2	3		7	65.4	23		7	457.9	4.2	29.3
9	2	8		8	74.9	22		6	449.4	4.3	25.9
10	2	12		9	34.2	14		5	170.8	3.5	17.7
11	2	21									
12	2	22							Totals		
13	2	23						61	4171.5		256.2
14	2	24									
15	3	8						Chi Square	1.56		
16	3	9						Critical value of			
17	3	10						Chi Square	11.03		

Measures of Variability: Bartlett's Test of Homogeneity of Variance

The range D2:F10 contains, for each level of the predictor variable, the variance in column E and the range in column F. You can see that the range increases as you move from 1 to 5 on the predictor variable, and then back down as you move from 6 to 9. The variances in column E are not so regular, and bounce up and down. It's the variances that the equal spread assumption is concerned with, and Figure 2.11 contains a statistical test of the assumption that is described next.

Earlier in this chapter I mentioned that some authors have recommended as many as several hundred observations for each predictor variable in a regression analysis. It may be that so large a number resulted from a concern for checking homogeneity of variance. With samples as small as, say, 10 observations at each point on the regression line, it's to be expected that they exhibit different variances.

The data in Figure 2.11 are a case in point. Notice in column E that the variances at different points along the predictor variable range from 34.2 to 89.7. Those are surely different, but do they mean that the homogeneity assumption has been violated?

If you have a very large sample, with hundreds of observations for each point on the regression line, you can probably answer that question without running a test. The more observations you have, the greater the likelihood that your sample is an accurate representation of the population.

If you don't have so large a sample, it's quite plausible that differences you see in the variances, such as those in E2:E10 of Figure 2.11, are due to sampling error; if you had 400 observations for point 1 of the predictor, another 400 for point 2, and so on, it's plausible that you would find the calculated residual variances to be very close to one another. But with only a few observations at each point, you can't get as accurate an estimate of the population value as you can with hundreds.

Still, you can run the test in Figure 2.11. The test is known as Bartlett's test for homogeneity of variance. The rationale for the test's procedures is not intuitively rich, so I simply describe the procedures here. All worksheet address references are to the worksheet shown in Figure 2.11.

1. Get the count of observations at each point measured for the predictor. Subtract 1 from each count to get the degrees of freedom for the group. (This value is frequently symbolized as v in writing about Bartlett's test.)

2. Get the sum of the squared deviations of each observation from the mean of the observations at that point. Use the worksheet function DEVSQ() to calculate this figure, as is done in cells I2:I10. For example, in I2, the formula is =DEVSQ($B2:$B7).

3. Take the natural log of the variance of each group, as is done in J2:J10. In J2, the formula is =LN(E2).

4. Multiply the value of v in column H and the log in column J. In cell K2, the formula is =H2*J2.

5. In cells H13, I13, and J13, take the sum of the values in the cells directly above them. Cell H13 contains the formula =SUM(H2:H10).

6. Calculate the value of a chi-square statistic. This is done in cell I15 with the following formula:

=H13*LN(I13/H13)-K13

This chi-square statistic, 1.56, has as its degrees of freedom the number of groups, minus 1—in this example, it has 8 degrees of freedom. The critical value for chi-square is returned in cell I17 by this formula:

=CHISQ.INV.RT(0.2,8)

In words, the formula asks for the value of the chi-square distribution with 8 degrees of freedom that cuts off the upper 20% of the area under its curve. Therefore, this test is run with an alpha of 0.2. It returns a value of 11.03. If the variances being tested are all the same in the population, 20% of the time you would observe a calculated chi-square value of 11.03 or greater. You could easily get the chi-square value of 1.56 that is calculated in this example when the population variances are equal. In this case, then, you conclude that you're dealing with homogeneous residual variances.

One reason for the importance of the assumption of homogeneous variances pertains to the accuracy of predictions you might make. Regression analysis routinely calculates something called the standard error of estimate, which I discuss later in this chapter in the section titled "Standard Error."

You use the standard error of estimate to help determine the amount of error you can expect in your forecasts. Suppose you forecast that 100 additional page hits translates to an additional $50 of revenue. You don't expect that forecast to be precise, but you do expect it to fall between certain brackets. You might want to report that your forecast has a margin of error of, say, $10 either way.

The larger the standard error of estimate, the larger those brackets. One of the factors used in calculating the standard error of estimate is the variance of the residuals. If the variance of the residuals is really different at different levels of the predictor variable, then you mislead yourself if you apply the same boundaries throughout the range of the predictor variable. If the residual variance in revenue is $5 when the number of hits is 5, but the residual variance is $10 when the number of hits is 10, then you shouldn't use the same brackets in both cases.

It's that situation that the issue of homogeneity of variance is intended to address. If Bartlett's test tells you that you're unlikely to have that homogeneity, you should be careful about reporting a single margin of error throughout.

Means of Residuals Are Zero

This assumption implies that in the full, unobserved population, the mean of the residuals should be zero at all points along the regression line. We don't have to assume that the mean of all the residuals is zero: That is always true because of the way they are calculated. The assumption is that their mean is zero at each point of the predictor variable, just as we assume that the variance of the residuals is homogeneous at all points along the regression line. And when the residual mean is zero at each point along the regression line, then the regression line between the actual values of the predictor variable and its forecast values is straight and the regression is indeed linear.

Normally Distributed Forecasts

It is also assumed that the residuals are normally distributed. There are several goodness-of-fit tests available to check that this assumption is met, but Bartlett's test for homogeneity of variance is so sensitive that it constitutes a good test for normality as well.

Good visual tests for these assumptions come from the various plots that are provided by the Regression tool. The next section covers that tool in detail.

Using Excel's Regression Tool

Since the mid-1990s, Excel has come with an add-in that is now called the Data Analysis add-in (for several years, it was called the Analysis ToolPak). This add-in makes available several tools for statistical analysis, some of them helpful time-savers and others that are not quite as well thought out.

One of the tools in the add-in runs a regression analysis for you. In several ways it's identical to the results of using the LINEST() worksheet function. But it includes some additional statistical analysis and corrects the problem with LINEST() involving the reversal of the order of the variables' coefficients.

A drawback is that the Data Analysis add-in's Regression tool provides static values. It's not "live" in the sense that LINEST() is live to changes in the underlying data set. If you change the value of a predictor or forecast variable, LINEST() recalculates; the results of the Regression tool don't.

The next two sections explain how to make the tools in the Data Analysis add-in available. I urge you to take the few minutes needed to install and access the add-in, if you haven't done so already. Chapter 3, "Forecasting with Moving Averages," and Chapter 4, "Forecasting a Time Series: Smoothing," base some of their discussions on the add-in's Moving Average and the Exponential Smoothing tools. Even the analysis tools that aren't implemented well can provide you with a comparison for your own solutions to problems in analytics.

Accessing the Data Analysis Add-In

Getting your hands on the Data Analysis add-in is a two-step process. The first step, which you or someone else might already have taken, is to install the add-in from the installation disc or downloaded file onto the computer where you're running Excel.

Simply installing the add-in on your computer isn't enough, though. You also need to alert Excel to the fact that the add-in is available so that Excel can put it on the Ribbon (or in the main menu) for you to use.

Accessing an Installed Add-In

You need to install add-ins yourself, but it's possible that the Data Analysis add-in has already been installed on the computer you want to use. To find out, open Excel 2007 (or a later version) and click the Ribbon's Data tab. If you see an Analysis group on that tab and Data Analysis as a member of that group, the add-in is already installed and accessible to Excel. Skip ahead to the "Running the Regression Tool" section later in this chapter.

If you're using a version of Excel prior to 2007, click its Tools menu. If you see Data Analysis in the Tools menu, the add-in is already installed and accessible; again, skip the remainder of this section.

If you can't find Data Analysis in the Ribbon, click the File tab and choose Options from the navigation bar. The Excel Options window appears; click Add-Ins on its navigation bar. Make sure that Excel Add-Ins appears in the drop-down at the bottom of the window and click Go. A dialog box similar to the one shown in Figure 2.12 appears.

If you see a checkbox labeled Analysis ToolPak, the add-in has been installed on the computer and you simply have to alert Excel to that fact. Fill the Analysis ToolPak checkbox—Analysis ToolPak is just an old name for the Data Analysis add-in—and then click OK. The Data Analysis tool is now available in the Analysis group on the Ribbon's Data tab.

Figure 2.12
Fill or clear the checkboxes to control which add-ins are immediately available from the Excel Ribbon or from Excel's main menu.

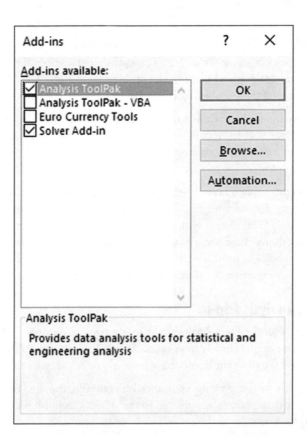

> **NOTE**
> As long as you have the Add-Ins dialog box open, you might as well check for the Solver Add-in. Solver is used extensively by the material in later chapters of this book. If you see it in the dialog box and it is unchecked, fill its checkbox. You'll want to use it later. If you don't see the Solver Add-In listed in the Add-Ins dialog box, install it as described next for the Analysis ToolPak, now termed the Data Analysis tool.

If you're using a version of Excel earlier than 2007, click Add-Ins in the Tools menu. You see the dialog box shown in Figure 2.12. If you see the Analysis ToolPak there, fill its checkbox and click OK.

Installing the Data Analysis Add-In on Your Computer

Regardless of the version of Excel that you're running, if you don't see the Analysis ToolPak checkbox in the Add-Ins dialog box shown in Figure 2.12, you have a bit more work to do. You need to rerun the Office installation software and it's usually best to do so from the Windows Control Panel—you should choose either Add or Remove Software, Programs and Features, or Apps & Features, depending on the version of Windows you're using.

Newer versions of Excel install the Data Analysis add-in automatically. If you're using an older version, expand the Excel portion of the installation tree by clicking the box with a plus sign inside it that's next to Excel. There's an Add-Ins box with its own expand box. Click it and choose to run the Analysis ToolPak from My Computer. Get back to Excel via the OK buttons. If Data Analysis is not automatically installed, continue as discussed earlier to open the dialog box shown in Figure 2.12, and you'll be ready to go.

Running the Regression Tool

Figure 2.13 shows the data set used in Figures 2.4 through 2.9. You should lay your data out in this way whether you expect to use the Regression tool, LINEST(), or both.

Figure 2.13
If you have them on your worksheet, include the cells with labels in the Input Ranges.

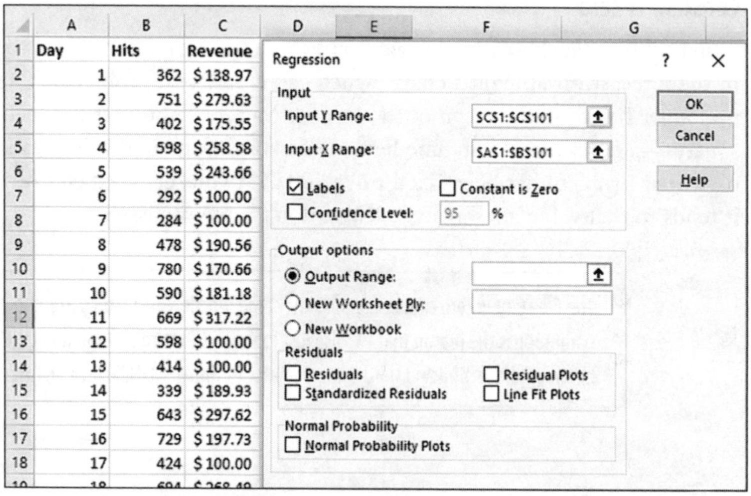

> **NOTE**
> In particular, if you have more than one predictor, you need to make sure that the predictor variables are in columns that are adjacent to one another. It doesn't matter if the forecast variable is to the right or to the left of the predictors, but the predictors must occupy one contiguous range of cells, beginning and ending in the same rows, in adjacent columns.

Understanding the Regression Tool's Dialog Box

Figure 2.13 also shows the dialog box that appears when you click the Ribbon's Data tab, click the Data Analysis item in the Analysis group, and choose Regression from the Data Analysis dialog box.

The purpose of each of the controls in the dialog box is described in the following sections.

Input Y Range

Click in this box and then enter the worksheet range where your forecast variable is located. In Figure 2.13, that's C1:C101. You can type the address or drag through the relevant cells.

Input X Range

The address of the variable or variables that you are treating as predictors goes in this box. In Figure 2.13, that's A1:B101. Again, if you have more than one predictor variable, the columns must all adjoin one another and must start and end in the same rows.

Labels

Fill this checkbox if you have labels in the first row of your forecast and predictor ranges—as is done in the range A1:C1 in Figure 2.13. If you include the cells with labels in your Input Y and Input X ranges, but you don't fill the checkbox, Excel tries to treat them as data points in your regression analysis.

Constant Is Zero

Don't fill this checkbox. Its purpose is to force the regression line through the zero point of the forecast variable on a chart, which can create real problems. The residual errors are no longer based on the mean of the forecast variable, and that can lead to negative sums of squares—a nonsensical outcome because no sum of squared values can be negative. (This particular problem has been fixed since 2007.) If you really expect the intercept to be zero, it tends to that value anyway even if you don't force the issue.

> **NOTE**
> The Constant Is Zero checkbox fulfills the same function as the third argument to LINEST(). The prior paragraph is the reason that I advise just ignoring the third argument in LINEST(), leaving it null between the second and third commas—for example, =LINEST(C2:C101,A2:B101,,TRUE).

Confidence Levels

A confidence level defines the size of a bracket around, in this case, regression coefficients. The brackets help you decide whether the regression coefficient might be zero, and that's important to know because if a regression coefficient is zero it adds no information to the regression equation. You might as well drop it from the equation, and in turn that means that you don't need the predictor variable itself in the LINEST() function or the Regression tool.

In the prior paragraph, I said that the regression coefficient *might* be zero. There, I'm referring to the regression coefficient in the population of values that you're really interested in. After all, the reason to do this sort of analysis is that you want to apply a regression equation to different data: the observations you make next week or next month, or that you make on some other (but probably similar) product, or on other potential buyers from the same market segment. So the question is not whether the calculated regression coefficient is zero—it almost certainly isn't—but whether the regression coefficient you'd get if you had access to an entire population of dates, products, or people would turn out to be zero.

That's what the brackets tell you. If the bracket's upper limit is greater than zero and the lower limit is less than zero, your bracket spans zero and you should consider dropping the variable in question. It might not be adding any useful information, and it's actually making the equation less accurate than it would otherwise be.

When you specify a confidence level, you also help specify the width of the bracket. Suppose you gathered your data 100 times, each time taking a different sample from a population. A 95% confidence level means that 95% of the 100 brackets you calculate from those 100 samples would capture the true population value of the regression coefficient. If the calculated bracket that you get from your actual sample does not span zero, that's pretty good evidence that the population's regression coefficient is not zero either.

You control the width of the bracket by specifying the confidence limit. A 95% level creates a bracket that's wider than a 90% bracket; a 99% level creates a bracket that's wider than a 95% bracket.

So, the greater the level of confidence that you require, the surer you can be that the bracket captures the true population value. The other side of the coin is that the wider the bracket, the more likely it is to span zero, *even if the true population value is not zero*. The bigger a target, the more likely you are to hit it, but if it's the side of a barn door, you might not be getting any useful information.

> **NOTE** The brackets I've described in this section are also called confidence intervals. It's probably more common to see confidence intervals applied to statistics such as mean values, but they work perfectly well with more complex statistics such as regression coefficients.

If you fill the Confidence Level checkbox, you can supply a different confidence level in the edit box. The Regression tool then shows the upper and lower limits for the 95% level as well as the upper and lower limits for the confidence level that you specify.

Output Range Options

These options enable you to select an existing worksheet, a new worksheet (a "worksheet ply" is just a new worksheet), or a new workbook. These options each come with an annoying result. When you select one of the option buttons, you normally expect the associated edit box to be made active so that you can enter a cell address or the name of a new worksheet. But that's not how the Regression tool (and several other Data Analysis tools, for that matter) behaves. When you choose one of the three output range options, the Input Y Range edit box is made active.

If you don't happen to notice that unexpected switch, you might think that you were using your mouse to click where you want the output to start, but you are actually changing the location of the Input Y Range data. In all likelihood you'll specify a blank cell and then the Regression tool will complain that you didn't give it any data to work with.

It's no calamity, just annoying, and if you keep this in mind you'll be able to save your patience for things that really need it.

Residuals

Fill these checkboxes to get plots of the residuals (the difference between the actual values of the forecast variable and the predicted values) and the values of the predictor variable or variables. Ideally, you'd like to see a random pattern of residuals against the predictors. If the pattern is something other than a spray of random markers on the chart, you might need to transform the predictor or forecast variables. An example of this kind of transformation is *differencing*, which is discussed at some length in Chapter 4.

Normal Probability Plot

Don't bother. The chart that the Regression tool supplies is not a normal probability plot. A probability plot is intended to display a straight, diagonal line when actual values are plotted against values that follow a normal distribution. The only way to do that in Excel is by way of a bar chart, the only chart in Excel with a vertical category axis. The Regression tool's Normal Probability Plot is not in conformance and is more likely to mislead you than to inform you.

Understanding the Regression Tool's Output

Figure 2.14 shows the results of running the Regression tool on the data in columns A:C.

The meaning of the numbers is described in the following sections.

Figure 2.14
Some cells have been reformatted so that the output fits on one printed page.

	A	B	C	D	E	F	G	H	I	J	K
1	Day	Hits	Revenue		SUMMARY OUTPUT						
2	1	362	$ 138.97								
3	2	751	$ 279.63		*Regression Statistics*						
4	3	402	$ 175.55		Multiple R	0.67					
5	4	598	$ 258.58		R Square	0.45					
6	5	539	$ 243.66		Adjusted R Square	0.44					
7	6	292	$ 100.00		Standard Error	127.12					
8	7	284	$ 100.00		Observations	100					
9	8	478	$ 190.56								
10	9	780	$ 170.66		ANOVA						
11	10	590	$ 181.18			*df*	*SS*	*MS*	*F*	*Significance of F*	
12	11	669	$ 317.22		Regression	2	1298771.49	649385.74	40.19	0.000	
13	12	598	$ 100.00		Residual	97	1567446.76	16159.24			
14	13	414	$ 100.00		Total	99	2866218.25				
15	14	339	$ 189.93								
16	15	643	$ 297.62			*Coefficients*	*Standard Error*	*t Stat*	*P-value*	*Lower 95%*	*Upper 95%*
17	16	729	$ 197.73		Intercept	-171.71	51.56	-3.33	0.001	-274.05	-69.37
18	17	424	$ 100.00		Day	1.79	0.44	4.06	0.000	0.92	2.66
19	18	694	$ 268.49		Hits	0.67	0.08	8.03	0.000	0.51	0.84

Multiple R

As already discussed in this chapter, this is the correlation between the composite variable made up of the best combination of the predictor variables, and the forecast variable. The Regression tool terms it a multiple R even if you have used only one predictor variable.

R Square

The R Square value, usually labeled R^2, is the workhorse of regression analysis. It shows up in many different contexts, more so than the Multiple R itself. It's important enough to have been given its own name, the *coefficient of determination* (which is a little misleading, because it tends to imply causation). Chapter 6 discusses its use in evaluating the quality of a forecast, and the remainder of this chapter refers to R^2 in its explanations of the Regression tool output.

The value of R^2 tells you the proportion of the variance in the forecast variable that can be accounted for by the predictor variable or variables. If your regression analysis returns a multiple R of 0.80, the multiple R^2 is 0.64. Because R cannot exceed 1.0 (or fall below −1.0), R^2 can range only from 0.0 to 1.0 and, as it turns out, it can be thought of as a percentage that ranges from 0% to 100%. So if R^2 is 0.64, you know that your predictor variable or variables account for 64% of the variance in your forecast variable.

Refer to Figure 2.10. The observations vary along the vertical scale. Because they have a general lower-left to upper-right orientation, it's clear that the observations follow the solid trendline inside the oval. Of their total variability on the vertical axis, the calculated R^2 of .58 tells you that 58% of their total variability on the vertical axis is associated with their variability on the horizontal axis—that is, the relationship between the two variables accounts for 58% of the variability in each.

NOTE Figure 2.10 uses a different data set than does Figure 2.14, and so the two figures have different values for R^2. You can show an R^2 value on a chart by right-clicking the charted data series, choosing to add a trendline from the shortcut menu, and filling the Display R-squared checkbox.

What of the remaining 42%? It might be simple random variation, or it might be associated with some other variable that wasn't included in the analysis.

Adjusted R Square

Toward the end of this chapter's section titled "Analyzing the Composite Variable," I noted that there is something called a shrinkage formula that helps you assess how stable the calculated R^2 is. The idea is to estimate the size of the R^2 value you would get if you ran the regression analysis on a different sample from the same population. The Regression tool calls it the Adjusted R Square. The formula is

$$\text{Adjusted } R^2 = 1 - (1 - R^2)\left((N - 1) / (N - k - 1)\right)$$

where N is the number of observations and k is the number of predictor variables.

A little thought will show that the adjusted R^2 must always be smaller than the calculated R^2. This is as it should be, because the way that the multiple R is determined assumes that the simple correlations (also called *zero-order correlations*) are free of errors of measurement and of sampling. Because that assumption is never true in practical applications, the R and R^2 values are always overestimates.

But the overestimates can be vanishingly small if you have a large sample (N) relative to the number of predictors (k). Otherwise, the R^2—and therefore the R—could shrink as much as is implied by the adjusted R^2 if you take another sample and recalculate the regression analysis.

Standard Error

The value labeled Standard Error is normally called the standard error of estimate. It is the standard deviation of the residuals: the differences between the predicted values of the forecast variable and its actual values (but see the following Note). As such, the standard error of estimate quantifies how accurate the predictions are, in their original scale of measurement.

One way to express the standard error of estimate is as follows:

$$\sqrt{\frac{SS_{resid}}{N - k - 1}}$$

In terms of the cell addresses in Figure 2.14, the formula is the following:

=SQRT(G13/F13)

Notice that formula returns the same value as given by the Regression tool in cell F7.

A standard deviation is the square root of the ratio of the sum of squared deviations to its degrees of freedom. That's what the prior formula returns. The sum of squares residual is the sum of the squares of the residuals (in G13), divided by their degrees of freedom (in cell F13). The square root of that ratio is the standard error of estimate: the standard deviation of the errors made in estimating the forecast variable from the predictor variables.

> **NOTE** You sometimes see the statement that the standard error of estimate is the standard deviation of the residuals. That's a good way to think of it, but it's a little oversimplified. If you merely get the residuals and calculate their standard deviation, you ignore the fact that you lose a degree of freedom for each predictor variable. The standard deviation of the residuals differs from the standard error of estimate by this factor:
>
> $$\sqrt{(N-1)/(N-k-1)}$$

ANOVA Table

The ANOVA (which stands for Analysis of Variance) table in the range E11:J14 is another way—besides gauging the adjusted R^2—to determine the reliability of the calculated R^2. It is what's called a *parametric* test because it tests the difference between, in this case, the calculated R^2 and what that R^2 actually might be in the population from which you have taken the sample.

> **NOTE** Statistical jargon distinguishes a value that's calculated using a sample from a value that's calculated using a population. For example, calculated on a sample, the mean is termed a *statistic*. Calculated on a population, the mean is termed a *parameter*.

The test determines the likelihood of getting an R^2 as large as the one observed if the R^2 in the population is really zero. Notice that an R^2 of zero would mean that there's no association between the predictor variables and the forecast variable.

The value labeled Significance of F, 0.000 in cell J12 of Figure 2.14, gives the likelihood of an observed R^2 as large as 0.45 when the R^2 in the population is really zero. In this case, the likelihood is extremely small and most would conclude that the population R^2 is larger than zero. (The 0.000 is the likelihood, remember, and it's not really a zero likelihood. It's just so small that it can't be shown accurately with only three visible decimals.)

In this chapter's "R Square" section, I pointed out that R^2 is the proportion of variability that can be accounted for by the regression with the predictor variables. One way to confirm that is to take the ratio of the sum of squares, or SS, for the regression (cell G12) to the total sum of squares (cell G14). The result is 0.45, which is the calculated R^2 in cell F5.

Regression Equation

Results that define the regression equation appear in Figure 2.14 in the range E16:K19. The terms used in the regression equation are in F17:F19. (The label *Coefficients* in F16 is mildly misleading; the intercept is not a coefficient, but the values in F18:F19 are.) The values shown are identical to those you would get by using LINEST() directly on the worksheet, but you don't have to contend with the reversed order of the coefficients that LINEST() imposes on you.

The values in G17:G19 are the standard errors of the intercept and the coefficients. If you divide each value in F17:F19 by the associated standard error in G17:G19, you get a t statistic—an inferential test of whether the figures in column F differ significantly from zero.

The t statistics appear in column H. By themselves, they don't tell you much. But combined with information about the degrees of freedom, they can help you infer whether a regression coefficient is really zero in the population you got your sample from.

For example, the value in cell I17 is 0.001. That indicates that there's about 1 chance in 1,000 that you would get a t statistic of −3.33 if the intercept in the population were really zero. You can get that p value yourself with this worksheet formula:

    =T.DIST.2T(ABS(H17),F13)

The "2T" part of the function name was introduced in Excel 2010, although it was included as one of the Options arguments to the older TDIST() function. The 2T indicates that you're using (just as the Regression tool does) a two-tailed or *nondirectional* test of the hypothesis that the coefficient or intercept is really zero in the population.

Also notice the use of the ABS() function in the prior formula. The T.DIST.2T() function does not accept a negative value for the t statistic, so it's best to convert it to a positive value via ABS(). Because it's a nondirectional test, the conversion has no effect on the probability level returned.

The lower and upper limits of the bracket, or the confidence interval, around the intercept and the coefficients are in J17:K19. You can calculate the limits for the intercept in F17 with these formulas:

    =F17-T.INV(0.975,F13)*G17

and

    =F17+T.INV(0.975,F13)*G17

The T.INV() function returns the t value for the particular confidence level (here, 0.975) and a given degrees of freedom (here, the value in cell F13). Multiply the t value by the value of the standard error in G17, and subtract and add the result to the value in F17, the intercept. The same pattern is followed for the regression coefficients.

The 0.975 level is specified because the 0.95 confidence level was chosen when the Regression tool was run. Because a two-tailed, nondirectional test is used, 2.5% of the area under the curve occupies each tail beyond the bracket limits. Therefore, we look for the value that cuts off 2.5% of the area, which includes 97.5% or 0.975 of the curve. Taken together, the 2.5% areas constitute the 5% area outside the 95% confidence interval.

The Regression tool's labels in cells J16:K16 are mildly misleading. To say, for example, "Upper 95%" is to imply that the associated value cuts off the upper 95% of the curve. In fact, as just discussed, the value cuts off the upper 2.5% of the curve. Similarly, the value under "Lower 95%" cuts off the lower 2.5% of the curve.

2

Forecasting with Moving Averages

3

The concept of a moving average is straightforward. You generally apply a moving average to a series of observations taken over time. The average moves forward with the data series. So, the first moving average might include Days 1 through 3, the second moving average might include Days 2 through 4, and so on. This chapter discusses some of the reasons why you might want to make those calculations.

If that were all there is to it, there wouldn't be much point to including the material in this chapter. However, the simple moving average forms the basis for much more sophisticated analyses. For example, the "MA" at the end of the acronym ARIMA (which codifies some fairly complicated forecasting procedures) stands for Moving Average. The varieties of exponential smoothing all rely on extensions of moving averages.

This chapter is therefore intended as background for discussions of predictive analytic techniques that you'll find in later chapters.

About Moving Averages

Any data series has, among other characteristics, an average value (or *mean*) and individual values that vary around that mean. A data series that consists of the sales made from a website last week has an average sales amount, measured in currency. It also has individual sales amounts, measured in currency, that vary around the mean.

Some individual sales amounts are higher than the mean and some lower. In some data series, the individual amounts steadily increase or decrease over time, pulling the mean up or down accordingly. In other series, the individual amounts vary randomly around a static mean value.

One of the questions that we would like to answer with forecasting is whether the mean value of the data series is increasing, decreasing, or merely remaining at the same level over time.

Signal and Noise

Most credible forecasting methods take notice of how the individual values vary, and whether they tend to drift generally up or down. Each forecasting method accounts for two components in the movement of the data series over time: the signal and the noise. Figure 3.1 shows a simple example.

Figure 3.1
The straight line represents the signal in this data series. The way that individual points vary around it represents the noise.

Two events happen over time with any data series that isn't just trivial:

- The average value remains the same, increases, or decreases. This is the signal. Generally, sales may be flat, rising, or declining, and you'd like to know which.

- The individual values vary, perhaps randomly, around the average value. This is the noise. You'd like to see through the noise to focus on the signal.

A *moving average* can help you distinguish random bounces in a data series from actual, fundamental changes in the signal. See Figure 3.2 for a data series that has a good bit of random fluctuation in its values.

When you calculate a moving average, you take the average of recent observations, and regard the average as the best estimate of what the series will do next.

For example, the first three values in the data series that's charted in Figure 3.2 are 855, 847, and 1,000. If you decide to take a moving average of length 3, you average those three values and let the result, 901, be your best estimate of where the series will be on the fourth day.

Figure 3.2
This data series bounces around quite a bit. You can eyeball what signal there is, but charting a moving average is usually better.

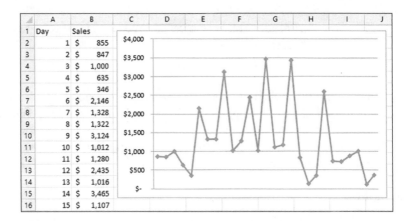

	A	B		C	D	E	F	G	H	I	J
1	Day	Sales									
2	1	$	855	$4,000							
3	2	$	847								
4	3	$	1,000	$3,500							
5	4	$	635	$3,000							
6	5	$	346								
7	6	$	2,146	$2,500							
8	7	$	1,328	$2,000							
9	8	$	1,322								
10	9	$	3,124	$1,500							
11	10	$	1,012	$1,000							
12	11	$	1,280								
13	12	$	2,435	$500							
14	13	$	1,016								
15	14	$	3,465	$-							
16	15	$	1,107								

Smoothing Out the Noise

The idea is that there is noise in the series, random events that knock the actual observations off their signal. Perhaps a couple of potential customers were under the weather on Days 1 and 2 and did not make the purchases that they were intending to make. The result was a loss of revenue on the first two days—random noise that pulled the actual sales down from the level that the signal says you could expect.

Those two customers were back at work on Day 3 and made their intended purchases, pushing the actual sales above the level that the signal would have led you to expect on Day 3.

By averaging the observations on Day 1 through Day 3, you might well get a better sense of the level of the data series as of Day 4. When Day 5 rolls around, you can average the observed values for Day 2, Day 3, and Day 4 to estimate the signal on Day 5—that's what makes it a moving average. With every additional time period that passes, the set of values that you average moves forward by one period.

Figure 3.3 shows the original data series and also the result of charting the three-day moving average.

Figure 3.3
The charted moving averages smooth out the noise in the data series.

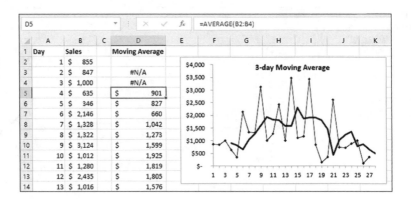

		D5					f_x	=AVERAGE(B2:B4)			

	A	B		C	D	E	F	G	H	I	J	K
1	Day	Sales			Moving Average							
2	1	$	855									
3	2	$	847		#N/A							
4	3	$	1,000		#N/A							
5	4	$	635		$ 901							
6	5	$	346		$ 827							
7	6	$	2,146		$ 660							
8	7	$	1,328		$ 1,042							
9	8	$	1,322		$ 1,273							
10	9	$	3,124		$ 1,599							
11	10	$	1,012		$ 1,925							
12	11	$	1,280		$ 1,819							
13	12	$	2,435		$ 1,805							
14	13	$	1,016		$ 1,576							

NOTE   See the section titled "Output Range," later in this chapter, for the reason that the first moving average cell, D2, is blank.

You can see that the chart of the moving averages is a good bit smoother than the chart of the original data series. It appears that the general drift is gently up and then gently back down. The smoothing that almost always results from calculating moving averages tends to locate the underlying level of the series at any given point, and the random events tend to cancel one another out.

Lost Periods

Nothing's free, though, and the principal cost of using moving averages is that you lose some observations at the start of the series. Look closely at the two data series that are charted in Figure 3.3. The actual observed values start at Day 1 and continue through Day 27. However, the moving averages start at Day 4—with a three-period moving average, you lose three periods at the start. In general, you lose as many periods at the start of a moving average as there are periods in the moving average.

Clearly, if you were to try to forecast a value for Day 3 using a moving average of three periods, you would want to find the average of Day 2, Day 1, and Day 0. But there is no Day 0.

There are different ways to deal with this problem, but nothing is as satisfactory as having a good long baseline of observations. That becomes clearer in Chapter 4, "Forecasting a Time Series: Smoothing," which discusses exponential smoothing.

Smoothing Versus Tracking

In general, the more observations you place in a moving average, the more smoothing you get. Compare the moving average charted in Figure 3.3 (which is a moving average of length 3) with the moving average charted in Figure 3.4 (which is of length 4).

Figure 3.4
Each moving average includes four actual observations.

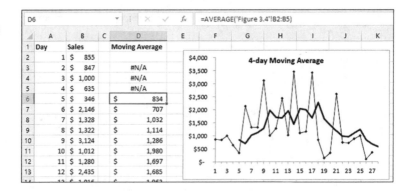

Notice first that the signal over time in this data series is somewhat clearer when you use a moving average of length 4. For example, in Figure 3.3, the moving average on Day 21 drops suddenly and temporarily from 1,470 to 441 and then picks back up to 1,030. The 441 value is the average of 836, 142, and 345 on Days 18 through 20.

But there is no such sudden and temporary dip in the moving averages shown in Figure 3.4. The reason is that the moving average is of length 4 rather than 3. With this data set, a moving average of length 4 is long enough that the moving average combines the three low observations on Days 18 through 20 with the relatively high observations on either Day 17 or Day 21.

Very likely, a temporary and random event threw the data series off its signal for a few days, after which it recovered, and the four-day moving average in Figure 3.4 smooths out the noise.

Of course, the cost of using a four-day average instead of a three-day average is that you lose an additional period at the start of the moving average. Notice that the four-day moving average starts on Day 5 in Figure 3.4, whereas the three-day moving average starts on Day 4 in Figure 3.3.

So far, I've discussed the useful effect of moving averages on smoothing out the random noise in a data series. There's another side to that issue: What's the effect of a longer moving average when an abrupt change in the level of a series isn't random noise but a real, persistent shift? See Figure 3.5.

Figure 3.5
The level of the series apparently drops during the final ten periods.

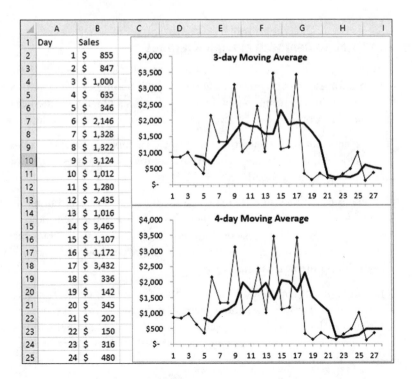

In Figure 3.5, I have changed some of the final ten observations from the values shown in Figures 3.3 and 3.4: In Figure 3.5 all ten values drop to the low hundreds. The moving average line in both charts also drops in response to the lower actuals.

But the moving average in the upper chart, which is based on three observations, catches up with the actuals on the twenty-first day. The moving average in the lower chart, where the basis is four observations, does not catch up to the drop in the actuals until the twenty-second day—one period later than the three-day moving average.

This difference is due to what's called *tracking*, which is the other side of the smoothing coin. Other things being equal, a moving average based on fewer actual observations tracks a change in the series level earlier and faster than one based on more actual observations.

You want the moving average to track faster when the change in the level of the series turns out to be real and persistent. Then your estimate of the signal reacts more quickly and accurately. You want the moving average to track more slowly when the change in the level of the series turns out to be temporary. Then your estimate of the signal won't get pulled off course—at least, not as far and not for as long.

The problem, obviously, is how to choose the best balance between smoothing and tracking, between suppressing an overreaction to temporary noise and failing to react quickly to a persistent change in the level of the series. There are objective ways to do that, which are covered in detail in Chapter 4.

First, it's a good idea to look at a couple of variations on moving averages, which have to do with *weighting*.

Weighted and Unweighted Moving Averages

Have you ever used QuickBooks? It's a popular, relatively inexpensive accounting application, intended for use primarily by small and very small businesses. Many of its versions include a cash flow projector, meant to look forward six weeks and tell you whether your current cash on hand plus projected weekly revenues will be enough to cover projected weekly expenses.

The expense side of the ledger is straightforward enough. Most small businesses know pretty closely how much they will have to pay for salaries, taxes, rent, utilities, supplies, and so on during the next month and a half.

Revenue is sometimes another matter. If the business is engaged in fulfilling a medium- to long-term contract, it's fairly sure when checks will arrive and for how much. A retail store or small professional services company, especially one without a track record covering several years, probably can't tell with much confidence how many dollars will come in weekly during the next month or two.

Therefore, one of your options in QuickBooks is to forecast the next weeks' worth of revenue on the basis of a weighted average of the prior six weeks. A weighted average multiplies each observation by a weight—usually, but not always, a different weight for each observation. The results are summed and divided by the number of weighted observations.

Figure 3.6 shows what this might look like in an Excel worksheet.

Figure 3.6
The weighted moving average typically assigns greater weight to more recent observations.

	A	B	C	D
			fx	=C9/6
1	Sales	Weight	Weighted sales	
2	$ 855.00	0.1875	$ 160.31	
3	$ 847.00	0.1875	$ 158.81	
4	$1,000.00	0.3750	$ 375.00	
5	$ 635.00	0.7500	$ 476.25	
6	$ 346.00	1.5000	$ 519.00	
7	$2,146.00	3.0000	$ 6,438.00	
8				
9		Sum:	$ 8,127.38	
10		Weighted average:	$ 1,354.56	
11		Unweighted average:	$ 971.50	

The sales figures in column A are the same as the first six figures shown in Figure 3.5. The weights shown in column B are the weights used by QuickBooks (and I might as well say right away that there's nothing magical about the particular weights that QuickBooks chooses to use).

Column C in Figure 3.6 shows the result of multiplying the sales figure in column A by the weight in column B. To get the weighted moving average, you sum the weighted sales figures in C2:C7. The result appears in C9. Then, divide by 6, which here is the total of the weights. The result, the weighted moving average, appears in C10.

The unweighted average in C11 is the simple average of the sales figures in A2:A7. (You could think of them as weighted if you wanted to: In a simple average, each of the six weights is 1.0.) Notice that the weighted moving average in C10 is about $383 greater than the unweighted average in C11. That's mostly because the largest sales figure, $2,146 in A7, is multiplied by the largest weight, 3.0 in B7. In the simple average shown in C11, the largest sales figure of $2,146 carries the same weight as each of the other five figures.

Apart from the fact that there's nothing magical about the weights themselves, there are a few points of interest, which are covered in the following sections.

Total of Weights

The weights total 6.0. This fact is largely a matter of convenience, given that the average is six periods long. You would get the same result if you doubled the size of each weight and at the end divided by 12.

Relative Size of Weights

It's a little easier to see the relative impact of the weights if you treat them as percentages, so that they total to 100%. Figure 3.7 translates the weights from Figure 3.6 into percentages.

So yesterday's actual value accounts for 50% of today's forecast; the value from the day before yesterday accounts for another 25%. Not at all unreasonable, but you'd like some more objective, substantive grounds for selecting the weights. Those grounds exist, and this chapter, along with Chapter 4, touches on them.

Figure 3.7
Expressed as percentages, these are called *normalized weights.*

	A	B	C	D	E	F
			C2 ▼ : × ✓ *fx* =B2/$B$9			

	A	B	C	D	E	F
1		Weight	Weight as percentage			
2		0.1875	3%			
3		0.1875	3%			
4		0.3750	6%			
5		0.7500	13%			
6		1.5000	25%			
7		3.0000	50%			
8						
9	Total	6.0000	100%			
10						

More Recent Weights Are Larger

The weight that's applied to the most recent observation is the largest. The farther back that an observation occurs, the smaller its weight is—until, in QuickBooks' scheme, you reach the first two weights. This makes pretty good sense: Unless there's some sort of seasonality in the data, the market conditions that were in place six periods back are less likely to represent the market conditions that were in place one period back. On the other hand, the more recent the observed value, the better it is as an indicator of the next, as-yet-unobserved value.

Until you get back to the first two weights used in Figure 3.7, each weight is exactly twice as large as the one preceding it. For example, 3.0 is twice as large as 1.5, 1.5 is twice as large as 0.75, and so on.

That's a problem, because there's nothing written down anywhere that says yesterday's value ought to have twice the weight as the value from the day before yesterday. When it comes to weighting past observations to get a weighted moving average, you want something more grounded in the data than a neat doubling sequence to determine the weights. The material on smoothing in Chapter 4 gets into that issue more deeply.

The pattern used by any weighting scheme, such as the one used by QuickBooks, has implications for how the moving averages track the actuals or smooth them out. Generally, when the more recent values are weighted more heavily, the moving average tracks more quickly. When the values are weighted equally, as are the moving averages in Figures 3.3 through 3.5, the moving average tends to smooth the original values more than it tracks them. You would probably reach that conclusion intuitively, but Figure 3.8 provides a visual example.

The data in columns A and B of Figure 3.8 is the same as in Figure 3.4. The chart is based on that data, on a six-day moving average and on a six-day weighted average.

Notice in Figure 3.8 that the six-day weighted moving average, shown with a dashed line in the upper chart, tracks the actual observations (solid line) rather closely and quickly. It has peaks and troughs one period following the actual observations.

Figure 3.8

The weighted moving average tracks the original data much more closely than does the unweighted moving average.

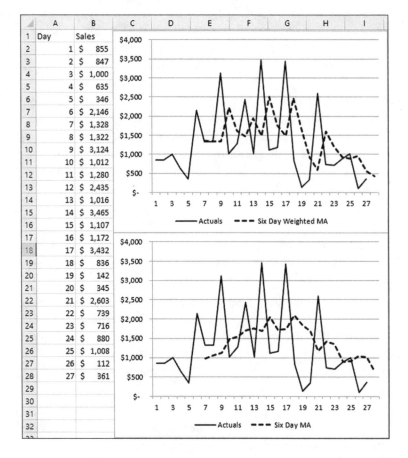

In contrast, the unweighted six-day moving average (shown as a dashed line in the lower chart) smooths the actuals, suppressing irrelevant noise—but at a cost. You might miss an important shift in the level of the series until it's too late to do anything about it.

Criteria for Judging Moving Averages

How should you decide on the number of values to use in a moving average—that is, should you use a moving average of length 2? 3? 5? Some other number? It's surprisingly difficult to make that choice by simply eyeballing a chart that shows the moving average against the actuals.

There are several objective methods, any of which could be thought of as a standard. Each of them depends, logically enough, on the difference between the forecast for a given period and the actual value observed for that period. That difference is calculated for each of the available periods, and the differences can then be analyzed in several ways.

For example, you might calculate the average difference between the forecast and the actual, and select the length of the moving average that results in the smallest average difference. One problem with this approach is that large swings tend to cancel one another out. The average error does not tell you that a given moving average resulted in some huge errors, some of them positive and some negative.

Mean Absolute Deviation

One way to get around that problem is to take the average of the absolute values of the errors. By treating all the errors as positive numbers, you avoid the problem of positive and negative errors cancelling each other out. This approach is usually called the *mean absolute deviation*. You would choose the length of your moving average that resulted in the smallest mean absolute deviation.

Least Squares

Another way of dealing with the problem of positive and negative errors is to square them. Both positive and negative errors, when squared, yield a positive result. This approach is called the method of *least squares*.

Least squares is likely the most popular approach to determining the optimal moving average length for forecasting a given data series. There are several reasons that this is so. One is that it is the same approach used in regression analysis (see Chapter 2, "Linear Regression," and Chapter 6, "Forecasting a Time Series: Regression"), and although it's not used as an inferential statistic in this context, its properties are well known and understood.

Another reason that analysts use the least squares criterion is that because the errors are squared, the least squares approach is more sensitive to large errors than are other approaches, such as the mean absolute deviation. In forecasting, it's often much more important to avoid a few large errors than it is to avoid many small errors. In business, for example, one serious error can sink you, whereas lots of little errors are virtually standard operating procedure.

Using Least Squares to Compare Moving Averages

Figure 3.9 shows two different moving averages calculated on the data series shown in Figure 3.4.

Figure 3.9
The six-day moving average in this case provides slightly more accurate forecasts than the three-day moving average.

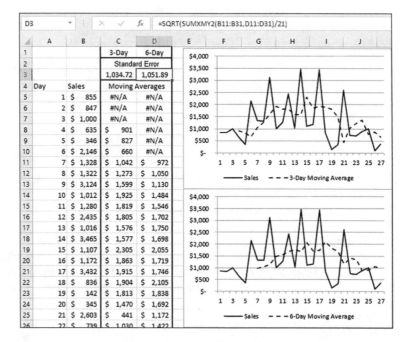

In Figure 3.9, columns A and B show on which day the data was measured and the data series itself. Column C, beginning in cell C8, contains the three-day moving average, and column D contains the six-day moving average beginning in cell D11.

It would be very difficult to judge, looking at the chart, whether a three- or a six-day moving average would provide the more accurate forecasts. But the two formulas in cells C3 and D3 quantify the difference between the two moving averages. The formula in C3 is as follows:

=SQRT(SUMXMY2(B8:B31,C8:C31)/24)

It uses Excel's SUMXMY2() function to get the sum of the squared differences (more often referred to as *deviations*) between the actuals and the three-day moving averages. (The meaning of the *SUM* part of the function name is self-evident. The *XMY* portion means "X Minus Y "—that is, the X values minus the Y values. The 2 means that the differences are squared before the summing takes place.)

The sum of the squared differences is divided by the number of moving averages, to get the average squared deviation. Finally, the square root is taken by means of Excel's SQRT() function, to get the result into the original scale of measurement.

The formula in D3 is as follows:

=SQRT(SUMXMY2(B11:B31,D11:D31)/21)

This formula analyzes the six-day moving average, just as the formula in C3 analyzes the three-day moving average. The average of the squared deviations of the six-day averages from the associated actuals is taken (notice that the divisor is 21, not 24, because there are three fewer moving averages). Then the square root is taken.

The results of this analysis indicate that, with this set of observations, the three-day moving average is slightly more accurate as a forecast than the six-day moving average. Lacking any special additional knowledge of the data series, I would certainly use the three-day average instead of the six-day average and take the bonus that I have three more averages to work with.

On the other hand, the three-day moving average is more accurate by a very slim margin. I would also continue the analysis for several more periods at least, until I felt satisfied that I was using the better moving average. The results could easily change after a few more days, and in that case I wouldn't hesitate to switch horses.

> **NOTE** Just because you use one method, such as the square root of the mean square error, doesn't mean that you can't buttress it with another method such as the mean absolute deviation. Particularly in close cases, such as the one shown in Figure 3.9, it's helpful to know if two different methods agree. If they don't, that's more reason yet to continue the analysis for a few more periods at least before making a firm decision to settle on a particular length for the moving averages.

Getting Moving Averages Automatically

In addition to the Regression tool and several others, the Data Analysis add-in described in Chapter 2 offers a Moving Average tool, which calculates and charts moving averages for you.

If you have already installed the Data Analysis add-in, continue with the next section. If you have not installed it, refer to the "Accessing the Data Analysis Add-In" section in Chapter 2. You need to do some installation prep work before you can use the add-in, but you need to do it once only. Chapter 2 walks you through the installation process.

I'm going to take some space in this chapter to describe how to use the Moving Average tool and to draw your attention to some of its idiosyncrasies. If you're new to the analysis of moving averages, you'll find the Moving Average tool a useful learning device. At the very least, you can use it to check the moving averages that you create yourself, along with their alignment as forecasts of the original data series.

Still, I expect that in time you will dispense with using the Moving Average tool and create your own forecasting analyses and charts.

Using the Moving Average Tool

The Data Analysis Add-In includes a tool that calculates a simple moving average for you. Optionally, it creates a chart with your original observations and the moving average that's based on them. You identify the location of your data series and how many periods (which the tool calls *intervals*) you want the moving average to include. The tool writes the moving averages (as formulas, not static values) to the worksheet and creates an embedded chart if you requested one.

Suppose your data is laid out as shown in Figure 3.10.

Figure 3.10
It's not usually a good idea to do so, but you could lay out your data to occupy a single row instead of a single column.

	A	B	C	D
1	Sales			
2	$ 838			
3	$ 346			
4	$ 540			
5	$ 682			
6	$ 155			
7	$ 872			
8	$ 705			
9	$ 677			
10	$ 535			
11	$ 715			

With the worksheet that has your data series active, click the Data tab and choose Data Analysis from the Analysis group. The dialog box shown in Figure 3.11 appears.

Figure 3.11
You'll have to scroll down to get to the Moving Average tool.

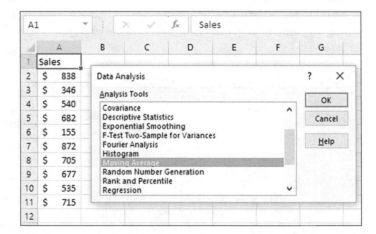

Click the Moving Average item in the list box to select it, and then click OK. The dialog box shown in Figure 3.12 appears.

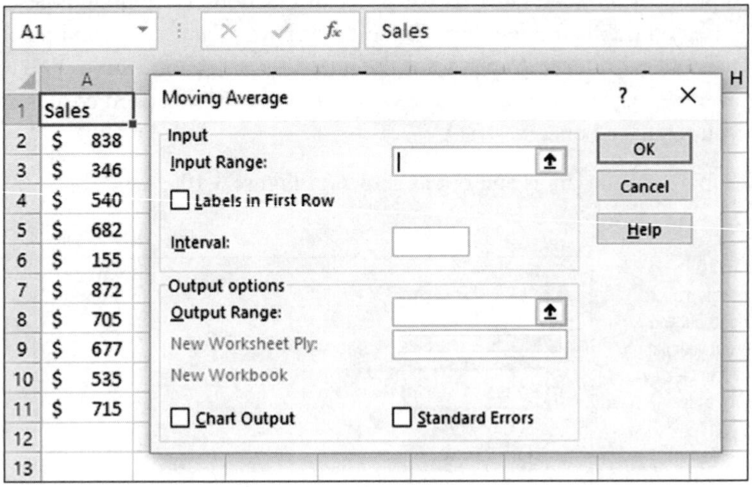

Figure 3.12
If you supplied a label for the data (such as in cell A1 in Figure 3.10), the tool's output does not display it.

To get the moving average analysis, follow these steps:

1. Click in the Input Range box and then drag through the range on the worksheet that contains your data. If there is a label at the start of the data series and if you include it in this step, you should take Step 2.

2. Fill the Labels in First Row checkbox if you used a label and included it in Step 1. (However, this has no effect on the output.)

3. Choose the number of values to include in each moving average. This is what the dialog box refers to as the Interval. Enter the number in the edit box.

4. Click in the Output Range edit box and then click in the worksheet cell where you want the moving averages to start.

5. Fill the Chart Output checkbox if you want the actuals and the moving averages to be charted. Fill the Standard Errors checkbox if you want them to appear along with the moving averages (more on this issue later in the chapter).

6. Click OK.

The results, based on the data in Figure 3.11, appear in Figure 3.13.

Figure 3.13
Notice that the label in cell B1 appears nowhere in the output.

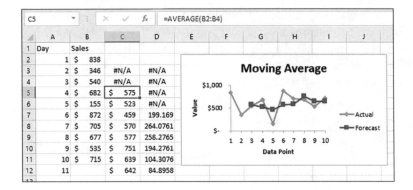

The following sections comment on using the dialog box and on the output.

Labels

Other tools in the Data Analysis add-in make good use of the Labels option. The Descriptive Statistics and Exponential Smoothing tools, for example, pick up any label that you supply at the start of a data range ("Sales" in Figure 3.13) and use it in the charts and tables that they provide.

The Moving Average tool doesn't behave similarly. It ignores your label. The only reason I mention the Labels option in the prior list of steps is to alert you to the possibility of an error. Suppose that you use a text label and include its cell in the Input Range without also filling the Labels checkbox. In that case, you get an error message; Excel's Moving Average tool can't use a text value as part of an average.

So, either omit the label from the input range or include it and select the Labels option. Either way causes Excel to ignore the label when it calculates the first moving average.

Output Range

I like to see the final moving average extend one row down from the final actual observation. That makes it a little clearer that the final moving average—quite legitimately thought of as a forecast—applies to the period immediately following the final actual observation.

To arrange that layout, I usually start the output in the row immediately following the first actual observation. As the actual observations are laid out in Figure 3.14, the first actual sales value is in cell B2. Therefore, I call for the output to start in cell C3; one column to the right to keep things tidy, and one row down to line up the moving averages properly with the actuals. More on that issue next.

Actuals and Forecasts

Notice that the embedded chart labels the original data series as "Actuals" and the moving averages as "Forecast." That's fair enough: Forecasting the next value in a data series is a primary rationale for running a moving average analysis in the first place.

But in that case, the chart should be lining up the data series differently. Notice in Figure 3.13 that the final moving average—or "forecast"—is aligned in the chart with the final actual observation. That's not a function of where you choose to start the output. You could tell Excel to start recording the calculated averages in cell AB757 and the charted data values would still line up as they appear in Figure 3.13's chart.

The problem with that alignment is that the final moving average should be the forecast for the *next* period (here, the next day). That final moving average is the average of the observations on Days 8 through 10. How, then, can a forecast for Day 10 be based in part on the actual observation for Day 10? By the time you have the actual value for Day 10, you no longer need a forecast for Day 10.

Therefore, if I use the Moving Average tool to create a chart, I like to adjust the chart as follows:

1. Select the forecast series in the chart by clicking it. The series address appears in the formula bar; in the chart shown in Figure 3.14, the address is $C$3:$C$12.

2. Edit the address in the formula bar so that it starts in $C$2 rather than $C$3. In this example, the address should now read as $C$2:$C$12.

3. Press Enter or click in some worksheet cell to deselect the chart.

(You could also adjust the range finder that appears around the worksheet cells when you select the data series. Just drag its handle so that it encompasses the range you want to chart.)

The effect of adjusting the data series address in this way is to push it one row down on the worksheet and therefore one period to the right on the chart. Figure 3.14 shows the result.

Figure 3.14
The forecast for the next period now extends beyond the end of the current period in the chart.

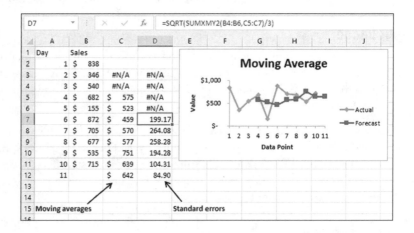

Now you can tell from looking at the chart what the moving average forecasts to be the next value.

Interpreting the Standard Errors—Or Failing to Do So

I never know what to say about the standard errors produced, if you select that option, by the Moving Average tool.

On one hand, there's nothing really wrong with them. They do not share the really awful problem with the standard errors produced by the exponential smoothing tool (see the "Standard Errors" section in Chapter 4 for a rant about those standard errors). They are not used in any way that's actually misleading.

On the other hand, they have almost nothing to contribute to the issue of moving averages, so I honestly have never understood what they're doing there.

There are various kinds of standard error, and the ones produced by the Moving Average tool are often called the *root mean square error*. It applies what you may have heard of as the *criterion of least squares*. The general approach is as follows:

- Find the difference between each actual value and the associated forecast. This difference measures the error in the forecast.

- Square the difference. This results in values that are all positive, so they can be summed without causing positive and negative errors to swallow one another up.

- Find the sum of those squares.

- Divide by the number of observations. This gives the average squared forecast error.

- Take the square root of the result. Doing so puts the result back into the original standard of measurement—that is, it reverses the effect of squaring the differences.

More concisely, Excel uses a formula following this pattern, for a moving average of length 3:

```
=SQRT(SUMXMY2(B4:B6,C5:C7)/3)
```

The formula uses the worksheet function SUMXMY2(). It calculates the sum of each difference in observed X values and Y values, and squares the difference. That formula is consistent with the definition of root mean square error.

However, limiting the observations and forecasts to as many as are involved in a given moving average is highly idiosyncratic. It gives you a sense of how much error there is in the moving average forecasts at any period in the data series. But that's seldom useful information. You normally want to get an estimate of the overall forecast error in the entire data series, not just in a small subset of the series.

In fact, if you are forecasting with regression instead of moving averages (see Chapter 5), one of the basic assumptions is that the variance is the same across the full set of data. In the population from which you have sampled, you assume that the variance during period 1 is the same as the variance during any other period in your data series.

You could test this assumption, but to do so with any degree of confidence you would have to include many more observations and forecasts at each point. That means calculating a series of moving averages, each of which encompasses a lengthy interval. Such a series of moving averages is likely to smooth out your data series so much that you wouldn't be able to pick up any meaningful trends in time to take advantage of them.

Therefore, there's little rationale for calculating the root mean square error at specific points in the data series. (There is a quantitative technique used in securities analysis called *Bollinger Bands*, which place limits around a moving average and which are based on standard deviations at each moving average. But they are not calculated in the way that the moving average add-in calculates the standard errors. The same is true of a more sophisticated procedure, Loess or Lowess curves.)

So, I suggest that you ignore the standard errors produced by the Data Analysis add-in's Moving Average tool. Or, better yet, just don't call for them in the tool's dialog box.

Chapter 4, on exponential smoothing, goes considerably further into the issue of predictive accuracy than does this chapter's background material.

Forecasting a Time Series: Smoothing

Chapter 3, "Forecasting with Moving Averages," shows you how the number of values that are included in a moving average controls the relative amount of smoothing and tracking that occurs. The more values in the moving average, the greater the amount of smoothing, and therefore the longer it takes the moving average to react to a change in the level of the series.

On the other hand, the fewer values in the moving average, the greater amount of tracking, and therefore the more quickly the moving average reacts to a change in the level of the series.

So there's an inevitable tension between smoothing and tracking. More smoothing helps to suppress the effect of random noise in the data series, but it slows the response to genuine changes. More tracking speeds up that response, but the result might be to overreact to noise.

One attractive way to deal with this issue is by way of weighted moving averages, as also discussed in Chapter 3. As described in that chapter, one of the problems with weighted moving averages is that there's usually no special reason to select any particular set of weights, although it's usual to make them total 100%. There might be nothing to support the choice of, for example, three weights of 30%, 30% and 40% instead of 20%, 30% and 50%.

But there is a family of techniques that are based on moving averages and smoothing, and that is appealing both theoretically and intuitively. At their simplest they are quite straightforward but they have intimidating-sounding names. You may have heard of them as Exponentially Weighted Moving Averages (often abbreviated as EWMA) or Exponential Smoothing.

Exponential Smoothing: The Basic Idea

Suppose that you have the data series laid out in Figure 4.1.

Figure 4.1

Each forecast combines the prior forecast with a correction that would have made the prior forecast more accurate.

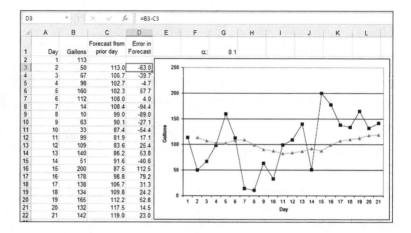

Notice in Figure 4.1 that the forecast on Day 2 is the same as the actual observation on Day 1: the forecast in cell C3 is the same as the actual observation in cell B2, 113 gallons. This is normal and standard at the start of a forecast based on smoothing (although there are other methods that this chapter touches on later).

Things change on Day 2 when it's time to forecast the value for Day 3. That forecast, 106.7, is in cell C4. There, the new forecast adds the prior forecast (113) to this error-correction term:

$$.1 * (50 - 113)$$

In that error-correction term, .1 is referred to as the *smoothing constant* (often termed *alpha* or α). The 50 is the actual on Day 2 and the 113 value is the forecast for Day 2 made on Day 1. The term multiplies the error (that is, the actual of 50 for Day 2 minus the forecast of 113 for Day 2) by the smoothing constant.

The error in the forecast for Day 2 is –63.0, as shown in cell D3. The negative 63.0 is the result of subtracting the forecast value of 113 from the actual value of 50. When you multiply the error of –63 by the smoothing constant of 0.1, you get –6.3. Finally, when you add –6.3 to the prior forecast value of 113, you get 106.7, as shown in cell C4 of Figure 4.1.

Now consider the forecast at Day 4. It is the sum of the prior forecast, 106.7, and the correction of the error in the prior forecast, which is the following:

$$.1 * (67 - 106.7)$$

The result is a forecast for Day 4, made on Day 3, as follows:

$$106.7 + .1 * (67 - 106.7) = 102.7$$

This version of the exponential smoothing formula emphasizes its error-correcting nature. The formula modifies the prior forecast by an amount *and in a direction* that would have made that prior forecast more accurate.

For example, on Day 3, a forecast of 102.7 was made for Day 4. Day 4's actual value turned out to be 98, so the forecast was an overestimate. The forecast would have been more accurate had it been lower. Therefore, the smoothing formula calculates the next forecast, for Day 5, by adding one tenth of the negative error amount to the prior forecast:

$$102.7 + .1 * (98 - 102.7)$$

or 102.3, as shown in cell C6 of Figure 4.1.

If you look at it in this way, you can think of exponential smoothing as a self-correcting forecast. The correction in the next forecast depends on the amount and the direction of the error in the prior forecast.

But this form of the smoothing equation makes it difficult to see how the actual, present value enters in. Here's how we get from the form discussed so far to another form, which is mathematically equivalent but emphasizes the role of the present value.

The forecast for, say, Day 4 is the sum of the forecast for Day 3 plus alpha times the error in the forecast on Day 3:

$$\hat{y}_{t+1} = \hat{y}_t + \alpha\varepsilon$$

Where:

- $\hat{y}_{t+1}$ is the forecast (indicated by the caret over the y) of the data series made at time t (say, Wednesday) for time $t + 1$ (say, Thursday).
- $\hat{y}_t$ is the forecast value of the data series for time t (again, Wednesday).
- α is the smoothing constant—here, and temporarily, we're using 0.1.
- ε is the error in the prior forecast.

Expand the error reference to show explicitly the difference between the actual on Day t, shown as y_t, and the forecast for Day t:

$$\hat{y}_{t+1} = \hat{y}_t + \alpha\,(y_t - \hat{y}_t)$$

Multiply the term in parentheses by alpha and rearrange the order of the terms:

$$\hat{y}_{t+1} = \alpha y_t + \hat{y}_t - \alpha\hat{y}_t$$

Finally, factor the forecast for Day t out of the second and third terms:

$$\hat{y}_{t+1} = \alpha y_t + (1 - \alpha)\,\hat{y}_t$$

That final version of the formula is often called the *smoothing equation.* It's interesting to notice that it really represents nothing more than a weighted average of the prior observation of y_t and the prior forecast, $\hat{y}_t$. The weights are, of course, alpha and (1 − alpha).

The exponential smoothing approach usually requires that alpha be between the values of 1 and 0, inclusive. So notice what happens if you set alpha to, say, 1.0. In that case, the quantity (1 – alpha) is 0, and the prior forecast is given no weight in the next forecast. In fact, the next forecast is precisely equal to the current observation, y_t. (Some people refer to that as *naïve forecasting*. Tomorrow's forecast is today's actual. There's more about naïve forecasting later in the chapter.)

On the other hand, if you set alpha to 0, each forecast is precisely equal to the prior forecast. Because the first forecast equals the first observation of 113, you wind up with a string of forecasts that each equal the first observation. Try it out in the Excel workbook for Chapter 4, on the worksheet for Figure 4.1—you can alter the value of alpha in cell G1 and watch what happens to the forecast series on the chart.

Of course, an alpha of 0 or 1 is likely to be of little value to you. When alpha equals 1, each forecast equals the prior observation and your forecast consists entirely of tracking— no smoothing. When alpha equals 0, you have no tracking because each subsequent observation carries no weight in the next forecast, and in that case the forecasts are smoothed to a horizontal line.

When alpha is between 0 and 1, though, you can get a useful balance of smoothing and tracking, and by "useful" I mean forecasts that track well without merely repeating the prior, actual observation, and that are not smoothed so ruthlessly that they ignore meaningful changes in the level of the series. We look at one good (and standard) approach to choosing the value of alpha later in this chapter.

Why "Exponential" Smoothing?

What's exponential about all this? None of the formulas mentioned in the prior section involve exponents. This section takes a slightly different look at the basic formula, in part to explain the term *exponential smoothing*, and in part to clarify the role of exponents in this kind of smoothing. You'll find that it's much more straightforward than the fairly pretentious name implies.

Suppose that you're at the end of the third day of measuring the water usage in a suburban home, and you're ready to forecast the water usage for the fourth day. You use this formula, which follows the smoothing form just discussed:

$$\hat{y}_4 = \alpha y_3 + (1 - \alpha)\hat{y}_3$$

That is, the forecast for Day 4 ($\hat{y}_t$) equals

> Alpha (α)
> Times the actual usage on Day 3 (y_3)
> Plus (1 – alpha)
> Times the forecast for Day 3 made on Day 2 ($\hat{y}_3$)

In actual values, this translates to the following:

Forecast usage, Day 4 = (.1) * (67) + (1 – .1)*(106.7)

Forecast usage, Day 4 = 6.7 + 96.0 = 102.7

Now, in the forecast for Day 4, replace the forecast for Day 3, $\hat{y}_3$, with its own calculation:

$$\hat{y}_3 = \alpha y_2 + (1 - \alpha)\,\hat{y}_2$$

So:

$$\hat{y}_4 = \alpha y_3 + (1 - \alpha)(\alpha y_2 + (1 - \alpha)\,\hat{y}_2)$$

Again using numbers instead of symbols, the forecast for Day 4 becomes:

Forecast usage, Day 4 = (0.1)*(67)+(1–0.1)*((0.1)*(50)+(1–0.1)*113)

Now, the forecast for Day 2 is the actual value observed on Day 1:

$$\hat{y}_2 = y_1$$

And therefore:

$$\hat{y}_4 = \alpha y_3 + (1 - \alpha)(\alpha y_2 + (1 - \alpha)\,y_1)$$

Expand the second term by multiplying through by (1 – alpha):

$$\hat{y}_4 = \alpha y_3 + (1 - \alpha)(\alpha y_2) + (1 - \alpha)(1 - \alpha)\,y_1$$

$$\hat{y}_4 = \alpha y_3 + (1 - \alpha)(\alpha y_2) + (1 - \alpha)^2\,y_1$$

Recall that any number raised to the zero-th power equals 1, and any number raised to the first power is the number itself. So you can rewrite the prior equation in this way:

$$\hat{y}_4 = (1 - \alpha)^0\,\alpha y_3 + (1 - \alpha)^1\,\alpha y_2 + (1 - \alpha)^2\,y_1$$

Finally, just rearrange the order of the terms in the prior equation to show the older observations on the left and the newer observations on the right. This makes it easier to see what's going on:

$$\hat{y}_4 = (1 - \alpha)^2\,y_1 + (1 - \alpha)^1\,\alpha y_2 + (1 - \alpha)^0\,\alpha y_3$$

In this example, I'm using a value of 0.1 for alpha. So, using numbers instead of $(1 - \alpha)$ raised to some power:

$$\hat{y}_4 = .81 y_1 + .9\alpha y_2 + 1\alpha y_3$$

You can see that each of the first three observations—y_1, y_2, and y_3—appears in the forecast for Day 4. The oldest observation, y_1, is multiplied by $.9^2$ or .81. The next oldest observation, y_2, is multiplied by $.9^1$, or .9. And the most recent observation, y_3, is multiplied by $.9^0$, or 1. The older the observation, the smaller its multiple, and therefore the smaller the observation's contribution to the current forecast.

Figure 4.2 shows how all this might play out in an Excel worksheet. You would not typically run the forecast using the approach shown in cells A13:G16 in Figure 4.2: It's tedious, error-prone and overkill. To get forecasts in C7:C9, all you need is something such as the range A5:B9 in Figure 4.2. The remainder of Figure 4.2 is meant solely to show how older actual observations continue to have an effect, however small, on the most recent forecast, and how that effect depends on raising the "damping factor" to higher and higher powers.

Figure 4.2
The results of the formulas appear in D14:G16. The formulas that return those results are in D21:G23.

C8 =C7+$B$1*D7

	A	B	C	D	E	F	G
1	α:	0.1					
2	1 – α:	0.9					
3							
4							
5	Day	Gallons	Forecast	Error			
6	1	113					
7	2	50	113.00	-63.0			
8	3	67	106.70	-39.7			
9	4	98	102.73	-4.7			
10							
11				Contribution from Day Number:			
12				1	2	3	
13	1 – α	Exponent	(1 – α)^Exponent				Total
14	0.9	0	1.00	113.00			113.00
15	0.9	1	0.90	101.70	5.00		106.70
16	0.9	2	0.81	91.53	4.50	6.70	102.73
17							
18				Contribution from Day Number:			
19				1	2	3	
20	1 – α	Exponent	(1 – α)^Exponent				Total
21	0.9	0	1.00	=$C14*B$6			=SUM(D14:F14)
22	0.9	1	0.90	=$C15*B$6	=Alpha*$C14*B$7		=SUM(D15:F15)
23	0.9	2	0.81	=$C16*B$6	=Alpha*$C15*B$7	=Alpha*$C14*B$8	=SUM(D16:F16)

Figure 4.3 shows all this for a ten-day series. You can see how complicated it could get if you had to extend each new forecast all the way back to Day 1.

It can help to see what happens to the weight that's applied to each observation as you go back toward the start of the data series. The farther back you go, the larger the exponent and the smaller the weight. That's consistent, of course, with the notion that older observations carry less weight in the next forecast. See Figure 4.4.

Figure 4.4 shows the value of the weights with three different smoothing constants, or alpha, as the observations get older. With an alpha of 0.1, the factor dies out rather slowly, and even an observation that's 20 periods old gets a weight of 0.12.

With an alpha of 0.9, the weight dies out almost immediately, and at three periods back it has dropped below 0.01.

An alpha of 0.5 occupies a middle ground, but it has just about vanished by the eighth period back.

Figure 4.3
Forecasts in C6:C14 are made with the error-correction formula and equal the forecasts in O19:O27, made by summing the components.

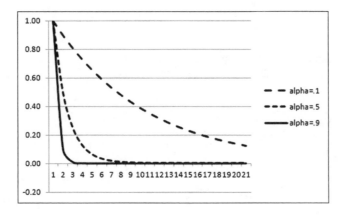

| J24 | | | ▼ | : | × | ✓ | fx | =Alpha*$E20*B$22 |

	B	C	D	E	F	G	H	I	J	K	L	M	N	O
4	Gallons	Forecast	Error											
5	113													
6	50	113.00	-63.0											
7	67	106.70	-39.7											
8	98	102.73	-4.7											
9	160	102.26	57.7											
10	112	108.03	4.0											
11	14	108.43	-94.4											
12	10	98.99	-89.0											
13	63	90.09	-27.1											
14	33	87.38	-54.4											
15														
16								Contribution from Day Number:						
17	Gallons				1	2	3	4	5	6	7	8	9	
18	113	1 – α	Exponent	(1 – α)^Exponent										Total
19	50	0.9	0	1.00	113.00									113.00
20	67	0.9	1	0.90	101.70	5.00								106.70
21	98	0.9	2	0.81	91.53	4.50	6.70							102.73
22	160	0.9	3	0.73	82.38	4.05	6.03	9.80						102.26
23	112	0.9	4	0.66	74.14	3.65	5.43	8.82	16.00					108.03
24	14	0.9	5	0.59	66.73	3.28	4.88	7.94	14.40	11.2				108.43
25	10	0.9	6	0.53	60.05	2.95	4.40	7.14	12.96	10.1	1.4			98.99
26	63	0.9	7	0.48	54.05	2.66	3.96	6.43	11.66	9.1	1.3	1.0		90.09
27	33	0.9	8	0.43	48.64	2.39	3.56	5.79	10.50	8.2	1.1	0.9	6.3	87.38
28														
29														
30					=$E24*B$18				=Alpha*$E19*B$23					

Figure 4.4
Larger smoothing constants result in weights that die out more quickly.

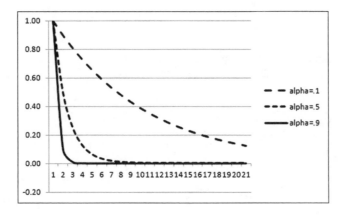

So, the larger you make the smoothing constant, the more quickly the effects of older observations die out. Make it as large as 0.9 and observations even three periods back have little influence on the next forecast value.

Using Excel's Exponential Smoothing Tool

Excel comes with an add-in (the same sort of extra that other applications call plug-ins) called the Data Analysis add-in, and you may already know it as the Analysis ToolPak. The Data Analysis add-in simplifies several statistical procedures such as the analysis of variance and multiple regression analysis. It also includes a tool that helps you carry out exponential smoothing.

If you have already installed the Data Analysis add-in, continue with the next section. If you have not installed it, refer to the "Accessing the Data Analysis Add-In" section in Chapter 2, "Linear Regression." You need to do some installation prep work before you can use the add-in, but you need to do it once only. Chapter 2 walks you through the installation process.

Understanding the Exponential Smoothing Dialog Box

After you have found the Data Analysis tool on the Ribbon, in the Data tab's Analysis group (or in an earlier version's Tools menu), it's easy to start the smoothing and forecasting process. Click the Data Analysis button to get the dialog box shown in Figure 4.5.

Figure 4.5
Scroll down in the dialog box to reveal another nine tools, including one for moving averages.

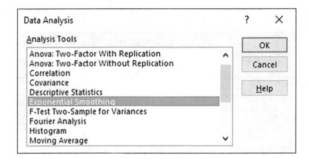

Click on the Exponential Smoothing item in the list box and then click OK. You get the Exponential Smoothing dialog box shown in Figure 4.6.

Figure 4.6
Some controls on this dialog box behave in unexpected ways.

	A	B
1	Day	Gallons
2	1	113
3	2	50
4	3	67
5	4	98
6	5	160
7	6	112
8	7	14
9	8	10
10	9	63
11	10	33
12	11	99
13	12	109
14	13	140
15	14	51
16	15	200
17	16	178
18	17	138
19	18	134
20	19	165
21	20	132
22	21	142

The way you fill the boxes in this dialog box controls the nature and the placement of the results. The following sections provide some clarification.

Input Range

This box should contain the worksheet address of the range of cells that contain your baseline data. Whether you supply a header cell for that range is up to you. The presence or absence of a header cell has no effect on the output—that is, if you include a header as part of the input range, the Exponential Smoothing tool makes no use of the header in either the charts or the lists it creates, so you might as well omit it from the input range. In Figure 4.6, the header is in cell B1 and the baseline itself is in the range B2:B22. You could enter B1:B22 as the Input Range to make sure that Excel captures the Gallons header, but there's no good reason to do so.

Labels

If you include a header, be sure to fill the Labels checkbox. If you use a header but don't fill the checkbox—and if the header contains any alphabetic characters—Excel complains and doesn't complete the analysis. If the header contains only numeric data, Excel thinks that the header is part of the baseline and will include it in the smoothing calculations—probably erroneously.

Damping Factor

The Damping Factor control causes confusion for no good reason. In the literature on exponential smoothing, the term "damping factor" is taken to mean 1 minus alpha, where alpha is the smoothing constant, just as discussed earlier in this chapter in the "Exponential Smoothing: The Basic Idea" section.

In the context of exponential smoothing, the term "smoothing constant" is used perhaps ten times as often as the term "damping factor," and it's unfortunate that the dialog box asks for the damping factor instead of the smoothing constant. It's not actually wrong to do so, but it's an unfamiliar, non-standard approach. (You might also see the term "discounting factor" in the literature on exponential smoothing; it means the same thing as "damping factor" and is equally rare.)

So, if you want to use 0.1 as the smoothing constant, you must enter 0.9 on the dialog box as the damping factor. Keep in mind that the smoothing constant must be between 0 and 1, and therefore the damping factor must also fall in that range, because the damping factor equals (1 − alpha). In general:

■ The greater the smoothing constant, the smaller the damping factor, and the *less* smoothing (and more tracking) that occurs. With a smoothing constant of, say, 0.99, a chart shows the forecasts as virtually identical to the actuals, just shifted forward by one time period.

■ The smaller the smoothing constant, the greater the damping factor, and the *more* smoothing (and less tracking) that occurs. A smoothing constant of 0.0 results in forecasts that lie on a straight horizontal line.

It's also a shame that you must enter a constant such as 0.9 or 0.3 in the Damping Factor box, because it would be very convenient to enter a cell address instead. That way, the Exponential Smoothing tool could create formulas using cell addresses instead of static values for the smoothing constant and damping factor. You could change the damping factor or smoothing constant to easily examine the effect of the change on your forecasts.

Most of the tools in the Data Analysis add-in provide their results as constant values. I regard that as a drawback because it makes it needlessly difficult to change something about the inputs—a single data value, for example, or a calculation option—and then view the effect of the alteration on the results of the analysis.

But the Exponential Smoothing tool writes formulas, not constant values, and that would make the tool a perfect candidate for viewing changes to the forecasts as you make changes to the smoothing constant (or, if you prefer, to the damping factor). However, the designers chose to force the selection of a constant number rather than a cell address, so you get formulas like this:

    =0.1*A3+0.9*B3

instead of this:

    =$F$1*A3+(1-$F$1)*B3

In the former case, if you want to know how things would look if you use a damping factor of 0.5 instead of 0.9, you have to run the tool again to supply a different damping factor. In the latter case, all you have to do is change the value in cell F1 from 0.1 to 0.5.

Of course, you can use Excel to search for and replace the constant in the forecast equations with a cell reference. In the prior example, you search the forecast range for 0.1 and replace it with $F$1 and then search for 0.9 and replace it with (1 – $F$1). I show you how to do that in the "Choosing the Smoothing Constant" section later in the chapter. But the exponential smoothing tool could have spared you those extra steps.

Output Range

You also need to specify the cell where you want the output to begin. Normally, you have set up your input data—that is, your baseline of observations—in an Excel list or table layout. That layout is defined as a given variable (such as gallons used) in a column, with different time periods represented in different rows. This is the setup used throughout this book, it is the standard approach, and it is as shown in Figure 4.6.

> **NOTE** The Exponential Smoothing tool accepts a range of input data arranged so that a given variable occupies a single row, with different time periods occupying different columns—that is, the data in Figure 4.6 rotated by 90 degrees. Conceivably you can come up with a good reason to arrange your data in that way, but that arrangement is pretty rare, and I suggest that you stick with the list or table layout. Most Excel functions and tools work best—and some work only—with the list layout.

Using a list layout, it's normally best to call for the output range to start in the first row of the baseline data. There can be no forecast for Day 1, because there is no baseline of data prior to Day 1, and therefore the Exponential Smoothing tool writes the #N/A value in place of the forecast of the first period's value. (However, you can subsequently use a procedure called "backcasting" to stretch the baseline out to earlier periods, and in that case you might want to start your output range elsewhere.)

By starting the output in the first row of the baseline data, you cause Excel to put the #N/A value in the same row as the first time period. Excel continues by putting the first forecast in the same row as the second time period, which is as it should be. The first actual forecast applies to the second time period, the second forecast to the third period, and so on.

This arrangement is convenient for several reasons. You often want to create your own chart to show both the actual data series and the forecasts, in preference to the one that the Exponential Smoothing tool optionally provides. Further, you frequently want to use the various worksheet functions that help analyze the nature and the quality of the forecasts. By aligning the actuals properly with the forecasts, you make that charting and analysis much more straightforward.

Chart Output

By filling this checkbox, you instruct Excel to create a chart of the actual values and the forecast values. The chart is embedded in the active worksheet (of course, you can put the chart on its own chart sheet later) as shown in Figure 4.7.

Figure 4.7
The chart aligns the forecasts properly with the actuals.

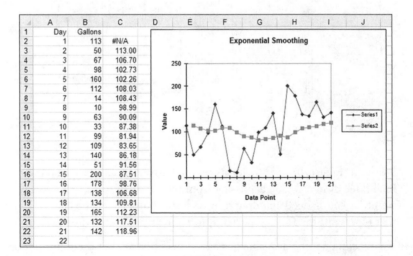

Even if you call for the forecasts to begin several rows or columns away from the actuals, the Exponential Smoothing tool aligns them correctly on the chart so that you can compare the actual baseline observations with their associated forecasts. (As Chapter 3 notes, the Moving Average tool does not align the forecasts properly on the chart.)

One aspect of all this analysis that I've ignored until now has to do with the final forecast. Notice in Figure 4.7 that the Exponential Smoothing tool does not provide a one-step-ahead forecast for the time period that follows the final actual observation. That is, in Figure 4.7 there are two figures for Day 21: an actual measurement, which you supply, and a forecast for Day 21, made by Excel on the basis of the actual observation and the forecast for Day 20. After you've recorded your actual observation for Day 21, your interest usually focuses on the forecast for Day 22.

The Exponential Smoothing tool doesn't provide that one-step-ahead forecast, but it's very easy to get. Assuming that your data appears as shown in Figure 4.7, just select cell C22— that's the forecast for Day 21—and copy and paste it (or drag it, using the cell's fill handle) into cell C23 to get the forecast for Day 22. As you've seen, with exponential smoothing the forecast for a given time period depends on data that's available at the end of the prior time period: the actual observation and the forecast for the prior period (see Figure 4.8).

Figure 4.8
Completing the one-step-ahead forecast.

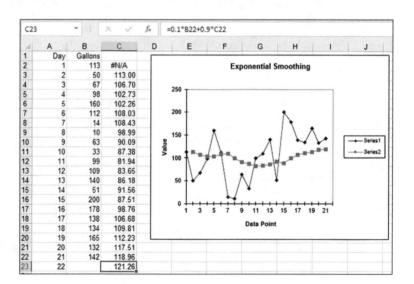

Notice in Figure 4.8 that the chart no longer reflects all the available data. In particular, the final forecast in cell C23 is missing from the chart. In some older versions of Excel, you can simply select that cell and drag it by its heavy border into the chart. Then the charted line that represents the forecasts extends forward an additional time period.

That technique isn't available in all versions of Excel, but the following one is. With the data and chart set up as in Figure 4.8, take these steps:

1. Click the chart to open it for editing.

2. Click to select the data series that represents the forecasts. Notice that the address of the worksheet range that contains the data series now appears in the Formula Bar. In Figure 4.8's chart, that address is $C$2:$C$22.

3. Edit the address in the Formula Bar so that it captures the newest forecast, and then click in the worksheet so that your edit takes effect. In this case, that forecast is in cell C23, so you would change this:

=SERIES("Forecast",,$C$2:$C$22,2)

to this:

=SERIES("Forecast",,$C$2:$C$23,2)

Notice that the charted data series that originally extended through cell C22 now extends through cell C23, and you can see the forecast for the as-yet-unobserved time period on the chart.

Another, and perhaps faster, way to adjust the address of a charted data series is to drag the range finder. That's the border that appears around the selected, charted range on the worksheet when you select a series in the chart. In this case, you would click on one of the two bottom corners of the range finder and drag down one row.

Neither of these two methods is necessary if you store your data in an Excel table rather than a list. The chart updates automatically when you add the final forecast. Again, the choice between a table and a list is usually a matter of personal preference. I find that the automatic update of charts is not worth the extra trouble involved in creating and using a table.

Standard Errors

This dialog box option provides something that the Exponential Smoothing tool calls "standard errors," but there's nothing standard about them. For each time period after the fourth in your data series, the add-in enters an equation that returns the "standard error" of the prior three periods—that is, a measure of the squared differences between the actual observations and the associated forecasts. See column C in Figure 4.9.

However, there is no rationale, whether theoretical or practical, for the way that the Exponential Smoothing tool goes about calculating standard errors. Here is an example of the formulas that the tool enters into the worksheet:

=SQRT(SUMXMY2(A3:A5,C3:C5)/3)

That formula does the following:

- It pairs the actual observations in the range A3:A5 with the associated smoothing forecasts in C3:C5.
- It applies the worksheet function SUMXMY2 to the ranges A3:A5 and C3:C5. That function, SUMXMY2, calculates the difference in each pair: A3 minus C3, A4 minus C4, and A5 minus C5. That's the "XMY" part of the function. It squares each difference (that's the "2" at the end of the function's name) and takes the total of the squared differences (the "SUM" at the start).
- The result is divided by 3, and the square root of the division is taken. That is what appears in each of the "standard error" cells.

Figure 4.9
The standard errors returned by the Exponential Smoothing tool are nearly meaningless.

	A	B	C	D	E	F	G
1	Gallons	Forecasts	Standard Errors				
2	113	#N/A	#N/A				
3	50	113.00	#N/A				
4	67	106.70	#N/A				
5	98	102.73	#N/A				
6	160	102.26	43.08				
7	112	108.03	40.55				
8	14	108.43	33.53				
9	10	98.99	63.94				
10	63	90.09	74.95				
11	33	87.36	76.53				
12	99	81.94	62.21				
13	109	83.65	36.43				
14	140	86.18	36.01				
15	51	91.56	35.73				
16	200	87.51	41.57				
17	178	98.76	75.71				
18	138	106.68	82.82				
19	134	109.81	81.48				
20	165	112.23	51.14				
21	132	117.51	38.08				
22	142	118.96	34.54				

C6 = SQRT(SUMXMY2(A3:A5,B3:B5)/3)

Here's the problem: Why 3? Why specifically three observations and the three associated forecasts? No credible source in the literature on exponential smoothing recommends that approach. Some source that isn't credible might recommend it, but I haven't been able to find it, and I've looked from time to time since 1995.

This isn't to say that standard errors aren't sensible and useful in exponential smoothing. But one of the basic ideas that underlie exponential smoothing is that observations starting with the first time period have some effect on the next forecast. After many time periods, the effects of the first few observations are quite small, but they are present and measurable. Nevertheless, the standard errors returned by the Exponential Smoothing tool take only the prior three observations and forecasts into account.

My recommendation is that you ignore the Standard Errors option in the Exponential Smoothing dialog box. All you'll get if you select it is additional clutter on your worksheet.

For a different and useful reason to calculate the standard error between a time series and the associated forecasts, see the next section on selecting a value for the smoothing constant, alpha.

Choosing the Smoothing Constant

The earlier section "Exponential Smoothing: The Basic Idea" shows how the smoothing constant alpha plays a significant role in determining the value of the forecasts returned by exponential smoothing. You can choose any value for alpha between 0.0 and 1.0, and therefore you would want to know what value will help make the most accurate forecasts.

You know that the closer alpha is to zero, the more that the forecasts are smoothed. In fact, an alpha of 0.0 returns a straight line for forecasts. On the other hand, an alpha of 1.0 returns the original data series, shifted forward one point in time.

You typically want a value of alpha somewhere between those two extremes, 0.0 and 1.0. That way you get a degree of smoothing to iron out some of the random noise that bounces the data series around. You also get some degree of tracking so that the movements in the series that are caused by the signal aren't completely suppressed.

One popular, standard, and theoretically sensible way to select a value for alpha is to choose the one that minimizes the squared deviations of the forecasts from the actuals—a minor twist on the least squares approach used in regression analysis. You select the value of alpha that results in forecasts whose squared differences from the associated actuals are smaller than any other value that you might select for alpha.

Excel provides a tool that helps you determine that optimum value. Used in this way, Excel's Solver tries different values for alpha until it finds the one that minimizes the total of the squared deviations between the actuals and the forecasts—that is, the alpha that results in the most accurate forecasts given the history you have on hand.

The basic approach uses the following general steps, which are detailed next:

1. Set up an exponential smoothing analysis, complete with an initial value for alpha and a set of forecasts.
2. On the same worksheet, enter an equation that's based on the sum of the squared differences between the forecast values and the associated actuals.
3. Install Solver if you haven't done so already. Use it to try out different values of alpha until the sum of the squared differences is minimized. Done manually, this search was once a tedious and error-prone process—but now it's automated by Solver.

Setting Up the Analysis

Figure 4.10 shows the result of running the Exponential Smoothing tool on the data shown in the prior figures in this chapter. As I discussed earlier, the tool uses fixed numeric constants as the smoothing constant alpha and as the value for (1 – alpha). The next step is to replace the constants in the smoothing formulas with cell references.

Notice that Figure 4.10 shows the values used by the Exponential Smoothing tool—for this example, 0.1 and 0.9. The user has entered those values on the worksheet, and they appear in cells F1 and I1.

Recall that the Exponential Smoothing tool asks the user to supply a "damping factor" on the tool's dialog box, along with other information such as the Input Range and whether to chart the results. The tool uses that damping factor to calculate the smoothing constant by subtracting it from 1.0. Then the formulas that return the forecasts are entered on the worksheet—in Figure 4.10, they are in column C.

Figure 4.10
Prepare to replace
numeric constants with
cell references.

	C4		▼	⋮	✕	✓	f_x	=0.1*B3+0.9*C3	

◢	A	B	C	D	E	F	G	H	I
1	Day	Gallons	Forecasts		α	0.1		(1 - α)	0.9
2	1	113	#N/A						
3	2	50	113.00						
4	3	67	106.70						
5	4	98	102.73						
6	5	160	102.26						
7	6	112	108.03						
8	7	14	108.43						
9	8	10	98.99						
10	9	63	90.09						
11	10	33	87.38						
12	11	99	81.94						
13	12	109	83.65						
14	13	140	86.18						
15	14	51	91.56						
16	15	200	87.51						
17	16	178	98.76						
18	17	138	106.68						
19	18	134	109.81						
20	19	165	112.23						
21	20	132	117.51						
22	21	142	118.96						

The problem is that the formulas use the smoothing constant and damping factor themselves. For example, the formula in cell C4 is the following:

=0.1*B3+0.9*C3

The presence of the constants in the formula means that you can't conveniently change the value of the smoothing constant—and therefore the damping factor—in the formulas. But if you replace the constants with cell references such as F1 and I1, you can change the values in those cells. Then the formulas with the forecasts automatically recalculate.

That's one good reason to edit the formulas. Another, related reason is that doing so makes it possible for you to use Solver on the problem, and I show how to do that in the next section.

To replace the numeric constants with the cell references, take these steps:

1. Select the range with the forecasts, C3:C22.
2. Click Find & Select in the Home tab's Editing group, and choose Replace in the drop-down menu.

3. In the Find and Replace dialog box, enter 0.1 in the Find What box and enter $F$1 in the Replace With box.

4. Click Replace All. This replaces all instances of the smoothing constant 0.1 with a reference to the cell $F$1.

5. In the Replace dialog box, enter 0.9 in the Find What box and enter $I$1 in the Replace With box.

6. Click Replace All. This replaces all instances of the damping factor 0.9 with references to the cell $I$1.

> **CAUTION**
>
> Be sure to supply the leading zeroes in the Find box. If you don't, Excel replaces, say, .1 with $F$1 and you wind up with a formula that includes the illegal expression 0$F$1.

In Figure 4.10, cell I1 contains this equation:

= 1 − F1

So whatever smoothing constant, or alpha, you put in cell F1, the "damping factor" or (1 − alpha) appears in I1. Cell F1 contains a numeric value between 0 and 1, so if you change F1 to 0.2, I1 immediately recalculates to 0.8. Put 0.3 in F1 and you get 0.7 in I1. If you try it out in the workbook for this chapter that's available from the publisher, you see that changing alpha in F1 not only changes the result shown in I1 but also the forecasts in C3:C22. (The forecasts change only if you have replaced the constant values of 0.1 and 0.9 with cell references, as described in the prior list of steps.)

Those forecasts depend on the values of alpha and of (1 − alpha), and you're about to use Solver to take advantage of those dependencies.

Using Solver to Find the Best Smoothing Constant

Solver (Excel uses the term "Solver" instead of the more natural "the Solver") is another add-in that you must install in the same way you install the Data Analysis add-in. Solver also comes with the Office installation disc or downloaded files.

Making Solver Available

You make Solver available to Excel by following the instructions given in Chapter 2 in the "Accessing the Data Analysis Add-In" section. In brief, you check the Ribbon's Data tab to see if Solver appears in the Analyze group. If it's there, you're all set. (In Excel 2003 or earlier, look for Solver in the Tools menu.)

Otherwise, Solver might have been installed on your computer but not yet made available to Excel. Click the File tab, choose Options, and then choose Add-Ins. If Solver Add-In is listed under Inactive Applications Add-ins, use the Go button at the bottom of the window to activate it.

If Solver is not listed in the Add-ins window, you have to use the Control Panel's Add or Remove Programs utility, or its Programs and Features utility, to physically install it on your computer.

Why Use Solver?

In most situations where you have a numeric problem to solve in Excel, you know what the conditions are and you rely on Excel to return the result. If you want know the sum of ten numbers, you supply the numbers and tell Excel to calculate the total.

But there are times when you know the result you want (or the kind of result you want, such as a maximum or a minimum value) and don't have the right inputs. For example, you might want to know the mix of management and line employees that minimizes both the fixed and variable costs of production during a given factory shift.

Certainly you could try out many different arrangements, noting which skills are available in each one, and total the resulting costs before selecting the one that's most cost effective. But that manual approach tends to be very tedious, and when most of us do something tedious we tend to make errors. Solver can automate a process such as that if you arrange things properly on the worksheet.

> **NOTE** Excel provides another tool named Goal Seek that can return results similar to those that Solver returns. But Goal Seek is a much more rudimentary tool. In the case of finding an optimal smoothing constant, Goal Seek does not enable you to call for a minimum result, and it does not allow you to establish constraints on the smoothing constant and damping factor.

When you're setting up an analysis that uses exponential smoothing, you have a series of actual observations and associated forecasts. As you saw earlier in this chapter, you choose a smoothing constant that Excel uses to calculate each forecast.

Up through the final period in your original data series, each period has both an actual observation and an associated forecast. You're in a position to evaluate the accuracy of those forecasts by comparing each one to its associated actual observation. If you decide that the accuracy is good enough, you can apply the same formula—including the same smoothing constant—to your final actual observation. That provides you a final forecast for the next period which you have not as yet observed.

Selecting a Criterion

So how do you decide whether the forecasts, and therefore your choice of smoothing constant, are good enough? The standard method is called a *least squares* criterion. In the context of forecasting, you subtract the value of the forecast from the value of the associated actual observation; the result is called the *error*. Then you square each error and take their sum. The result is the sum of squared errors, which you sometimes see abbreviated as SSE.

Some analysts like to take the average of the squared errors, called the *mean squared error* or *MSE*, and stop there. Other analysts go one step further and take the square root of the

MSE to get what's called the *standard error*. That type of standard error is often abbreviated *RMSE*, for *root mean square error*.

Any of those three—the SSE, the MSE or the standard error—can be used as a criterion to decide whether the smoothing constant you choose is good enough. You're looking for the smoothing constant that will minimize the value of the criterion you use. And if you minimize the SSE, you will have also minimized the MSE, and also the standard error or RMSE. I use the standard error in this book because many people find it a more useful statistic than the other two: The standard error is a type of standard deviation that is easy to visualize. The SSE and MSE are expressions of the variance, which can be more difficult to visualize.

Other Types of Criteria

You might wonder why you wouldn't simply add up the errors and try to minimize their sum to find the best smoothing constant. You could do so by subtracting each forecast from its associated actual to find each error amount, and totaling the errors. The problem is that some of the errors will be positive numbers and some negative. Their total is frequently close to zero *regardless* of the smoothing constant you choose, and so the simple total of the errors is next to useless as a criterion for a smoothing constant.

Of course, you could take the absolute value of the errors, so that they're all positive, and find the average error amount. Some analysts do just that, and the result is called the *mean absolute deviation* or *MAD*. That's better than the simple total of the raw errors, but it's not as good as the standard error, which involves totaling the squared errors.

Squared errors are often preferred to absolute values of errors because they emphasize larger differences. An error of, say, 10 units contributes 10 units to the sum of the absolute error values. But it contributes 100 units to the sum of the squared error values. It's usually better to arrive at a forecast that minimizes large errors, even if that tends to maximize small errors. Therefore, a criterion that focuses on and minimizes the larger errors tends to be more effective than one that does not.

Minimizing the Criterion Value

After you have your worksheet set up properly, you can invoke Solver and tell it to minimize the criterion value—usually the standard error, but if you prefer you can use the SSE or the MSE—by repeatedly trying different values for the smoothing constant and noting the resulting value of the standard error. You tell Solver to stop trying new smoothing constants when it has minimized the standard error.

Figure 4.11 shows a typical layout. In Figure 4.11, the two critical cells are F1 and F5. Cell F1 contains the current value of the smoothing constant. That value, in combination with the damping factor, determines the forecasts.

Cell F5 contains the RMSE, or standard error, and you can see the Excel formula in the Formula Box. It uses the SUMXMY2() function to get the sum of the squared errors (the differences between the actuals and the forecasts) in the ranges B3:B22 and C3:C22.

Figure 4.11
This layout has all that Solver needs: variable cells and an objective cell.

| | F5 | | ⋮ | × | ✓ | f_x | =SQRT(SUMXMY2(B3:B22,C3:C22)/20) | |

	A	B	C	D	E	F	G	H
1	Day	Gallons			α	0.1		
2	1	113	#N/A					
3	2	50	113.00		(1 - α)	0.9		
4	3	67	106.70					
5	4	98	102.73		Objective cell:	54.28833		
6	5	160	102.26					
7	6	112	108.03					
8	7	14	108.43					
9	8	10	98.99					
10	9	63	90.09					
11	10	33	87.38					
12	11	99	81.94					
13	12	109	83.65					
14	13	140	86.18					
15	14	51	91.56					
16	15	200	87.51					
17	16	178	98.76					
18	17	138	106.68					
19	18	134	109.81					
20	19	165	112.23					
21	20	132	117.51					
22	21	142	118.96					

NOTE

The Exponential Smoothing tool does not supply the formula in cell F5. Although the tool optionally supplies standard errors, they are a "moving" standard error and as such are useless for this analysis along with most others. The user must supply the formula that Solver uses as a target cell.

The worksheet is set up to provide these results:

■ If you change the smoothing constant's value in cell F1, the damping factor changes in response. Its formula, in F3, is 1 – F1, and entering, say, 0.3 in F1 forces a recalculation in F3 to 0.7.

■ Similarly, changing the value of the smoothing constant changes the values of the forecasts, which depend in part on the value of the smoothing constant.

■ When the forecasts change, there's a change in the value of the standard error.

■ A change to the smoothing constant can increase, or it can decrease, the value of the standard error.

With the worksheet set up as shown in Figure 4.11 (or with any layout that includes the smoothing constant, the actuals, the forecasts, and the standard error), you can cause Solver to find the value of the smoothing constant that minimizes the standard error. This often turns out to be the best forecast. Because the method depends on finding the smallest value of the standard error, it is one of a family of methods called *least squares*.

Running Solver

With the worksheet as shown in Figure 4.11, click the Ribbon's Data Analysis tab and then click Solver. You see the dialog box shown in Figure 4.12.

To get the optimal value for alpha from Solver in an exponential smoothing problem, take the following steps in the Solver dialog box:

1. Click in the Set Objective box to make it active, and then click in cell F5 to identify it as Solver's objective.

2. Click the Min button. You want Solver to minimize the standard error that's calculated in the objective cell, F5.

Figure 4.12

In addition to the Objective and Variable cells, in this case you also need to supply a couple of constraints.

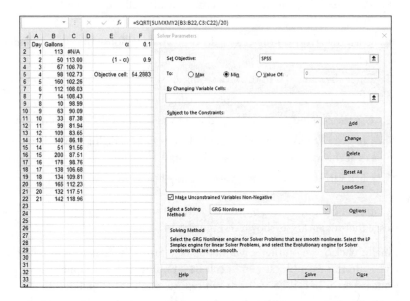

3. Click in the box labeled By Changing Variable Cells, and then click in cell F1 to identify it as the cell that Solver changes as it seeks a minimum value in F5.

4. Click the Add button next to the Constraints list box. The Add Constraint dialog box shown in Figure 4.13 appears.

Figure 4.13
You want to constrain cell F1's value for alpha to a number between 0 and 1.

5. With the Cell Reference box active, click in cell F1 to establish a constraint on that cell's value. (In this layout, cell F1 contains alpha, but of course you could choose some other cell for alpha.)

6. Don't change the less than–equal to operator in the center drop-down.

7. Enter the value 1.0 in the Constraint box.

8. Click the Add button to clear the boxes. Your choices are written to the main Solver dialog box.

9. With the Cell Reference box active, click in cell F1 to establish another constraint on that cell's value.

10. Click the arrow on the center drop-down and choose the greater than–equal to operator from the list.

11. Enter the value 0.0 in the Constraint box.

12. Click OK to return to the Solver dialog box.

13. Use the Solving Method drop-down to select the GRG Nonlinear method.

14. Click the Options button to get Solver's Options dialog box. Click the GRG Nonlinear tab at the top, and fill the Use MultiStart checkbox.

15. Click OK to return to the Solver dialog box.

Before you click the Solve button to start the solution process, review the Solver dialog box to see that it appears as shown in Figure 4.14.

Finally, click Solve on the Solver dialog box. Solver iterates through the possible values for alpha—in this example, stored in cell F1—until it finds the alpha that results in a minimum standard error in cell F5. Solver then reports that it has found a solution that conforms to the instructions you provided, and puts that solution in—again, in this case—cell F1 (see Figure 4.15).

Understanding Solver's Requirements

A couple of the steps listed in the preceding section require a little more explanation.

Setting Constraints

One assumption made by the exponential smoothing technique is that the smoothing constant is some fraction between 0.0 and 1.0. (The same assumption is made regarding the "damping factor," but that's inherent in the definition of the damping factor as 1 – alpha.)

Figure 4.14
Solver requires that
you identify at least
an Objective cell that
contains a formula, and
one or more Variable cells
that contain static values
that Solver can change.

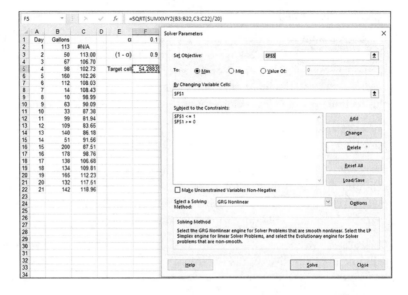

Figure 4.15
The optimum value for
the smoothing constant,
given the baseline of
values in B2:B22, now
appears in cell F1.

▲	A	B	C	D	E	F	G	H	I
1	Day	Gallons			α	0.3875			
2	1	113	#N/A						
3	2	50	113.00		(1 - α)	0.6125			
4	3	67	88.59						
5	4	98	80.22		Objective cell:	51.305			
6	5	160	87.11						
7	6	112	115.35						
8	7	14	114.05						
9	8	10	75.29						
10	9	63	49.99						
11	10	33	55.03						
12	11	99	46.49						
13	12	109	66.84						
14	13	140	83.18						
15	14	51	105.19						
16	15	200	84.19						
17	16	178	129.07						
18	17	138	148.03						
19	18	134	144.14						
20	19	165	140.21						
21	20	132	149.82						
22	21	142	142.91						

F5 • : × ✓ fx =SQRT(SUMXMY2(B3:B22,C3:C22)/20)

It's entirely possible that you might present Solver with a baseline of observations that
would result in Solver returning an optimum alpha less than 0.0 or greater than 1.0.
Therefore, it's a good idea to set constraints on alpha to keep it within those limits.

That's the reason for steps 4 through 12 in the prior list. After you establish those constraints,
Solver does not try out values for alpha that are less than 0.0 or greater than 1.0.

Choosing the Method

Unless you want to start learning a lot about the math that underlies simulations, feel free to skip this section. As long as you know that you should select the GRG Nonlinear method as suggested in step 13 of the prior list, you really need to know nothing else regarding the solution method. I don't want to get into the gory details here, but the rest of this section explains a little more about the implications of your choice.

Solver offers you three methods to reach a solution, and it's up to you to use your knowledge of the data to choose the best method.

Simplex LP   Choose this method if the relationship between the values in your Variable cells and the results in your Objective cell is linear—that is, if the relationship is described by a straight line. Solver can reach a solution for this sort of problem very quickly and there's seldom any ambiguity about the solution.

GRG Nonlinear   Choose GRG Nonlinear if the relationship between values in the Variable cells and the Objective results is a smooth curve. Figure 4.16 shows the relationship between the values of alpha and the resulting standard errors in the problem used so far in this chapter.

Figure 4.16
The relationship is nonlinear but smooth.

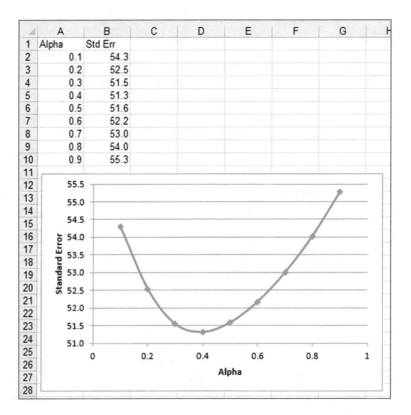

It's a little tedious, but you could create a list of values that underlie the relationship shown in Figure 4.16 yourself, directly on the worksheet, without resorting to Solver at all. Using the results you could then get a rough-and-ready estimate for the optimum value of alpha. But I've always found Solver to be a lot faster and a lot less error prone than I am when it comes to trying out different possibilities directly on the worksheet. And when you have several different variable cells (not just one as here), you really should be using Solver to manipulate the variable cell values.

Evolutionary If the relationship between the variable values and the objective value is nonlinear and is not also smooth, use the Evolutionary method. That can come about when you can't represent the relationship with a straight line, and the line jumps around or doesn't even exist for some spans of one variable or another. The likelihood of getting a feasible solution with that sort of relationship is often substantially smaller than with a linear or smooth nonlinear relationship.

Using MultiStart In the prior list of steps to take with Solver, step 14 advised you to select the MultiStart option. That option instructs Solver to choose several different starting points to begin its evaluation of the Objective cell results.

A nonlinear relationship such as you see in Figure 4.16 can cause Solver to think that it has found the best solution possible when in fact there are better solutions available.

For example, suppose that Solver started with the value 0.01 for alpha. It then might try 0.00 and 0.02 and finds that 0.00 improves the objective outcome but 0.02 doesn't. Solver might stop at that point and tell you that 0.00 is the optimum value for the variable cell. But if it had tried 0.03 it would have found a more desirable value in the objective cell. Because 0.02 turned out worse than 0.01, Solver didn't look further in that direction.

If you choose MultiStart, Solver tries several different randomly selected values as starting points. Then you're much less likely to see Solver stop prematurely with a suboptimal result.

The Point

What's the point of doing all this? Here's a quick review of what this chapter so far has suggested that you do:

1. Lay out your baseline data as an Excel list or table.
2. Install the Data Analysis add-in and make it available to Excel.
3. Install the Solver add-in and make it available to Excel.
4. Run the Data Analysis add-in's Exponential Smoothing tool on your baseline.
5. Replace the constant values in the exponential smoothing forecast formulas with cell references so that you can easily change alpha and the "damping factor," and so that Solver can work with the results.
6. Run Solver on the exponential smoothing results to optimize the value of alpha and make the forecasts overall more accurate.

Looked at that way, all at once, it does seem like a lot of work to get one simple forecast. But consider the following:

■ You need to install and make available the Data Analysis add-in once only, and the same is true of the Solver add-in. Nevertheless, if you're concerned with running any sort of analytics in Excel, you'll use both add-ins over and over.

■ If you're satisfied with the accuracy of the forecasts, you can continue making forecasts very easily: Just enter the new actual or actuals, and copy the forecasting formula down to get the next one.

■ From time to time, you can run Solver just to fine-tune the value of alpha, or to take account of unanticipated changes in the nature of the baseline.

Getting ready to make exponential smoothing forecasts for the first time, and to run Solver for the first time, represents most of the work that's needed. After that's done, the mechanics of generating a new forecast for the next period go very quickly.

Is it worth even that much effort? You have to answer that question for yourself. But with the baseline that this chapter has used so far, suppose that you shrugged your shoulders and just stuck a value of 0.90 into the Exponential Smoothing dialog box as the damping factor—therefore, a value of 0.10 as the smoothing constant. You'd get a forecast of 121.26 for the 22nd period.

But if you run Solver and use the optimal value of 0.39 for alpha, you'd get a forecast of 142.57 as the next forecast—a difference of 21.31 in the two forecasts, or about 0.4 standard errors. That's quite a difference. If it's also true that you're getting more forecasts that turn out to be more accurate, it's surely worth the little extra time and effort required to optimize the smoothing constant.

Handling Linear Baselines with Trend

The methods and the Excel tools that the first major section of this chapter describes are best suited to a *horizontal* baseline—that is, a baseline of values that do not head up or down for a long period of time. A horizontal baseline is more typically called a *no-trend* or *stationary* time series, to distinguish it from a baseline with trend, or a *trended* time series.

Characteristics of Trend

Figure 4.17 shows a series with trend.

There's no reason that you couldn't use exponential smoothing on this time series, just as this chapter has already described. But a problem arises when it's time to choose a smoothing constant. With a baseline like the one in Figure 4.17, the smoothing constant that results in the smallest amount of forecast error is either 1.0 or a value very close to that, such as 0.99. Here's what happens:

When a data series drifts up or down, as it does in Figure 4.17, the correlation between one actual observation and the next is likely to be very strong. That is also true of a data series that drifts up for a while, and then down for a while, and that's typical of a business cycle.

Figure 4.17
This company's number of customers trends up over the long term.

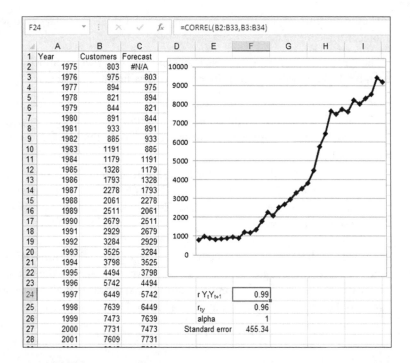

Notice cell F24 in Figure 4.17. It contains the correlation between each observation and the next in the data series, which you find using this Excel formula:

=CORREL(B2:B33,B3:B34)

That correlation is 0.99, a huge value when you consider that the maximum possible value for a correlation coefficient is 1.0. And it tells you that the best predictor of the next value in the series is the current value. Let's verify that.

Figure 4.17 also provides a formula to calculate the standard error of the forecasts. It's in cell F27 and it uses the formula discussed earlier in this chapter:

=SQRT(SUMXMY2(B3:B34,C3:C34)/32)

The formula is altered, of course, to take account of the location and length of the baseline. When you use Solver to calculate the alpha that minimizes the standard error, Solver returns an optimum value for alpha of 1.0. Let's revisit the smoothing equation from earlier in this chapter:

$$\hat{y}_{t+1} = \alpha y_t + (1 - \alpha)\hat{y}_t$$

The forecast for time $t + 1$ is alpha times the actual observation for time t, plus 1 – alpha times the forecast value for time t.

If alpha equals 1, the equation simplifies to this:

$$\hat{y}_{t+1} = y_t$$

That is, the forecast for tomorrow is the observed value for today—and we encounter naïve forecasting once again.

The term *naïve forecasting* sounds condescending, so it's worth noticing that naïve forecasts can be the best available. Two situations are best handled using naïve forecasts:

- The level of the time series holds steady for a substantial period of time. The cost of part of an assembly might remain constant for months, then rise by, say, 5%, and then hold steady again for months. In that sort of case, the best forecast for tomorrow's cost is today's cost.

- The time series drifts up or down, as shown in Figure 4.17, or up and down, as shown in Figure 4.18. In each case, the correlation between each observation and the one that follows—one type of *autocorrelation*—is so strong that you can't improve on using one observation to forecast the next.

In cases like these, the best predictor for the next observation turns out to be the value of the prior observation, and so when you use Solver to minimize the standard error of the forecasts, Solver winds up setting alpha to 1. That means that all the weight in the forecast goes to the prior observation, and none at all to the prior forecast.

Figure 4.18
This sort of pattern is termed autocorrelative drift.

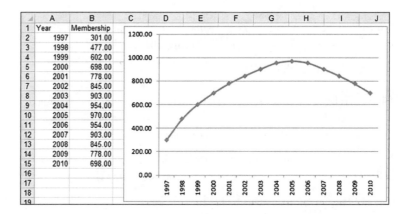

So why not use naïve forecasting exclusively? Because there are other patterns that you see in time series that don't resemble the two just discussed, steady values and drifting values. Naïve forecasting doesn't work well with those other patterns because it tracks noise in the series perfectly. Figure 4.19 shows just one example.

Two sets of forecasts are calculated and charted in Figure 4.19. The first set of forecasts is in column B and appears in the upper chart. It is based on naïve forecasting; notice that each forecast is identical to the prior actual observation. The value of alpha used, shown in cell B18, is 1.0, and the standard error of the forecasts is 444.0, in cell B20.

Figure 4.19
When you're dealing with noise, naïve forecasting is seldom as good as smoothing.

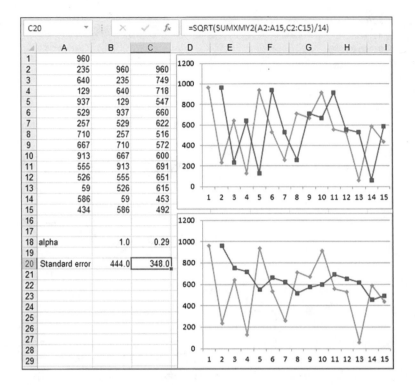

The second set of forecasts is based on exponential smoothing using an optimized alpha of 0.29 (cell C18). The standard error of the forecasts is a substantial improvement over naïve forecasting—348.0 shown in cell C20.

This happens largely because of extreme swings such as on period 5, when the observed value is 937 and the naïve forecast is 129. The squared difference between the observation and the forecast is $(937 - 129)^2$ or 652,864. In contrast, using smoothing, the squared difference on period 5 is $(937 - 547)^2$ or 152,413.

> **NOTE** Until you've become familiar with the nature of a given time series, it's difficult to know what sort of forecasting method will work best. Even then, as time passes and more and more observations arrive, you sometimes find that it's helpful to change horses and start using a different approach.

First Differencing

So, should you use naïve forecasting when you encounter a time series such as the one shown in Figure 4.20?

In cases such as the one in Figure 4.20, it's possible that you should just use the prior observation as the best forecast of the next observation. But possibly not, and in fact you often find that the best approach is to "stationarize" the data series first: that is, make it horizontal. And that's where *differencing* comes into the picture.

Figure 4.20
This customer census is clearly a strongly trended time series.

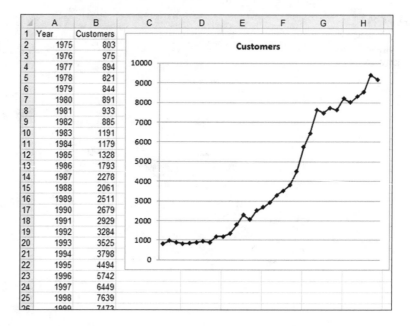

	A	B
1	Year	Customers
2	1975	803
3	1976	975
4	1977	894
5	1978	821
6	1979	844
7	1980	891
8	1981	933
9	1982	885
10	1983	1191
11	1984	1179
12	1985	1328
13	1986	1793
14	1987	2278
15	1988	2061
16	1989	2511
17	1990	2679
18	1991	2929
19	1992	3284
20	1993	3525
21	1994	3798
22	1995	4494
23	1996	5742
24	1997	6449
25	1998	7639
26	1999	7473

Suppose that you subtract the value of each observation from the value of the one that immediately follows. Using the data in Figure 4.20, for example, you could subtract 803 from 975, 975 from 894, 894 from 821, and so on. The results of those subtractions are called *first differences* and they appear in column C of Figure 4.21.

Notice the two time series on the chart in Figure 4.21. The upper series is the original, raw data. The lower series represents the first differences of the original series and does not exhibit any particular upward or downward trend.

In that case we can use exponential smoothing to forecast the next first difference. It may well be that if we forecast the differences and then reassemble the original series based on the forecast differences, we might wind up with better forecasts than we get from naïve forecasting.

The next step, then, is to use exponential smoothing on the first differences, putting Solver to work so as to find the optimum value for the smoothing constant. After the forecasts of the first differences have been optimized, the original series can be reintegrated. All this is shown in Figure 4.22.

The first important feature in Figure 4.22 is that there's a forecast based on reintegrated first differences that's more accurate overall than the forecast that's based directly on the original data series. Notice the forecast standard error in cell G3, based on forecasts developed from the first differences and reintegrated in column D. Its value of 377.0 is substantially smaller than the standard error shown in cell L3, 455.3, which is based on naïve forecasts of the original time series.

Figure 4.17 shows how the naïve forecasts are created from this time series and also shows the forecast standard error. The following steps show how the forecasts based on first differences are developed in Figure 4.22.

Figure 4.21

The first differences of a trended data series often describe a stationary series.

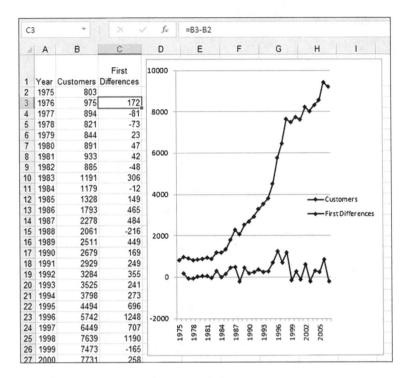

Figure 4.22

The standard error of the forecasts of the reintegrated series is less than the standard error of the direct forecasts.

	A	B	C	D	E	F	G	H	I	J	K	L
		First	Forecast	Integrated		Analysis using first			Direct	Analysis using raw	
1	Customers	differences	differences	series		differences			forecast	observations	
2	803					Alpha:	0.12			Alpha:	1.00
3	975	172		803		Standard error:	377.0		803	Standard error:	455.3
4	894	-81	172	1148					975		
5	821	-73	142	1036					894		
6	844	23	116	937					821		
7	891	47	104	949					844		
8	933	42	98	989					891		
9	885	-48	91	1024					933		
10	1191	306	74	958					885		
11	1179	-12	102	1293					1191		
12	1328	149	88	1267					1179		

G3 fx =SQRT(SUMXMY2(A3:A34,D3:D34)/32)

1. Calculate the first differences of the original time series. Enter this formula in cell B3:

   =A3–A2

2. Copy and paste cell B3, or use cell B3's fill handle, to put its formula through the remainder of the series, of course with appropriate adjustments to the cell addresses. In the worksheet used for Figure 4.22, B3 is copied into cells B4:B34. The range B3:B34 now contains the first differences of the original time series found in column A.

3. Enter the value 0.1 in cell G2. This will be used as the starting value for the smoothing constant that Solver will optimize. If you prefer, you can enter any other value between 0.0 and 1.0.

4. Enter this formula in cell C4:

   =B3

5. Enter this formula in cell C5:

   =($G$2*B4)+(1–$G$2)*C4

   That formula is one version of the smoothing formula. It multiplies the smoothing constant times the prior observation, and adds the product of the damping factor and the prior forecast.

6. Copy and paste (or autofill) the formula in cell C5 into the range C6:C34. You now have the forecast values of the first differences in column C.

7. Reassemble the forecast values for the original series by adding the forecast first differences to the original series. Enter this formula in cell D3:

   =A2+C3

   Copy and paste or autofill that formula into the range D4:D34.

8. To get the forecast standard error, enter this formula in cell G3:

   =SQRT(SUMXMY2(A3:A34,D3:D34)/32)

9. Use Solver as described earlier in this chapter to minimize the value of the standard error in cell G3 by changing the value of the smoothing constant in cell G2.

You now have forecasts of the original series in column D, and you can extend that forecast by one time period by copying the formula in cell D34 into D35. The forecasts are different, and more accurate in the aggregate, than the naïve forecasts made on the original time series: compare their forecast standard errors.

> **NOTE**
>
> Of course you could use the Data Analysis add-in's Exponential Smoothing tool to forecast the first differences instead of entering the formulas directly as in steps 4 through 6 of the preceding list. But then you would have to replace the smoothing constant in the tool's formulas with a cell reference. Use whichever method you prefer—the results are equivalent—but when you feel as though you're on familiar ground with the formula, I think you'll find it more straightforward to enter it directly instead of relying on the Exponential Smoothing tool.

Here's a much briefer and more conceptual summary of what is done in Figure 4.22. By taking the first differences of the time series in column A, we have created a new time series in column B that is not trended; in forecasting terms, we have *detrended* the original time series. Glance back at the chart in Figure 4.21 and notice that the original time series shows a pronounced upward trend, but that the first differences chart as a horizontal series.

What's left in the series of first differences is—in theory and usually in practice—random fluctuations around a mean of zero.

Those fluctuations, which are more often called *errors*, are also supposed to be independent of one another: that is, the value of any given error should be unrelated to the value of any other error in the series. That's not true of a trended series, and if you enter these two formulas on the worksheet for Figure 4.22:

    =CORREL(A2:A33,A3:A34)

and

    =CORREL(B3:B33,B4:B34)

you'll find that the correlation between one original observation and the next is nearly perfect in the original time series (A3:A34), but not significantly different from zero (that is, no reliable correlation) in the series of first differences in B3:B34.

These characteristics of first differences—stationarity and mutual independence—make them appropriate for forecasting with exponential smoothing. We run the first differences through the exponential smoothing process and then use Solver to optimize the smoothing constant, so that the forecast errors of the first differences are minimized.

Finally, we take our best forecasts of the first differences and, again using forecasting terminology, *integrate* them with the original starting point (in this example, the value 803 in cell A2) to re-create the original series with the best forecast of the period-to-period differences. In this case, and in the cases of many other trended time series, this approach turns out to be more accurate than naïve forecasting—which is what direct exponential smoothing of the original trended series often equates to.

4

NOTE

You may have been wondering about second differences. They exist (as do third differences), and you create second differences by taking the first differences of the first differences. This procedure is sometimes necessary when the original trended series has such a strong, pronounced, nonlinear growth trend that the first differences themselves still display trend or autocorrelation. It's relatively rare, but when it occurs you can take differences of the differences until you have a stationary series with independence of observations, and use that as the basis for your forecast. Then reintegrate the smoothed differences all the way back to the original raw observation. But keep in mind that differencing induces additional and undesirable dependency from one time period to the next, so don't use differencing unnecessarily. (By the way, the second, *d* parameter in the ARIMA(p,d,q) model refers to the number of differences that must be taken to make a time series stationary. This book has more to say about ARIMA models in later chapters.)

More Advanced Smoothing Models

Holt's Linear Exponential Smoothing

One way to account for a trend when you're smoothing a time series is to use differencing, as discussed in the prior chapter. Most often, first differencing is enough to remove the trend from the time series, but sometimes second or even third differencing is needed to produce a stationary series.

I used the phrase "remove the trend" in the prior sentence because that's what differencing does, and more advanced approaches to forecasting, such as Box-Jenkins ARIMA models, require that any trend be removed by differencing. But you can take a simpler approach, often called *Holt's method* or *linear exponential smoothing*.

> **NOTE**
> Just because a method is simpler doesn't mean it's less effective or less accurate. Holt's method is a good, robust way to forecast values in a trended time series and can easily outperform other, more sophisticated approaches. Your choice of method ought to be based on the nature of the data in the time series and your experience with it, not on a method's apparent level of sophistication.

Holt's method handles trend in a time series by accounting for and quantifying the trend. As you see shortly, you can smooth a trend just as you smooth a level when you use simple exponential smoothing. In Holt's method, you expect to get useful estimates of the trend in a data series. You combine the trend with estimates of the level in the time series to generate your forecast.

About Terminology and Symbols in Handling Trended Series

It's something of a headache in statistics and analytics generally, and in forecasting particularly, that terminology and symbols are not standardized. You find different sources using different symbols for identical concepts, and you often find them using different terms for the same ideas. Probably things will settle down some as the field becomes more mature, but in the meantime you are likely to encounter terms and symbols in one source, such as this book, that conflict with terms and symbols in other books, in journals, or in articles that you find on the Internet.

Two concepts are particularly important in Holt's linear smoothing:

■ The current level of a time series
■ The current slope of a time series

By "level," I mean that if a residence uses 60 gallons of water on the tenth day in your time series, the time series' level is 60 on Day 10. By "slope," I mean that if a residence uses 60 gallons on Day 10 and 65 on Day 11, the time series' slope is 5 (that is, 65 − 60) on Day 11.

To give you an idea of what I'm complaining about as to terminology, one well-known book on forecasting techniques uses the term "trend" to mean the level of a time series, and "slope" to mean its slope. Most people think of a tendency to move up or down when they think of a trend, so it's needlessly confusing to use the word to represent the level of a time series. Furthermore, the same book uses an uppercase T to represent trend, and a lowercase t to represent a time period, and that tends to cause more confusion in an expression such as $T_t(t-1)$, which that book uses to represent the level T of the series at time t, as of time $t-1$.

I reserve the word *trend* to mean a consistent change in the level of a data series over time—that's to help distinguish it from a stationary series. I use *level* to mean the value of a series at a particular time, and *slope* to mean the amount of change in the level of a series between two time periods.

Using Holt's Linear Smoothing

Figure 5.1 shows the trended data series used in Figures 4.20 through 4.22 of Chapter 4.

As in simple exponential smoothing, one way to obtain the first forecast is to set it equal to the first observation. At the outset there is no slope to calculate for the first observation, so the first forecast is taken to be the first observation. In Figure 5.1, that's how the first forecast of the series' value in cell G2 is calculated.

Figure 5.1
Because Holt's method smooths two parameters, level and slope, you need two smoothing constants—one for each parameter.

	G2			▾	:	×	✓	f_x	=C2+D2					

▲	A	B	C	D	E	F	G	H	I	J	K
					Forecast from prior		Forecast for next				
1	Period	Customers	Level	Slope	day	Error	period		Alpha	Gamma	RMSE
2	1	803	803.0	0			803.0		0.1	0.1	1555.6
3	2	975	820.2	1.7	803.0	172.0	821.9				
4	3	894	829.1	2.4	821.9	72.1	831.6				
5	4	821	830.5	2.3	831.6	-10.6	832.8				
6	5	844	834.0	2.4	832.8	11.2	836.4				
7	6	891	841.9	3.0	836.4	54.6	844.9				
8	7	932	853.6	3.9	844.9	87.1	857.4				
9	8	884	860.1	4.1	857.4	26.6	864.2				
10	9	1,190	896.8	7.4	864.2	325.8	904.2				
11	10	1,178	931.6	10.1	904.2	273.8	941.7				
12	11	1,327	980.2	14.0	941.7	385.3	994.2				
13	12	1,793	1,074.1	22.0	994.2	798.8	1,096.1				
14	13	2,277	1,214.1	33.8	1,096.1	1,180.9	1,247.9				
15	14	2,061	1,329.2	41.9	1,247.9	813.1	1,371.1				
16	15	2,510	1,485.0	53.3	1,371.1	1,138.9	1,538.3				
17	16	2,679	1,652.4	64.7	1,538.3	1,140.7	1,717.1				
18	17	2,928	1,838.2	76.8	1,717.1	1,210.9	1,915.0				
19	18	3,284	2,051.9	90.5	1,915.0	1,369.0	2,142.4				
20	19	3,524	2,280.6	104.3	2,142.4	1,381.6	2,384.9				
21	20	3,797	2,526.1	118.4	2,384.9	1,412.1	2,644.5				

> **NOTE** It turns out that showing each forecast twice in the worksheet is important to an understanding of the forecasting process. In Figure 5.1 and in other figures in this chapter, I have shown the forecast both in the period when it is made (for example, cell G2 in Figure 5.1, which takes place in Period 1) and in the period to which the forecast applies (for example, cell E3 in Period 2). The formulas in column E do not recalculate the forecast: Each one merely points to the cell in column G that's one row up. So, for example, the formula in cell E4 is
>
> =G3

In Holt's method, each forecast after the first is the sum of the prior level estimate and the prior slope estimate. Therefore, in Figure 5.1, the forecast of 821.9 in cell G3, for Period 3, is the sum of the level estimate 820.2 in cell C3 and the slope estimate 1.7 in D3, both made during Period 2.

Here's how that level estimate and slope estimate are calculated. Cell C3 calculates the second estimate of level with this formula:

    =Alpha*B3+(1–Alpha)*E3

> **NOTE** The prior formula uses the defined name *Alpha*. I have used Excel's defined names capability in Figure 5.1 to give the name *Alpha* to cell I2 and the name *Gamma* to cell J2. (Click in cell I2 and then in J2, noting what shows up in the Name box.) Now that we are dealing with not one but two smoothing constants, using cell names instead of addresses makes it easier to see what's going on in the smoothing formulas. One way to name a cell is to select it, click in the Name Box to the left of the Formula Box, and then type the name you want. This method is quick but doesn't give you as much control over the name's characteristics as clicking Define Name in the Names group on the Ribbon's Formulas tab.

5

Just as in simple exponential smoothing, the smoothing constant Alpha is multiplied by an actual observation (here, in cell B3). The product is added to (1–Alpha) times a forecast (here, in cell E3). The result of the full formula for the series' estimated level is 820.2 in cell C3.

The first estimate of the slope is in cell D3. Its formula is as follows:

=Gamma*(C3-C2)+(1-Gamma)*D2

> **NOTE** Sources vary, but many refer to the smoothing constant for the slope using Holt's method as *Gamma*, and I follow that usage here.

Again, the smoothing constant Gamma is multiplied by an actual observation, but here the actual observation is the difference in level—that is, the slope—from C2 to C3. The result is added to (1 − Gamma) times the prior forecast of the slope. One acceptable estimate of the slope at period 1 is zero, as shown in cell D2.

The result of adding the smoothed level to the smoothed slope is 803.0, shown in both cell G2 and cell E3, as the sum of cells C2 (the estimated level) and D2 (the estimated slope).

It's not strictly necessary to calculate the forecast error explicitly, but Figure 5.1 does so in column F. It is the difference between the actual observation in column B and the forecast in column E.

The remaining estimates of the series' level and slope, and the resulting forecasts and errors, are calculated by simply copying and pasting the formulas in the range C3:G3 into the range C4:G34.

Notice that the forecast for the 34th period, which has not yet come to pass, is 9,026.2 in cell G34 in Figure 5.2. To get it, just copy the formulas in cells E34 and G33 and paste them into E35 and G34. The value shown changes after the next phase, when we use Solver to find the optimum values for Alpha and Gamma.

Choosing Alpha and Gamma

Finding Alpha and Gamma is done just as it is in simple exponential smoothing, but now we have Solver modify two values, Alpha and Gamma, instead of Alpha only as in simple exponential smoothing (see Figure 5.2).

I've changed the mechanics of the worksheet a bit in Figures 5.1 and 5.2. In other figures, such as Figure 4.15, I placed both the smoothing constant Alpha and (1 − Alpha) directly on the worksheet. Alpha was entered as a constant to be changed by Solver, and (1 − Alpha) was entered explicitly as a worksheet formula that reacts to changes in Alpha. Putting both on the worksheet helps make what's going on a little clearer when you're getting used to the ideas involved in smoothing.

Figure 5.2
The values for Alpha and Gamma have now been optimized. The forecast for the next, as-yet-unobserved period is 9,474.2.

C7				f_x	=Alpha*B7+(1-Alpha)*G6					
	A	B	C	D	E	F	G	H I	J	K
1	Period	Customers	Level	Slope	Forecast from prior day	Error	Forecast for next period	Alpha Gamma		RMSE
2	1	803	803.0	-			803.0	0.95 0.21		375.5
3	2	975	966.7	34.4	803.0	172.0	1,001.1			
4	3	894	899.2	13.0	1,001.1	(107.1)	912.1			
5	4	821	825.4	(5.2)	912.1	(91.1)	820.1			
6	5	844	842.9	(0.5)	820.1	23.9	842.4			
7	6	891	888.7	9.2	842.4	48.6	897.9			
8	7	932	930.4	16.1	897.9	34.1	946.4			
9	8	884	887.0	3.6	946.4	(62.4)	890.6			
10	9	1,190	1,175.6	63.4	890.6	299.4	1,239.0			
11	10	1,178	1,180.9	51.2	1,239.0	(61.0)	1,232.2			
12	11	1,327	1,322.4	70.2	1,232.2	94.8	1,392.6			
13	12	1,793	1,773.7	150.2	1,392.6	400.4	1,924.0			
14	13	2,277	2,260.0	220.8	1,924.0	353.0	2,480.8			
15	14	2,061	2,081.2	136.9	2,480.8	(419.8)	2,218.1			
16	15	2,510	2,496.0	195.2	2,218.1	291.9	2,691.2			
17	16	2,679	2,679.6	192.8	2,691.2	(12.2)	2,872.4			
18	17	2,928	2,925.3	203.9	2,872.4	55.6	3,129.2			
19	18	3,284	3,276.6	234.8	3,129.2	154.8	3,511.4			
20	19	3,524	3,523.4	237.4	3,511.4	12.6	3,760.8			
21	20	3,797	3,795.3	244.6	3,760.8	36.2	4,039.9			
22	21	4,494	4,472.1	335.4	4,039.9	454.1	4,807.5			
23	22	5,741	5,696.1	522.0	4,807.5	933.5	6,218.1			
24	23	6,449	6,437.9	568.1	6,218.1	230.9	7,006.0			
25	24	7,638	7,607.6	694.5	7,006.0	632.0	8,302.0			
26	25	7,473	7,512.9	528.7	8,302.0	(829.0)	8,041.6			
27	26	7,731	7,745.9	466.7	8,041.6	(310.6)	8,212.6			
28	27	7,608	7,637.1	345.8	8,212.6	(604.6)	7,982.9			
29	28	8,214	8,202.9	392.0	7,982.9	231.1	8,594.9			
30	29	8,006	8,034.3	274.3	8,594.9	(588.9)	8,308.6			
31	30	8,315	8,314.7	275.6	8,308.6	6.4	8,590.3			
32	31	8,546	8,548.1	266.7	8,590.3	(44.3)	8,814.8			
33	32	9,408	9,379.5	385.3	8,814.8	593.2	9,764.7			
34	33	9,178	9,206.2	268.0	9,764.7	(586.7)	9,474.2			
35	34				9,474.2					

But when we get to two-parameter smoothing, as we do with Alpha and Gamma in Holt's method, it's time to get a little more parsimonious, and I show Alpha and Gamma directly on the worksheet, but not (1 – Alpha) or (1 – Gamma); the cells are named Alpha and Gamma, as discussed in the two prior Notes. The damping factors that are associated with the two smoothing constants are calculated in the formulas themselves, rather than in worksheet cells. For example, in Figures 5.1 and 5.2, the formula for the series level in cell C3 is

=Alpha*B3+(1–Alpha)*G2

and the formula for the series slope in cell D3 is

=Gamma*(C3–C2)+(1–Gamma)*D2

where the name Alpha refers to cell $I$2 and Gamma refers to cell $J$2. You could of course use the absolute cell references instead of the names in the formulas, but using the names helps make the formulas more self-documenting.

5

Figure 5.3 shows how the Solver dialog box would be set up to optimize the values for Alpha and Gamma. Chapter 4 shows how to set up the worksheet and complete Solver's dialog box with one smoothing constant. The differences when you have to smooth two constants, Alpha and Gamma, instead of just one are

- Provide the cell addresses of both smoothing constants in the Variable Cells edit box.
- Constrain both constants to stay between 0 and 1.

Other settings, such as specifying the Target cell as the standard error, or RMSE, and the solution method as Generalized Reduced Gradient (GRG), remain as shown in Chapter 2.

> **NOTE** In the context of exponential smoothing, the standard error statistic is more frequently termed *root mean square error*, or *RMSE*, and I follow that convention here.

Figure 5.3
Remember to set constraints for both Alpha and Gamma.

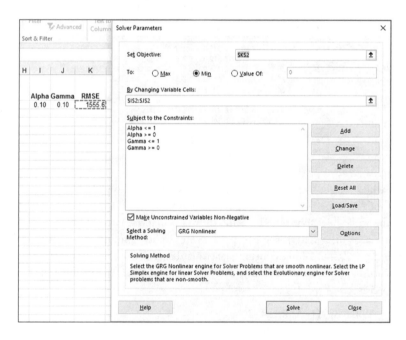

After using Solver to find the optimum values of Alpha and Gamma, the forecast RMSE is reduced from 1,555.6 as shown in Figure 5.1 to 375.5 in Figure 5.2.

You would bear that in mind when you looked at the values for the next forecast. The values of 0.1 for Alpha and Gamma result in a forecast RMSE of 1,555.6, whereas the values of 0.95 and 0.21 result in a forecast RMSE of 375.5—overall a much more accurate forecast. It is more sensible to adopt 9,474.2, the next forecast from the optimized smoothing constants, than to adopt 9,026 as the next forecast, based on the less accurate smoothing constants.

Choosing the Initial Level and Slope

When you have a very short time series—say, five to ten observations—then the way you make the first forecast can have a greater effect on later forecasts than you would like. The problem is that there's no value at hand from before the first observation; if there were, that prior value would be the first observation itself.

If the first observation is an outlier, a value that is quite high or quite low compared to other early observations, that outlier can exert an undue influence on the early smoothed values.

Using an Early Average   To deal with that problem, some forecasters like to take the average of the first few observations as the initial forecast. You can certainly do the same if the spirit moves you. As a matter of personal preference I don't subscribe to that practice: I would have to decide how many early observations to include in the average, and if I do that, I'm inserting my own judgment into a process that is better driven by the numbers, not by my own assessments.

Using a Backcast   Another approach involves *backcasting*. In effect, you reverse the time series and use smoothing to forecast to period zero. Then you use that forecast of time zero to calculate the smoothed value for period 1. I believe that approach has a good bit more to be said for it than averaging the first few observations because the role of the forecaster's judgment isn't overdone. More important, Box and Jenkins (who originated ARIMA models) themselves suggest the use of backcasting, and I'm not likely to argue with them.

Using the First Observation   You can also use the first observation as the first forecast, as has been done so far in this chapter. That's generally my own preference. If I do anything else, I'm inserting myself into the process and I need a compelling reason to do that.

Even if that first observation looks like an outlier, I have no special reason to believe that it doesn't belong there. And the farther that the smoothing process gets through the time series, the less influence the first observation has on the next forecast. That, of course, is due to the effect of the exponentiation that was illustrated in Chapter 4 in Figures 4.2 and 4.3.

This is one reason that it pays to have a lengthy series of actual observations for a baseline. Your interest usually centers on the next forecast for the time period that you haven't yet observed because it hasn't yet occurred.

At period 2, your forecast is based entirely on the first observation. At period 10, its influence on the next forecast is somewhere between 15% and 45%, depending on the value you're using as Alpha. At period 50—which you can often get to if you have four years of monthly data—the influence of the first observation is vanishingly small. And in that case there's little reason to worry about letting an oddball observation at period 1 have undue influence on your forecast for period 50.

5

Using Manual Smoothing   Finally, and particularly when Holt's linear exponential smoothing is in use, some forecasters like to use averages of particular observations for the first four smoothed estimates of the slope. The usual recipe is as follows:

Slope 1: 0

Slope 2: $y_2 - y_1$

Slope 3: $(y_3 - y_1)/2$

Slope 4: $((y_2 - y_1) + (y_4 - y_3))/2$

Beginning with the fifth period, the slope is smoothed as described in the prior section.

I'm sure there are some time series that benefit from this approach to managing the first few smoothed values for the slope, but I've never encountered one—not even when the time series was relatively short. I have found that typically the forecast RMSE is larger when I use the recipe outlined in this section than when I used zero as the first smoothed slope and then calculated the remaining slopes according to the standard formula given earlier, and used in Figures 5.1 through 5.3:

New slope=Gamma*(C3-C2)+(1–Gamma)*D2

That is, Gamma times the difference between the two prior level estimates, plus (1 – Gamma) times the prior smoothed slope.

Holt's Method and First Differences

You probably have noticed a similarity between Holt's method of determining the slopes between observations in a baseline and the method of first differences. Chapter 4 discusses first differences as a means of moving from a trended baseline to a stationary baseline. Once that's done, you can use simple exponential smoothing to forecast the differences and then reintegrate the forecasts back into the baseline.

Similarly, Holt's method calculates the differences between consecutive baseline estimates and calls them "slopes" rather than first differences. It's at this point that the two approaches part company. If you're forecasting with first differencing, you use smoothing, but not on the *level* of the baseline—only on the differences between consecutive levels. Once smoothed, the differences are added back into the original baseline to get the trended forecast. The reason for jumping through these hoops is that simple exponential smoothing often results in naïve forecasting when you use it with a trended series. The optimized Alpha turns out to be 1 and each forecast equals the prior actual observation. Strong autocorrelation in the baseline is the cause of this behavior (autocorrelation is the Pearson correlation between, say, observations 1 through 49 and observations 2 through 50).

Holt's slopes differ from first differences in other ways, despite the fundamental outcome of smoothing period-to-period differences. I noted earlier that Holt's method calculates the differences between consecutive baseline estimates. That means that each slope is the difference between two consecutive *smoothed* baseline values, whereas first differences are between two consecutive actual observations.

Furthermore, Holt's method smooths both the slopes and the levels, but first differencing smooths the differences only. And when it comes time to optimize Alpha and Gamma, the smoothing constants, Holt's method optimizes both constants simultaneously.

Figures 5.4 and 5.5 show the two methods, with the smoothing constants optimized by Solver, so that you can more easily compare the results. For example, if you contrast the RMSE for Holt's method in cell J4 of Figure 5.4 with the RMSE returned by first differencing in cell H3 if Figure 5.5, you see that the two values are quite close: 376.9 versus 375.5.

Figure 5.4
Notice that Alpha, the smoothing constant for the level of the series in Holt's method, is close to 1.0.

C3 =HoltAlpha*B3+(1-HoltAlpha)*E3

	A	B	C	D	E	F	G	H	I	J
1	Period	Customers	Level	Slope	Forecast (Holt's method)	Error	Forecast for next period		Analysis using Holt's method	
2	1	803	803	0			803.0		Alpha:	0.95
3	2	975	966.7	34.4	803.0	172.0	1001.1		Gamma:	0.21
4	3	894	899.2	13.0	1001.1	-107.1	912.1		RMSE	375.5
5	4	821	825.4	-5.2	912.1	-91.1	820.1			
6	5	844	842.9	-0.5	820.1	23.9	842.4			
7	6	891	888.7	9.2	842.4	48.6	897.9			
8	7	932	930.4	16.1	897.9	34.1	946.4			
9	8	884	887.0	3.6	946.4	-62.4	890.6			
10	9	1,190	1175.6	63.4	890.6	299.4	1239.0			
11	10	1,178	1180.9	51.2	1239.0	-61.0	1232.2			
12	11	1,327	1322.4	70.2	1232.2	94.8	1392.6			
13	12	1,793	1773.7	150.2	1392.6	400.4	1923.9			

Figure 5.5
Here we forecast the differences only, so there's just one smoothing constant.

E5 =B4+D5

	A	B	C	D	E	F	G	H
1	Period	Customers	First differences	Forecast differences	Forecast (first differences)		Analysis using first differences	
2	1	803					Alpha:	0.12
3	2	975	172		803		RMSE	376.9
4	3	894	-81	172	1147			
5	4	821	-73	141	1035			
6	5	844	23	115	936			
7	6	891	47	104	948			
8	7	932	41	97	988			
9	8	884	-48	90	1022			
10	9	1,190	306	74	958			
11	10	1,178	-12	102	1292			
12	11	1,327	149	88	1266			
13	12	1,793	466	95	1422			
14	13	2,277	484	140	1933			
15	14	2,061	-216	182	2459			

The slight difference in RMSE values tells the story: With this data, or any similar, strongly trended data set, the results you get from first differencing are likely to be very similar to those you get from Holt's method. As I pointed out in Chapter 4, when the autocorrelation in the time series is strong (and here it's .99) then the best estimate of the series level at time *t+1* is its level at time *t*. In that event, there's a strong case to use naïve forecasting.

TIP If you want to check the autocorrelation in the baseline shown in Figures 5.1 through 5.5, use this formula:

=CORREL(B2:B33,B3:B34)

But as Chapter 6 shows, that formula is an approximation (albeit a close one) of the autocorrelation function used in Box-Jenkins analysis.

Naïve forecasting is tantamount to using an Alpha smoothing constant of 1.0 to forecast the next level in Holt's method. And the result of that is to base the slopes calculated between consecutive observations on the observations themselves: With an Alpha of 1.0, the smoothed estimate is precisely equal to the actual observation.

And the result of *that* is to make the calculated slopes precisely equal to the first differences—with an Alpha of 1.0, you wind up with an analysis that's identical to a first difference analysis, just as described in Chapter 4. You can demonstrate this using Figure 5.4: Change Alpha to 1.0, and run Solver again, deleting Alpha as a variable cell. As Alpha approaches 1.0, then the results of Holt's method approach those returned by first differencing.

Another way of looking at the same outcome is to compare the charted forecasts. See Figure 5.6.

Figure 5.6
The charted forecasts are nearly impossible to distinguish.

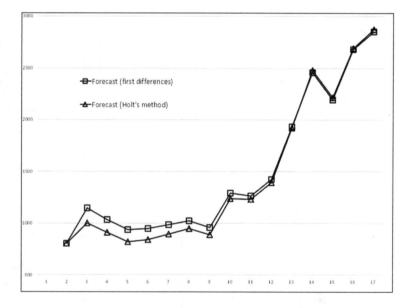

The forecasts are so close to one another that the final 6 of the 16 forecasts can't be told apart on the chart. The takeaway is that when a baseline has substantial autocorrelation, there's not much to choose from between first differencing and Holt's method. With weaker autocorrelations in other baselines, you might want to try both methods and choose, at least tentatively, the one that returns the smaller RMSE. Of course, as autocorrelation weakens, the argument for treating the baseline as trended also weakens.

The differencing method for dealing with a trended baseline is an integral part of several ARIMA models, and it might appear simpler to use than Holt's method, but that's a deceptive simplicity. You sometimes have a baseline that's characterized by both trend *and* seasonality: That is, the baseline's trend might be generally increasing or decreasing up or down over a span of years, but display regular seasonal variation within years. Then, you likely want to use another method, called Holt-Winters, to account for both the trend and the seasonality.

It's entirely possible to deal with seasonality in a set of first differences, but it turns out to be a good bit more straightforward to adapt the Holt method to the Holt-Winters method, so that you're smoothing three components of the baseline simultaneously: the level, the trend, and the seasonal component. This chapter works through an example of that procedure in the section named "Holt-Winters Models: Dealing with Trend and Seasonality."

Seasonal Models

When you consider events that follow a seasonal pattern, it's normal to think of calendar seasons: spring, summer, fall, and winter. And certainly plenty of interesting phenomena follow the calendar: flu cases peak during the winter months, home sales peak during the spring, water usage climbs in the summer, and back-to-school sales rise during the fall.

If there is a regular tempo to this seasonal variation, we should be able to take advantage of it in our predictions. If we can rely on median home sales prices to be $10,000 higher during the spring than their annual median, then we're in a position to make more accurate forecasts than we would be if we didn't know about the seasonality, or if the seasonal effect differed radically every year.

But those four calendar seasons are not the only ways that time periods can rotate and repeat. For example:

- Night shifts at a hospital might require more staff for nighttime traffic accidents than day or evening shifts.
- Power requirements at factories often depend on the time of day.
- U.S. air passenger traffic peaks during the third quarter and hits bottom during the first quarter.
- Many local governments experience a major inflow of tax receipts as a function of the annual or biannual schedule for the payment of property taxes.

By looking at a baseline of data—even just a single rotation of the "seasons," you can establish seasonal effects. (These seasonal effects are often termed *seasonal indexes*—or, if aiming to sound especially elegant, *indices*.) By adding these effects, both positive and negative, to the current level of a series, you might be able to forecast the next actual observation with good accuracy. Furthermore, because you'll have estimates of a full rotation available, you won't be locked into one-step-ahead forecasts. You can add the seasonal indexes to the series' current level and get a reasonable forecast for as many seasonal periods into the future as you have seasons.

Estimating Seasonal Indexes

Several methods for forecasting purely seasonal models exist, but this book focuses on the seasonal smoothing method. This is largely because you're more likely to come across the smoothing method than any of the others, but it's also because it fits well with both simple exponential smoothing discussed in Chapter 4, and with baselines that are both seasonal and trended. This chapter's section on Holt-Winters smoothing discusses that situation, but first let's take a look at how to smooth baselines that have seasonality but no trend.

Figure 5.7
The effects of being in each of the six seasons during the first year appear in H2:H7.

H2 =D2-Year_1_Mean

	A	B	C	D	E	F	G	H	I	J	K	L
1	Year	Season	t	Observ-ations				Seasonal Effect				
2	2014	1	1	7950				-220.8				
3		2	2	7304				-866.8			Year 1 Mean	8170.8
4		3	3	8071				-99.8				
5		4	4	9374				1203.2				
6		5	5	8819				648.2				
7		6	6	7507				-663.8				
8	2015	1	7	7307								
9		2	8	7383								
10		3	9	8035								
11		4	10	9084								
12		5	11	9076								
13		6	12	7944								
14	2016	1	13	7477								
15		2	14	7307								
16		3	15	7963								

5

Figure 5.7 shows a baseline of data in the range D2:D16. Each year in the baseline consists of six two-month seasons. Cell L3 uses this formula:

=AVERAGE(D2:D7)

to return the mean of the six seasons during 2014.

The seasonal effects for the first year in the baseline appear in H2:H7. So, the effect of being in the first season is to reduce the level of the observations by 220.8 from the annual mean. This is the formula used in cell H2:

=D2-Year_1_Mean

(For clarity, I have given the name Year_1_Mean to cell L3.) Similarly, the effect of being in the second season of the first year is found in cell H3 with this formula:

=D3-Year_1_Mean

Estimating the Series Level and First Forecast

With those values in hand, you can begin to create actual forecasts, as shown in Figure 5.8.

Figure 5.8
It takes one full turn of the seasons before you can start smoothing in this model.

In Figure 5.8, cell G7 (in addition to cell L3) contains the mean of the first six seasonal observations, which estimates the level of the time series at the end of the first year. Because you are treating this baseline as a horizontal series—one without trend—it's plausible to use the average of the Year 1 seasonal observations as the best estimate of the series level at the start of the smoothing process.

You now have the two estimates you need to make the first forecast: an initial estimate of the series level in cell G7, and an estimate of the effect of the first season in cell H2. It's the end of 2014 and you're about to get your forecast for Season 1 of 2015. That forecast is in cell I7, and it also appears in cell E8. The formula in I7 is

=G7+H2

It's the sum of the estimated level—the average of 2014's seasonal observations—plus H2, the most recent estimate available of the seasonal effect of being in Season 1.

That forecast is carried forward from the end of Season 6, when it is made in cell I7, into Season 1 of 2015, cell E8, which is the season to which the forecast actually applies. Cell E8 contains the simple linking formula =I7.

At the end of Season 1 in 2015, you have the necessary information to record the actual observation for that period, 7307, in cell D8, and you can now evaluate the accuracy of the first forecast. Cell F8 does so by subtracting the value of the forecast in E8 from the value of the actual observation in cell D8:

=D8-E8

Extending the Forecasts to Future Periods

In preparation to make the forecast for the next period, Season 2 in 2015, you need to get an estimate of the baseline's current level and trend. Recall from Chapter 4 that the way to smooth the series' level is to multiply the most current actual observation by Alpha, the level smoothing constant; then add to that (1 – Alpha) times the most recent forecast. In Figure 5.8 you do that by means of this formula in cell G8:

=Alpha*(D8-H2)+(1-Alpha)*G7

If this were simple exponential smoothing, as you might use on a baseline that shows neither seasonality nor trend, you might instead expect the formula to be the following:

=Alpha*D8+(1-Alpha)*G7

where cell D8 contains the current observation and G7 contains the most recent estimate of the level. But here you're dealing with a baseline that displays seasonality (but not trend). Therefore, the current observation is a combination of the current level of the baseline plus the effect of the current season. To "observe" the current level, you subtract the most recent effect of the current season (in cell H2) from the current observation (in D8). Then you multiply the difference between the observation and the seasonal effect—the observed level—by Alpha.

Finally, multiply the most recent forecast of the baseline level in G7 by (1 – Alpha). Add the result to Alpha*(D8-H2) to get the smoothed estimate of the baseline's current level, in cell G8.

You now have calculated the first term in the forecast, the estimated level. The second term in the formula for the forecast, the estimated seasonal effect, is found in cell H8 in Figure 5.8:

=Delta*(D8-G8)+(1-Delta)*H2

The formula employs the seasonal smoothing constant Delta, which operates much like the constant Alpha does for the series level, and like the constant Gamma does for the series slope in this chapter's first section on Holt's Linear Smoothing. In Figure 5.8, Delta is located in cell L2 (which is named Delta).

The pattern is the same as is used to calculate the level estimate in cell G8: the seasonal smoothing constant Delta times the observed current seasonal effect, plus (1 – Delta) times the most recent seasonal estimate. Again, you're analyzing this baseline as a horizontal time series, with no trend but with seasonality. Therefore you can back into an observation of the current seasonal effect by subtracting the current estimated level in G8 from the current observation in cell D8. The difference is the current "observed" seasonal effect, which you multiply by Delta.

The second term calculates (1 – Delta) times the most recent estimate of the effect of the current season. That estimate is found in cell H2. Cell G8 treats that value as an actual observation: It's used as a means of getting the current observed level by means of D8-H2. But just as the first forecast in simple exponential smoothing is taken to be the first actual observation, the first observed seasonal effects stand in for seasonal forecasts until you get far enough into the baseline that the estimated seasonal effects are truly estimated. As shown in Figure 5.9, this occurs in cell H14, which picks up the first smoothed estimate of the seasonal effect in cell H8.

Combine the two terms as shown in cell H8 of Figure 5.8 to get the current estimate of the seasonal effect. To get the forecast for the next period, Season 2 of 2015, sum cells G8 and H3. The result appears in cell I8.

Finishing the One-Step-Ahead Forecasts

At this point, you can copy the range E8:I8 down into the range E9:I16. You'll see the result in Figure 5.9.

Figure 5.9
The baseline runs out of observations at period 15—the third season of 2016.

	A	B	C	D	E	F	G	H	I	J	K	L
					Forecast				Forecast			
				Observ-	for this		Estimated	Seasonal	for next			
1	Year	Season	t	ations	period	Error	Level	Effect	period	Alpha		0.1
2	2014	1	1	7950				-220.8		Delta		0.3
3		2	2	7304				-866.8		Year 1 Mean		8170.8
4		3	3	8071				-99.8				
5		4	4	9374				1203.2		RMSE		321.6
6		5	5	8819				648.2				
7		6	6	7507			8170.8	-663.8	7950.0			
8	2015	1	7	7307	7950.0	-643.0	8106.5	-394.4	7239.7			
9		2	8	7383	7239.7	143.3	8120.9	-828.1	8021.0			
10		3	9	8035	8021.0	14.0	8122.3	-96.1	9325.4			
11		4	10	9084	9325.4	-241.4	8098.1	1138.0	8746.3			
12		5	11	9076	8746.3	329.7	8131.1	737.2	7467.3			
13		6	12	7944	7467.3	476.7	8178.8	-535.1	7784.3			
14	2016	1	13	7477	7784.3	-307.3	8148.0	-477.4	7319.9			
15		2	14	7307	7319.9	-12.9	8146.7	-831.6	8050.7			
16		3	15	7963	8050.7	-87.7	8138.0	-119.7	9276.0			
17		4	16		9276.0							
18		5	17									
19		6	18									
20	2017	1	19									

The range D8:E16 provides all the information you need to prepare to optimize the Alpha and Delta smoothing constants. In fact, if you maintain the formulas in F8:F16, to show the error in each forecast, you can use this formula for the RMSE (cell L5 in Figure 5.9):

=SQRT(SUMSQ(F8:F16)/9)

That formula sums the squares of each of the errors in F8:F16, gets the average of the squares by dividing by 9, and takes the square root of the result.

If you don't want to bother with getting each individual forecast error on the worksheet, you can use a formula such as this one instead:

=SQRT(SUMXMY2(D8:D16,E8:E16)/9)

The SUMXMY2( ) function finds the differences between the values in D8:D16 and E8:E16 for you, squares them and sums the squares. Both the two previous formulas can be entered normally and need not be entered as array formulas.

With the RMSE in hand and the Alpha and Delta smoothing constants in place, you can use Solver to optimize Alpha and Delta just as discussed earlier in this chapter, in "Using Holt's Linear Smoothing." The only difference is that you identify Alpha and Delta as the variable cells, rather than Alpha and Gamma.

Extending the Forecast Horizon

With the data as shown in Figure 5.9, you can forecast into one more period: The forecast for Period 17 is in cell I18. But you can't use the same procedures for Period 17, 18 and so on as you used for Periods 7 through 15. The reason is that the smoothing forecasts you've been building rely on the actual observations in column D to calculate the level estimates in column G. For example, the formula in cell G8 is

=Alpha*(D8-H2)+(1-Alpha)*G7

and the value in cell D8 accounts for most of the first term in the formula. After the third season of 2016, however, there's no value in column D to contribute to a new estimate of the baseline's level.

Furthermore, if you examine the estimates of seasonal effects in column H, you'll see that the way they're calculated changes in Season 7, from simple deviations from the Year 1 mean in seasons 1 through 6 to smoothing formulas thereafter. You need to initialize each season's effect at the outset, and the way I've chosen to do so for this example is to calculate the difference between the observations in each of the first six seasons, less the mean of the first six seasons.

> **NOTE**
> I mentioned earlier in this chapter that several methods exist for initializing the seasonal effects, including simple averages, moving average and linear regression. I chose this method because it is straightforward and does not distract from the main point of the example, the combination of smoothing the baseline's level with smoothing the seasonal effects after they have been initialized.

So, the formula used for the seasonal effect in Season 6 is

=D7-Year_1_Mean

or the difference between the Season 6 observation and the mean observation for the first year. But at that point, you're about to forecast Season 1 of Year 2, and by then you have in hand, in cell H2, an estimate of the effect of being in the first season. So in cell H8 you can replace the simple difference between a season's observation and the year's mean (as in H2:H7) with this smoothing formula:

=Delta*(D8-G8)+(1-Delta)*H2

But you do have enough raw material to forecast into Season 4 of 2016, and all you need to do is drag cell E16 into E17. That gives you the final one-step-ahead forecast of 9276.0.

Now: Given that you're out of the new observations that would allow you to continue smoothing the level of the baseline, is it possible to make credible forecasts beyond the one-step-ahead forecast into the seventeenth period?

Yes, it's possible. And here's where it can start to get a little tricky, but only just a little. See Figure 5.10.

Figure 5.10
The assumption is that the estimated level remains constant as of Period 15.

	H17				f_x	=H16							
	A	B	C	D	E	F	G	H	I	J	K	L	M	N
1	Year	Season	t	Observ-ations	Forecast for this period	Error	T₁(t)	Estimated Level (Smoothing) T₁(t-1)	Season i	Seasonal Index (Smoothing)	Forecast for next period		Alpha	0.1
2	2014	1	1	7950					1	-220.8			Delta	0.3
3		2	2	7304					2	-866.8			Year 1 Mean	8170.8
4		3	3	8071					3	-99.8				
5		4	4	9374					4	1203.2			RMSE	321.6
6		5	5	8819					5	648.2				
7		6	6	7507				8170.8	6	-663.8	7950.0			
8	2015	1	7	7307	7950.0	-643.0	8170.8	8106.5	1	-394.4	7239.7			
9		2	8	7383	7239.7	143.3	8106.5	8120.9	2	-828.1	8021.0			
10		3	9	8035	8021.0	14.0	8120.9	8122.3	3	-96.1	9325.4			
11		4	10	9084	9325.4	-241.4	8122.3	8098.1	4	1138.0	8746.3			
12		5	11	9076	8746.3	329.7	8098.1	8131.1	5	737.2	7467.3			
13		6	12	7944	7467.3	476.7	8131.1	8178.8	6	-535.1	7784.3			
14	2016	1	13	7477	7784.3	-307.3	8178.8	8148.0	1	-477.4	7319.9			
15		2	14	7307	7319.9	-12.9	8148.0	8146.7	2	-831.6	8050.7			
16		3	15	7963	8050.7	-87.7	8146.7	8138.0	3	-119.7	9276.0			
17		4	16		9276.0		8138.0	8138.0	4		8875.2			
18		5	17		8875.2			8138.0	5		7602.9			
19		6	18		7602.9			8138.0	6		7660.6			
20	2017	1	19		7660.6			8138.0	1		7306.4			
21		2	20		7306.4			8138.0	2		8018.2			

In Figure 5.10, notice that the estimated level of the baseline becomes constant in cell H17 and remains at 8138.0 through H21. Allowing the estimated level to remain constant is an assumption, of course, but by making it you can rationally forecast another full turn of the seasons, through the third season of 2017. You won't be smoothing the series level as you had been, and so you won't have the advantage of making corrections to the level of the baseline. But by relying on seasonal variation around a now-constant level, you're likely to have more accurate forecasts than you would if you simply extended the most recent smoothed forecast out by several periods.

As to the worksheet mechanics, one way of forecasting several periods past the end of the actual observations is to freeze the reference to the final smoothed level using a fixed reference. Cell K17 in Figure 5.10 contains the first forecast after smoothing the baseline level has ended. It could contain this formula:

=$H$17+J12

That formula returns the sum of the level (8,138.0 in cell H17) and the smoothed slope (737.2 in cell J12). The smoothed slope in J12 belongs to the fifth season (see cell B12) and cell K17 provides the forecast for the fifth season in 2016.

If you were to copy that formula down into K18:K21, the results would combine the value in H17 with those in J13, J14, J15, and J16. Because the reference to H17 in the previous formula is fixed, it's not necessary to repeat the value in H17 in H18:H22.

But if you wanted to be as explicit as possible, you could repeat the final smoothed level in H16 down through H21 (as shown in Figure 5.10). Then do not freeze K17's reference to H17, and allow the references to levels in K18:K21 to adjust from H17 to H18 through H21.

Using Additive Holt-Winters Models

Chapter 4 introduced the basic idea of exponential smoothing as a way of forecasting the next level of a time series or baseline. That chapter focused on horizontal models—those without a persistent upward or downward trend—that also bear no particular evidence of seasonality. The first section of this chapter showed how to use smoothing to account for the presence of a trend in the baseline, and the chapter's second section showed how to use smoothing with a baseline that responds to the effects of seasons.

The present section deals with what are often called *Holt-Winters* models, which apply exponential smoothing techniques to baselines that display both trend and seasonality. (You might occasionally see the procedures described as *triple exponential smoothing*, owing to its use of three smoothing constants, for the level, the trend, and the seasons.) In the late 1950s, Charles Holt wrote the original paper on forecasting trends by means of exponential smoothing. In 1960, an article by Peter Winters showed how the same approach could be applied to seasonality in a trended time series—hence the term "Holt-Winters smoothing."

The Holt-Winters approach to forecasting is often discussed using what Box and Jenkins, in their initial work on ARIMA forecasting, called "Series G," a baseline of monthly counts of Australian airline passengers between 1949 and 1960. I use the same data set here, partly because it provides a striking example of a baseline that's both trended and seasonal, and partly because it's so popular an example that the statistical application R includes it in its package of sample data sets.

Figure 5.11 shows a chart of the air passenger data set.

You can see how, over time,

- The monthly number of passengers (measured in thousands) increases at a slightly accelerating rate.
- The seasonal component recurs each year. A larger chart would show the annual maximum in August and the annual minimum in November.

Figure 5.12 illustrates how you might analyze the air passengers data set in Excel using the Holt-Winters method.

Figure 5.11
Both the baseline's seasonality and its trend are apparent in the chart.

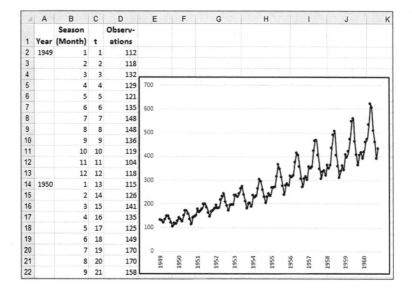

⌿	A	B	C	D	E	F	G	H	I	J	K
		Season		Observ-							
1	Year	(Month)	t	ations							
2	1949	1	1	112							
3		2	2	118							
4		3	3	132							
5		4	4	129							
6		5	5	121							
7		6	6	135							
8		7	7	148							
9		8	8	148							
10		9	9	136							
11		10	10	119							
12		11	11	104							
13		12	12	118							
14	1950	1	13	115							
15		2	14	126							
16		3	15	141							
17		4	16	135							
18		5	17	125							
19		6	18	149							
20		7	19	170							
21		8	20	170							
22		9	21	158							

Figure 5.12
Accounting for both trends and seasonality requires an added column and smoothing constant.

G14 f_x =Alpha*(D14-I2)+(1-Alpha)*(G13+H13)

⌿	A	B	C	D	E	F	G	H	I	J	K	L	M
					Forecast				Estimated	Forecast			
				Observa-	for this		Estimated	Estimated	Seasonal	for next			
1	Year	Season	t	tions	period	Error	Level	Trend	Index	period		Alpha	0.24796
2	1949	1	1	112					-14.7			Gamma	0.03453
3		2	2	118					-8.7			Delta	1
4		3	3	132					5.3			Year 1 Mean	126.67
5		4	4	129					2.3			Year 1 Trend	0.55
6		5	5	121					-5.7			RMSE	13.01
7		6	6	135					8.3				
8		7	7	148					21.3				
9		8	8	148					21.3				
10		9	9	136					9.3				
11		10	10	119					-7.7				
12		11	11	104					-22.7				
13		12	12	118				126.7	0.5	-8.7	112.5			
14	1950	1	13	115	112.5	2.5	127.8	0.6	-12.8	119.7			
15		2	14	126	119.7	6.3	129.9	0.6	-3.9	135.9			
16		3	15	141	135.9	5.1	131.8	0.7	9.2	134.8			

Notice that Figure 5.12 includes three smoothing constants, as follows:

- The level smoothing constant Alpha, in cell M1
- The trend smoothing constant, Gamma, in cell M2
- The season smoothing constant, Delta, in cell M3

> **NOTE**
> Different sources use different Greek letters to identify the smoothing constants. Although Alpha is almost universally used to identify the level smoothing constant, the trend constant is sometimes termed Beta, sometimes Gamma, and sometimes Delta. The same is true of the seasonal constant. My sense is that most sources use Gamma for the trend and Delta for the seasons, and that's the usage I've adopted in this book.

5

Also, notice that Figure 5.12 calculates the level estimates in column G, the trend estimates in column H, and the seasonal effect estimates in column I. The forecasts themselves are the sum of the associated values in those three columns, although—just as in this chapter's section on seasonal time series—the associated seasonal estimate is farther up the worksheet than the forecast it helps calculate. For example, the forecast in cell J13 of Figure 5.12 is

=G13+H13+I2

because I2 contains the most recent estimate of the effect of season 1 at the time that the forecast for season 1 in 1950 is made in J13.

The baseline level is initialized as shown in the prior section on seasonal smoothing: It is simply the mean of the observations during 1949, the first year. That value is calculated in cell M4 as

=AVERAGE(D2:D13)

and is named Year_1_Mean.

The baseline trend is initialized in a different fashion than is illustrated earlier in this chapter, where several figures show its initial value to be zero. In Figure 5.12, largely to show that different initialization methods are available to you, the trend is initialized by taking the difference between the observations in Year 1's first and last months, and dividing by 11, the number of month-to-month differences in one year. Here's the formula used in cell M5:

=(D13-D2)/11

where it's named Year_1_Trend.

And you've seen the method used to initialize the seasonal effects in this chapter's section on seasonal smoothing. There are twelve such effects to initialize because we're working with monthly data. Each cell in the range subtracts the mean observation for the first year from the actual observation for the month. So the estimate of the first month's effect, initialized in cell I2, is calculated as follows:

=D2-Year_1_Mean

and that formula is copied down through cell I13.

The exponential smoothing methods discussed in Chapter 4 and earlier in this chapter have used what are usually termed *smoothing formulas*. Smoothing formulas follow the general pattern of multiplying the most recent observation by a smoothing constant (Alpha, Gamma, or Delta), and the most recent forecast by 1 minus a smoothing constant (such as 1 − Alpha or 1 − Delta). The smoothing construct emphasizes a smoothed value as weighted average of an observation and a forecast. The size of the smoothing constant determines the weight given to the previous observation and the weight that goes to the previous forecast.

The alternatives to smoothing forms are usually termed *error correction formulas*. In this form, you add a previous forecast to the product of the smoothing constant and the error in the prior forecast. The error correction forms emphasize how the new forecast takes into account the error in the prior forecast.

To keep matters consistent, I have used the smoothing formulas throughout this book. The use of three terms instead of just one requires that you modify the basic form of the smoothing formula, but the general approach of a weighted average of an observation and a forecast remains in place. The smoothing and the error correction forms are algebraically equivalent and return identical results.

In Figure 5.12, smoothing begins in row 14. There are three terms to smooth: level, trend and season.

Level

Cell G14 contains the first smoothed level estimate. It uses this formula:

=Alpha*(D14-I2)+(1–Alpha)*(G13+H13)

Here, you multiply Alpha by the difference between the current observation in D14 and the most recent instance of the effect of the first season in cell I2. By subtracting the seasonal effect for Season 1 from the actual observation, you arrive at the current observed level of the baseline, free of the influence of the observation's seasonal effect.

Then you multiply (1 – Alpha) by the sum of the prior estimate of the level and the prior estimate of the trend. (For the first smoothed period, of course, the prior estimates are the initialized values of the level and the trend.) The sum of these two terms is the current estimate of the baseline level.

Trend

The first smoothed estimate for the trend appears in cell H14. It uses this formula:

=Gamma*(G14-G13)+(1-Gamma)*H13

In English: Take as the current trend the difference between the current estimate of the baseline level, in G14, and the prior estimate of the level, in G13. This difference is the observation of the current trend and is multiplied by the trend smoothing constant. Notice that because the difference is between consecutive *level* estimates, it's not influenced by an estimate of the current season's effect.

Then, multiply the prior estimate of the series trend in H13 by (1 – Gamma). Add the two terms together to get the current trend estimate.

5

Season

The third estimate to smooth is the seasonal effect. It looks a trifle more complicated than the smoothed estimates of the level and the trend, but it's still straightforward. The formula used in cell I14 is

=Delta*(D14-G14)+(1-Delta)*I2

The formula takes the difference between the current observation in cell D14 and the current estimate of the baseline level in cell G14. This difference is taken to be the currently observed seasonal effect, and it's multiplied by Delta, the seasonal smoothing constant.

The second term in the formula, (1 − Delta) * I2, looks different at first from the level and the trend smoothing formulas. They rely on estimates that take place in the prior period: The second term in the smoothed level in cell G14 involves the values in G13 and H13, while the smoothed trend in cell H14 involves the prior trend estimate in H13. In contrast, the seasonal smoothing formula in cell I14 picks up its prior estimate from cell I2.

The reason, of course, is that we're not just smoothing the prior season constant, but the prior season constant for the first season. With monthly data in which each month is regarded as a different season, you always look back 12 periods to pick up the most recent instance of a given seasonal effect. This accounts for the structure of the formula as it's provided, generically, in various sources:

$$s_t = \delta(y_t - l_{t-1}) + (1 - \delta)s_{t-m}$$

where t indexes the time period and m is the number of periods in an encompassing time period such as a year. So, if you're smoothing the fifteenth time period in a baseline of monthly seasonal observations, you would use the seasonal effect in the $t - m = 15 - 12 = $ 3rd period.

Some sources give the smoothing formula for the seasonal effect as follows:

$$s_t = \delta'(y_t - l_{t-1} - b_{t-1}) + (1 - \delta')s_{t-m}$$

where:

- s_t is the seasonal effect for period t
- y_t is the actual observation at period t
- l_{t-1} is the estimated level at period $t - 1$
- b_{t-1} is the estimated trend at period $t - 1$
- s_{t-m} is the estimated seasonal effect at period $t - m$
- m is the number of seasons in one encompassing period

Note that the only apparent difference between the prior formula and the one provided at the start of this section is that the second formula subtracts the most recent trend estimate in the formula's first term. The two formulas return equivalent results *if* you set δ' equal to $\delta/(1-\alpha)$ where α is Alpha, the level smoothing constant.

Formulas for the Holt-Winters Additive and Multiplicative Models

In the early 1900s, the Dow Jones Industrial Average (DJIA) typically stayed under 100 points. At the beginning of 1902, the DJIA stood at 64. At the beginning of 1908, the average was about 60. An increase or decrease of two points was regarded as significant. Notice that two points is about 3% of a DJIA of 60.

Today, when the DJIA stands at more than 20,000, a swing of two points is regarded as not even negligible. But a swing of 600 points, 3% in today's terms, would be regarded as quite large.

The issue is that the size of the swing in the DJIA is proportional to the level of that index. In such a case, it's usually best to express and calculate the size of the swing in percentage terms, rather than in absolute terms. The Holt-Winters model provides for either an additive or a multiplicative seasonal component:

■ The additive method, discussed in the prior section, provides for seasonality by adding or subtracting the seasonal effect, measured in the same scale as the actual observations.

■ The multiplicative method provides for seasonality by multiplying or dividing by the seasonal effect, measured as a percentage of the actual observations.

You generally use the additive method when the seasonal variation is roughly the same regardless of the level of the series. Figure 5.13 has an example of the sort of situation that would normally call for the use of the additive method. Notice that the level of the time series is increasing as time passes, but the size of the seasonal swings is roughly the same regardless of the annual level of the series.

Of course, if the level of the series were not increasing, you probably would not be using Holt-Winters at all, but rather a simple seasonal smoothing approach such as that discussed earlier in this chapter.

When the seasonal swings vary as the level of the series changes, you generally prefer the multiplicative method to the additive method, although the advantage may turn out to be very slight. Figure 5.14 as an example of the times series that might cause you to choose the multiplicative method.

Notice in Figure 5.14 that as the level of the series increases, so does the size of the seasonal swings. This is the sort of situation I described at the start of the section, in which daily swings in the DJIA and are much larger when the index is in the range of 20,000 than when it's in the range of 100.

Figure 5.13
The level of the series increases but the seasonal swings do not.

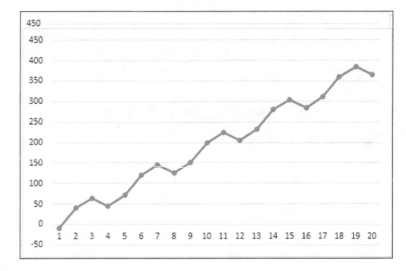

Figure 5.14
The size of the seasonal effects varies with the level of the time series.

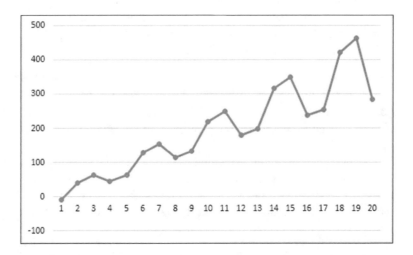

Formulas for the Additive Model

The formulas for the level, trend, and seasonal effects are typically given as follows. The smoothing versions of the formulas follow the usual pattern of a smoothing constant (such as α) times the current level, trend or seasonal effect, plus 1 minus the smoothing constant times the prior estimate of the level, trend, or seasonal effect.

The error correction versions of the formulas are provided along with the smoothing versions. They combine the previous estimate with the product of one or two constants and the error in the current forecast.

Level

The level smoothing formula is

$$l_t = \alpha(y_t - s_{t-m}) + (1 - \alpha)(l_{t-1} + b_{t-1})$$

Here, the first term in the formula multiplies α times the difference between the current observation, y_t, and the current seasonal effect, s_{t-m}. That difference is taken to be the current observation of the estimated level of the series. The second term in the formula multiplies $1 - \alpha$ times the total of the prior level estimate (l_{t-1}) and the prior trend estimate (b_{t-1}), which, combined, provide the prior estimate of the series level. Notice the subscript for the season, $t - m$. The letter t identifies the number of the current observation and the letter m identifies the number of seasons in the encompassing period. So if we're forecasting for January, we would want to use last January's estimated seasonal effect, and we get that from the subscript $t - m$.

In its error correction form, the formula is

$$l_t = (l_{t-1} + b_{t-1}) + \alpha\varepsilon_t$$

where ε_t is the error in the forecast at time t.

Trend

The trend smoothing formula is

$$b_t = \gamma(l_t - l_{t-1}) + (1 - \gamma)b_{t-1}$$

In this case, the first term in the formula multiplies the trend smoothing constant γ times the difference between the current estimated level and the prior estimated level. That difference is taken to be the observation of the current trend in the series. The second term in the formula multiplies one minus the trend smoothing constant by the prior estimate of the series trend.

Here's the error correction form of the trend formula:

$$b_t = b_{t-1} + \alpha\gamma\varepsilon_t$$

Seasonal Effect

The seasonal smoothing formula is

$$s_t = \delta(y_t - l_{t-1} - b_{t-1}) + (1 - \delta)s_{t-m}$$

Here, the current seasonal effect is calculated by subtracting the prior level of the series and the prior trend in the series from the current observation. The result of those subtractions is taken to be the current seasonal effect and is multiplied by δ. The second term multiplies one minus δ times the seasonal effect that was calculated the last time this season occurred—that is, $t - m$ seasons earlier.

In its error correction form:

$$s_t = s_{t-m} \delta(1 - \alpha)\varepsilon_t$$

The one-step-ahead forecast equation—regardless of whether the current estimates are based on the smoothing or the error correction forms of the equations—is then

$$\hat{y}_t = l_t + b_t + s_t$$

Formulas for the Multiplicative Model

Suppose that you're working with a trended time series, one that also exhibits apparent seasonality. If it appears to you as though the sizes of the seasonal effects are roughly proportional to the current level of the times series, consider using a multiplicative model rather than an additive model.

> **NOTE**   One way to check that proportionality is to take first differences of the time series as described in the prior chapter. Then calculate the Pearson correlation between the absolute values of the first differences and the level of the series at the point where each difference was taken. Even a moderate correlation would suggest that proportionality is present and that you should consider a multiplicative model.

The principal difference between additive and multiplicative models is that in the process of correcting for the seasonal effect, and of correcting the seasonal effect itself, the multiplicative model *divides* by the correction factors whereas the additive model *subtracts* the correction factors.

Following are the formulas for level, trend, and seasonality in the multiplicative model for Holt-Winters. Again, both the smoothing and the error correction forms of the equations are provided.

Level

In its smoothing form, the multiplicative model's level estimate is as follows:

$$l_t = \alpha(y_t / s_{t-m}) + (1 - \alpha)(l_{t-1} + b_{t-1})$$

Compare that to the level estimate in the additive model:

$$l_t = \alpha(y_t - s_{t-m}) + (1 - \alpha)(l_{t-1} + b_{t-1})$$

The only difference in the two formulas is that the additive model removes the seasonal effect from the current observation by subtraction. The multiplicative model removes the seasonal effect from the current observation by division.

Following is the error correction version of the same formula:

$$l_t = l_{t-1} + b_{t-1} + \alpha \varepsilon_t / s_{t-m}$$

Again, we divide by the seasonal effect, rather than by subtracting it as is done in the additive model.

Trend

The trend is not affected by the seasonality, and in consequence there is no difference between the trend equation in the additive model and that in the multiplicative model. Here is the trend equation for both the additive and multiplicative models, in its smoothing form:

$$b_t = \gamma(l_t - l_{t-1}) + (1 - \gamma)b_{t-1}$$

The error correction form of the multiplicative version is as follows:

$$b_t = b_{t-1} + \alpha\gamma\varepsilon_t / s_{t-m}$$

Seasonal Effect

The smoothing form of the seasonality equation in the multiplicative method is

$$s_t = \delta y_t / (l_{t-1} + b_{t-1}) + (1 - \delta)s_{t-m}$$

The error correction form of the formula for the seasonality effect in the multiplicative model is

$$s_t = s_{t-m} + \delta(1 - \alpha)\varepsilon_t / s_{t-m}$$

The Models Compared

Let's have a look at how these two models work out in practice on the same data set. Figures 5.15 and 5.16 illustrate the models as applied to the Box-Jenkins Series G data set, which contains 10 years of monthly data on the number of airline passengers in Australia. Figure 5.15 shows the additive model applied to that data set.

It's pretty clear from the chart that as the level of the series increases from around 100 to around 600, the size of the seasonal effects also increases, from around 50 in 1950 to more than 200 in 1960. Nevertheless, the additive method does a reasonably good job of forecasting this behavior.

It does so, however, by setting the value of the seasonal smoothing constant, δ, to 1.0. Notice that the value of δ, as optimized by Solver, is 1.0 in cell M3. That means that each successive seasonal value is based completely on the actual current observation, and not at all the on the prior seasonal estimate. As far as the seasonal effects are concerned, this is tantamount to naïve forecasting.

Figure 5.15
The seasonal swings are proportional to the series level.

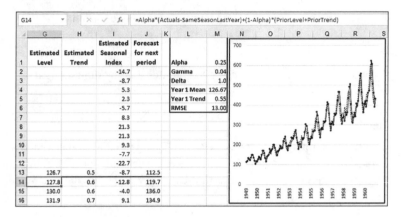

| G14 | | ▼ | ⋮ | × | ✓ | fx | =Alpha*(Actuals-SameSeasonLastYear)+(1-Alpha)*(PriorLevel+PriorTrend) |

	G	H	I	J	K	L	M
1	Estimated Level	Estimated Trend	Estimated Seasonal Index	Forecast for next period		Alpha	0.25
2			-14.7			Gamma	0.04
3			-8.7			Delta	1.0
4			5.3			Year 1 Mean	126.67
5			2.3			Year 1 Trend	0.55
6			-5.7			RMSE	13.00
7			8.3				
8			21.3				
9			21.3				
10			9.3				
11			-7.7				
12			-22.7				
13	126.7	0.5	-8.7	112.5			
14	127.8	0.6	-12.8	119.7			
15	130.0	0.6	-4.0	136.0			
16	131.9	0.7	9.1	134.9			

Figures 5.15 through 5.17 make extensive use of named cells and ranges. I have found that the use of descriptive names makes it much easier to tell what is going on in smoothing formulas than the use of actual cell addresses such as G14. The names that I have used are as follows:

- **Actuals**—In Figure 5.15, the name Actuals refers to the actual observations, found in cells D2:D145. The formulas that refer to the range named Actuals make use of Excel's implicit intersection. Therefore, if a formula in cell A20 refers to the range named Actuals, the value returned from that range is the value in the same row—that is, the value in cell D20.

- **Levels**—The name Levels refers to the range G13:G145. It is used in various formulas by means of the implicit intersection, just as the name Actuals is used in that fashion.

- **PriorLevel**—This is a relative range name—that is, the location of the cell with that name depends on the location of the cell that uses the name. So if I use the name PriorLevel in the cell G14, it refers to value in cell G13. PriorLevel is always located one row up from the cell that uses the name, and in column G.

- **PriorTrend**—This is another relative range name and, like PriorLevel, refers to the cell one row up from the cell that uses the name, in column H.

- **SameSeasonLastYear**—Another relative range name. This name refers to the value in column I that is 12 rows up from the cell that uses it. Recall that several smoothing formulas employed the seasonal effect from the prior instance of that season. Therefore, we need to look one year back to find the seasonal effect that we're interested in. So, if I am in cell G14, which is in Month one of 1950, I need to pick up the value of the seasonal effect in Month one of 1949. That's what SameSeasonLastYear does for you.

- **NextSeasonLastYear**—When it comes to actually calculating the forecast for the next season, we need to look one season further down than we get from SameSeasonLastYear. This relative range name looks 11 months back, not 12, in column I.

I strongly recommend that you consider using names such as these if you intend to do any forecasting based on exponential smoothing in Excel. It takes a little more time at the outset to define the names, but it pays off in the long run because your formulas will be more self-documenting, and you will find it much easier to locate and correct errors.

One more point regarding Figure 5.15: The value of RMSE is 13.00. Compare this information with what you see in Figure 5.16.

Figure 5.16
The multiplicative model provides somewhat greater accuracy with this data set.

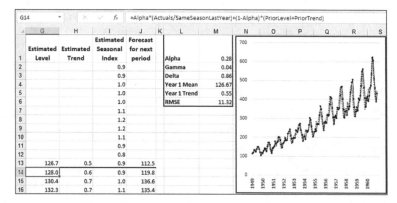

| G14 | | | | f_x | =Alpha*(Actuals/SameSeasonLastYear)+(1-Alpha)*(PriorLevel+PriorTrend) | | | | | | | | | |

	G	H	I	J	K	L	M	N	O	P	Q	R	S
1	Estimated Level	Estimated Trend	Estimated Seasonal Index	Forecast for next period		Alpha	0.28						
2			0.9			Gamma	0.04						
3			0.9			Delta	0.86						
4			1.0			Year 1 Mean	126.67						
5			1.0			Year 1 Trend	0.55						
6			1.0			RMSE	11.32						
7			1.1										
8			1.2										
9			1.2										
10			1.1										
11			0.9										
12			0.8										
13	126.7	0.5	0.9	112.5									
14	128.0	0.6	0.9	119.8									
15	130.4	0.7	1.0	136.6									
16	132.3	0.7	1.1	135.4									

Comparing Figure 5.16 to Figure 5.15, you can see that the multiplicative method is slightly more accurate than the additive method with this data. The smoothing constants have been optimized by Solver and the RMSE in cell M6 is 11.32, almost two points more accurate than the value returned by the additive model. And although the optimized solution relies rather heavily on a large value for the seasonal smoothing constant, it is still less than 1.0. Therefore, we're not relying on naïve forecasting for the seasonal forecasts.

Damped Trend Forecasts

One difficulty with trended data series, whether they include a seasonal component or not, is that their forecasts tend to overshoot the actual observations. This difficulty tends to occur with data that pertains to product introductions, which are often characterized by explosive growth early on, but which is not maintained in the long run. The estimated trends do slow down eventually, but not as quickly as do the actual observations. The difficulty appears more often with forecasts that employ a multiplicative model rather than an additive one.

One popular solution to this difficulty has been the addition of a damping parameter to the smoothing formula, along with the level, trend, and smoothing constants. The damping parameter, often signified by the Greek letter phi (Φ), is raised to successively higher powers according to the length of the forecast horizon. In Holt-Winters multiplicative models, the damping parameter appears in the estimates for the level, the trend, and the seasonality components of the forecast equation.

Here are the formulas for each component, shown in the smoothing form for a data series assuming additive trend and multiplicative seasonality:

- Level: $l_t = \alpha(y_t/s_{t-m}) + (1 - \alpha)(l_{t-1} + \Phi b_{t-1})$
- Trend: $b_t = \gamma(l_t - l_{t-1}) + (1 - \gamma)\Phi b_{t-1}$
- Season: $s_t = \delta y_t/(l_{t-1} + \Phi b_{t-1}) + (1 - \delta)s_{t-m}$

The one-step-ahead forecast for a damped, additive trend with multiplicative seasonality is given by this formula:

$$\hat{y}_t = (l_t + \Phi b_t)s_{t-m}$$

The Box-Jenkins Series G example data set of Australian airline passengers does not provide an especially good test bed for the use of the phi parameter. This is because the baseline represents neither explosive growth nor the slowing trend: Rather, it's a straight line.

Nevertheless, Series G is analyzed using phi, in Figure 5.17, so that you can compare it directly with an analysis that does not involve a damped trend, such as the one in Figure 5.16. Both figures analyze Series G.

Notice that all three smoothing constants are virtually the same in both figures. Excel's Solver set them to those values in the process of optimizing the RMSE. In this case, that Phi parameter does not improve the forecast. Notice in figure 5.17 that Phi equals 1. That means that any equations that use Phi remain unaffected, and it would be surprising to see a difference in Alpha, Gamma, Delta, or RMSE, when Solver has set Phi to 1.0.

By opening the workbook for this chapter and activating the worksheet named Fig 5.17, you'll be able to see how the formulas for level, trend, and seasonality are modified by the inclusion of the Phi parameter. Try different values and see the results on the charted forecasts.

Figure 5.17
Reducing Phi on the worksheet bends the forecast curve downward.

Forecasting a Time Series: Regression

Smoothing approaches to forecasting, such as simple exponential smoothing and Holt's linear smoothing, belong to a branch of analytics usually known as *nonparametric* techniques. That means that you are not calculating a statistic from a sample and evaluating it in light of your knowledge about the measure's distribution in a population.

But analytics also includes many parametric methods, and one of them is regression analysis. Regression is often a plausible alternative to smoothing when you want to forecast from a baseline of observations. It involves some tests that are considered parametric—t-tests, for example, which you can apply to decide whether a predictor variable is useful as a predictor. We take up two regression approaches, standard linear regression and autoregression, in this chapter.

Chapter 4, "Forecasting a Time Series: Smoothing," discussed one general approach to forecasting: exponential smoothing. Whether you use simple exponential smoothing, Holt's method or another approach to exponential smoothing, each actual observation has some weight in the value of the next forecast. Older observations carry less weight, and new observations more weight, because the older the observation, the larger the exponent that's applied to the smoothing fraction. For example, 0.2 raised to the 30th power puts much less weight on a value that's thirty periods old than does 0.2 raised to the 5th power on a value that's five periods old.

Forecasting with Regression

There's a different approach to forecasting, termed *regression*, and mathematically it's the same linear regression that you might have studied in a college statistics class. In forecasting work, there are several different ways to use regression. Two of the most frequently used are *linear regression* (usually just termed *regression*) and *autoregression*.

When you use linear regression as a forecasting tool, the variable that you forecast is a sequence of observations, just as in the smoothing methods discussed in Chapters 4 and 5. The predictor variable is often the period during which the observation was made: the hour, or the day, or the month, and so on. The first period is typically designated 1, the second period 2—and so on.

> **NOTE** This general approach can turn out to involve non-linear, also called *curvilinear*, regression. This can happen when, for example, a product's sales accelerate each month for several months. Then, the trend in the data would describe a curve instead of a straight line. Although this is an important subset of analytic techniques, non-linear regression is beyond the scope of this book.

When you identify the periods by their order in the time series, you can calculate a correlation between the period and the variable that you have measured and want to forecast. That correlation quantifies the relationship between the time variable and the forecast variable. By specifying which time period you want to forecast into, you can use the relationship to calculate a new forecast—in the language of forecasting, you're *regressing* the forecast variable onto the predictor variable.

Another general approach to forecasting with regression is called *autoregression*. Using autoregression, instead of associating each observation with its time period, you associate each observation with another observation that's one period back, two periods back, and so on. Again in the language of forecasting, you're regressing the forecast variable onto itself. You saw autoregression in a slightly different guise in Figure 4.17, where it is termed autocorrelation.

> **NOTE** The terms *autoregression* and *autocorrelation* are very nearly equivalent, but you tend to find "autocorrelation" used when the emphasis is on quantifying the relationships in a time series, and "autoregression" when the emphasis is on forecasting values based on those relationships.

You might decide to use autoregression if it's characteristic of your time series that the current observation tends to depend heavily on the value of one or more recent observations. For example, suppose that you are tracking the value of a business's inventory. The effect of a large purchase to inventory tends to linger in the valuation of goods or materials on hand for a few periods after the purchase is made.

Exponential smoothing is one way to deal with this effect. It concentrates the weights on the most recent observations and causes the weights to die out gradually as you go back farther in the baseline. On the other hand, autoregression enables you to control which observations in the baseline are to receive the most weight, based on the strength of their correlations with later observations, not solely on how recently the prior observations occurred.

A particularly large value might have a greater effect than other observations on the next forecast, but that is a function of the value of the observation, not on how recently (or how long ago) in the baseline that it occurs.

In contrast to autoregression, linear regression spreads the weight that's assigned to the predictor variable equally across all the records in the baseline. (That weight, of course, comes in the form of the regression coefficient, which is applied to all records in the data set).

> **NOTE** The general regression technique comes in a variety of flavors: simple linear regression, autoregression, multiple regression, stepwise, forward and backward regression, and so on. Despite these different types, regression itself is a basic statistical technique that isn't difficult to grasp. Nevertheless, it takes considerable space to cover the basics thoroughly, and my page budget for this book doesn't allow for that. This book does discuss how to use Excel to perform linear regression, and it discusses some regression theory in ways that assume a background in the basics. But this book does not provide extensive coverage of the basic theory and concepts of regression. If you're new to the concept of linear regression, I urge you to get yourself grounded with one of many excellent books on basic-to-intermediate statistics. My book *Regression Analysis: Microsoft Excel*, published by Que, is one example.

Linear Regression: An Example

Figure 6.1 shows how you might use linear regression to forecast from a time series that is trended. There's a lot going on in Figure 6.1. The information in columns A through D, and in the chart, is as follows:

Column A

Column A contains a number that identifies a record's location in the time series—such as the number of each of the first 11 months in the year.

Column B

Column B contains monthly observations, such as the number of gallons of water used to irrigate a vegetable garden each month. I'll return to columns C and D shortly.

Trend Chart

The chart shows that during the first eight periods the number of gallons used generally increases. Those measures drop during the final two periods, but there's not enough data yet to tell whether that is seasonal variation that will subsequently turn back up or that it's random departure from the general upward trend, perhaps due to heavier than normal rain during those two periods.

Figure 6.1
The straight diagonal line in the chart is called a trendline. Excel provides it if you call for it.

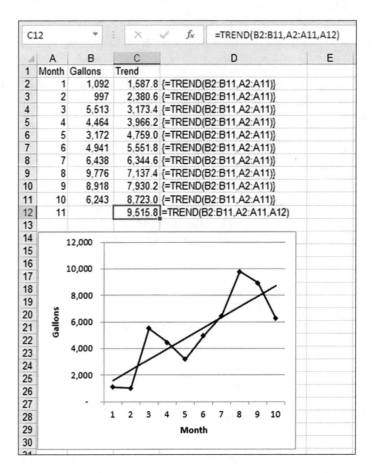

The chart also displays a straight, diagonal line called a *trendline*. If you created (as you do later in this chapter) an equation that forecasts water usage from the number of the month, that equation would describe a straight line when you chart its results. The equation is called the *regression equation*. Excel can calculate that equation for you and display the resulting straight line on the chart, and I show you how to do that, too.

Column C

Column C contains forecasts of the number of gallons that the regression equation calculates for each value of Month. In Excel, one way to get linear regression forecasts is by using the TREND() worksheet function. In Figure 6.1 you would array-enter the function using these steps:

1. Select the range C2:C11.
2. Type =TREND(B2:B11,A2:A11), but don't press Enter just yet.
3. Hold down the Ctrl and the Shift keys and then press Enter. Release the keys.

When you look at the worksheet, you see that the results have filled the array of cells that you began by selecting in Step 1. If you select one of the cells in that array, Excel's Formula Box shows what you typed in Step 2, but the formula is surrounded by curly brackets.

The curly brackets let you know that the formula has been entered as an *array formula*. One of the purposes of array formulas is to fill an array of cells with a formula that, as here, returns an array of different results.

> **NOTE** Don't type the curly brackets yourself. If you do, Excel treats the formula as text, not as an equation to be evaluated.

You have now entered a formula in cells C2:C11 that returns the results of a linear regression equation. Excel calculates the relationship between Month and Gallons, and returns an idealized version of that relationship in the cells where you array-enter the formula.

The formula uses two arguments, which Excel refers to as the *known_y's* and the *known_x's*. The known_x's are the values that you want to forecast from: in this example, the month numbers 1 to 10 in the range A2:A11. The known_y's are the values in your baseline that are associated with those month numbers: the values in B2:B11. So this formula:

    =TREND(B2:B11,A2:A11)

tells Excel to calculate the relationship between the known_y's in B2:B11 and the known_x's in A2:A11, and return the forecasts implied by that relationship.

If you added the results in column C to the chart, you would get the straight diagonal trendline that appears in Figure 6.1. Excel can chart that trendline for you automatically, without requiring you to perform the intermediate calculations.

The formula in C12 is not part of the array formula in C2:C11 and it must be entered as a separate formula.

> **NOTE** The formula in C12 calculates one result only, occupies only one cell. It is not handed an array of values where it normally expects one value only. Therefore, it need not be array-entered.

6

Cell D12 shows that the formula in C12 is the following:

    =TREND(B2:B11,A2:A11,A12)

Notice that the formula includes a third argument to the TREND( ) function, A12. It's an optional argument that Excel terms *new_x's*. In this example, you have a new month number, an x- or predictor-value, that you want to use as a basis for the forecast. Notice that the value in A12 has no corresponding value in B12. By supplying A12 as a new_x, you tell Excel "Calculate the relationship between the values in A2:A11 and B2:B11 and apply that relationship to the new_x in A12." This becomes your forecast for the as-yet-unobserved eleventh month. You aren't forced to limit the forecast to one month ahead, as I've done in Figure 6.1. You could, for example, enter a 12 in A13 and a 13 in A14. You would also change the formula in B12 to make the references to the observed values absolute:

    =TREND($B$2:$B$11,$A$2:$A$11,A12)

Then just copy the formula from B12 into B13 and B14.

But the farther you go out from the most recent observation that's available to you, the less confidence you should place in the forecast. Should something happen in the intervening time periods to alter the relationship between the known_x's and the known_y's, the forecast could turn out to be way off base. This sort of thing can easily happen when your baseline captures only the upward—or only the downward—swing of a seasonal cycle. For example, it would probably be a mistake to forecast the sales of skis in June on the basis of ski sales made from November through March.

Column D

Column D in Figure 6.1 shows you the formula in each cell in the C2:C12 range. Notice that C2:C11 each have the same formula, and yet they return different results. That's because it's one array formula occupying ten cells—so the formula's the same—but it returns different results in each cell because the forecast is different for each observation.

Using the LINEST( ) Function

To this point I have referred somewhat vaguely to a "relationship" between a predictor variable and a forecast variable—a regression equation—without specifying exactly what I meant. Excel offers several worksheet functions that pertain to the regression equation, but the most comprehensive and powerful is the LINEST() function.

Entering the LINEST( ) Function

Figure 6.2 shows how LINEST() works. Figure 6.2 shows the same data baseline that appears in Figure 6.1, but the figure shows the results of LINEST() rather than those of the TREND() function.

Cells A14:B14 contain the regression equation based on the data in cells A2:B11. The formula, visible in the Formula Box, is the following:

    =LINEST(B2:B11,A2:A11,,TRUE)

It is also an array formula, so once again you select a range of cells (here, A14:B14), type the formula, and then enter it with Ctrl+Shift+Enter instead of simply Enter. When you do so, the curly brackets appear around the formula in the Formula Box.

Figure 6.2

The results of the LINEST( ) function always put the regression coefficient on the left, and the intercept on the right.

| A14 | | ▼ | : | × | ✓ | *fx* | {=LINEST(B2:B11,A2:A11,,TRUE)} |

⊿	A	B	C	D	E	F	G
1	Month	Gallons					
2	1	1,092					
3	2	997					
4	3	5,513					
5	4	4,464					
6	5	3,172					
7	6	4,941					
8	7	6,438					
9	8	9,776					
10	9	8,918					
11	10	6,243					
12							
13	Coefficient	Intercept					
14	792.8	795					
15							
16	11	9515.8					

The first two arguments to LINEST( ) are the same as the first two arguments to TREND( ): the known_y's in B2:B11 and the known_x's in A2:A11. The third argument is missing—its absence is indicated by two commas with nothing between them—and the fourth argument is TRUE. As used in Figure 6.2, the fourth, TRUE argument, is not really necessary, but in most situations it is needed. I suggest that you always use it so that you don't forget to do so when you want it. Its purpose is to notify Excel to calculate some additional results that aren't shown in Figure 6.2 but that appear in Figure 6.3.

The value 792.8 that you see in cell A14 is termed the *regression coefficient*, and the 795 value on the right is the *intercept*. The coefficient gives the slope of the regression line and the intercept tells you the value of the forecast variable when the value of the predictor is zero—so in this example, it would be the number of gallons forecast for the nonexistent Month 0.

> **NOTE**
> It's called the *intercept* because it's the point where the regression line crosses, or *intercepts*, the vertical axis, given that the horizontal and vertical axes cross at their {0, 0} point. The intercept is also often termed the *constant*.

So you could forecast the value for gallons in the eleventh month by applying the equation returned by the LINEST( ) function. That was done in Figure 6.1 using the TREND( ) function in cell C12, which returns 9515.8. As shown in cell B16 of Figure 6.2, you could get the same result using this formula:

=A14*A16+B14

6

That is, multiply the value of Month (A16) that you're interested in by the regression coefficient (A14), and add the value of the intercept (B14). You get the predicted value for Gallons in Month 11.

You could do the same thing with the other values of Month that you have in A2:A11, and your results would be the same as the values shown in column C of Figure 6.1.

More generally, the regression equation in a single predictor situation looks like this:

Forecast = (Regression coefficient × Predictor value) + Intercept

In sum: The TREND( ) function calculates a regression equation from the values of a predictor variable and from the values of a variable that you want to forecast. TREND( ) does not show the equation itself, but rather the results of applying the equation to the values of the predictor variable. Those predictor values can include a value or values that were not used to calculate the regression equation (for example, cell A12 in Figure 6.1). The LINEST( ) function calculates the regression equation; it shows you the equation, as TREND( ) doesn't, but doesn't show you the equation results, as TREND( ) does.

In the prior paragraph, I mentioned that you can apply the regression equation to values that weren't used in the calculation of the equation. Just because you can, though, doesn't mean that you should. Referring to Figure 6.2, you could enter the value 36, say, in cell A16 instead of the value 11. The formula in cell B16 would update to apply the regression equation in A14:B14 to Month 36. You would get 29,335.8.

In that case, you would be determining the relationship between measures of month number and gallons used for 11 months, and applying that relationship to a month that would not come to pass for another two years. Many things could happen during the intervening two years, including the cost of water increasing so much that using almost 30,000 gallons would be prohibitively expensive. Or, as I implied earlier, the upswing in usage during the 11 months shown in the figures could be nothing more than the growth part of a periodic cycle that is about to turn down.

The point is that you need more than 11 data points to forecast 36 periods into the future. Rely too heavily on a regression equation and it's likely to break.

Choosing to Use LINEST( )

You're usually interested in the forecasts you can get from a regression analysis, and less so in the equation itself. So why would you even bother with LINEST( )?

I haven't yet shown you all that LINEST( ) can do for you. Figure 6.3 shows the full set of LINEST( ) results that you can get from the data set used in this section.

In Figure 6.3, the results of the LINEST( ) function occupy the range A13:B17. Therefore the user would select a two-column by five-row range and array-enter the LINEST( ) function in a formula, just as before:

=LINEST(B2:B11,A2:A11,,TRUE)

Figure 6.3
LINEST() can return up to five rows of useful information.

	A	B	C	D	E	F	G
A13			f_x	{=LINEST(B2:B11,A2:A11,,TRUE)}			
1	Month	Gallons					
2	1	1,092					
3	2	997					
4	3	5,513					
5	4	4,464					
6	5	3,172					
7	6	4,941					
8	7	6,438					
9	8	9,776					
10	9	8,918					
11	10	6,243					
12							
13	792.8	795.0		Coefficient	Intercept		
14	194.1	1204.5		SE of coefficient	SE of intercept		
15	0.7	1763.2		R²	SE of estimate		
16	16.7	8		F ratio	DF residual		
17	51853876.8	24870427.6		SS Regression	SS Residual		

Remember that you use Ctrl+Shift+Enter, not simply Enter, to array-enter a formula. Because LINEST() uses one formula to return a variety of different results, array-entry is necessary. And in this case you *need* to supply TRUE as the fourth argument, because otherwise LINEST() would not return any results other than the coefficient and the intercept.

I'm going to sketch the meaning of the additional results, and where you can find them, very briefly, because if you're still with me then you very likely know their meanings already.

Regression Coefficients and Intercept   In Figure 6.3, cell A13 shows the regression coefficient, and cell B13 shows the intercept. Therefore, cells A13 and B13 together give you the constant components of the regression equation, given the data provided to the LINEST() function.

Standard Errors   Cell A14 contains the standard error of the regression coefficient. You can use it in conjunction with the degrees of freedom and the t distribution to decide whether the coefficient is significantly different from zero. If you decide that the coefficient in the population might be zero, you are in effect deciding that your predictor variable adds no useful information to your forecast.

Cell B14 contains the standard error associated with the intercept. There are occasions when you want to test the statistical significance of the intercept—that is, whether it is significantly different from zero in a statistical sense—but these occasions come up very rarely in forecasting. As a practical matter, in forecasting you can ignore the test of the intercept and therefore also ignore the standard error of the intercept.

R² and Standard Error of Estimate   Cell A15 contains R^2, which can be interpreted as a proportion or percent of variance. In this example, it is 0.7 or 70%, which means that 70% of the variability in the known_y's—in this case, Gallons—is associated with variability in the known_x's—in this case, Month number.

6

Cell B15 contains the standard error of estimate, an expression of the variability of the errors made in the forecasts (also called the *residuals*). For a given scale of measurement, the smaller the standard error of estimate, the more accurate the forecasts and therefore the better the regression equation. It's convenient, if not strictly accurate, to think of the standard error of estimate as the standard deviation of the residuals. The formal and accurate equation for the standard error of estimate is the following:

$$SE_{est} = \frac{\sqrt{SS_{res}}}{N-k-1}$$

where:

- SS_{res} is the residual sum of squares, also returned by LINEST() as described shortly.
- N is the number of observations—10 in this example.
- k is the number of predictors—1 in this example.

Suppose that you calculate the residuals by getting the forecasts with TREND() and subtracting the forecasts from the associated actuals. If you put the residuals in, say, F2:F11, the Excel formula to calculate the standard error of estimate would be

=SQRT(DEVSQ(F2:F11)/(10–1–1))

where:

- DEVSQ(F2:F11) calculates the sum of squared deviations of the residuals from their mean (which is always zero or vanishingly close to zero).
- (10–1–1) is the number of observations, less one for the predictor, less one for the grand mean—in other words, the degrees of freedom for the regression.

I'm specifying the actual equation and formula partly because they provide more insight into the nature of the standard error of estimate than words do, and partly so that you can see how the loss of an additional degree of freedom distinguishes it from a "typical" standard deviation.

F Ratio and Degrees of Freedom   Cell A16 contains the F ratio, or the mean square regression divided by the mean square residual. The F ratio is closely related to R^2, and provides a means of testing statistically whether the regression equation explains a meaningful proportion of the variance in the forecast variable.

Cell B16 contains the degrees of freedom for the residual. You can use it in conjunction with the F ratio and worksheet functions such as F.DIST() to test the statistical significance of the regression.

Sums of Squares   Cells A17 and B17 contain the sums of squares for the regression and for the residual, respectively. In most cases this information is redundant, because the main use for these two sums of squares is to calculate the F ratio (each sum of squares divided by its degrees of freedom equals its mean square, and the F ratio results from dividing the mean square regression by the mean square residual).

A Word on Multiple Regression

Some of what I've written here regarding LINEST( ) is intended to suggest that LINEST( ) can accommodate more than just one predictor variable, such as Month in the example used in the last several sections. LINEST( ) can handle more than one predictor, and if there were two predictor variables in, say, A2:B30, and a forecast variable in C2:C30, you could array-enter LINEST( ) as follows:

=LINEST(C2:C30,A2:B30,,TRUE)

Notice that the argument for the known_x's now refers to two columns, A and B. Therefore, you need to begin by selecting a range with three columns instead of just two and up to five rows. The LINEST( ) results include coefficients and standard errors for two predictors, not just one, as well as the intercept. (A regression equation includes one intercept only, no matter how many regression coefficients it includes.)

Most straightforward forecasting situations that use regression have only one predictor variable, so you enter LINEST( ) in two columns only. You might be forecasting on the basis of a single date-or-time variable such as Month. Or you might be using autoregression (discussed shortly) and forecasting on the basis of an observation one period back, or sometimes two periods back. These are garden variety, bread-and-butter forecasting situations, and they usually call for no more than one predictor variable.

But some situations require two or more predictors. For example, it might turn out in an autoregression context that you need to make forecasts based on values that occur both one period and two periods before the period to be forecast. In that case, you need to make provision for two predictors.

More frequently, you might have a time series that exhibits seasonality, with values spiking once a year, or once a quarter, or on some other regular basis. In that case you need to provide a predictor that accounts for the period (a day, perhaps, or a week) and another that accounts for the season. If so, you need to use LINEST( ) with multiple predictors. I have more to say about this in the section on autoregression.

Reverse English

One final point for now regarding LINEST( ): It's a powerful function, and used properly it's much more flexible and has much broader scope than anything in the Data Analysis add-in. But it has one frustrating drawback: In a multiple regression situation it returns coefficients and standard errors backward.

Suppose you have predictor variables in A1:B50, and your forecast variable in C1:C50. You might array-enter LINEST( ) in, say, A56:C60. If you did, the regression coefficient for the predictor variable in column A would appear in B56 (and its standard error in B57). The regression coefficient for the predictor variable in column B would appear in cell A56 (and its standard error in A57).

This effect holds true for any number of predictor variables. Suppose your predictor variables are in columns A through F. If you array-enter the LINEST( ) function in columns H:M, the coefficient for the variable in column A shows up in column M, the coefficient for the variable in column B shows up in column L, and so on. The order of the results is the reverse of the order of the arguments.

This makes for an unnecessary difficulty in interpreting the results. LINEST() should return the coefficient for the leftmost predictor in its first column, and the next predictor in the second column, and so on. There is no acceptable reason, theoretical or practical, statistical or programmatic, for this inconsistency. But it's existed in Excel since Version 3 in the 1990s, and to change it now would cause problems in countless users' workbooks. So, it's not going away, and you need to get used to it. I'm just sayin'.

Forecasting with Autoregression

The whole concept of autoregression is intuitively appealing, just as is the concept of smoothing. If you're going to forecast a time series—say, membership in a recently opened golf course—what better variable is there to use as a predictor than the prior period's number of members? Next month you're likely to have the same members that you had this month, plus some unknown number of new members. That might well be a better approach than forecasting on the basis of a date, as was done with water usage in the prior section.

Problems with Trends

But there are also problems that come along with the intuitive appeal of autoregression. To get a clearer sense of one of them, consider a different problem: forecasting a child's weight from knowledge of what grade he's attending in elementary school.

Suppose you take a sample of grade school children and record each child's weight and current grade in school. You could then calculate the correlation in your sample between weight and grade level, and you would very likely get a correlation somewhere around 0.90: a very strong correlation. And you could pump the data through Excel's LINEST() function to get a regression equation that predicts weight from grade with quite a high degree of accuracy.

Does that mean that you could jump a child's grade level from, say, third grade to fourth and watch his weight increase by ten pounds as a result? Of course not. You might as well try to increase his weight by changing his home's street address: Weight and address have no *causal* relationship, and neither do weight and grade in school.

So how is it that unrelated variables such as weight and grade can be so strongly correlated that you can predict weight from grade with good accuracy? It's sometimes called *spurious correlation*. Both weight and grade are trended: As a typical child's age increases, the weight increases—and so does the grade level. Both increases are a function of the passage of time. Time is the third variable that has a causal relationship with weight and grade and might make it appear that variables such as weight and grade level have a causal relationship when they really don't.

Correlating at Increasing Lags

What does that have to do with autoregression? When you use autoregression to forecast the next value in a series on the basis of a preceding value, you depend on the correlation between one set of consecutive observations and another set of observations from the same series. See Figure 6.4 for an example.

The same data series appears twice in Figure 6.4, once in A1:A25 and once in B1:B25. This formula is used in cell D1:

> =CORREL(A1:A24,B2:B25)

The formula determines the correlation between the first 24 values in the series (found in A1:A24) and the final 24 values in the series (found in B2:B25). You can see which worksheet ranges are involved by looking at the range finders that Excel uses to surround the appropriate ranges.

As used in Figure 6.4, the CORREL( ) function pairs up the first observation in A1:A24 with the first observation in B2:B25—that is, A1 with B2. Then it pairs up A2 with B3, and A3 with B4, and so on. It calculates the correlation between the first 24 values with the set of 24 values that immediately follows, or *lags*, the first 24. This is called a *lag 1 autocorrelation*.

Figure 6.4
When you edit a formula, range finders surround the cells or ranges that it uses as arguments.

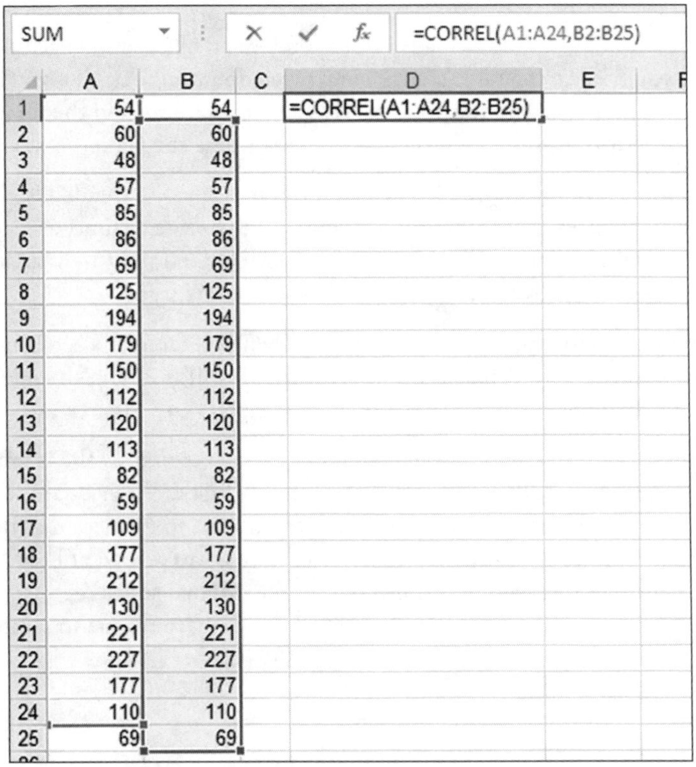

SUM		× ✓ ƒx	=CORREL(A1:A24,B2:B25)

	A	B	C	D	E	F
1	54	54		=CORREL(A1:A24,B2:B25)		
2	60	60				
3	48	48				
4	57	57				
5	85	85				
6	86	86				
7	69	69				
8	125	125				
9	194	194				
10	179	179				
11	150	150				
12	112	112				
13	120	120				
14	113	113				
15	82	82				
16	59	59				
17	109	109				
18	177	177				
19	212	212				
20	130	130				
21	221	221				
22	227	227				
23	177	177				
24	110	110				
25	69	69				

6

I put the data in two columns to make it a little easier to see what's going on. There's no reason that you couldn't use just the one data series in A1:A25 and use this formula instead:

=CORREL(A1:A24,A2:A25)

Both the formula in cell D1 and the formula just given express the lag 1 autocorrelation in the data series found in A1:A25. (Actually, it's very close to but not quite an autocorrelation—a small tweak is needed and we'll get to it, but the tweak obscures the concept so I'm ignoring it for the moment.)

You can and usually do calculate autocorrelations for other lags: lag 2, lag 3, and so on. For example, this small change in the prior formula calculates the lag 2 autocorrelation:

=CORREL(A1:A23,A3:A25)

and here's the lag 3 autocorrelation:

=CORREL(A1:A22,A4:A25)

Notice that in each case, the first argument ends one row earlier and the second argument starts one row later. That's because as the lags increase, the farther away from one another the two series begin and end. In a lag 1 autocorrelation, you're correlating values that are one period apart. In a lag 2 autocorrelation, you're correlating values that are two periods apart.

One result of increasing the lags is that you lose an observation each time you increase the lag. If you tried to calculate a lag 2 autocorrelation using A1:A24, you'd run out of data because you'd be trying to correlate A1:A24 with A3:A26, and there's no data in cell A26. So each series has to be shortened by one, each time the lag increases by one.

What if the series were trended? If the series in A2:A25 is trended, so is the series in A1:A24. If the reason for the trend is simply the passage of time, as it tends to be for a child's weight and grade in school, the autocorrelation might well be due to a variable, time, that causes the series to increase (or decrease) as time passes.

Therefore, one of the early steps you take when you forecast a series using the series itself as the predictor is to decide if the series is trended. If it is, you should first remove the trend by differencing, just as was shown in Chapter 4, in Figures 4.20 through 4.22.

Figure 6.5 shows a data series in column B and, in column C, the result of first differencing on the series. Both the original series and its first differences are shown and charted in Figure 6.5. Each charted series includes a trendline and it's clear that the original series has a strong trend, whereas the first differences have a weak trend at best. If you test the regression coefficient returned by LINEST() for the original series regressed on the Day variable, you find that it is strong and extremely unlikely to be due to sampling error.

Figure 6.5
First differencing removes the trend from the series and makes it stationary—that is, horizontal.

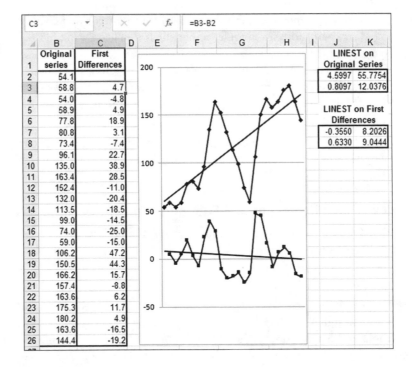

	B	C	D	E	F	G	H	I	J	K
	Original series	First Differences							LINEST on Original Series	
1				200					4.5997	55.7754
2	54.1								0.8097	12.0376
3	58.8	4.7								
4	54.0	-4.8								
5	58.9	4.9		150					LINEST on First	
6	77.8	18.9							Differences	
7	80.8	3.1							-0.3550	8.2026
8	73.4	-7.4							0.6330	9.0444
9	96.1	22.7								
10	135.0	38.9		100						
11	163.4	28.5								
12	152.4	-11.0								
13	132.0	-20.4								
14	113.5	-18.5		50						
15	99.0	-14.5								
16	74.0	-25.0								
17	59.0	-15.0								
18	106.2	47.2		0						
19	150.5	44.3								
20	166.2	15.7								
21	157.4	-8.8								
22	163.6	6.2								
23	175.3	11.7		-50						
24	180.2	4.9								
25	163.6	-16.5								
26	144.4	-19.2								

C3 f_x =B3-B2

In contrast, in this example the regression coefficient for the differenced series, regressed on the Day variable, is not significantly different from zero. The trendline in the chart of first differences is not precisely horizontal, but it's close enough to zero that it's entirely reasonable to decide that there's no trend in the first differences.

Why am I making a big deal of the regression coefficients and the slope of the trendlines? Recall that the regression equation with a single predictor looks like this:

Forecast = (Regression coefficient × Predictor value) + Intercept

If the regression coefficient is zero—if there is no relationship between the predictor variable and the forecast variable—this equation tells us that no matter what value is selected for the predictor value, the forecast always equals the intercept. Any variation in the observed values of the variable to be forecast is therefore due to random fluctuations around the equation's intercept.

6

NOTE   To add a trendline to a chart, right-click the charted data series and choose Add Trendline from the shortcut menu. You get several choices, such as Linear, Polynomial and Moving Average. The trendlines shown in Figure 6.5 are linear. You can also choose to display the R^2 value and the equation itself in the chart. Excel often includes too many decimal places in the R^2 and in the equation, but you can select and format them to display fewer decimal values.

That is true of standard linear regression—that is, if there's no reliable relationship between a predictor and a forecast variable, you might as well leave it out of the equation and use the constant intercept as the sole forecast value. But it is also true, of course, for autoregression. If there is no reliable correlation between a series of values and another series that follows the first, there is no point in forecasting the second series from the first: for example, to forecast February through December using January through November.

And in that case you might do well to forget about using autoregression with your time series. It still might be possible to get good forecasts leaving the trend in place (rather than by using differences) and regressing the time series on time values (months, quarters, days, whatever).

A Review: Linear Regression and Autoregression

It's helpful to stop at this point and review some points regarding linear regression and autoregression.

Terminology

The use of the terms *linear regression* and *autoregression* tends to imply that autoregression is not linear, but autoregression frequently is linear. The term *linear regression* is used to emphasize that the variable that is forecast bears a linear relationship to some other variable, often dates or times of day. *Autoregression* denotes the use of the same variable as the predictor and the forecast, but the values used as predictors precede the forecast values in time. (As I noted earlier, autoregression is often linear, despite the fact that you seldom see the term *linear autoregression*.)

Trends and Autocorrelation

A trend is not the same as autocorrelation, although the two may well be closely related. A series that is trended—that moves steadily up or down over time—does have autocorrelation. If a series moves steadily from relatively low values to relatively high values, earlier low values are paired with other early, low values, and the same is true of the pairing of later, higher values. That sort of pairing results in autocorrelation.

The reverse is not necessarily true. A series that has autocorrelation does not necessarily have trend throughout. It may drift up for several periods, then down, and you often see that pattern with seasonal sales.

As you proceed with diagnosing the nature of your data series, you want to remove a trend if one exists. The reason is that you would like to investigate any autocorrelation in the data series, unabetted by the trend. So you detrend the series, often by taking first differences, and then testing for autocorrelation in the differenced series.

If autocorrelation exists after the series has been differenced and made stationary, you make use of the autocorrelation in a regression equation to forecast the *differenced series*. After you have forecast the differences, you rebuild the series by "undifferencing" it. This process is usually called *integrating* the series.

Autocorrelation without trend shows up in Figure 6.6.

Figure 6.6
The series drifts both up
and down.

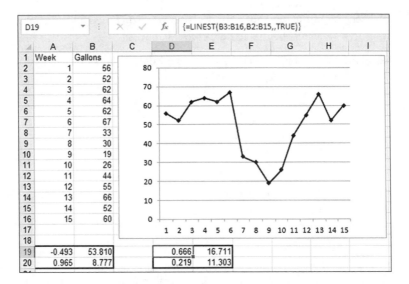

A trended series must have autocorrelation, but a series whose values are autocorrelated is not necessarily trended. Figure 6.6 shows a data series that displays what's called *autocorrelative drift*. The level of the series drifts gradually down and then up, and consecutive values are correlated. But the series in general is not trended.

I have included two instances of LINEST() in Figure 6.6. One, shown in the range A19:B20, shows the regression of Gallons in column B on Week number in column A. Looking at the chart, you would not expect that the series has a trend: It drifts up and down and has no upward or downward slope throughout.

That visual impression is confirmed by LINEST(), which gives the regression coefficient in cell A19 as −0.493 and the standard error of the coefficient in cell A20 as 0.965. The value of the coefficient is therefore less than one standard error from zero and few would regard that as a reliable difference. The series is not trended.

On the other hand, the LINEST() formula in the range D19:E20 regresses the Gallons in Weeks 2 through 15 onto the Gallons in Weeks 1 through 14. As used there, LINEST() is testing the reliability of any autocorrelation in the series. The coefficient in cell D19 is 0.666 and the standard error of the coefficient is 0.219: A two-tailed t-test indicates that the coefficient is different from zero at below the .01 confidence level. It is as always partly a subjective decision, but I'd put my money on significant autocorrelation in this data series.

Because the series is not trended, there's no need to difference it before looking further into the autocorrelation.

Adjusting the Autocorrelation Formula

I mentioned in the "Correlating at Increasing Lags" section earlier in the chapter that the formula for the autocorrelation function (or *ACF*) isn't quite what you'd expect, and the simple correlation between one set of values and another that lags the first set has to be tweaked. It's not necessarily a big deal and you won't miss a lot if you skip this section, but it's worth knowing about, and here's what happens:

Standard correlation coefficients adjust the values being correlated by adjusting them for their own mean. You begin by calculating the *covariance*, and then dividing by the standard deviation of each variable. The formula for the covariance with two different variables, X and Y, is

$$s_{xy} = \sum_{i=1}^{N} \frac{(X_i - \overline{X})(Y_i - \overline{Y})}{N-1}$$

and you calculate the correlation as follows, dividing the covariance by the standard deviation of each variable:

$$r_{xy} = s_{xy} / (s_x s_y)$$

Notice that the numerator of the covariance subtracts the mean of X from each value of X, and the mean of Y from each value of Y. But in autocorrelation, we are working with different values of the same variable. Partly for this reason and partly due to other matters, both of theory and feasibility, the ACF uses the mean of all the observations in the time series:

$$\sum_{i=2}^{N} \frac{(Y_i - \overline{Y})(Y_{i-1} - \overline{Y})}{N-1}$$

If the ACF conformed perfectly to the usual Pearson correlation, the mean of, say, the first through the twenty-fourth values would be subtracted from each of those values. The mean of the second through twenty-fifth values would be subtracted from each of *those* values. The results of each subtraction would be multiplied together and their products summed.

But as ACFs are actually calculated, only one mean is used: the mean of all the observations. Furthermore, instead of calculating the standard deviations of the two sets of values to move from the covariance to the ACF, a single measure of variability is used, based on all the values in the time series.

If you have a time series that's reasonably long, the difference between a Pearson correlation coefficient and the ACF is negligible. But if you have a very short time series—say, five or six values—then it's possible to get problematic results, even ACFs that exceed 1.0, and that's not a possible outcome with a Pearson correlation.

I have included this bit of esoterica about ACFs in part so you know what's going on if you see a difference between an ACF and what you get using something such as this:

=CORREL(A1:A24,A2:A25)

and in part to give you another reason to use good, lengthy time series to base your forecasts on.

Using ACFs

You don't generally calculate just one ACF to help diagnose what's going on in a time series. The prior discussion focused on a lag 1 ACF, but as I mentioned earlier you can calculate a lag 2 ACF, a lag 3 ACF, and so on.

Excel's relative and absolute addressing makes it easier to calculate the ACFs for different lags than it would be if all addressing were relative, but we can do better yet. One of the files available for you to download from the publisher's website is called ARIMA.xls; it calculates and charts the lagged ACFs for you. Figure 6.7 shows an example of the results.

Figure 6.7
The lower chart shown here is called a correlogram.

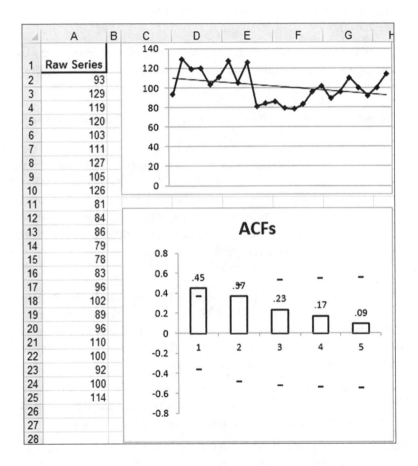

Figure 6.7 contains two charts. The upper chart is a standard line chart showing the data series over time. The lower chart is a special sort of chart called a *correlogram*. In the correlogram, the column markers that extend above the zero point on the vertical axis show the magnitude of the ACF at each lag. So, the lag 1 ACF is .45, the lag 2 ACF is .37, and so on. The numbers just below the horizontal axis identify the lag, and the decimal fractions

associated with each column marker tell you the size of the ACF at that lag. (There are none shown for this data series, but you very often see negative ACFs that extend below the zero point on the vertical axis.)

Notice also the dashes in the correlogram. The location of each dash indicates the location of approximately two standard errors above and below the zero point on the vertical axis. Any ACF column marker that extends beyond its associated dash can be considered significantly different from zero at the 95% confidence level.

So, in the case of the correlogram in Figure 6.7, the first ACF of .45 can be considered significant because it extends beyond its associated dash mark (which is at .36). None of the other ACFs extends beyond two standard errors from zero, and you can disregard them for the moment.

The conclusion you could reach from this correlogram is that only the lag 1 autocorrelation function is significant: that you need to pay attention only to the relationship between one value and the next value (not two periods later, not three periods later) to develop your autoregression forecast. That conclusion might well be correct, but you would want to also look into the PACFs, discussed in the next section, before you made up your mind about it.

> **NOTE** Notice that the dashes in the ACF correlogram extend further from 0 as the number of lags increases. This is normal behavior and is a function of the cumulative proportion of variance shared by the two data series as the lags progress from 1 to 2, to 3, and so on. The result is that the ACFs must also be larger as the lags increase if you are to regard them as reliable, or "statistically significant." An ACF must exceed the value shown by the associated dash (which represents two standard errors from 0) to be regarded as statistically significant at the .05 level.

One further point will later prove important: Notice that the ACFs decline gradually as the number of lags increases. This is characteristic of autoregressive data series, as distinct from a data series that's better defined by moving averages. In an autoregressive series, the strength of the autocorrelation gradually drops off as the distance between the two series, as measured by the number of lags, increases.

As you'll see, when a data series is defined by *shocks* that linger via moving averages in the series' level (such as inventory levels after major supply purchases), the ACF signature drops sharply instead of declining gradually, as in the present example.

Besides ACFs, the other major diagnostic tool in autocorrelation is *partial* autocorrelation, measured by partial autocorrelation functions or PACFs. I introduce PACFs next.

Understanding PACFs

Don't let the term "partial autocorrelation function" throw you; those are just words. If you have a reasonable comfort level with standard Pearson-type correlations, it's just a small step to the partial autocorrelations. Conceptually, PACFs are pretty straightforward. Computationally they're a pain in the neck, but that's what computers are for.

A Review: Correlation and Shared Variance

One point is particularly important to understanding PACFs, though, and it's so fundamental that it deserves its own soapbox. The correlation coefficient between two variables is closely tied to the percent of variance that the two variables share, or have in common. In general, the square of the correlation coefficient between two variables, or r^2, expresses the percent of variance that the two variables share. Another way of putting this concept is to say that if the correlation between two variables is 0.80, they share 0.80 * 0.80 = 0.64, or 64% of their variance.

Take height and weight. Suppose those two variables, measured on children who are still growing, have a correlation of 0.60. In that case, 36% of the variance in weight can be *accounted for*, or *explained*, or *predicted* given knowledge of a child's height.

Now suppose that in addition to the weight and height of several children, you also know each child's age in months. You analyze all three variables and find that the correlation between age and weight is 0.70, and between age and height it's 0.30.

So according to these statistics (which I have made up in order to provide a crisp example), 0.70^2 or 49% of the variability in children's weight can be explained by knowledge of their age. We've already posited that 36% of the variability in children's weight can be explained by knowledge of their height.

Can we therefore explain 49% + 36% = 85% of children's weight from knowledge of their height and age? No. The problem with simply adding up the percentages of explained variance is that height and age are themselves correlated, that they also share variance. This example assumes a height-age correlation of 0.3, and therefore 9% variance in common between height and age.

Some of the variance that height shares with weight is also shared with age. So if we simply add the two values of r^2—49% and 36%—together, we'll be adding some of it twice.

Furthermore, we'd be assigning some of the variability in weight to height, variability that it also shares with age. But how much of the variability in weight is assigned to height, and is therefore no longer available for assignment to age?

Partial Correlations and Unique Variance

Partial correlations help out with this sort of problem, and it's the approach that's usually meant when you hear or read about how some variable such as education or income is "held constant" in a statistical analysis. The general idea is to remove the effects of one variable on two others; then analyze the relationship given what's left over.

Continuing the example of age, weight, and height, you might use the relationship between age and weight to predict weight from age. Then subtract measured weight from predicted weight to get what are called *residual* measures of weight.

You do the same thing with height. Use the age-height relationship to predict height from age. Subtract the actual, measured heights from predicted heights to get residual measures of height.

6

Finally, analyze the relationship between residual height and residual weight. Because you have removed, by subtracting the predicted values, the effect of age from both weight and height, what remains of each variable is independent of age. Figure 6.8 uses Venn diagrams to show, conceptually, how this works.

Figure 6.8
What's left after removing the effect of age is the partial correlation between height and weight.

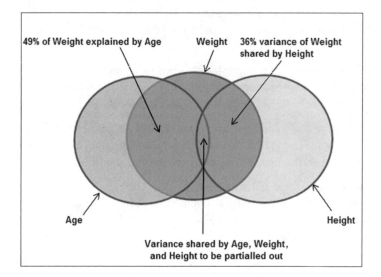

The partialling process removes from height the effects of age, and therefore removes the variability in height that it shares with age. It also removes from weight the variability that it shares with age. The result is that when you evaluate the relationship between the residuals, your analysis is not made ambiguous by the problem of the variance that age shares with height and with weight.

> **NOTE**
>
> You may have also seen references to something called *semipartial* correlations. They are similar to partial correlations, but they are used when you want to remove the effect of a third variable from only one of two others. Continuing the example used by this section, if you removed the effect of age from weight but not from height, and then calculated the correlation between the residual values of weight with the original values of height, that would be a semipartial correlation. Semipartial correlations are sometimes called *part correlations*—which is unfortunate, because that term doesn't convey the fact that you are removing the effects of a third variable from only one of two others.

ACFs and PACFs

So far we've looked at ACFs, the correlations between sequences of values that are farther and farther apart from one another in a data series.

We've also looked at partial correlations, which you use to examine the relationship between two variables after you have removed, or *partialled out*, the influence of a third variable on both. The example used was the relationship between children's height and weight after the effect of age had been removed from both.

You've seen that the correlation between a set of values that lags another set by one point in time can be fairly strong, and that the correlation between sets separated by two lags can be a little weaker, by three lags weaker still, and so on.

But what of the correlations between those earlier sets? Suppose that you have been measuring daily hits on a website during the month of May, and it's now June 1. You can calculate the lag 1 autocorrelation between the values from May 1 to May 30, and the values from May 2 to May 31. You can also calculate the lag 2 autocorrelation between the values from May 1 to May 29, and the values from May 3 to May 31 (see Figure 6.9).

In cell F4, you can see that the lag 1 ACF is 0.55, and in cell G5 the lag 2 ACF is 0.38. The ACFs decline as they often do (compare with Figure 6.7).

Figure 6.9
Cells F4 and G5 show the lag 1 and lag 2 ACFs, respectively, as of the morning of June 1.

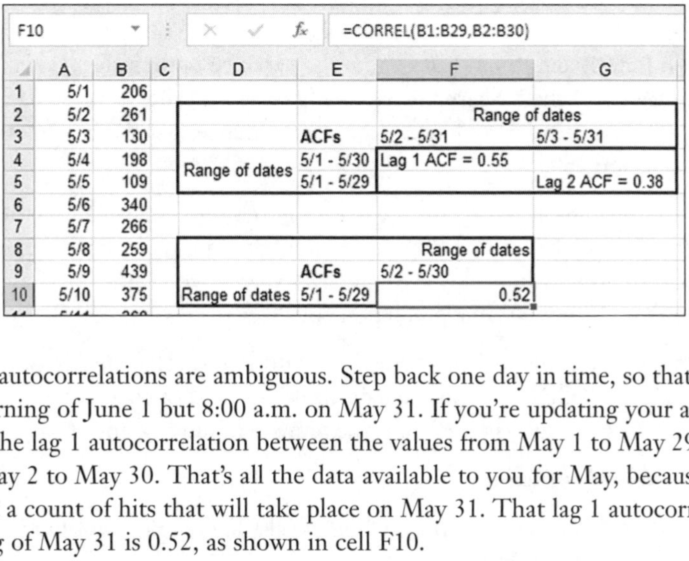

But those two autocorrelations are ambiguous. Step back one day in time, so that it's no longer the morning of June 1 but 8:00 a.m. on May 31. If you're updating your analysis daily, you get the lag 1 autocorrelation between the values from May 1 to May 29 and the values from May 2 to May 30. That's all the data available to you for May, because you haven't yet got a count of hits that will take place on May 31. That lag 1 autocorrelation as of the morning of May 31 is 0.52, as shown in cell F10.

So, on June 1 you can see that there's an appreciable autocorrelation, 0.52, between what are now the lag 2 values (5/1 through 5/29) and the lag 1 values (5/1 through 5/30). That means that the two earlier sets of values share variance. In fact, with the ACF of 0.52 shown in cell F10, the two sets of values share 0.52^2, or 27% of their variance.

The lag 2 ACF is 0.38. The square of 0.38 is 0.14, so 14% of the variability in the 5/3 through 5/31 values is shared with the values from two days earlier.

The lag 1 ACF is 0.55. The square of 0.55 is 0.30, so 30% of the variability in the 5/2 through 5/31 values is shared with the values from one day earlier.

But the correlation between the lag 1 and the lag 2 values is 0.52. If you remove—partial out—the effect of the lag 1 values from the lag 2 values, and also from the most recent set, you wouldn't be surprised to see the lag 2 ACF drop from 0.38 to a lower figure.

Therefore, the amount of shared variance in the lag 1 and lag 2 ACFs in cells F4 and G5 is not unique to each:

■ The values from May 1 through May 30 do not explain *a unique* 30% of the variance in the values from May 2 through May 31 (lag 1).

■ The values from May 1 through May 29 do not explain *a unique* 14% of the variance in the values from May 3 through May 31 (lag 2).

What's needed is a way to remove the shared variance, and that's what the partial autocorrelation coefficient does. The lag 1 ACF is calculated normally, and is identical to the lag 1 PACF because as yet there's no third variable to partial out of the other two.

But when it comes time to calculate the lag 2 results, the shared variance is all allocated to the lag 1 ACF. It is *partialled out* of the lag 2 ACF, which is then referred to not as an ACF but as a PACF.

Another way of saying this is that we cannot simply add the 30% of the shared variance implied by the lag 1 ACF on June 1 to the 14% of the shared variance implied by the lag 2 ACF on June 1, and think that 44% of the variance in the values from May 2 through May 31 has been explained. Shared, overlapping variance exists in those data series, and to simply add the variances is to double-count the variance that the predictors have in common with one another.

More to the point, when there's a correlation between the lag 1 and the lag 2 values, it's entirely possible that the lag 2 values do not correlate well with the current values if you first remove the relationships with the lag 1 values. And if the lag 2 autocorrelation is weak, you don't want to use it in a prediction equation.

Most applications that calculate autocorrelations also calculate partial autocorrelation functions, or PACFs. You can evaluate all the PACFs, of course, but here's how you might evaluate the lag 1 and lag 2 PACFs; the same reasoning extends to PACFs at greater lags.

There are four possibilities:

■ The lag 1 and lag 2 PACFs are both weak. There's no point in trying to forecast using values that are 1 or 2 lags back.

■ The lag 1 PACF is strong and the lag 2 PACF is weak. This constitutes evidence that you can forecast using the lag 1 values. You're unlikely to improve the forecast by also regressing on the lag 2 values.

■ The lag 1 PACF is weak but the lag 2 PACF is strong. This situation is more typical of a moving average model than an autoregressive model, and exponential smoothing is more likely to provide good forecasts than is regression.

■ Both the lag 1 and the lag 2 PACFs are strong. This indicates that the lag 2 values retain a useful relationship with the current values, even when the effect of the lag 1 values has been removed from both. You probably should forecast using a regression equation that predicts on the basis of values that are both one and two lags back.

The result of managing things in this way—of calculating PACFs in addition to ACFs—is that you have a much less ambiguous way of evaluating the lag 2 (and lag 3, lag 4, and so on) autocorrelations. Calculating the partial autocorrelation for lag 2 given lag 1 means that if there's still a sizable lag 2 PACF, you can pay attention to it. In that case there's a relationship remaining between the most current values and the values from two time periods back.

But it often happens that the PACFs cut off—in other words, drop down below the level of statistical significance indicated by the dashes on the correlogram, or even close to the horizontal zero line on the correlogram. In Figure 6.10 the PACFs cut off after lag 1, and that tells you that if you forecast using regression, your predictor variable should be the lag 1 values only; you should not go further back to lag 2, lag 3, and so on for your predictors.

Figure 6.10
A typical first order autoregressive process: The ACFs decline gradually and the PACFs drop to insignificant levels after the first lag.

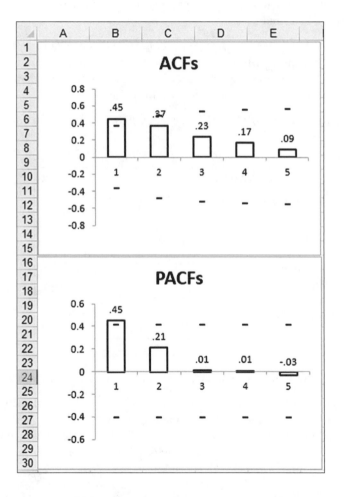

In sum, the correlogram of the ACFs in Figure 6.10 tells you whether you have a data series that is well suited to forecasting using regression. The ACFs decline gradually as the lag length increases. The correlogram of the PACFs tells you which lag or lags you should use as your predictor or predictors in the forecast.

Using the ARIMA Workbook

On the book's website, you can find an Excel workbook that calculates ACFs and PACFs for you, and creates correlograms for both ACFs and PACFs.

The file is named ARIMA.xls. To use it, you need an Excel workbook with a sequence of observations in a single column, as shown in Figure 6.7. (You can have date or time identifiers along with the actual observations, as shown in Figure 6.6, but the ARIMA utility ignores them.)

Open ARIMA.xls, and then open the workbook with your data in it. You'll see a worksheet with some comments about ARIMA.xls. Switch your data workbook to make it active. If you're using a version of Excel that precedes Excel 2007, look in the Data menu for the ARIMA menu item, and click it.

If you're using Excel 2007 or a later version, Excel adds a new tab labeled Add-Ins to the Ribbon. You find an ARIMA item in the Add-Ins group; click it. ARIMA.xls is not formally an add-in, so it does not require the special installation procedures that, for example, Solver does. Nevertheless, Excel puts it in the Add-Ins group.

When you have clicked ARIMA, the dialog box shown in Figure 6.11 displays.

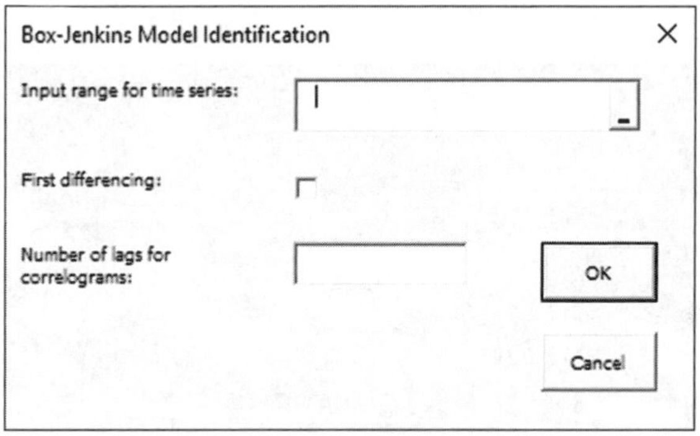

Figure 6.11
The Input Range and the Number of Lags are required.

Click in the Input Range box and drag through the data series that you want to analyze.

If the series has trend, fill the First Differencing checkbox. Excel calculates first differences in your data series before it begins determining the ACFs and PACFs. If you need more than first differencing, the best approach is to difference the series as many times as necessary to achieve stationarity. Do that directly on the worksheet before you start ARIMA, and leave the First Differencing checkbox blank.

Decide on the number of lags you want the correlogram to show and enter that number in the box labeled Number of Lags for Correlograms. I like to base that decision on the level of measurement I'm using. For example, if I have monthly data, I enter 12 to make sure that I can spot any seasonality by month.

Click OK to continue, or Cancel to stop the analysis. Assuming that you click OK, you get a new workbook after a few seconds. That workbook contains the following sheets:

- A chart sheet labeled ACFs with the ACF correlogram, as shown in the upper chart in Figure 6.10.

- A chart sheet labeled PACFs with the PACF correlogram, as shown in the lower chart in Figure 6.10.

- A worksheet named Sheet1 that contains the data for the ACF and PACF charts. That worksheet appears in Figure 6.12.

Figure 6.12
This data matrix forms the basis for the correlograms.

A1				f_x	0.518653415137606	
	A	B	C	D	E	F
1	0.518653	0.30712	-0.30712	0.518653	0.359211	-0.35921
2	0.351136	0.445479	-0.44548	0.11236	0.359211	-0.35921
3	0.058	0.479865	-0.47987	-0.22435	0.359211	-0.35921
4	-0.25703	0.480769	-0.48077	-0.35678	0.359211	-0.35921
5	-0.26688	0.498184	-0.49818	0.039069	0.359211	-0.35921

The data matrix has as many rows as the number of lags you requested in the ARIMA Model Identification dialog box. It always has six columns, as follows:

- Column A contains the ACFs.
- Column B contains the upper two standard errors from zero for the ACFs.
- Column C contains the lower two standard errors from zero for the ACFs.
- Column D contains the PACFs.
- Column E contains the upper two standard errors from zero for the PACFs.
- Column F contains the lower two standard errors from zero for the PACFs.

I have left the VBA code in the ARIMA.xls workbook unprotected. If you'd like to see just how it goes about the business of calculating the ACFs and PACFs, how it calculates and analyzes first differences, and how it creates the charts, you can do so. If your mind turns that way, you can also tweak the code so that it does other things—for example, automating the calculation and analysis of second or higher order differencing if your data set calls for that. (However, few trended data sets require more than first differencing.)

The ARIMA.xls workbook is saved in the pre-Excel 2007 format so that you can use and edit it even if you're using, say, Excel 97. To get to the VBA code, no matter what version of Excel you're using, just open ARIMA.xls and then press the Alt key and F11 to open the Visual Basic Editor. Click the ARIMA project's ARIMA Module in the project pane to open, view and edit its code.

6

Logistic Regression: The Basics

7

Let me get this off my chest right off the bat: Logistic regression, as carried out by most of those who use it, is completely unrelated to regression.

That's better. (Thank you.) Now let's take a look at what logistic regression really is, and why it's needed.

Traditional Approaches to the Analysis

Fifty years ago, and more, people were interested in the ways that dichotomous variables behave, every bit as much as they are today. Then as now, people wanted to know more about binomial variables such as buys/doesn't buy, survives/doesn't survive, married/single, Democrat/ Republican, female/male, and so on.

Until the mid- to late-1960s, one standard way of dealing with that sort of situation was by way of something called the *Central Limit Theorem*. In some other situations, something else called the *chi-square goodness of fit test* was used. I'm going to inflict some information about these approaches on you. That's not because I think you should necessarily use them. It's because understanding something about them, and a bit about why they are now less frequently used, is important to understanding the rationale for logistic regression.

Z-tests and the Central Limit Theorem

The Central Limit Theorem is a characteristic of how averages—specifically, arithmetic means—behave. Suppose that you have a population that is distributed in any fashion, such as a skewed distribution of housing prices, or a binomial distribution such as acceptable/unacceptable.

For this example, I'm using a buy/doesn't buy dichotomy. You take a sample of 200 recent visits to a website and find that 120 visits resulted in a purchase from the site and 80 did not. Therefore your site has, in this sample, a 60% buy rate. What is the likelihood that the buy rate in a full population of users who might visit your site is also 60%? Put another way: Is the 60% buy rate you observed characteristic of the population? Or is the buy rate in the population really something like 40% and you're being misled by sampling error?

You can approach this problem using the Central Limit Theorem. It turns out that if you take repeated, sufficiently large samples such as the one I just described, calculate each sample's mean, and chart the results, you get a normal distribution. The underlying distribution can be of any shape—dichotomous in this case—but the distribution of the means of repeated samples turns out to be normal.

So you can act as though the buy/doesn't buy dichotomy is actually distributed normally, just as though it were a continuous variable such as height or weight.

Furthermore, you can get an estimate of the standard deviation of the sample means based on a dichotomy. That turns out to be

$$s_p = \sqrt{p(1-p)/n}$$

where s_p is the standard deviation of the means of repeated samples, p is the proportion in the sample you took, and n is the size of the sample you took. So, in this example with a 60% buy rate based on 200 observations, the estimated standard deviation of sample means taken from a population whose mean value is .6 is

$$\sqrt{.6(1-.6)/200} = 0.0346$$

Suppose that your sample mean is 0.6: a buy rate of 60%, and that you have a decision rule to go live with a web site only if it promises to result in a buy rate greater than 50%. Is the new site's buy rate in the population really, for example, 50% instead of the 60% indicated by your sample? Using what's called a z-test, you can answer that at, say, the 99% confidence level. You calculate a z statistic using this formula:

$$z = (.6 - .5)/.03535$$

where .6 is the rate you observed in your sample, .5 is the rate you might hypothesize for the full population, and .03535 is the standard deviation of sample means of size 200 from a population whose mean is .5—that is, your hypothesized value:

$$\sqrt{.5(1-.5)/200}$$

The result in this case is 2.83:

$$z = (.6 - .5)/.03535 = 2.83$$

In Excel 2010 and more recent versions, you use the function NORM.S.DIST() to access the normal distribution. Using that function, you learn that if the population rate is 0.5

then you would observe a rate of .6 in only 0.2% (two-tenths of one percent) of 200-record samples from that population. The formula is

=1-NORM.S.DIST(2.83,TRUE)

or, using a version prior to Excel 2010, the formula is

=1-NORMSDIST(2.83)

Both these formulas return the value 0.0023, or 0.2%.

So, if you adopted a confidence level of 99% before obtaining and analyzing your sample, you would reject the hypothesis that the population buy rate is really 50%. A 99% confidence level implies that you would reject that hypothesis if your result could occur only 1% of the time when the hypothesis is true. But this analysis indicates that it could occur only 0.2% of the time, so your decision rules tell you to reject that hypothesis.

It is rational to assume that your sample came from some population with a mean buy rate that's greater than 50%. It is irrational to conclude that you got your digital hands on a sample that would occur only 0.2% of the time if a purchase from this web page is really a 50-50 proposition.

What's the problem with this analysis? Actually, there are several difficulties, discussed next.

Sample Size and Observed Rate

Some sources state that you should not use this z-test approach if either np or $n(1 - p)$ is less than 5. So, if you have 100 observations in your sample and the observed proportion is 4% or .04, np is 4 and the accuracy of the procedure is suspect. Other sources tell you that both np and $n(1 - p)$ should be greater than 10. It's not a good idea to unquestioningly adopt a procedure that's dogged by major discrepancies about the conditions under which it should be used.

Binomial Distribution

For decades the principal reason for using a normal curve test on a dichotomy has been the difficulty of calculating the exact binomial distribution. Many continuous variables follow a normal distribution, and probability statements about those variables are relatively easy to arrive at because the normal curve is a standard.

But dichotomous variables are different: There's a different binomial distribution for every value of p. The actual formula for the binomial distribution is

$$\text{Probability} = \binom{n}{r} p^r q^{n-r}$$

In this formula, and for the example used in this section

- n is the number of page hits—that is, your sample size.
- r is the number of buys made by the sample.

7

- $\binom{n}{r}$ is the number of combinations. You might know it as the *nCr* formula, or "*n* things taken *r* at a time."

- *p* is the probability of "buy" in the population.

- *q* is (1 − *p*), or the probability of "doesn't buy" in the population.

The number of combinations is obtained in part by finding the factorial of both *n* and *r*. So, if your sample size is 50, you would have to calculate $50 \times 49 \times 48 \times \ldots \times 3 \times 2$. That's very tedious.

But when the use of personal computers and analysis applications such as Excel came along, it became much easier to compute exact binomial probabilities. There's no need to calculate factorials; you simply use Excel's BINOM.DIST( ) function (prior to Excel 2010, it's the BINOMDIST( ) function). In the case we've been considering, the Excel formula would be

   =BINOM.DIST(80,200,0.5,TRUE)

This exact formulation returns slightly different probabilities than does the z-test. The discrepancies for different samples versus a population mean of 0.5 appear in Figure 7.1. The differences between the distributions occur largely because the normal distribution is continuous (it allows the logical impossibility of, say, 1.5 hits to a web page) but the binomial is not (for example, it goes directly from one hit to two).

So the broad availability of cheap computing power has rendered pointless the primary rationale for using a z-test on a proportion—the difficulty of calculating the exact binomial distribution. There is no longer a need to appeal to the Central Limit Theorem in order to avoid having to calculate the factorials of even relatively small sample sizes.

Only One Comparison

Perhaps the most serious difficulty with using a z-test to assess the probability of an event is that you can use it to test only two values: your sample value and another value, which might be a hypothetical ("We got a 60% buy rate in our sample. Is the buy rate in the population really 50%?") or the observed value from a different sample ("We got 60% buy rate on page 1, but a 50% buy rate on page 2. Is that difference reliable or is it just sampling error?").

But in practice you often find that you need to make comparisons based on more than just two values. You might have results from three or more web pages to compare, not just two. Or you might need to compare sales results from different ZIP Codes and different age groupings. This additional level of complexity is another reason to move beyond z-tests as appropriate tests of differences between proportions. The chi-square statistic, discussed next, has been (and continues to be) used both for the more elementary two-proportion comparisons and in more complex situations, including this chapter's main topic, logistic regression.

Figure 7.1
The probabilities returned
assuming a normal curve
differ from those based
solely on the use of a
binomial distribution.

	A	B	C	D	E	F
1	π	n	Standard error			
2	0.5	200	0.0354			
3						
4	p	1-p	z	Probability of z	Binomial Probability	Difference
5	0.05	0.95	-12.73	0.000	0.000	0.000
6	0.1	0.9	-11.31	0.000	0.000	0.000
7	0.15	0.85	-9.90	0.000	0.000	0.000
8	0.2	0.8	-8.49	0.000	0.000	0.000
9	0.25	0.75	-7.07	0.000	0.000	0.000
10	0.3	0.7	-5.66	0.000	0.000	0.000
11	0.35	0.65	-4.24	0.000	0.000	0.000
12	0.4	0.6	-2.83	0.002	0.003	0.001
13	0.45	0.55	-1.41	0.079	0.089	0.011
14	0.5	0.5	0.00	0.500	0.528	0.028
15	0.55	0.45	1.41	0.079	0.069	-0.010
16	0.6	0.4	2.83	0.002	0.002	-0.001
17	0.65	0.35	4.24	0.000	0.000	0.000
18	0.7	0.3	5.66	0.000	0.000	0.000
19	0.75	0.25	7.07	0.000	0.000	0.000
20	0.8	0.2	8.49	0.000	0.000	0.000
21	0.85	0.15	9.90	0.000	0.000	0.000
22	0.9	0.1	11.31	0.000	0.000	0.000
23	0.95	0.05	12.73	0.000	0.000	0.000

Using Chi-Square

Another way to reach the conclusion reached by the z-test, discussed in the prior section's example, is by using a chi-square (pronounced *kai square*) statistic instead of a z statistic.

Let the symbol π represent the hypothesized proportion you're interested in; the example discussed in the prior section uses 0.5, or 50%, as that hypothetical value. Continuing the same example, a chi-square analysis would use this Excel formula:

$$= 200*((0.6 - 0.5)^\wedge 2/0.5 + (0.4 - 0.5)^\wedge 2/0.5)$$

or, using symbols instead of numbers:

$$= n * ((p - \pi)^\wedge 2/\pi + (q - \pi)^\wedge 2/\pi)$$

7

With the values as just given, the result of the formula is 8. That is exactly the square of the result of the z-test described earlier in the "Z-tests and the Central Limit Theorem" section:

$$2.83 = (.6 - .5)/.0354$$

And 2.83 squared equals 8.

> **NOTE** This is generally true: When you are comparing only two percentages, the result you get for the z statistic is the square root of what you get for the chi-square statistic.

Figure 7.2 compares the results of the z-test with those of chi-square for different sample means, again assuming that the population mean is 0.5.

Figure 7.2
The probabilities returned by chi-square for the two-group case are exactly twice those returned by the z-test.

G5		⋮ × ✓ f_x	=2*D5-F5			

	A	B	C	D	E	F	G
1	π	n	Standard error				
2	0.5	200	0.0354				
3							
4	p	1-p	z	Probability of z	χ^2	Probability of χ^2	$2p(x)-\chi^2$
5	0.05	0.95	-12.73	0.0000	162	0.0000	0.00000
6	0.1	0.9	-11.31	0.0000	128	0.0000	0.00000
7	0.15	0.85	-9.90	0.0000	98	0.0000	0.00000
8	0.2	0.8	-8.49	0.0000	72	0.0000	0.00000
9	0.25	0.75	-7.07	0.0000	50	0.0000	0.00000
10	0.3	0.7	-5.66	0.0000	32	0.0000	0.00000
11	0.35	0.65	-4.24	0.0000	18	0.0000	0.00000
12	0.4	0.6	-2.83	0.0023	8	0.0047	0.00000
13	0.45	0.55	-1.41	0.0786	2	0.1573	0.00000
14	0.5	0.5	0.00	0.5000	0	1.0000	0.00000
15	0.55	0.45	1.41	0.0786	2	0.1573	0.00000
16	0.6	0.4	2.83	0.0023	8	0.0047	0.00000
17	0.65	0.35	4.24	0.0000	18	0.0000	0.00000
18	0.7	0.3	5.66	0.0000	32	0.0000	0.00000
19	0.75	0.25	7.07	0.0000	50	0.0000	0.00000
20	0.8	0.2	8.49	0.0000	72	0.0000	0.00000
21	0.85	0.15	9.90	0.0000	98	0.0000	0.00000
22	0.9	0.1	11.31	0.0000	128	0.0000	0.00000
23	0.95	0.05	12.73	0.0000	162	0.0000	0.00000

Compare, for example, cells D12 and F12 or D14 and F14. The values of the chi-square probability in column F are exactly twice the corresponding values in column D.

When you use a z-test to analyze the difference between two means, you treat a negative difference separately from a positive difference. That is, this value for z:

$$2.83 = (.6 - .5)/.0354$$

is positive and occupies a point in the right tail of the normal curve, whereas this point:

$$-2.83 = (.4 - .5)/.0354$$

is negative and occupies a point in the left tail of the normal curve. So, to determine the total probability of getting a sample mean of .6 or larger, or .4 or smaller, you total the two probabilities. This is sometimes termed a *two-tailed test*.

In contrast, if you use a chi-square test instead, you find this value:

$$8 = 200*((.6 - .5)^2/.5 + (.4 - .5)^2/.5)$$

With chi-square, you are accumulating squared values, which of course are always positive. So the probability of sample means of .4 and less, and .6 and more, are both found in the right tail of the chi-square distribution.

And because the normal curve is symmetric, the probability of a chi-square value for means of .4 and less and .6 and more is exactly twice the probability of a z score for either .4 or .6.

Preferring Chi-Square to a Z-test

One fundamental reason that you would want to use chi-square instead of a z-test is that a z-test is limited to testing two proportions: two observed proportions (such as the percent of Republicans voting for a particular proposition, contrasted with the percent of Democrats), or an observed proportion and a hypothetical value (for example, the prior section contrasted an observed proportion of 0.6 with a hypothetical proportion of 0.5).

But what if you have more than two proportions to contrast? You might want to contrast Republicans' support for a proposition with that of both Democrats and Independents. Or you might want to compare the buying behavior of those who land on a given web page from more than just one other site. A z-test is not designed to make those sorts of contrasts. It compares two values only, not three or more.

But a chi-square test is well suited to that sort of question. One way to use chi-square is as a test of independence of classifications in a contingency table. Figure 7.3 illustrates this usage.

Figure 7.3 shows how many men and how many women were either admitted or denied admission to graduate programs at the University of California at Berkeley in 1973. The question is whether women were denied admission in disproportionately large numbers, which according to the lawsuit would be evidence of sex discrimination. The actual distribution that was observed is shown in cells B3:C4 of Figure 7.3.

Figure 7.3
The figures are taken from a lawsuit filed in Berkeley, California in the 1970s.

H3		:	×	✓	f_x	=$D3*B$5/$D$5			
⊿	A	B	C	D	E	F	G	H	I	J
1			Observed						Expected	
2		Admitted	Denied	Total	Percent admitted			Admitted	Denied	Total
3	Men	3738	4704	8442	44%		Men	3461	4981	8442
4	Women	1494	2827	4321	35%		Women	1771	2550	4321
5	Total	5232	7531	12763	41%		Total	5232	7531	12763
6										
7										
8									Expected	
9								Admitted	Denied	Total
10							Men	=D3*B5/D5	=D3*C5/D5	=H3+I3
11							Women	=D4*B5/D5	=D4*C5/D5	=H4+I4
12							Total	=H3+H4	=I3+I4	=J3+J4

Under the chi-square test of independence, you determine how you would expect the observations to be distributed if there is no relationship between the dimensions of a table. If the observed frequencies are sufficiently different from the expected frequencies, you conclude that the dimensions—here, sex and admission status—are somehow related: That is, the dimensions are not independent.

The expected frequencies are determined according to the formulas in cell H10:I11 of Figure 7.3. Generally, you multiply the total frequency in a cell's row by the total frequency in its column, and divide by the total frequency. So the expected frequency of men who were denied admission is

8,442 * 7,531 / 12,763 = 4,981

Now you have, in this case, four calculated frequencies that you expect under a null hypothesis that there is no relationship between sex and admission status. If there were a relationship, one of the outcomes that you might find is that men are admitted more frequently than the expectation you get from the marginal frequencies. And that would imply that women were admitted less frequently than you would expect.

This is just a matter of comparing one proportion with another, as discussed in the prior section, extended to a situation in which there are several proportions to compare. You will probably recognize the pattern in the following equation from the earlier discussion of the chi-square statistic:

$$\sum_{k=1}^{K}\left[\frac{(f_{o,k}-f_{e,k})^2}{f_{e,k}}\right]$$

where:

- k indexes each cell in the table.
- $f_{o,k}$ is the observed count, or the frequency, in each cell.
- $f_{e,k}$ is the expected frequency in each cell.

So to get the value of chi-square, you do the following for each cell—in this case, there are four cells:

1. Take the difference between the expected and the observed cell frequency.
2. Square the difference.
3. Divide by the expected cell frequency.

These calculations are shown in cells C8:C11 of Figure 7.4.

When you have the result of step 3 for each cell, total the results to get the value of chi-square for your table. Suppose that the total is in cell C13. You then find the probability of obtaining your chi-square value, assuming no relationship between the table's dimensions, with this formula:

> CHISQ.DIST.RT(C13,1)

The first argument to the function is the chi-square value itself. The second argument is the degrees of freedom. In this sort of test, the degrees of freedom is the product of the number of categories in one dimension, minus 1, and the number of categories in the other dimension, minus 1. There are two categories of admission status and two categories of sex, so the degrees of freedom is

> (2–1)*(2–1)

or 1. In a table that has three categories for one dimension and two categories in another dimension, the degrees of freedom would be

> (3–1)*(2–1)

or 2.

In this case, the CHISQ.DIST.RT() function returns a probability smaller than one one-thousandth. This is apparently very strong evidence that the dimensions of sex and admission status are not independent of one another in the context that the data was collected.

NOTE

It's more complicated than I've made it appear here. Researchers looked more deeply into the numbers and found that something called the Yule-Simpson effect was at work, making the evidence look as though the selection process was biased, when in fact the evidence pointed in another direction.

It's usually a mistake to take a convenience sample, as was done at Berkeley in the 1970s, and almost mindlessly apply a statistical technique to it. Inferential statistics such as those discussed in this section are *meaningless* without strong experimental designs to provide a context for the numbers.

7

Figure 7.4
This sort of analysis can be misleading if it's not based on a true experimental design.

| C8 | | × ✓ fx | =(B3-H3)^2/H3 | | | | | | |

◢	A	B	C	D	E	F	G	H	I	J
1			Observed						Expected	
2		Admitted	Denied	Total	Percent admitted			Admitted	Denied	Total
3	Men	3738	4704	8442	44%		Men	3461	4981	8442
4	Women	1494	2827	4321	35%		Women	1771	2550	4321
5	Total	5232	7531	12763	41%		Total	5232	7531	12763
6										
7										
8	Men	Admitted	22.22							
9	Men	Denied	15.44							
10	Women	Admitted	43.42							
11	Women	Denied	30.17							
12										
13		Total (chi-square)	111.25							
14		Probability of chi-square if dimensions are independent	<.001							

So, chi-square provides a way to test the differences between proportions that applies to a broader range of situations than does a simple z-test. And as you'll see, chi-square is fundamental to the branch of analytics known as logistic regression.

That is why I have drawn out the analysis shown in Figure 7.4 as I did. Excel has another worksheet function that's related to chi-square: CHISQ.TEST() in Excel 2010 and later, or CHITEST() in Excel 2007 and earlier. This function returns the probability of a chi-square value for a given number of degrees of freedom, if there is no difference between the observed frequencies and the expected frequencies.

It's much faster to use something such as this:

=CHISQ.TEST(B3:C4,F3:G4)

than to go through the various calculations shown in Figure 7.4. But all you get from the CHISQ.TEST() function is the probability, which obscures what's really going on with the test: the accumulation of the squared differences between the actual and the expected frequencies. And that's important to understanding what logistic regression is up to.

Although chi-square is by itself a step up from a simple z-test of two proportions, it's still somewhat limited compared to the regression analyses discussed in Chapter 2, "Linear Regression," and Chapter 6, "Forecasting a Time Series: Regression."

So why not develop a regression equation that uses variables such as sex, admission status, web page requests, and so on to forecast percentages? The next section gets into the reasons you shouldn't.

7

Regression Analysis on Dichotomies

Chapter 2 spent quite a bit of ink on the topic of assumptions that are built into regression analysis, both simple two-variable regression and the slightly more complicated multiple regression analysis. The purpose was not to overwhelm you with a list of must-haves that you need to meet before running a regression analysis. The purpose was to lay the groundwork for a discussion of why you need to deal with logistic regression at all. As you'll see, running a regression on a dichotomy with just two possible outcomes makes it impossible to meet some of those assumptions—assumptions that are easily met, or that turn out to be unimportant, when the forecast variable is a continuous one such as blood pressure or revenue dollars.

Here's a review of the assumptions I have in mind along with a discussion of the reasons that a dichotomous forecast variable makes them difficult to deal with.

Homoscedasticity

In the part of Chapter 2 titled "Assumptions Made in Regression Analysis," a subsection titled "Variability" discusses the ugly word *homoscedasticity*, which means equal spread and has to do with the differences between predicted values and observed values.

Predicted Versus Error, Ordinary Least Squares

Suppose you are looking into the relationship between the number of dollars that customers spend on your products during two consecutive calendar quarters. You have a sample of 20 customers and you run a regression analysis as shown in Figure 7.5.

Figure 7.5
The relationship between the predicted values and the errors is essentially random.

D2 {=TREND(A2:A21,B2:B21)}

	A	B	C	D	E
1	Spent *Second* Quarter	Spent *First* Quarter		Predicted values	Error (Residuals)
2	$ 19	$ 20		24.1	-5.1
3	$ 65	$ 100		76.1	-11.1
4	$ 18	$ 66		54.0	-36.0
5	$ 79	$ 91		70.2	8.8
6	$ 35	$ 22		25.4	9.6
7	$ 48	$ 41		37.8	10.2
8	$ 23	$ 23		26.1	-3.1
9	$ 64	$ 80		63.1	0.9
10	$ 44	$ 38		35.8	8.2
11	$ 43	$ 50		43.6	-0.6
12	$ 38	$ 38		35.8	2.2
13	$ 19	$ 16		21.5	-2.5
14	$ 94	$ 67		54.7	39.3
15	$ 5	$ 26		28.0	-23.0
16	$ 34	$ 41		37.8	-3.8
17	$ 81	$ 48		42.3	38.7
18	$ 63	$ 84		65.7	-2.7
19	$ 54	$ 84		65.7	-11.7
20	$ 32	$ 51		44.3	-12.3
21	$ 13	$ 12		18.9	-5.9

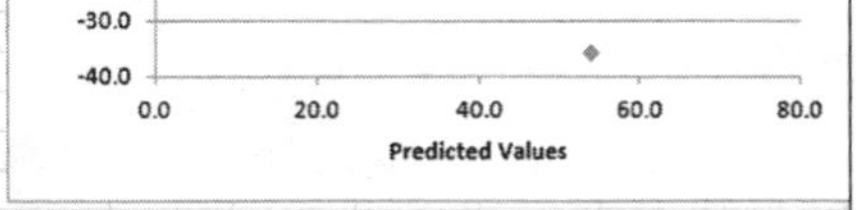

The observed values for your small sample of dollars spent are in columns A and B. The cells in the range D2:D21 contain the TREND() function

=TREND(A2:A21,B2:B21)

array-entered. (The TREND() function is discussed in some detail in Chapter 2.) The results of the TREND() function show the predicted values of the dollars spent during the second quarter based on the relationship between the actual dollars spent during the first and the second quarters.

The values in column E are the differences between the predicted second quarter values and the observed second quarter values; these differences are sometimes called *errors*, sometimes *residuals*, and sometimes *errors of estimate*. (I tend to prefer *residuals* to avoid the negative implication of the term *error*.)

It's often useful to analyze the residuals, and one of the more informative analyses involves the relationship between the predicted values and the residuals. If the regression equation accounts for the systematic variability in the predicted variable, what's left in the residuals is random and an XY chart of the residuals against the predicted values should look something like the chart in Figure 7.5.

> **NOTE** It is also often useful to examine the relationship between the residuals and the predictor variable (or, in the case of multiple regression, the predictor variables). The Data Analysis add-in's Regression tool provides the appropriate XY charts of the residuals by the predictors, but does not provide an XY chart of the residual Y values by the predicted Y values. You have to create that chart yourself, as shown in Figure 7.5.

Figure 7.6, in contrast, shows a chart of residuals on the vertical axis by predicted values on the horizontal axis taken from an analysis of a dichotomous variable. Clearly it looks nothing like the residuals versus predicted values chart in Figure 7.5.

Why does a dichotomous predicted variable result in such a different chart of residuals against predicted values? Consider how the residuals are calculated:

Residual = Actual – Predicted

In the case of a dichotomous variable that's scored as 1 or 0, that results in this:

Residual = 0 – Predicted

when the actual observation is 0, and this:

Residual = 1 – Predicted

when the actual observation is 1. The result of those two equations is two straight lines, one unit apart and parallel to one another—precisely what you see in Figure 7.6.

Figure 7.6
You get something very similar to this pattern whenever you plot least squares residuals of a dichotomous variable against the predicted values.

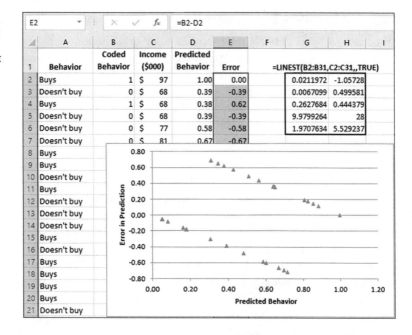

Furthermore, it's clear that the least-squares assumption of homoscedasticity is violated. Up to about a predicted value of 0.3 on the horizontal axis, the residuals fall on one straight line, and the same is true above the 0.8 value for the predicted values. The variability of the residuals is constrained in the upper and lower ranges of the predicted values.

But in the center of the range of predicted values, from 0.3 through 0.8, there's much more variability in the residuals. They still occupy straight lines, but there are two straight lines through that range of predicted values. Clearly there is much more variability in residual values between 0.3 and 0.8 on the horizontal axis than there is outside that range. Compare with Figure 7.5, where the variability on the vertical axis exists throughout the range of predicted values.

Why is that important? Because the assumption is that the standard error is the same throughout the range of predictor values. Suppose that you were using men's heights to predict their weights. You might find that the standard error of estimate is 15 pounds. Thus, your prediction of a man's weight on the basis of his height could easily be off by 30 pounds in either direction: two standard errors of estimate above and below the predicted weight. Furthermore, ordinary, least-squares regression analysis would lead you to believe that the standard error of estimate is the same for a man who stands five feet five inches as it is for a man who stands six feet five inches.

In the context of regression analysis, that's what "equal spread" means. But it clearly does not apply to a situation where your predicted variable is dichotomous: Figure 7.6 demonstrates that.

7

Residuals Are Normally Distributed

Another assumption, closely related to the assumption of homoscedasticity, is that residuals are normally distributed around the predicted values. Suppose you took many residual values, each associated with the same predictor value—continuing the prior section's example of predicting weight from height, you might choose all the residuals, actual weight minus predicted weight, associated with men who stand five feet eleven inches. If you then plotted the frequency of each of those residuals, the assumption of normally distributed residuals would lead you to expect that they would resemble a normal curve.

But Figure 7.6 once again demonstrates that the residuals do not resemble a normal curve at any point along the horizontal axis. As discussed earlier, with a dichotomous predicted variable, residuals can take on only two values. Those values are 1 minus the predicted value and 0 minus the predicted value. For any given point on the horizontal axis the predicted value is constant for all records at that point, so there can be only two distinct residuals at each point on the horizontal axis. When you subtract a single predicted value from an observed value of 1, and then the same predicted value from an observed value of 0, you wind up with two residual values only at each point on the horizontal axis. Two values do not a normal distribution make.

Restriction of Predicted Range

The third issue that arises when you use regression to predict a dichotomous variable has to do with the values that the dichotomy can take on. Of course there are only two possible values—that's the meaning of the term "dichotomy." It's never wrong, and it's often convenient, to designate the two values as 1 and 0. For example, a particular customer's probability of buying a given product is, *a priori*, 1 or 0, 100% or 0%.

But when you plug those values into a regression equation as the predicted variable, you often run into problems. Although the possible range of the predicted variable might be 1.0, from 0.0 to 1.0, the range of the predictor variable or variables is not necessarily restricted.

Figure 7.7 adds three predicted values, based on the data shown in Figure 7.6. Notice that the raw data in columns A and B of Figure 7.7 is the same as in Figure 7.6. The LINEST() function shown in the range E2 has the same results as the one in the range G2:H6 in Figure 7.6. In each case, the higher the income, the greater the likelihood of buying. As Figure 7.6 shows in cell D2, an income of $97,000 predicts a likelihood of buying of 1.00.

But in Figure 7.7, the same regression equation is applied to two other income amounts: $110,000 in cell H3 and $40,000 in cell H4. If you apply the regression equation to those two amounts, you get a probability of buying of 127% and –21%, respectively.

That's a problem. What does a probability of 127% mean? For that matter, what does a negative probability of buying mean?

Figure 7.7
This sort of difficulty
leads mainly to logical
conundrums.

	A	B	C	D	E	F	G	H	I	J
		Coded	Income					Income	Predicted	
1	Behavior	Behavior	($000)		LINEST()			($000)	Behavior	
2	Buys	1	$ 97		0.021197	-1.05728		$ 97	100%	=$E$2*H2+$F$2
3	Doesn't buy	0	$ 68		0.00671	0.499581		$ 110	127%	=$E$2*H3+$F$2
4	Buys	1	$ 68		0.262768	0.444379		$ 40	-21%	=$E$2*H4+$F$2
5	Doesn't buy	0	$ 68		9.979926	28				
6	Doesn't buy	0	$ 77		1.970763	5.529237				
7	Doesn't buy	0	$ 81							
8	Buys	1	$ 74							
9	Buys	1	$ 80							
10	Doesn't buy	0	$ 64							

E2 · : × ✓ *fx* {=LINEST(B2:B31,C2:C31,,TRUE)}

There is no constraint on the income variable. It can range from $0 to millions of dollars—and depending on how you measure it, income can consist of a negative quantity. There's no difficulty with that, whether mathematical or logical.

The difficulty comes in when you apply a linear regression equation with a variable whose values are unconstrained, to predict a variable whose values *are* constrained. The trendline extends as far in either direction as the predictor variables (here, income) require, and the predicted value comes along for the ride, regardless of whether the predicted values stop making sense at some point.

Ah, But You Can Get Odds Forever

The previous section discussed three genuine problems that arise when you try to use a dichotomy as the predicted variable in a regression analysis:

- The residuals don't exhibit equivalent variability across the different values of the predictor variable.

- The residuals are not normally distributed at different values of the predictor variable.

- The predictor variable can range, in theory, from negative to positive infinity. Even when the predictor's range is more limited, the regression equation can easily take you out of the realm of logical outcomes into a Neverland of negative probabilities and likelihoods greater than 100%.

An alternative is needed. There is a good one, and it starts with the odds.

Probabilities and Odds

There's a close relationship between probability and odds, and it's clearest when there are just two possible outcomes, as is the case with a dichotomous variable. The *odds* is the ratio of two complementary probabilities.

7

Suppose that you have a fair coin—that is, a coin that is somehow known not to favor one side or the other when you flip it. Therefore, before you flip it, the probability that it will come up heads is 0.5, or 50%.

And in consequence, the probability that it will come up tails is also 0.5 or 50%. The odds are therefore 0.5/0.5, or 1 to 1, that the coin will come up heads.

What are the odds of getting heads on two consecutive flips? When two events are independent of one another (and two flips of a fair coin are independent events), the probability that they will both occur is the product of the individual probabilities. So, the probability of getting two consecutive heads (or two consecutive tails, for that matter) is 0.5*0.5, or 0.25. Similarly, the probability that you will *not* get two consecutive heads is 1 – 0.25, or 0.75.

(It's easy to count the cases that result in these probabilities. There are only four possible outcomes in four flips: H/H, H/T, T/H, and T/T. Only one of the four outcomes, H/H, represents two heads, so its probability is 0.25. Three of the outcomes involve at least one tails, so their cumulative probability is 0.75.)

The ratio of the probabilities, 0.25 to 0.75, is 1:3. The odds are 1 to 3 in favor of two consecutive heads, or as it is often phrased, 3 to 1 against.

It's easy enough to go back and forth between probabilities and odds. Going from probabilities to odds, here's the general equation:

$$Odds = P / (1 - P)$$

where P is the probability of an event. So if the probability is 0.8, the odds are 4 to 1:

$$4 = .8 / (1 - .8)$$

Going from odds to probabilities, the general equation is

$$P = Odds / (1 + Odds)$$

So if the odds are 4:

$$.8 = 4 / (1 + 4)$$

and the probability is .8.

The odds change as a function of the probabilities. Figure 7.8 shows the relationship between the probabilities and the odds for a dichotomous variable such as *buys/doesn't buy*.

(The formulas used in Figure 7.8's C3:C10 are shown in D3:D10.) Notice that although, as was discussed earlier in this chapter, the probability ranges only from 0.0 through 1.0, the odds can be considerably larger. Because in theory the probability can come infinitely close to 1.0, the odds can in theory go all the way to infinity. This feature of odds handles the problem, shown in the prior section, of predicting a probability that's larger than 1.0. No matter how high the odds get, they never imply a probability greater than 1.0.

7

Figure 7.8
The relationship between probabilities and odds is not a linear one.

	A	B	C	D	E
B3			f_x	=A3/(1+A3)	
1	**Odds on Success**	**Prob of Success**	**Delta Probability**		
2	0.0001	0.01%	#N/A		
3	0.001	0.10%	0.09%	=B3-B2	
4	0.01	0.99%	0.89%	=B4-B3	
5	0.1	9.09%	8.10%	=B5-B4	
6	1	50.00%	40.91%	=B6-B5	
7	10	90.91%	40.91%	=B7-B6	
8	100	99.01%	8.10%	=B8-B7	
9	1000	99.90%	0.89%	=B9-B8	
10	10000	99.99%	0.09%	=B10-B9	

We haven't yet dealt with the problem of keeping the probability above 0.0, and that will have to wait a bit—it's covered in the later section titled "Moving on to the Log Odds." In the meantime, it's important to take a closer look at how the probabilities change as the predictor values change.

How the Probabilities Shift

Figure 7.9 shows more graphically how the type of regression equation used in Figure 7.7 would work out.

Figure 7.9
A straight line is not normally representative of how probabilities fluctuate.

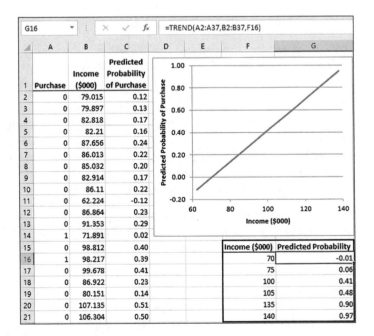

One of the characteristics of linear regression is that its predicted values are, well, linear. If you give it just a bit of thought, it will be clear why that's often unhelpful in a case such as a buy/doesn't buy decision.

Leave aside for the moment the problems of the negative probabilities that are predicted for incomes less than $70,000. Also ignore that the probability of a purchase would exceed 100% if income exceeded, say, $150,000. For the moment, consider the implications of the straight line between the points that represent $70,000 and $80,000 of income in Figure 7.9's chart.

Suppose that the purchase in question in Figure 7.9 is that of a house whose asking price is $600,000. Even with the historically low interest rates prevailing in 2017, it seems highly unlikely that person making $70,000 will purchase the house via a mortgage. You don't need Excel to tell you that. You merely need to ask yourself where a person who grosses roughly $6,000 per month is going to get the $3,000 per month to service the mortgage.

And the regression analysis in Figure 7.9 supports that conclusion. It says that given the data in columns A and B, someone making less than $70,000 has a negative probability of making the purchase. Let's just say that the probability is effectively zero.

What of someone who earns $75,000 instead of $70,000? The same regression analysis says that instead of a 0% probability of purchase, the person whose income is $75,000 stands a 6% likelihood of making the purchase (see cell G17 in Figure 7.9).

Does that make sense? The person whose income is $75,000 has less than $500 more per month available than the person whose income is $70,000, and yet the regression analysis says that person's purchase probability is 6% instead of 0%. Instead of making a $3,000 mortgage payment on a monthly income of $6,000, it takes place on a monthly income of $6,500. No, that doesn't make sense: The extra $500 a month of income does not result in 6% higher probability of purchase.

But what about the person whose income is $100,000? The analysis says that the probability of purchase in that case is about 41%. It also says that the probability of purchase by someone whose income is $105,000 is 48%—that is, the same 6% difference as between $70,000 and $75,000 income.

That makes somewhat more sense. Someone who grosses $8,500 a month is in a reasonable position to afford a $3,000 mortgage payment. Bump the gross monthly income to $9,000 and it's rational to anticipate that the probability of purchase might rise by 6%, from 42% to 48%. That extra $500 a month could come in handy for paying, say, property taxes on the house and convince a buyer who would otherwise be on the fence.

And at the high end of income? The regression analysis in Figure 7.9 indicates that someone who grosses $135,000 stands a 90% likelihood of making the purchase, while someone grossing $140,000 has a 97% likelihood.

This outcome is also irrational. A monthly gross of $11,000 is easily capable of meeting a monthly mortgage payment of $3,000, and an additional $500 a month is scarcely likely to move a buyer from a 90% probability of purchasing to a 97% probability. More likely, a buyer who is 90% likely to buy will stay at that level regardless of an additional $500 in monthly income.

The problem here is that ordinary, least-squares regression produces a straight line that might provide accurate predictions in the middle range of the predictor variable but mis-estimates probabilities at the low end and the high end.

Figure 7.10 shows the regression line from Figure 7.9 along with a curve that more realistically portrays the situation.

Figure 7.10
The curve provides more realistic projections than does the straight line.

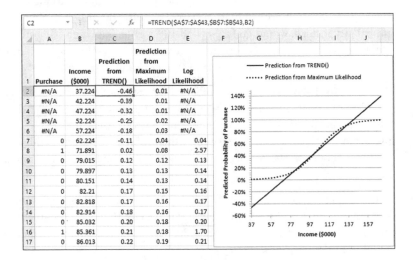

There are three main points to note about the two charted data series in Figure 7.10:

■ Both lines represent the relationship between income and probability of purchase. The solid, straight line is calculated by least-squares regression, and the dotted, curved line is calculated on odds using techniques that I discuss in the next chapter.

■ The straight regression line takes you into negative probabilities at the low end of income and probabilities that exceed 100% at the high end of income. The curved line does neither, and would not do so even if you extended the range of income to much lower and much higher values.

■ The differences in probabilities as you move gradually from one income level to another are smaller in the tails for the curved line. The changes in probability are constant in the straight line.

So if it's possible to estimate probabilities in a way that keeps them within a range of 0% to 100%, and recognizes that they behave differently near 0% and 100% than they do in the middle, then we're in a much better position than we are using ordinary regression to predict raw probabilities.

Moving On to the Log Odds

The prior section shows how it's desirable to quantify probabilities in a way that results in plausible outcomes:

- No negative probabilities
- No probabilities greater than 100%
- Changes in probabilities that make sense in terms of changes to the predictor variable

As you'll see, moving from raw probabilities to odds is an important step in the right direction. When you cast probabilities in terms of odds, you deal with a metric that, were it probability instead, would go far beyond 100%. But such high odds still represent probabilities that make sense. For example, Figure 7.8 shows that as the odds move from 100 to 10,000, the associated probabilities move only from 99.01% to 99.99%.

And the odds have a lower bound of 0.0. They cannot get smaller than that. You can't have a probability smaller than 0.0. Therefore the numerator of the odds (which is a probability) can be no smaller than 0.0, and neither can the odds itself. But if you used odds as the predicted variable, you would encounter the problem of negative odds just as if you were using probability as the predicted variable. Negative odds are as meaningless as negative probabilities.

The way to manage that problem, one that has gained general acceptance since the 1930s when this approach was first proposed, is by way of the log odds—that is, the natural logarithm of the odds. Figure 7.11 repeats the data in Figure 7.8 but includes the log odds in addition to the raw odds.

Figure 7.11
The log odds can vary in theory from negative to positive infinity.

A2			×	✓	f_x	=LN(C2)	

	A	B	C	D	E
1	**Log Odds**	**Delta Log Odds**	**Odds on Success**	**Prob of Success**	**Delta Probability**
2	-9.210		0.0001	0.01%	#N/A
3	-6.908	2.303	0.001	0.10%	0.09%
4	-4.605	2.303	0.01	0.99%	0.89%
5	-2.303	2.303	0.1	9.09%	8.10%
6	0.000	2.303	1	50.00%	40.91%
7	2.303	2.303	10	90.91%	40.91%
8	4.605	2.303	100	99.01%	8.10%
9	6.908	2.303	1000	99.90%	0.89%
10	9.210	2.303	10000	99.99%	0.09%

Using log odds instead of raw odds allows the bottom end of the scale to fall as far as necessary in order to represent a very low probability of success (more generally, a very small probability in the numerator of the odds).

Notice that although the odds shown in column C of Figure 7.11 approach 0.00 but can never get below 0.00, the log odds can and do. This means that there is no theoretical lower limit, and similarly there is no theoretical upper limit, so the predicted log odds can go as far up or down as predictor variables can take them. And yet the associated probability levels never venture beyond their logical limits of 0% and 100%.

If you haven't worked with transformed values such as the logarithms of a predicted variable in the past, it is likely to seem a strange thing to do. Is there some sort of intuitively meaningful result that you can derive by generating an equation that predicts log odds instead of, say, the probability of a given web page of making a sale? Or the probability that a person taking a given medication will recover from a disease?

Unless you're unusually fluent in thinking about these matters—and few of us are—the answer to those questions is "No." So it's helpful to follow this general sequence:

1. Convert probabilities to odds.

2. Convert odds to log odds.

3. Derive an equation that results in the combination of predictor variables that best predicts the log odds.

4. Convert the predicted log odds back to predicted odds, and the predicted odds to predicted probabilities.

In the process of getting comfortable—or regaining a sense of comfort—with logarithms, odds, and log odds, it can help to consider these aspects of the data in Figure 7.11:

- The probabilities shown in column D form a nonlinear series. Solely because of the values I chose to show, they would form an s-shaped curve if you charted them.

- The odds shown in column C form a geometric progression; each value is ten times larger than the preceding value.

- The log odds shown in column A form an arithmetic progression; each value is 2.303 larger than the preceding value.

- What we are doing in converting odds (column C) to log odds (column A) is to change a series that goes up by multiplying by 10 to a series that goes up by adding 2.303 (column B)—converting a curve to a straight line.

Before developing more of the theory of the logistic model, it will help to see how all this works out in an example, which you'll find at the beginning of the next chapter.

This chapter has discussed some of the reasons that using ordinary least-squares approaches is usually a poor idea when your outcome, predicted variable is a dichotomy. These reasons also apply to situations in which the outcome has more than two values (Democratic, Republican, Independent; or Ford, GM, Toyota), and Chapter 9 discusses how logistic regression handles the multinomial problem. The next chapter details how you use logistic regression to solve the problems that this chapter points out.

7

Logistic Regression: Further Issues

Chapter 7, "Logistic Regression: The Basics," concerns itself with issues pertaining to the difficulties that a binomial (that is, dichotomous) variable presents when you want to predict the probabilities of one value or the other: buy/don't buy, survive/don't survive, vote/don't vote, and so on.

When you think of predicting outcomes that are measured on a continuous numeric scale such as blood pressure, dollars of revenue, or batting averages, you usually think of using regression to generate the predictions.

But binomial outcome variables present special problems that standard, least-squares regression simply does not handle well. These problems range from the violation of theoretical assumptions such as equal variances and normally distributed residuals to more bread-and-butter issues such as winding up with probabilities that are greater than 100% or less than 0%.

Chapter 7 presents arguments for, and illustrations of, the use of odds and their logarithms to solve these problems. This chapter demonstrates how you can apply logistic regression to take advantage of the benefits of using odds and their logs. It also shows you how you can do so from within the comfortable environment of Excel, without having to venture into the (possibly unfamiliar) user interfaces of SAS, Stata, R, and other popular, purely statistical applications. However, you'll also find a couple of examples that show how to use R functions to carry out logistic regression on binomial outcome variables.

8

An Example: Predicting Purchase Behavior

Figure 8.1 shows data collected by a real estate marketing company on prospects who either purchased or declined to purchase properties in the company's portfolio.

Figure 8.1
Just as a matter of personal preference, I prefer using lists to tables.

	A	B	C	D	E
1	Purchase	Income	Age	Zip	
2	0	79.015	50	1	
3	0	79.897	50	1	
4	0	82.818	47	1	
5	0	82.210	49	1	
6	0	87.656	42	1	
7	0	86.013	47	1	
8	0	85.032	49	1	
9	0	82.914	55	1	
10	0	86.110	51	1	
11	0	62.224	52	2	
12	0	86.864	52	1	
13	0	91.353	55	1	
14	1	71.891	49	2	
15	0	98.812	54	1	
16	1	98.217	55	1	
17	0	99.678	53	1	
18	0	86.922	44	2	
19	0	80.151	54	2	
20	0	107.135	53	1	
21	0	106.304	56	1	
22	1	85.361	57	2	
23	0	93.090	51	2	
24	0	93.830	53	2	
25	1	120.007	51	1	

The data is laid out as an Excel list, as follows:

■ There are 36 prospects. If you open the workbook for this chapter, available from www.quepublishing.com/title/9780789758354, you'll find that the list extends from row 1 through row 37.

■ Each prospect's purchase decision is coded as a 0, for did not purchase, or as a 1, for purchased. These values are shown in column A.

- Each prospect's income is in column B. The income values are shown in thousands of dollars. The reason is that the data will be passed to Excel's EXP() function, which returns the antilog of its argument. The EXP() function returns the #NUM! error value if its argument is approximately 710 or larger. The income values are scaled down to avoid that error. (I discuss EXP() and antilogs later in this chapter.)

- The prospect's age appears in column C.

- The prospect's current ZIP Code is in column D. In this example, there are only two ZIP Codes. They are recorded because the realty company believed that there were significant and meaningful demographic differences between the two geographic areas represented by the ZIP Codes. (The actual ZIP Codes are not used. Instead, a 1 and a 2 are used to distinguish them.)

If we had a continuous variable to predict (for example, the amount of money each prospect might spend on a purchase), we might use a standard multiple regression analysis with that amount of money as the predicted variable, and income, age, and ZIP Code as three predictors.

But as Chapter 7 shows, with a dichotomous variable (such as purchase/doesn't purchase) as the predicted variable, ordinary multiple regression is not a good choice. Instead, we can apply logistic regression as described next.

Using Logistic Regression

We're after an equation similar to a regression equation, something like this:

$$Y = B_0 + B_1 X_1 + B_2 X_2 + B_3 X_3$$

where:

- Y is the predicted variable—here, purchase/doesn't purchase.
- B_0 is the intercept, sometimes termed the *constant*.
- B_1 is a coefficient, a constant that multiplies all the available values of the variable X_1.
- X_1 is a variable—in this case, Income.
- B_2 and B_3 are coefficients, constants that multiply all the available values of the variables X_2 and X_3.
- X_2 and X_3 are variables—in this case, Age and ZIP Code.

One end result of logistic regression, a prediction equation, is thus very similar to one end result of ordinary single or multiple regression: a prediction equation. The difference lies in how you get there.

Least Squares Versus Maximum Likelihood

Ordinary least squares arrives at the best combination of predictor variables using this matrix expression:

$$(X'X)^{-1} X'y$$

That's a compact way of saying to do the following:

1. Premultiply the matrix of X values by its transpose.
2. Find the inverse of the result.
3. Premultiply the y values (the variable to be predicted) by the transpose of the X matrix.
4. Premultiply the result of step 3 by the result of step 2.

You can do that on an Excel worksheet if you really want, by using Excel's MMULT(), TRANSPOSE(), and MINVERSE() functions. But LINEST() relieves you of having to do all that. Whichever approach you take, you get the intercept and coefficients (in this case, B_0, B_1, B_2, and B_3) that define the regression equation.

In contrast, logistic regression uses what's termed the *maximum likelihood estimate* approach. Logistic regression tries out different values for the intercept and the coefficients until it finds the value that results in probabilities—that is, *likelihoods*—that are closest to the actual, observed probabilities. (Formally, probability and likelihood are two different things, and I touch on the distinction a little later in this chapter.)

> **NOTE** This is the reason that I began Chapter 7 by stating that logistic regression has almost nothing to do with regression. The workhorse of regression is correlation: Conceptually, correlation and regression are opposite sides of the same coin. You don't bother with correlations in logistic regression, unless you are calculating some ancillary results such as Wald statistics. The workhorse of logistic regression is the odds.

In Figure 8.1, notice that the values for the Purchase variable in column A are all 0 or 1: 0 for did not purchase, 1 for did purchase. This type of coding, 0 and 1, is usual in binomial logistic regression. Using the values 0 and 1 is helpful for several reasons. Among those reasons is that the values can be interpreted as probabilities. That is, if a person did not purchase, and therefore has a value of 0 in the Purchase variable, that person's probability of having bought is 0%. Similarly, a person who did buy, and has a 1 on the Purchase variable, has a 100% probability of having bought.

And taking the average of all the Purchase values returns the overall likelihood of any given person in this sample having purchased. In this example, 14 of 36 people purchased. Therefore the average value for Purchase is 14/36 or 0.3889—the probability that any randomly selected person (from the population that this sample of 36 people represents) made a purchase is, *a priori*, 38.89%.

More generally, when you assign the value 1 to one possible outcome and the value 0 to the other possible outcome, the average across all the cases is the probability that the variable's value is 1 in any particular case.

We would like to find a coefficient for each of the predictor variables—here, those are income, age, and ZIP Code—that in combination result in an estimated probability that comes closest to the actual value (0 or 1) for any given case.

Conceptually, if a person has greater income, the probability that he or she will purchase is greater than if the person has less income. Logistic regression seeks to find the combination of the predictor variables that results in the most accurate estimate of the likelihood that people will buy (or vote for a particular political party, or survive a medical procedure).

Ordinary least squares analysis does something similar, but the results, as Chapter 7 points out, are for various reasons inept. Logistic regression takes a different approach, often termed *maximum likelihood estimation.*

In logistic regression, you maximize the likelihood of an accurate prediction when you find the set of coefficients that result in the greatest overall likelihood of obtaining this particular set of outcome values. This is done not by a set of relatively simple matrix equations, as discussed at the beginning of this section, but by an iterative process that tries out different values for the coefficients until the likelihood is maximized. Excel comes with an add-in called *Solver* that automates this process for you.

About Solver

You can install Solver from the factory disc or from the software that you downloaded to put Excel on your computer. Solver helps you backtrack to underlying values when you want them to result in a particular outcome.

For example, suppose you have ten numbers on a worksheet, and their mean value is 25. You want to know what the tenth number must be in order for the mean to equal 30 instead of 25. Solver can do that for you. Normally, you know your inputs and you're seeking a result. When you know the result and want to find the necessary values of the inputs, Solver is one way to do so.

The example in the prior paragraph is trivially simple, but it illustrates the main purpose of Solver: You specify the outcome and Solver determines the input values needed to reach the outcome.

You could use another Excel tool, Goal Seek, to solve this particular problem. But Solver offers you many more options than does Goal Seek. For example, using Solver you can specify that you want an outcome maximized, or minimized, instead of solving for a particular outcome value. That's relevant here because we want to find the values for the coefficients so as to maximize the likelihood estimate.

Finding and Installing Solver

It's possible that Solver is already installed and available to Excel. To use Solver in Excel 2007 or later, click the Ribbon's Data tab and find the Analysis group. If you see Solver there, you're all set. (In Excel 2003 or earlier, check for Solver in the Tools menu.)

If you don't find Solver on the Ribbon or the Tools menu, take these steps in Excel 2007 or later:

1. Click the Ribbon's File tab and choose Options.
2. Choose Add-Ins from the Options navigation bar.

3. At the bottom of the View and Manage Microsoft Office Add-Ins window, make sure that the Manage drop-down is set to Excel Add-Ins and click Go.

4. The Add-Ins dialog box appears. If you see Solver Add-in listed, fill its checkbox and click OK.

You should now find Solver in the Analysis group on the Ribbon's Data tab.

If you're using Excel 2003 or earlier, start by choosing Add-Ins from the Tools menu. Then complete step 4.

If you didn't find Solver in the Analysis group on the Data tab (or on the Tools menu in earlier Excel versions), and if you did not see it in the Add-Ins dialog box in step 4, then Solver was not installed with Excel on your computer. You will have to re-run the installation routine, and you can usually do so via the Programs item in the Windows Control Panel.

The sequence varies according to the operating system you're running, but you should choose to change features for Microsoft Office. Expand the Excel option by clicking the plus sign by its icon and then do the same for Add-Ins. Click the drop-down by Solver and choose Run from My Computer. Complete the installation sequence. When it's through, you should be able to make the Solver add-in available to Excel using the sequence of four steps provided earlier in this section.

We'll return to Solver and how you use it shortly, in the section titled "Running Solver on the Logistic Regression Problem."

Product of All Probabilities Is Likelihood

In Chapter 7, a section titled "Probabilities and Odds" discusses how the product of the probabilities of two or more independent events equals the probability that they both occur. So the probability that a fair coin will come up heads is 0.5, and the probability that it will come up heads in two particular flips is 0.5 * 0.5 or 0.25.

Similarly, the likelihood of purchases by 36 prospects is the product of the probability that Prospect 1 will buy, times the probability that Prospect 2 will buy, . . ., times the probability that Prospect 36 will buy.

Because probabilities can range only from 0 to 1, you're finding the product of—in this example—36 fractions. In the usual course of analyzing probabilities, whether of economic behavior, political preferences, or susceptibility to disease, that product tends to be extremely small. Even a sample of just eleven people, each of whom stands a 50% chance of purchasing, returns an overall likelihood of 0.5^{11}, or less than one twentieth of one percent.

That makes good sense, given that each person (or record, or patient, or whatever your unit of analysis is) acts independently of each other person. That assumption of independent events is a crucial one. That caveat in mind, the task is to come up with coefficients that maximize the likelihood that the predicted probability is closest to the observed behavior. So, we would want coefficients for, in the present example, income, age, and ZIP Code that behave as follows:

- They predict a probability closer to 0.0 than to 1.0 for those who don't purchase.
- They predict a probability closer to 1.0 than to 0.0 for those who do purchase.

After we have those predicted probabilities, there's a simple modification that makes them more interpretable. When that modification has been made, you might have the two outcomes outlined next.

Probability of No Purchase Joe, who did not purchase and therefore has a 0 on the Purchased variable, has a predicted probability of 2% that he will purchase. This is as it should be: He didn't purchase, and the coefficients we arrive at tell us that his probability is only 2% that he would purchase.

Probability of Purchase Jane, who did purchase and therefore has a 1 on the Purchased variable, has a predicted probability of 94% that she will purchase. Again, this is as it should be. We want our coefficients to result in a relatively large probability when the actual behavior, a purchase, is represented by a 1.

Putting the Probabilities on a Common Footing

A minor problem exists. The probabilities are of two different events: *No Purchase* and *Purchase*. We need to express one of the two measures as a new variable so that we can also work with a different sort of probability—that of accurately predicting the outcome, whichever one it is.

That's easily done. Right now we have two probabilities, 2% and 94%, for two different people, and the probabilities express the chance that each will make the purchase: Put in terms of numbers, the chance that each will have a value of 1 on the Purchased variable.

That's close to what we want, but it's not quite it. What we have is a way of predicting the probability that someone will buy. But for the purpose of assessing the validity of the logistic regression equation, we also want the probabilities that we're predicting each person's behavior accurately. John, for example, does not purchase, and we predict that his probability of purchasing is 2%. Because there are only two possible outcomes (*No Purchase* and *Purchase*, or 0 and 1), we can simply calculate 100% – 2%, or 98%, as the probability that John would *not* purchase.

If we cast the probability in that way, we can still be reasonably happy with our predictions. In Jane's case, it's 94% that she purchases (and she does). In John's case, it's 98% that he *doesn't* purchase, and he doesn't.

There are various accepted ways to convert the probability of purchasing to the probability of a correct prediction, and they're all equivalent. Suppose the actual outcome, 0 or 1, is

8

in column A and the predicted probability is in column G. An obvious and entirely correct way of making the conversion in Excel is to put this formula in cell H3:

=IF(A3=1,G3,1–G3)

Suppose John's record is in row 3. He didn't purchase, so he has a 0 in cell A3. Our coefficients tell us that he has a 2% chance of purchasing. Because he has a 0 in A3, the formula returns a value of 1 – 0.02, or 98% in cell H3. That is no longer the probability that John purchases, but the probability that he doesn't purchase—in other words, the probability that our coefficients predict the actual outcome.

But if Jane's record is in row 3, then because she purchased, cell A3 contains the value 1. Cell G3 contains 94%, the probability that our coefficients led us to predict. Now the formula in cell H3 returns the value 94% because Jane's record passes the logical test that cell A3 contains the value 1.

I mentioned that there are various ways to reach the same result. I have seen code for logistic regression that was written in the late 1970s when FORTRAN was still the programming language of choice for numeric analysis (but was starting to be supplanted by C). FORTRAN implemented IF-THEN-ELSE structures relatively awkwardly. So, the code used a statement that would look like this if translated into an Excel formula:

=(G3^A3)*(1-G3)^(1–A3)

If Jane is in row 3, with a 1 in A3 and a 94% in G3, then this formula would evaluate as follows:

=(.94^1)*(1–.94)^(1–1)

=.94*(.06^0)

=.94

because any real number (except zero itself) raised to the zero-th power equals 1.

If instead John is in row 3, the formula evaluates as follows:

=(.02^0)*(1–.02)^(1–0)

=1*(.98^1)

=.98

This approach is not as self-documenting as the IF structure in an Excel worksheet formula, and I recommend that you use the IF structure. I have discussed the older approach, based on exponents, so that if you encounter it in some other source, you'll recognize it for the simple conversion that it is, instead of some mysterious mathematical wizardry.

Sum of Log Probabilities Is Log Likelihood

Over hundreds of records, the product of the predicted probabilities can get inconveniently small. These very small numbers are handled pretty easily using current software such as Excel, but historically analysts have preferred to work with logarithms.

> **NOTE**
>
> This is an unfortunate source of some confusion to those who are just starting to study logistic regression. The use of logarithms as a convenient way to measure the overall likelihood *has nothing to do with* the use of logarithms to solve the problems associated with a dichotomous dependent variable.
>
> Early sections of Chapter 7 discussed the problems that arise when neither the probability nor its close cousin, the odds, can take on values smaller than zero. The use of the logarithm of the odds, which this chapter takes up shortly, is necessary to carry out logistic regression.
>
> Using logarithms to measure likelihoods, both individual and overall, is a separate procedure. It is not necessary to use them in this way in order to carry out a logistic regression analysis. It is primarily a convenience, but to quantify likelihood in logarithmic form is conventional in most logistic regression reports that you'll see.

By converting each predicted probability to a logarithm, you can add the results instead of multiplying them. Figure 8.2 shows how this is done.

In Figure 8.2, the range B2:B13 contains hypothetical predicted probabilities for each of 12 records. Their overall likelihood—the likelihood of correctly predicting the outcomes of all twelve records—is the product of all the probabilities.

You can do that in Excel using the PRODUCT( ) worksheet function, and you can find its result, as used here, in cell B16 in Figure 8.2. (The formula itself appears in cell B17.) Even with only 12 records, the product of the probabilities is less than half of one percent; with a more realistic sample size of 100 or more, the product would be considerably smaller.

That's not necessarily a problem for Excel, but you might find it inconvenient to work with such small numbers. An alternative, one that is normally followed in most studies that use logistic regression, is to work with the logs of the probabilities. They also appear in Figure 8.2, in the range D2:D13. It's normal to use the natural logarithm of the probabilities, and the Excel worksheet function that returns the natural log is LN( ). The formulas used to get the natural logarithms are in D2:D13 and are shown, as formulas, in E2:E13.

The sum of the logarithms is in cell D16. It is usually termed the *log likelihood*, although there are some minor transformations and other designations that I'll list shortly.

Figure 8.2
The log of a number less than 1.0 is always negative.

◢	A	B	C	D	E
1		**Predicted Probability**		**Log Predicted Probability**	
2		0.92		-0.083381609	=LN(B2)
3		0.94		-0.061875404	=LN(B3)
4		0.86		-0.15082289	=LN(B4)
5		0.77		-0.261364764	=LN(B5)
6		0.95		-0.051293294	=LN(B6)
7		0.41		-0.891598119	=LN(B7)
8		0.56		-0.579818495	=LN(B8)
9		0.38		-0.967584026	=LN(B9)
10		0.54		-0.616186139	=LN(B10)
11		0.44		-0.820980552	=LN(B11)
12		0.42		-0.867500568	=LN(B12)
13		0.77		-0.261364764	=LN(B13)
14					
15		**Product of Probabilities**		**Sum of Logs**	
16		0.003647291		-5.613770625	
17		=PRODUCT(B2:B13)		=SUM(D2:D13)	
18					
19		**Log of Product**			
20		-5.613770625			
21		=LN(B16)			

Notice that the sum of the logarithms in cell D16 is equal to the value that appears in cell B20. That's the way that logarithms behave: The sum of the logs of the individual probabilities equals the log of the product of the individual probabilities. In Excel worksheet function terms, these two formulas are equivalent:

=LN(PRODUCT(B2:B13))

=SUM(LN(B2:B13))

> **NOTE**
> You would have to enter the latter formula as an array formula because the LN( ) function normally expects a single value, not an array of values, as its argument.

This value, the log likelihood, is the one that we want to maximize. Equivalently, we could maximize the product of the probabilities shown in cell B16.

The log likelihood performs a role that's similar to R^2 in ordinary regression analysis, whether multiple or single. R^2 ranges from 0 to 1.0, and can be considered as a percentage of variability. An R^2 of 1.0—or 100%—means that 100% of the variance in the predicted variable can be explained by variability in the predictor variable or variables.

Of course, such a situation would be completely artificial or trivial. No real-world analysis ever returns an R^2 of 1.0, unless it's a bogus data set or something trivial such as regressing height in inches against height in centimeters. Similarly, an R^2 of 0.0, which means that none of the variability in the dependent variable is explained by variability in the independent variable(s), is bound to be a fantasy. Even simple measurement or sampling error will induce an R^2 that's at least slightly greater than 0.0 (such as 0.01 or 0.02).

You can expect that an R^2 of, say, 0.80 means that you have analyzed variables that are strongly related: When you can predict 80% of the variability because you know the values of the predictor variables, you have put your hands on a strong relationship. And if your calculated R^2 is something like 0.10, you don't have much to work with. Unless you're working with a large sample, an R^2 of 0.10 is not significantly different from 0.0, using criteria that most people would feel comfortable with.

The log likelihood is not bounded in the same way that R^2 is bounded by the minimum and maximum possible values of 0.0 and 1.0. But as you'll see, the closer to 0.0 a log likelihood, the better the fit. Put differently, the closer to 0.0 the log likelihood, the closer you've come to maximizing the estimate of the likelihood.

Calculation of Logit or Log Odds

I've thrown a lot of theory at you in the last few sections of this chapter. I'm not comfortable with that, but it turns out worse if you try to step through the procedures of logistic regression without an overview of where you're trying to get to. This section starts to tie things together with an example, but first a brief recap.

Our goal is to find coefficients for our predictor variables that do the best job of estimating the probability that each member of our data set behaves as he or she actually did. When we get those coefficients, we would like to apply them to a different sample with some confidence that we will therefore know who will purchase and who won't (or who will get sick and who won't, or who will vote and who won't, and so on).

We find the best coefficients by trying out different values for each coefficient, using Solver to help us get the best outcome.

We use the log likelihood as our criterion for the "best" coefficients. The closer that log likelihood is to zero, the closer the product of all the predicted probabilities is to 1.0. And you can get 1.0 as a product of all the probabilities only if they are all 1.0—that is, if your predictions are correct in all the cases. That's an unrealistic goal, of course, but it's the value that we want to shoot at.

Figure 8.3 starts us off. It repeats the raw data that appears in Figure 8.1, along with a place to put the intercept and the coefficients in the range A3:D3. The labels associated with each coefficient are in A2:D2.

> **NOTE**
>
> I have referred to "coefficients" in this chapter as though that term subsumes the intercept along with the coefficients. I have done that to avoid needlessly complicating the text. From this point on, I use the term *intercept* to refer to it, and *coefficients* to refer only to the numbers that are used as coefficients.

Notice the Name Box in Figure 8.3—that's the box to the left of the f_x Insert Function button on the Formula Bar. In Figure 8.3, it contains the name IncomeBeta. I have given that name to cell B3, which is also the active cell. If the active cell has been named, as here, that name appears in the Name Box.

As you'll see, a fair amount of the vocabulary of logistic regression is not standardized. However, many (not all) people who use logistic regression employ the term *beta coefficient* to mean the coefficients that I have mentioned throughout this chapter. Many other writers reserve the term *beta coefficient* for the standardized coefficients and call the coefficients for unstandardized variables *b-coefficients*. I won't get as persnickety as that here. I'll use the term *coefficients*, unencumbered by "beta" and "b-" because it's simpler and avoids the mild confusion sometimes induced by distinguishing raw from standardized variables.

Figure 8.3
It's useful to name the cells that contain the coefficients.

	IncomeBeta	▼	⋮	✕	✓	f_x	0	

	A	B	C	D	E
1		Coefficients			
2	Intercept	Income	Age	Zip Code	
3	1	0	0	0	
4					
5	Purchase	Income ($000)	Age	Zip Code	Logit
6	0	79.015	50	1	1
7	0	79.897	50	1	1
8	0	82.818	47	1	1
9	0	82.210	49	1	1
10	0	87.656	42	1	1
11	0	86.013	47	1	1
12	0	85.032	49	1	1
13	0	82.914	55	1	1
14	0	86.110	51	1	1
15	0	62.224	52	2	1
16	0	86.864	52	1	1
17	0	91.353	55	1	1
18	1	71.891	49	2	1
19	0	98.812	54	1	1
20	1	98.217	55	1	1
21	0	99.678	53	1	1

However, it's convenient to give the coefficients names in the Excel worksheet. I use "beta" as a tag to the variable name; thus, *IncomeBeta* refers to the coefficient used with the variable named Income.

In any case, you multiply the values of the predictor variables by their respective coefficients and add the results together to obtain what's termed the *logit* of the predicted variable for a particular record. For example:

> Logit = Intercept + Beta1*Age + Beta2*Income + Beta3*ZipCode

To distinguish the coefficient that's used with the Age variable from the Age variable itself, I have named the cell that will contain the coefficient for Age as AgeBeta. Similarly, the cells for the Income coefficient and the ZipCode coefficient have been named IncomeBeta and ZipBeta. I have also named cell A3 as Intercept. Using those names, I can create a formula for the logit that looks like this, to avoid the uninformative Beta1, Beta2, and Beta3:

> Logit = Intercept + AgeBeta*Age + IncomeBeta*Income + ZipBeta*ZipCode

In versions of Excel that precede Excel 2007, one way to name a cell is by way of Insert, Name, Define. In Excel 2007 and later, you click the Formulas tab on the Ribbon; then, click Define Name in the Defined Names group.

One more issue regarding defining names to refer to the coefficients: For reasons that I get into later in the chapter, it's often a good idea to run logistic regression analysis on the same data set more than once (the reason has to do with comparing different models). When you do that, you expect to wind up with different values for the coefficients.

Therefore, I like to carry out those different analyses on different worksheets. In turn, it's helpful to use the same names for the beta coefficients on the different worksheets, but to define them as local to the worksheet itself. In that way, the name AgeBeta (for example) can refer to the value in cell C3 when *Sheet1* is active, and to a different value in C3 (or some other cell, for that matter) when *Sheet2* is active.

You make a defined name local to a particular worksheet in the New Name dialog box, which appears when you choose Define Name from the Ribbon's Formulas tab. Choose the worksheet you want from the Scope drop-down box.

Calculating the Logits

Figure 8.3 adds a column to those shown in Figure 8.2. Column E has the label *Logit* in cell E5. The logit is the unit that we want to calculate using the intercept, plus the coefficients multiplied by their associated variables. It is the natural log of the odds, just as discussed in Chapter 7, in the section titled "Moving on to the Log Odds."

We'll find the values for the intercept and coefficients that result in logits, odds, and probabilities that best fit the actual purchase behavior. The process involves setting up these formulas:

- Formulas for the logit values
- Formulas that convert the logit values to odds
- Formulas that convert the odds to probabilities

Logistic regression's approach is to change the values of the intercept and the coefficients. As those changes occur, they bring about changes in the logits (which depend on the intercept and the coefficients), and thus in the odds (which depend on the logits) and thus in the probabilities (which depend on the odds).

At each step, Excel compares the new, trial set of probabilities with the actual behavior (0 or 1, 0% or 100% probability of purchasing) associated with each record. The analysis ends when Excel has determined that any further changes to the intercept and coefficient will be unable to improve the fit between the calculated probabilities and the actual probabilities.

The logits are converted to odds using formulas similar to this:

Odds = EXP(logit)

The logit, as discussed in prior sections, is the log of the odds. That is, using natural logarithms as implied by the use of the LN( ) worksheet function, you raise the base 2.718 to the power of the logit to get the associated odds. Excel does this for you by means of its EXP( ) worksheet function, which is the complement of the LN( ) function.

For example, assume that the odds is 2.0 (in English, that's two-to-one, so the probability is 66.67%). Then the logit, the log of the odds, is returned by this formula:

=LN(2)

which returns 0.6931.

Suppose that the process of running a logistic regression analysis results in a logit of 0.6931, calculated by using the intercept and the products of the coefficients and the predictor variables. Then you can find the odds associated with that logit value by means of this formula:

=EXP(.6931)

which returns 2, or the *odds*, or the *antilog* of .6931.

> **NOTE**
>
> If you want to delve more deeply into the relationship between logs and antilogs, the next section dips gently into that topic. If you feel no strong urge to do so, you can certainly skip it without missing anything crucial about logistic regression.

When we have the odds from the logit, we can use formulas similar to this one in order to convert the odds to probabilities:

Probability = Odds / (1+Odds)

So, after you have given names to the cells that contain the intercept and coefficients, you can enter a formula such as this in cell E6 to get the logit for the record in row 6 (given the layout used in Figure 8.3):

=Intercept+IncomeBeta*B6+AgeBeta*C6+ZipBeta*D6

Then simply copy cell E6 and paste it into the range E7:E41. You get a series of the value 1.0, because as I've set up the worksheet—in particular, the values for the intercept and the coefficients—the formula resolves to this in cell E6:

=1+0*B6+0*C6+0*D6

and similarly in rows 7 through 41. The intercept has been manually set to 1, and the coefficients have each been manually set to 0. We'll be using Solver to replace the 1 and 0's with best-fit values for the intercept and the coefficients.

Logs and Antilogs

Recall from Chapter 7's section titled "Moving on to the Log Odds" that the logit is defined as the logarithm of the odds. Moving in the other direction, we can obtain the odds from the logit by taking the antilog of the logit. In Excel, the EXP() worksheet function returns the antilog, using 2.71828, the base of the natural logarithms.

That can be a little confusing at first, and this is a good place to review the relationship between logs and antilogs.

The logarithm of a number A is the power, or exponent, to which you raise another number B to get A. The number B is called the *base* and using natural logarithms, B is 2.71828.

Now, the natural logarithm of the number 10 is 2.3026:

LN(10) = 2.3026

In that case:

2.71828^2.3026 = 10

The *antilog* reverses this, and Excel's EXP() function returns the antilog. So:

EXP(2.3026) = 10

And in that case, this is still true:

2.71828^2.3026 = 10

When you use 2.71828 as the base, you are using natural logarithms. Excel's worksheet function LN() returns the natural logarithm of its argument. LN(2.71828) = 1, because 2.71828 raised to the first power is 2.71828.

(There are bases other than 2.71828 that are often used, including 2, the binary logarithm, and 10, the common logarithm. The natural logarithm is useful for a variety of reasons that aren't strictly relevant to this discussion.)

Given the relationship between a number and its logarithm, we can get the odds from the logit. Recall that the logit is defined as the log of the odds:

LN(Odds) = Logit

8

Therefore:

EXP(Logit) = Odds

Using Defined Names Instead of Cell References in the Logit Formulas

Earlier you saw that the formula used to calculate the logit in cell E6 of Figure 8.3 looks like this:

=Intercept+IncomeBeta*B6+AgeBeta*C6+ZipBeta*D6

If you have not given names to the cells that contain the intercept and the beta coefficients, then the formula that calculates the logit in cell E6 might look like this:

=$A$3+$B$3*B6+$C$3*C6+$D$3*D6

Notice first that the addresses of the cells that contain the intercept and the beta coefficients, A3 through D3, have replaced the defined names in the formula. That forces you to check that you're multiplying the right variable by the right coefficient.

Then, the cell addresses have been made absolute. If they were relative addresses—say, A3 instead of $A$3—then copying the formula down would result in this formula in E7:

=A4+B4*B7+C4*C7+D4*D7

and you'd wind up with the wrong cells for the intercept and the coefficients.

In contrast, defined names are absolute references by default. You can make them relative if you want to, but if you don't do anything special then the defined name is an absolute reference.

So, naming the cells that contain the intercept and the coefficients requires a little extra work at the outset. But it saves you work in the long run, it makes your formula more self-documenting, and it helps guard against mistakes in the addresses of the intercept and coefficients.

> **NOTE**
> The word *logit*, the value that we are calculating, is pronounced in various ways. If you go searching for "logit" and "pronounce" on the Web, you'll find posts from experienced statisticians plaintively asking for a good, solid reference for the proper pronunciation of the word. Some pronounce the "o" as a long "a" as in "saw." Others pronounce it as a long "o" as in "flow." Some use a soft "g" as in "page" and others use a hard "g" as in "grasp." For what it's worth, the Shorter Oxford English Dictionary recommends "law-git." The word itself is apparently a contraction of *logarithmic unit*, much as *bit* is a contraction of *binary digit* (a usage attributed to the eminent statistician John Tukey).

From the Logit to the Odds and Probability

Figure 8.4 takes the process to the next-to-last step by incorporating the formulas described in the prior section to obtain the odds and the associated probabilities.

Column F in Figure 8.4 contains the odds that are based on the logit. For example, cell F6 contains this formula:

=EXP(E6)

Because of the relationship between odds and probabilities, we can calculate the probabilities from the odds, and that takes place in column G. The formula for odds from probabilities (originally shown in Chapter 7) is

$Odds = P/(1-P)$

Figure 8.4
The figures for odds and probabilities won't make sense until we solve for the proper intercept and coefficients.

	A	B	C	D	E	F	G	H	I
1			Coefficients						
2	Intercept	Income	Age	Zip Code		Sum Log Likelihood:	-33.2774		
3	1	0	0	0					
4									
5	Purchase	Income ($000)	Age	Zip Code	Logit	Odds	Predicted Probability that Y = 1	Predicted Probability that Y = Y	Log Likelihood
6	0	79.015	50	1	1	2.71828	0.7311	0.2689	-1.3133
7	0	79.897	50	1	1	2.71828	0.7311	0.2689	-1.3133
8	0	82.818	47	1	1	2.71828	0.7311	0.2689	-1.3133
9	0	82.210	49	1	1	2.71828	0.7311	0.2689	-1.3133
10	0	87.656	42	1	1	2.71828	0.7311	0.2689	-1.3133
11	0	86.013	47	1	1	2.71828	0.7311	0.2689	-1.3133
12	0	85.032	49	1	1	2.71828	0.7311	0.2689	-1.3133
13	0	82.914	55	1	1	2.71828	0.7311	0.2689	-1.3133
14	0	86.110	51	1	1	2.71828	0.7311	0.2689	-1.3133
15	0	62.224	52	2	1	2.71828	0.7311	0.2689	-1.3133
16	0	86.864	52	1	1	2.71828	0.7311	0.2689	-1.3133
17	0	91.353	55	1	1	2.71828	0.7311	0.2689	-1.3133
18	1	71.891	49	2	1	2.71828	0.7311	0.7311	-0.3133
19	0	98.812	54	1	1	2.71828	0.7311	0.2689	-1.3133
20	1	98.217	55	1	1	2.71828	0.7311	0.7311	-0.3133
21	0	99.678	53	1	1	2.71828	0.7311	0.2689	-1.3133

where the letter *P* stands for probability. You reverse the process, getting the probability from the odds, with this formula:

Probability = $O/(1+O)$

where the letter *O* stands for Odds. More specifically, in Figure 8.4, you get the probability using the following formula in G6, which is then copied and pasted into G7:G41:

=F6/(1+F6)

As shown in Figure 8.4, that formula returns 0.7311 for all records. That's because the intercept and coefficients have not yet been optimized. With an intercept of 1.0 and each coefficient at 0.0, as shown, the logit must equal 1.0 (see the prior discussion in the section titled "Calculating the Logits"). That inevitably leads to odds of 2.718, the base of the natural logarithms, because EXP(1) equals 2.718; the associated probability is 0.7311, the result of 2.718/(1+2.718).

Furthermore, the calculated probability is 0.7311 in all cases. As discussed in this chapter's section titled "Putting the Probabilities on a Common Footing," the probability shown in column G is the probability that the record's value on the Purchase variable in column A is 1. That's conceptually and arithmetically different from the probability that the logit leads to a correct decision about the record's actual value on Purchase.

When we omit the Income, Age, and ZIP Code variables from the logit equation—and that's what we are doing when their coefficients are each set equal to zero—then we're predicting on the basis of the intercept alone. And because the intercept is set to 1.0, each record has the same calculated value for probability of Purchase.

But the intercept hasn't been optimized yet either. When it is, when you run the logistic regression on the basis of the intercept alone, the result is as shown in Figure 8.5.

Figure 8.5
Using only an optimized intercept, the predicted probability in column G is the mean of the predicted variable—here, Purchase.

| G6 | | | f_x | =F6/(1+F6) | | | | |

	A	B	C	D	E	F	G	H	I
1			Coefficients						
2	Intercept	Income	Age	Zip Code		Sum Log Likelihood:	-24.056945		
3	-0.45199	0.00000	0.00000	0					
4									
5	Purchase	Income ($000)	Age	Zip Code	Logit	Odds	Predicted Probability that Y = 1	Predicted Probability that Y = Y	Log Likelihood
6	0	79.015	50	1	-0.45	0.63636	0.3889	0.6111	-0.4925
7	0	79.897	50	1	-0.45	0.63636	0.3889	0.6111	-0.4925
8	0	82.818	47	1	-0.45	0.63636	0.3889	0.6111	-0.4925
9	0	82.210	49	1	-0.45	0.63636	0.3889	0.6111	-0.4925
10	0	87.656	42	1	-0.45	0.63636	0.3889	0.6111	-0.4925
11	0	86.013	47	1	-0.45	0.63636	0.3889	0.6111	-0.4925
12	0	85.032	49	1	-0.45	0.63636	0.3889	0.6111	-0.4925
13	0	82.914	55	1	-0.45	0.63636	0.3889	0.6111	-0.4925
14	0	86.110	51	1	-0.45	0.63636	0.3889	0.6111	-0.4925
15	0	62.224	52	2	-0.45	0.63636	0.3889	0.6111	-0.4925
16	0	86.864	52	1	-0.45	0.63636	0.3889	0.6111	-0.4925
17	0	91.353	55	1	-0.45	0.63636	0.3889	0.6111	-0.4925
18	1	71.891	49	2	-0.45	0.63636	0.3889	0.3889	-0.9445
19	0	98.812	54	1	-0.45	0.63636	0.3889	0.6111	-0.4925
20	1	98.217	55	1	-0.45	0.63636	0.3889	0.3889	-0.9445
21	0	99.678	53	1	-0.45	0.63636	0.3889	0.6111	-0.4925

(I show you how to get the optimized value for the intercept, as well as for the coefficients, shortly.) After the value of the intercept is optimized, the probability, shown in column G, that the record has a Purchase value of 1.0 is a constant 0.3889. That's the average value of the Purchase variable across all the cases in the analysis. Without any information about income, age or ZIP Code, the best you can do to predict any given record's value on Purchase is the average of all the values. Conceptually, this is very similar to the notion of the expected value of the dependent variable in ordinary least-squares analysis. Absent additional information, the best prediction—the expected value—is the mean of the predicted variable. But the probability that a given record has a Purchase value of 1.0 isn't all we're after. We also want the probability, based on the intercept plus the three predictor variables, that the record has the Purchase value that was actually observed.

Therefore, column H adjusts the probability from column G according to whether the Purchase value is 1 or 0. (This adjustment is discussed earlier in this chapter, in the section titled "Putting the Probabilities on a Common Footing.") If it's 1, we use the column G probability. If it's 0, we use 1 minus the column G probability. The formulas in column H follow this pattern:

=IF(A6=1,G6,1–G6)

As in columns E through G, we copy and paste that formula into the range H7:H41.

From the Probability to the Log Likelihood

Finally, we come to the calculation of the log likelihood for any given record. This formula is in cell I6 of Figure 8.5:

=LN(H6)

It is copied and pasted down into I7:I41. The natural logarithm of each probability is referred to as the log likelihood. Somewhat confusingly, so is the sum of those logs—that is, the total of the individual log likelihoods is also often called the log likelihood.

We'll be working with the logs of the probabilities, particularly with their sum. The logic of the relationship between the probabilities and their logs is important and I discuss it next.

Excel has three worksheet functions that return logarithms:

- LOG10() returns logarithms to base 10, or common logs.
- LN() returns logarithms to base 2.718, or natural logs.
- LOG() returns logarithms to a base that you specify in the function's arguments (see the following Note).

The log of 1 is 0 regardless of the base in use. That's because, as discussed earlier in this chapter, any number other than 0 raised to the zero-th power equals 1. A logarithm is an exponent. Therefore, whether you use base 10 for common logs or 2.718 for natural logs or 2 for binary logs, the base raised to the zero-th power is 1:

LOG10(1) = 0, and 10^0 = 1

LN(1) = 0, and 2.718^0 = 1

LOG(1,2) = 0, and 2^0 = 1

And the log of a number smaller than 1 is less than zero. Again in terms of exponents:

LOG10(.9) = –0.046, and 10^–0.046 = 0.9

LN(.9) = –0.105, and 2.718^–0.105 = 0.9

LOG(.9,2) = –0.152, and 2^–0.152 = 0.9

> **NOTE** You're not likely to have much use for this nicety in logistic regression, but the Excel worksheet function LOG( ) enables you to specify any base for the logarithm. So, in the prior example, LOG(.9,2) calls for the logarithm of 0.9 to base 2.

As discussed in Chapter 7, there is no defined lower limit to a logarithm. The closer that a fractional number is to 0, the larger its (negative) logarithm. So:

LN(.1) = –2.3

LN(.01) = –4.6

LN(.001) = –6.9

Now, the probabilities that are derived in column H of Figure 8.5 are all less than 1.0. All such probabilities must by definition be less than or equal to 1.0, and greater than or equal to 0.0. Therefore, the logarithm of a probability must be a negative number.

What if the probabilities in column H were all close to 1.0? That is, what if the coefficients we use result in estimates that are very close to the actual Purchase behavior? The closer that each individual probability is to 1.0, the closer the product of all the probabilities is to 1.0. So, the product of smaller probabilities such as these:

.65 * .72 * .59 * .68 * .71 = .13

is closer to 0.0, but the product of larger probabilities such as these:

90. * .95 * .87 * .94 * .88 = .61

is closer to 1.0.

Each of the first set of probabilities just given is smaller than each of the probabilities in the second set. The result is that the product of all the first set of probabilities is smaller than the product of the second set.

One of the properties of logarithms is that the log of the product of several numbers is the sum of the logs of the individual numbers. So, using the set of probabilities just shown, the sum of the logs is

$$LN(.90) + LN(.95) + LN(.87) + LN(.94) + LN(.88) = -0.486$$

which equals the log of their product:

$$LN(.61) = -0.486$$

All this gets us here: We would like to set our coefficients to values that result in each individual record probability in column H being as close to 1.0 as possible. That outcome would cause the overall product of all the individual probabilities to be as close to 1.0 as possible.

> **NOTE** You'll sometimes see that product operation referred to as the *continued product*. It is symbolized as Π, the uppercase Greek letter pi. It works much as Σ does in summation: ΣX_i means the sum of i values of X, and ΠX_i means the product of i values of X. Excel's worksheet function to return that product is, helpfully, PRODUCT( ).

Furthermore, setting each probability as close as possible to 1.0 would cause the sum of the logarithms of the probabilities to be as close to 0.0 as possible. Bear in mind that:

- The logarithm of 1.0 is 0.0.
- The logarithm of a product is the sum of the logarithms of the product's factors.

Therefore, coefficients that result in an overall product of the probabilities that is as close as possible to 1.0 will also result in a logarithm of the overall product that is as close to 0.0 as possible.

The next step in the process is to use Solver to find the best coefficients—those that result in a continued product of column H probabilities that comes as close as possible to 1.0. However, particularly when you are working with a large number of observations, that continued product can become excruciatingly small—so small that it's difficult for the software's algorithms to successfully reach the best set of coefficients.

But if you hand the sum of the *logarithms* of those probabilities over to Solver and ask it to find the coefficients that cause the sum to be as close as possible to 0.0, the algorithms have a much easier time. This is the reason that column I in Figure 8.5 calculates the logs of the probabilities.

Those logs are summed in cell H2. Because the probabilities are by definition positive fractional values, their logarithms must all be negative values. Their sum, the log likelihood, is therefore a negative number, and the task is to find a set of coefficients that results in a log likelihood that is close to 0.0. A log likelihood of –20 would be better than –50. A log likelihood of –10 would be better than –15.

Next up: How to get Solver to find regression coefficients that bring the sum of the logarithms in H2, the log likelihood, as close as possible to 0.0—the logarithmic equivalent of getting the product of the probabilities as close as possible to 1.0.

Running Solver on the Logistic Regression Problem

You need your data laid out in a fashion similar to that shown in Figure 8.4 or Figure 8.5. You also need to have Solver installed in Excel, as shown earlier in this chapter in the section titled "About Solver." Then take these steps:

1. With the exact layout shown in Figure 8.5, select cell H2. More generally, select the cell in your worksheet that contains the sum of the logarithms that you want to bring as close as possible to 0.0.

2. Click the Ribbon's Data tab.

3. Click Solver in the Analysis group. The dialog box shown in Figure 8.6 appears.

4. Because you began by selecting your criterion cell, its address appears in the Set Objective (or Target Cell) edit box. Click the Max radio button to signal Solver that you want to maximize the (negative, as we've seen) value in the criterion cell—that is, bring it from its current negative value to as close to 0.0 as possible.

5. Click in the By Changing Variable Cells box.

6. Drag through cells A3:D3, or wherever you have placed the intercept and coefficients, so that the address of that range appears in the By Changing Variable Cells box.

7. Make sure that the Make Unconstrained Variables Non-Negative checkbox is cleared.

8. Choose GRG Nonlinear in the Solving Method drop-down box. (If you're using Excel 2007, click the Options button and make sure that the Assume Linear Model box is cleared.)

Figure 8.6
Solver's dialog box labels your criterion cell as Target Cell or as Set Objective, depending on the Excel version you're running. Its purpose is the same regardless of the label.

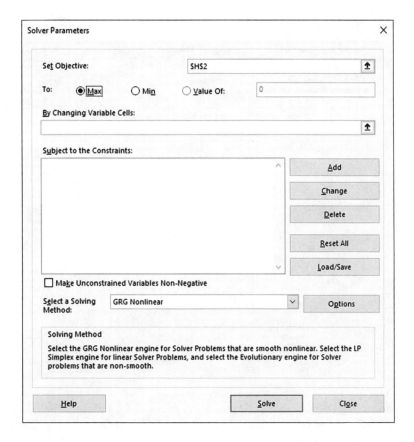

9. Click the Options button to get the Options dialog box. (If you're using Excel 2010 or later, click the GRG Nonlinear tab box; see Figure 8.7.) In the Derivatives area, click the Central button. Click OK to return to the main Solver dialog box.

10. Click Solve.

Figure 8.7
The dialog box looks different in versions prior to Excel 2010, but the Central Derivatives option is available in all versions.

Solver tries various values for the intercept and the coefficients until it maximizes the value of the criterion cell, H2 in this example, so that the sum of the log likelihoods is as close to 0.0 as it can come with this data. Solver reports the result by way of the dialog box shown in Figure 8.8.

Figure 8.8
If Solver does not report that it has found a solution, you should usually choose Restore Original Values and Return to Solver Parameters Dialog.

Solver Results   ✕

Solver found a solution. All Constraints and optimality
conditions are satisfied.   Reports

                                                             Answer
⊙ Keep Solver Solution   Sensitivity
                                                             Limits
○ Restore Original Values

☐ Return to Solver Parameters Dialog   ☐ Outline Reports

  ⎡   OK   ⎤   Cancel   Save Scenario...

Solver found a solution. All Constraints and optimality conditions are satisfied.

When the GRG engine is used, Solver has found at least a local optimal solution. When Simplex LP
is used, this means Solver has found a global optimal solution.

If all looks good in the Solver Results dialog box, click OK to return to the worksheet. (If not, refer to the following Note.)

If you're comfortable with Excel's Scenario Manager, consider saving the Solver's results as a scenario. The Variable Cells you identify in Solver become Changing Cells in the Scenario Manager. In this way, you can save different combinations of coefficients as different scenarios. Although this approach can work well, my personal preference is to save the different sets of coefficients and their outcomes on different worksheets.

The result of all this is to locate an intercept and coefficients that best predict the actual purchase outcomes. Figure 8.9 shows the best outcome for this set of data.

The logistic regression equation that you wind up with is this one, applied to the values for the first record in row 6:

$$= -20.001+.091*B6+.127*C6+2.584*D6$$

That equation returns the maximum-likelihood estimate logit in cell E6. To convert it to a probability is easy enough. We've been through this before, in the section titled "From the Logit to the Odds and Probability," but it's helpful to review the process with the actual values after Solver has optimized the intercept and coefficients.

First use the logit's antilog to get the associated odds:

$$=EXP(E6)$$

Figure 8.9
The values in A3:D3 have been set to optimal values for this logistic regression problem.

	A	B	C	D	E	F	G	H	I
H2				fx	=SUM(I6:I41)				
1			Coefficients						
2	Intercept	Income	Age	Zip Code			Sum Log Likelihood:	-14.160149	
3	-20.0005	0.09112	0.12669	2.5843					
4									
5	Purchase	Income ($000)	Age	Zip Code	Logit	Odds	Predicted Probability that Y = 1	Predicted Probability that Y = Y	Log Likelihood
6	0	79.015	50	1	-3.8824	0.02060	0.0202	0.9798	-0.0204
7	0	79.897	50	1	-3.8021	0.02232	0.0218	0.9782	-0.0221
8	0	82.818	47	1	-3.916	0.01992	0.0195	0.9805	-0.0197
9	0	82.210	49	1	-3.718	0.02428	0.0237	0.9763	-0.0240
10	0	87.656	42	1	-4.1086	0.01643	0.0162	0.9838	-0.0163
11	0	86.013	47	1	-3.6249	0.02665	0.0260	0.9740	-0.0263
12	0	85.032	49	1	-3.4609	0.03140	0.0304	0.9696	-0.0309
13	0	82.914	55	1	-2.8938	0.05537	0.0525	0.9475	-0.0539
14	0	86.110	51	1	-3.1093	0.04463	0.0427	0.9573	-0.0437
15	0	62.224	52	2	-2.5747	0.07618	0.0708	0.9292	-0.0734
16	0	86.864	52	1	-2.9139	0.05426	0.0515	0.9485	-0.0528
17	0	91.353	55	1	-2.1248	0.11945	0.1067	0.8933	-0.1128
18	1	71.891	49	2	-2.0739	0.12569	0.1117	0.1117	-2.1923
19	0	98.812	54	1	-1.5719	0.20765	0.1719	0.8281	-0.1887

in cell F6. You can then convert the odds in F6 to the associated probability in cell G6:

=F6/(1+F6)

The value calculated in cell G6 is still the probability that the record in row 6 was a purchaser—that is, has a 1 in column A instead of a 0. So we keep that probability, or p, in column H if there's a 1 in A6, and otherwise put $(1 - p)$ in H6: the probability that the record has a 0 in A6.

=IF(A6=1,G6,1-G6)

Finally we put the log likelihood for the particular record detailed in row 6 into cell I6:

=LN(H6)

With the intercept and the coefficients optimized, you are in a position to classify new, prospective purchasers. With data on income, age, and ZIP Code for, say, one thousand prospects, you can use the logistic regression equation to assign a logit to each prospect, and then quickly convert the logit to a probability for each prospect that he or she will purchase.

But please finish this chapter first.

NOTE

There are various ways that Solver—or any nonlinear solution tool, for that matter—can go wrong and inform you that it can't find a solution. If this happens to you, you should first restore the original values (see Figure 8.8). Then check the options you have set for Solver. Make sure that the maximum time to solution and the maximum number of iterations are not set to some absurd levels.

At times it can help to give Solver an assist by setting the beginning values of the intercept and the coefficients differently—closer, perhaps, to the values that you think they will converge to.

Most important, make sure that the logic of your analysis makes sense. For example, don't tell Solver to minimize a negative log likelihood; you're likely to wind up trying to raise 0 to the 0th power (0^0), which many, apparently including Excel's architects, regard as an indeterminate quantity.

Comparing Excel with R: A Demonstration

It's one thing for you to read about this analysis and examine the worksheets available from the publisher's download site (www.quepublishing.com/title/9780789758354). It's quite another to arrange a benchmark: to compare the results you get from Excel with a different analysis package.

I want you to be able to make that kind of comparison, in order to convince yourself that you can get a reasonably sophisticated statistical analysis from Excel. More important, you should feel comfortable that my descriptions of what happens inside a logistic regression done in Excel do in fact lead to the same outcome as you get from a specifically statistical application such as SAS or R.

But you've already bought Excel and it's not fair to ask you also to buy SAS or SPSS or Stata or some other expensive application. Fortunately, the freeware application R is generally available for download. This section briefly describes how to obtain R if you don't have it already. You can then benchmark the results that Excel provides, as shown in the prior section, against R's results for the same data set.

I show you R's results, and how to get them, in this section, so that you can run the analysis in a different environment. Or, if you prefer, you can make the comparison without obtaining R; this section shows you R's results on the data set analyzed in the prior section.

Getting R

You can download R itself from this site: http://cran.r-project.org/.

That site gives you free access to R's base system. You need that if you want to run R itself. However, the base system includes only the software needed to run logistic regression with a binary (also termed *binomial*) outcome variable. That software consists of a function named *glm* and this chapter includes an example of its use. To handle a data set with three or more outcomes (usually termed *multinomial*) you need to download and install a software package specifically designed for that sort of outcome variable. In R, that package is named *mlogit* and again you'll find an example of its use in this chapter.

Much of R's functionality is available in the form of what R terms *contributed packages*: software that R can use, much like an Excel add-in, to extend its analysis capabilities. As I write this in early 2017, the R site has more than 3,500 contributed packages available for download, with names ranging from *A3* to *zyp*. Both R itself and the contributed packages are freeware.

You can download the contributed logistic regression package named mlogit by choosing Install Packages from R's Packages menu. There are other contributed packages for R that compute logistic regression analyses. I do not necessarily recommend mlogit over the others. I am simply more familiar with mlogit and in general have confidence in its results.

The site http://cran.r-project.org/ has instructions for installing R and contributed packages.

Running a Logistic Analysis in R

This section describes how you can get a logistic regression analysis from R, assuming that you have a data set to analyze, and that you have obtained and installed the R base system and the mlogit contributed package. Before going into the details, though, you might wonder why you would bother to use Excel for logistic regression instead of R.

I think that there are some pretty good reasons to use Excel, although they're not what one would think of as technical reasons.

User Interface

One reason I use Excel is that I have to steel myself to deal with R's user interface. It's clunky (as you'll soon see). I know that there are plenty of graphic user interfaces for R that have been devised to overcome this drawback, but I don't like them either.

Charts

Another reason is that Excel's charting capabilities are so strong. R does have charting capabilities that go well beyond the simple text-based charts offered by the early versions of, for example, Systat. But I prefer not to have to jump through hoops necessary to get the charts in R, and I just don't regard R's charts as at the same level of visual impact, automatic response to recalculations, and ease of use as Excel's.

Live Data

I frequently work with data that's live, using updates that are no more than an hour old. I find it convenient to have Excel workbooks linked to the live data sources: sometimes via xml scripts, sometimes via ODBC links to relational databases. I find it much easier to set those up in Excel than it is in R.

Diagnostics

R's diagnostics are occasionally obscure or even missing. For example, it can happen that you define an object, such as a data set, using a name that's the same as one already reserved and used by a contributed package. Although this can happen in virtually any programming language (certainly including Excel), most languages will let you know that you've tried to use a reserved word. R does not necessarily do this, and might simply terminate processing with an obscure, uninformative error message.

Nevertheless, there are reasons that I like to use R to supplement analysis that I do in Excel. R gives me access to certain multiple comparison procedures such as the Tukey HSD test that rely on reference distributions (in the HSD test, that's the q distribution) that Excel does not offer. R is a good resource for checking the results of statistical analyses that I run in Excel. And there's no question that R is much faster for any analysis, such as logistic regression, that would require considerable setup on an Excel worksheet.

That said, let's get on to a demonstration of using R for a logistic regression. First we need some data.

Importing a csv File into R

Two good ways to get a data file into an R data frame involve importing a comma separated values, or csv, file, and pulling the data in directly from an open Excel workbook. This section describes how to get data from a csv file; the next section shows you how to get the data directly from Excel.

You should start out with a worksheet that contains your data only: an Excel list with variable names in the first row of each column followed by rows that represent individual records. Figure 8.1 is in general a good example of the sort of layout you should use, but I recommend that, as shown, you stick with simple, one-word headers in the first row, and that you avoid special characters such as dollar signs. There's no point in getting involved with how R might interpret, for example, a tilde in a column header.

> **NOTE** R has some idiosyncratic rules about how it handles variable names. In general, for example, a variable name that begins with a period followed by a number (such as `.3factor`) causes an error if you submit it to a statistical function—for example, `mean(.3factor)`. But a disallowed name causes no problem if you submit its data frame to a function, such as `str`, that merely lists the data frame's contents or structure.

With that worksheet active, save the workbook as a .csv file. (The .csv extension stands for *comma separated values*.) The steps are easy enough:

1. Activate the worksheet with your data.
2. Click the Ribbon's File tab, and choose Save As from the navigation bar on the left.
3. On the Save As dialog box, locate the Save as Type drop-down box at the bottom of the window. Click its down-arrow and choose CSV (Comma delimited) (*.csv).
4. Enter a different name for the file, if you wish, in the File Name edit box, and click Save. Note the location where you have saved the file, so that you can pass it along to R.

If your workbook contains more than one worksheet, Excel warns you that CSV files cannot save more than one sheet. That's okay—all you want is the one sheet. Click Save.

Excel might then warn you that a CSV file cannot support certain Excel features, such as charts or pivot tables, that might be in the worksheet you want to save. If your worksheet contains data only, as I recommended earlier in this section, go ahead and click Yes. Otherwise, if it's important to retain those features, you might copy the data to a new workbook and initiate the save from there.

When the file has been saved as a CSV file, exit Excel or simply switch to Windows, and then start R. You'll get some preliminary information about R, and then the command prompt: >. You enter R commands following each prompt; you get a new prompt after each command that you enter.

What follows is the sequence of R commands—along with comments—needed to execute a logistic regression analysis on the data last shown and analyzed in Figure 8.9. The commands that you submit to R all begin with a > mark.

```
> mydata <- read.csv("C:/Documents and Settings/t/Desktop/Purchases.csv")
```

The prior statement instructs R to read a CSV file, identified by its path and name within the parentheses and double quote marks.

> **NOTE**
> R requires that you use forward slashes (/) instead of backslashes (\) in file paths. You can also use two consecutive backslashes in place of a single backslash—for example, C:\\Documents and Settings\\t\\Desktop\\Purchases.csv. If you'd like to avoid the complexities involved in specifying the file's full path in the read.csv statement, you can use the Change Dir item in the R's File menu to re-set the default directory. Then just use this:
>
> mydata <– read.csv("Purchases.csv")

The data in the CSV file is assigned to a data frame that you have declared just by using its name, *mydata* in conjunction with the read.csv function. The assignment is carried out by one of R's assignment operators, <–. Note that the assignment operator consists of two characters: the "less than" symbol, <, and the dash, –.

You now have imported the contents of the CSV file into a data frame named *mydata*. Before I move ahead with analyzing the data I like to look at the structure and at least some of the data frame's contents, just to reassure myself that I'm working with what I expect the data frame to contain. In preparation for checking the data I've imported, I often find it convenient to use R's attach function. Doing so is not a requirement but it can be helpful. In this case you might use this:

```
> attach(mydata)
```

The data frame named *mydata* is added to R's search path. Using the attach function can make life a little easier. After a data frame has been attached, you can use the names of variables in that data frame without qualifying them by means of the data frame's name. When you have attached *mydata*, for example, your R commands could refer to the variable Purchase.

But if you haven't attached *mydata*, you need to refer to the variable as mydata$Purchase. The use of the *mydata* variable tells R where to look for the variable named Purchase; the dollar sign ($) is used to separate the name of the data frame from the name of the variable.

> **NOTE**
> Be careful if you attach more than one data frame. Suppose you have a variable named Purchase in a data frame named *mydata1* and also in another named *mydata2*. If you attach *mydata1* first and then attach *mydata2*, R tells you that Purchase is masked from *mydata1*. If you see that sort of message, either don't attach both data frames, or change any duplicate variable names before you attach them. You can unattach a data frame by using the detach function.

```
> names(mydata)
```

R is asked to report back the names of the variables in the file. These are the same as the headers in the Excel list that was saved to the CSV file: Purchase, Income, Age, and Zip. R responds by listing the variable names:

```
[1] "Purchase" "Income" "Age" "Zip"
> table(Purchase)
```

R is told to display a table showing the number of instances (22 and 14 in the CSV file) for the values in the Purchase variable. R responds as follows:

```
Purchase
 0  1
22 14
```

There are 22 instances of the value 0 for Purchase, and 14 instances of the value 1. By using the attach function first, you can use table(Purchase) instead of table(mydata$Purchase).

The str function returns information about the variables in a data frame:

```
> str(mydata)
```

R responds:

```
'data.frame':   36 obs. of  4 variables:
 $ Purchase: num  0 0 0 0 0 0 0 0 0 ...
 $ Income  : num  79 79.9 82.8 82.2 87.7 ...
 $ Age     : num  50 50 47 49 42 47 49 55 51 52 ...
 $ Zip     : num  1 1 1 1 1 1 1 1 1 2 ...
```

The sort of information you can get from functions such as the names, the table and the str functions can assure you that the data you imported has come across to R properly.

Importing From an Open Workbook Into R

The preceding section discusses how to import into an R data frame a CSV data file, typically created by another application such as Excel, Access, or even QuickBooks. That approach to getting data into R usually works perfectly well, but it can be annoying to have to specify the path to the CSV file. Back in the day, it was possible simply to specify something such as C:\mydata.csv. Today, you probably have to navigate through a thicket of folders including one that identifies the user, possibly a Documents folder, and a hierarchy of any project folders that you might have set up. This is so even if you are using the Change Dir command in R's main menu to navigate from one working directory to another.

Add to all that the necessity of replacing backslashes in the file's address with either forward slashes or double backslashes, and even users with more patience than I have find it an annoying way to get data from another application into R.

There's another way that I'm partial to, largely because my clients and I make heavy use of Excel for various analyses. R's DescTools package includes a function named XLGetRange that imports a range of data in the active Excel worksheet directly into an R data frame.

To use XLGetRange, you first have to install it—it's a contributed package. You also need a package named RDCOMClient, so you might as well install it as long as you're installing from R's site.

NOTE You need to install RDCOMClient specifically, but when it comes time to use it, the function XLGetRange calls RDCOMClient automatically. As of early 2017, RDCOMClient does not work with Excel running on Apple computers, so if that's your setup you need to opt for another way to pull data into an R data frame.

After DescTools and RDCOMClient are installed, you can use them to import data directly from an Excel workbook using these steps:

1. Open the Excel workbook that contains the data you want to import.

2. Activate the worksheet that contains the data you want to import.

3. Select the range of data to import. Include column headers if you want, but it's best to omit special characters from the headers.

4. Switch to R. Enter these two commands:

```
> library(DescTools)
> MyDataFrame <- XLGetRange(header = TRUE)
```

You should now have available in R a new data frame named MyDataFrame that contains the records and variables that are selected on Excel's active worksheet. You can use functions such as names, table and str to make sure that the data entered the data frame as you expected.

Understanding the Long Versus Wide Shape

Suppose that you are analyzing the behavior of prospective customers who are shopping for a new car, a particular model of Ford sedan. You're interested in a simple, binary outcome variable: whether or not the customer makes the purchase. But you have three variables that might help predict that behavior: the customer's income, whether the customer has a trade-in, and the new car's sticker price.

In this sort of situation, matters are straightforward. The customer either makes or does not make the purchase of that model. The customer's income does not vary as a function of whether the purchase is made. The sticker price may vary with the customer—because different customers patronize different car dealers—but not with the purchase decision. And the customer either has or doesn't have a trade-in.

So all the available and pertinent information regarding a particular customer can be contained in a single record in a data frame: the customer's decision (yes/no), the customer's income, the presence of a trade-in, and the sticker price.

Now suppose that you are not analyzing a simple binary outcome such as Yes versus No, but one in which the customer is choosing either a Ford, a GM, or a Toyota. In this case, things get more complicated. You probably want to account for different sticker prices for each make of car. And, of course, the outcome variable is no longer buys versus doesn't buy; it's the chosen make of car instead. (With more than two possible outcomes, this is a multinomial rather than binomial design. To keep the multinomial discussion simpler, I'm ignoring the possibility that the customer will make no purchase at all.)

Now you have a choice to make regarding how you store your data. A flat-file structure, such as one usually adopted in Excel workbooks or R data frames, has one sort of record. In this example, that's the customer. It would be typical to store the customer's choice in one variable, the cost of the Ford in another variable and the cost of the other two makes of car in two additional variables.

One drawback to this approach is that you generally need to reserve at least one variable for each possible choice. And three months into your data-gathering process, you suddenly find that you need to include some customers who decide to buy a BMW instead of a Ford, GM, or Toyota. Now you need to add a variable for the BMW's sticker price to all the records of customers who never considered a BMW.

Relational database systems solve this problem by arranging for *parent* and *child* records. In this case the customer would be the parent record, which would include information on the customer's income and whether a trade-in was involved. Each parent record would be associated with child records, which would store the name of the make of car and its sticker price. The association would be maintained by record IDs: So, each child record would also contain the record ID of the parent record it belongs to.

In this way, a relational database does not need to reserve a different field or fields to accommodate each possible choice of car. If a customer looks at additional makes, the database merely adds a new child record for that customer.

R's mlogit package prefers the general approach taken by the relational database, in which different choices are represented by different rows in the data frame. That approach is termed the *long shape*, because it generally contains more rows than the alternative (which is termed the *wide shape*). As more alternatives are added, more rows are created in the long shape, whereas more columns are created in the wide shape.

The rationale for using the long shape is different in mlogit than in relational databases, but mlogit does prefer the long shape. You can use either shape, but you need to specify in an argument which shape your data frame assumes. And it's entirely possible to create a data frame with the wide shape and have R convert it to a long shape using a preliminary function (mlogit.data).

With the data imported into R and the distinction between the wide and the long shapes made, you can begin your logistic regression analysis using either the mlogit or the glm function. We continue here with an example of using glm.

Running Logistic Regression Using glm

In large measure because it handles only data sets with a binary outcome variable, glm is much easier to use than R's other logistic regression functions such as mlogit. Compared to the alternatives to glm, it's easy to understand the use of glm's arguments. And because glm handles binary outcome variables only, there's no need to make any special arrangements concerning the long or wide shape of the data frame. (See the previous section named "Understanding the Long Versus Wide Shape.")

You also save a step because glm is part of R's base *stats* package, so there's no need either to download a contributed package nor to load it via the *library* function.

With the Purchase data set (last shown in Figure 8.9) established in R as the data frame named Pchsdata, enter the glm function:

```
> glm(formula = Purchase ~ Income + Age + Zip, family = "binomial",
data=Pchsdata)
```

The syntax in the `glm` command just shown presents three arguments to the function, described next.

Formula

This argument is

```
formula = Purchase ~ Income + Age + Zip
```

In words, this argument states that the `glm` function should calculate an equation that treats the probability of a purchase as a function of the simultaneous effects of income, age and zip code.

Family

The `glm` function is capable of working with a variety of error distributions, including the gaussian, the Gamma, and the binomial. Here, we're working with the binomial distribution.

Data

The `Data` argument simply tells `glm` where to find the four variables specified in the `Formula` argument.

The results appear in the R console as shown in Figure 8.10.

Figure 8.10
The results are identical to those returned by Excel—see Figure 8.9.

```
> library(DescTools)
> Pchsdata <- XLGetRange(header=TRUE)
Loading required namespace: RDCOMClient
> head(Pchsdata)
          Purchase  Income   Age      Zip
     1        0     79.015    50        1
     2        0     79.897    50        1
     3        0     82.818    47        1
     4        0     82.21     49        1
     5        0     87.656    42        1
     6        0     86.013    47        1

> glm(formula = Purchase ~ Income + Age + Zip, family = "binomial",data=Pchsdata)

Call: glm(formula = Purchase ~ Income + Age + Zip, family = "binomial",
   data = Pchsdata)

Coefficients:
(Intercept)  Income    Age        Zip
  -20.0005   0.09112   0.12669   2.58431

Degrees of Freedom: 35 Total (i.e. Null); 32 Residual
Null Deviance:            48.11
Residual Deviance:       28.32          AIC:       36.32
```

Running Logistic Regression Using mlogit

The `mlogit` function is found in a contributed package, `mlogit`. Therefore you need to tell R to make `mlogit` accessible before you can run the `mlogit` function. Assuming that you have downloaded and installed the `mlogit` package, your first step is to tell R to search the `mlogit` package for the `mlogit` function when you invoke it. You give that information to R by means of the library function:> library(`mlogit`)

R is told to make the mlogit package available. R's response, assuming it's done so successfully, is

```
Loading required package: maxLik
```

The mlogit package requires the maxLik package and you are notified that it's been loaded along with mlogit. Your system has access to maxLik if you have downloaded and installed the R base system as well as the mlogit package. Depending on the version of R you have installed on your computer, you might see additional messages that other required packages have been loaded.

Using `read.csv` or `XLGetRange`, pull the data shown starting in row 6, in columns A:D, of Figure 8.9 into a data frame named, for this example, mydata. After you have established mydata as a data frame, treat the `Purchase` variable as a factor—that is, as a nominal variable with categories, not as a numeric variable with continuous values:

```
> mydata$Purchase<-as.factor(mydata$Purchase)
```

Get the data frame ready for use by the `mlogit` function by means of the mlogit package's `mlogit.data` function. Specify the mydata data frame as the data source. Identify `Purchase` as the choice variable that represents the binomial (1 or 0, Yes or No, Survive or Die) or multinomial (Democratic, Independent, Republican) outcome. The shape = "wide" specification informs R that the data has all the alternatives for the choice variable on the same row (the shape is wide) or distributed across different rows(the shape is long). (Again, see the earlier section named "Understanding the Long Versus Wide Shape.")

With those arguments specified, assign the result to a new data frame, Pchsdata:

```
> Pchsdata<-mlogit.data(mydata,choice="Purchase",shape="wide")
```

Specify the model for mlogit to use, and store the result in mlogit.model:

```
> mlogit.model<-mlogit(Purchase~1|Income+Age+Zip,data=Pchsdata)
```

I'll walk through the syntax used by the preceding instance of the mlogit function shortly. First, it's important to discuss the function's basic structure.

The mlogit function's syntax can be considerably more complex than `glm`'s syntax. Its arguments begin with the name of the choice variable (here, `Purchase`) followed immediately by the tilde, to indicate that the value of `Purchase` is a function of what follows the tilde.

Multinomial, as distinct from binomial, situations require some specialized terminology. Again, suppose that in our example the customer chooses among three makes of car (it's a multinomial situation) rather than between buying and not buying a car. We now have variables such as customer income and customer age which vary among customers, but which do not vary with the make of car. These are termed *individual-specific* variables.

However, if we were analyzing which of three makes of car is chosen (rather than whether the customer buys) then sticker price would certainly be an important variable. Price varies along with the make of car. Ford, GM and Toyota are the alternatives in this example, and the sticker price of each make is termed an *alternative-specific* variable.

If you're familiar with the analysis of covariance, or ANCOVA, you likely recall that an important test in ANCOVA is for homogeneity of regression coefficients. Suppose that you are testing whether men or women have the higher average diastolic blood pressure, and you are using a measure of low density lipoproteins (LDL) as a covariate. Before you use the same regression coefficient for blood pressure on LDL with both sexes, you should test whether it's plausible that the regression coefficient calculated for men is the same as the regression coefficient calculated for women.

Conceptually it's the same sort of issue in multinomial logistic regression. Although the customer's age might not vary with the make of car, the *coefficient* for customer age might vary with the make of car.

I have more to say about this sort of matter in Chapter 9, "Multinomial Logistic Regression." I have introduced the concepts here so that the syntax of the mlogit function will seem less mysterious.

The syntax of the mlogit function calls for a three-part formula to follow the tilde (I *said* it's complex). The syntax calls for a three-part map to the formula in this way:

Outcome Variable ~ Part 1 | Part 2 | Part 3

where

- In this example, the Outcome Variable is Purchase. It is followed by a tilde, indicating that the outcome variable is a function of whatever follows the tilde, up to the first comma. In the mlogit function, the three-part formula comes between the tilde and the first comma.

- Part 1 of the three-part formula comes between the tilde and the first instance of the | (the vertical line often termed the *piping symbol*). Part 1 consists of any alternative-specific variables that you want to use as predictors with a single, generic coefficient. This is analogous to using the same regression coefficient for males and females.

- Part 2 of the formula follows the first piping symbol. Use Part 2 to specify any individual-specific variables as predictors with alternative-specific coefficients.

- Part 3 of the formula follows the second piping symbol, if there is one. Use Part 3 to specify any alternative-specific variables that will get alternative-specific coefficients.

Back to the actual function used in this example, repeated here for convenience:

```
> mlogit.model<-mlogit(Purchase~1|Income+Age+Zip,data=Pchsdata)
```

The first part of the formula comes between the tilde and the first piping symbol, and contains alternative specific variables that take a generic coefficient—that is, the coefficient is the same regardless of the alternative. In the Pchsdata data frame there are no alternatives; it implies a binomial logistic regression. The number 1 is inserted between the tilde and the first piping symbol as a sort of placeholder.

Part 2 of the formula follows the first piping symbol and in this case consists of the three individual specific variables Income, Age, and ZIP. The mlogit syntax allows for these individual specific variables to be multiplied by alternative specific coefficients, but here we have no alternatives and therefore no alternative specific coefficients.

Part 3 of the formula is absent in this example. It's optional and can be used when alternatives exist in the data frame. Here, there are none, so mlogit does not complain. Notice that there is no piping symbol to separate Part 2 from a Part 3, so mlogit can tell that we have omitted Part 3.

The next argument to the mlogit function specifies the source of the data, in this example Pchsdata.

A summary of the logistic regression results is requested by means of the summary function. Notice that the estimates of the coefficients returned by mlogit are identical to those returned by glm, and by Excel in Figure 8.9.

```
> summary(mlogit.model)
```

The results of the summary function appear in Figure 8.11.

Figure 8.11
The mlogit function returns the same coefficients and log likelihood as the glm function.

```
> mlogit.model<-mlogit(Purchase ~ 1 | Income+Age+Zip,data=Pchsdata)
> summary(mlogit.model)

Call:
mlogit(formula = Purchase ~ 1 | Income + Age + Zip, data = Pchsdata,
    method = "nr", print.level = 0)

Frequencies of alternatives:
              0          1
      0.61111    0.38889

nr method
6 iterations, 0h:0m:0s
g'(-H)^-1g = 1.38E-06
successive function values within tolerance limits

Coefficients :
                 Estimate  Std. Error  t-value    Pr(>|t|)
1:(intercept  -20.0005     8.595602    -2.3268    0.019974  *
1:Income        0.091115   0.032594     2.7955    0.005182  **
1:Age           0.126686   0.120781     1.0489    0.294229
1:Zip           2.584307   1.057398     2.444     0.014524  *
---
Signif. codes: 0 '***' 0.001 '**' 0.01 '*' 0.05 '.' 0.1 ' ' 1

Log-Likelihood: -14.16
McFadden R^2: 0.41139
Likelihood ratio test : chisq = 19.794 (p.value = 0.00018731)
```

In Figure 8.11, notice the table with the headings Estimate, Std. Error, t-value, and Pr(>|t|). The four values under the Estimate heading are, in order from top to bottom, the intercept, the Income coefficient, the Age coefficient, and the ZIP Code coefficient. They are the values that, used in the equation discussed earlier in the section titled "Running Solver on the Logistic Regression Problem," most accurately predict the likelihood of purchase by each of the 36 records in the sample.

Notice also that the intercept and the coefficients are trivially different from those that are returned by Solver and that are shown in Figure 8.9. The differences, which do not tend to appear until the fifth decimal place, are very likely due to minor changes in the criterion for convergence to the minimum value for the log likelihood.

Statistical Tests in Logistic Regression

Before you rush off to bounce these coefficients off data on a thousand new prospects, you really should check whether the variables, multiplied by their coefficients, actually enhance the accuracy and reliability of your decision making.

Models Comparison in Multiple Regression

Among the techniques used by ordinary least squares, in particular the methods of multiple regression, is one that's often termed *models comparison*. Here's the basic idea.

Suppose you have a random sample of 500 adults. You have three measures on each of them: sex, number of years of school that each has taken, and annual income. You run a (fairly simple) multiple regression analysis on your data, regressing income against sex and education. You have several objectives for this project, among which are these three:

- Your main objective is to determine how accurately you can predict income from knowledge of a person's sex and years of education.

- Another objective is to test whether there is an *interaction* between sex and education that gets expressed in income: that is, does years of education have a different effect on men's income than on women's income?

- You would like to know if you can safely discard either education or sex from the analysis without reducing whatever predictive power the analysis has. There are various reasons, both pragmatic and technical, for this objective, but the general goal is sometimes called *parsimony*. As long as you don't lose a significant amount of accuracy in the prediction, the fewer predictor variables you have hanging around, the better.

Figure 8.12 shows how the data might be laid out.

Figure 8.12
A models comparison approach to deciding whether to keep a predictor in the regression equation.

	A	B	C	D	E	F	G	H	I	J	K
			Educ-	Inter-							
1	Income	Sex	ation	action							
2	0.50	1	11	11		0.01308	0.02326	-0.29759	0.23226152		
3	0.41	0	11	0		0.01568	0.01565	0.23701	0.22235522		
4	0.44	0	11	0		0.69644	1.29066	#N/A	#N/A		
5	0.66	1	11	11		379.32063	496	#N/A	#N/A		
6	0.93	0	11	0		1895.61823	826.23736	#N/A	#N/A		
7	0.08	1	11	11							
8	0.98	1	11	11		0.03627	-0.12542	0.061477			
9	0.20	0	11	0		0.00108	0.11624	0.086426			
10	0.33	0	11	0		0.69602	1.29026	#N/A			
11	0.98	1	11	11		568.98264	497	#N/A			
12	0.42	0	11	0		1894.46051	827.39508	#N/A			
13	0.60	0	11	0							
14	0.41	0	11	0		Source of Variation	Prop. of variance	df	(Prop. of Variance) / df	F	p
15	0.31	1	12	12		R^2 increment	0.0004	1	0.0004	0.6950	0.4049
16	0.31	1	12	12		Residual	0.3036	496	0.0006		

Cell reference: F2 f_x {=LINEST(A2:A501,B2:D501,,TRUE)}

Calculating the Results of Different Models

To meet these objectives in this particular case, you run your regression analysis twice. The first time, you create an additional variable to represent the interaction between sex and education. This is pretty simple. Your Sex variable represents the females in your sample with a 1 and the males with a 0; the Education variable simply shows the years of school each person has completed.

To create an interaction term, you multiply the value on Sex by the value on Education. Then you run a regression analysis of Income on Education, Sex, and the interaction of Education and Sex.

You array-enter the LINEST() function in the range F2:I6 shown in Figure 8.12. Your analysis returns an R^2 of 0.69644 (see cell F4). That means that in your sample, nearly 70% of the variability in Income is associated with variability in the best linear combination of Education, Sex, and their interaction. This is sometimes called an *unrestricted* or *full model*, because it includes in the regression equation all the available variables and their interactions.

The possibility of a difference in Income that's due to an interaction between Education and Sex ought to be eliminated if it's insignificant. If an interaction is present, you'll want to account for it. But if it's absent, then leaving it in a regression equation is a needless complication, and doing so unnecessarily can make the equation less stable—and even less interpretable.

You can test the possibility that an interaction is present by dropping the interaction term from the equation. Run your multiple regression again, but this time you should regress Income against Education and Sex only, leaving the interaction term out of the equation. In Figure 8.12, this has been done by array-entering LINEST() in the range F8:H12.

This time, your regression analysis returns an R^2 of 0.69602 (see cell F10). That's almost as strong a relationship between Income and the predictor variables as you got from the full model, which included the interaction term. The two R^2 values are only 0.0004 apart and the difference is not a meaningful one, but it's easy enough to test whether it's a reliable difference in a statistical sense.

Testing the Difference Between the Models

The range F14:K16 in Figure 8.12 shows that test in an Analysis of Variance context. Cell G15 contains 0.0004, which is the difference in the two values for R^2, and represents the increment in proportion of explained variance that you can attribute to the interaction term.

The value in cell G16 is the proportion of residual, unexplained variability in the Income variable for the full model. It's obtained easily by subtracting the value in cell F4 from 1.0. Cell F4 contains the proportion of explained variance in the full model, so 1.0 less that proportion is the unexplained, residual variance.

The F-test, which you often see used in the analysis of variance and in regression analysis, tests the statistical reliability of the difference between two proportions of variance. The difference is measured not by subtraction but as a ratio. In this case, we're going to find the ratio of the incremental variability in G15 to the residual variability in G16. We'll use Excel's F.DIST.RT( ) function to find the probability of getting a ratio as large as the one we observe, if the two variances are in fact the same in the population.

First, though, we have to adjust for the degrees of freedom in the two measures of variability. The degrees of freedom for the incremental variability is 1, and the degrees of freedom for the residual is 496, the same value as returned by LINEST( ) in cell G5. The two values for degrees of freedom are shown in H15:H16 of Figure 8.12. The results of dividing each proportion of variance in G15:G16 by the degrees of freedom in H15:H16 appear in I15:I16. These values, designated *Proportion of Variance/df*, are commensurate with the mean squares we would calculate if we were bringing sums of squares (which is just a constant multiple) along with the proportions of variability.

Finally, the ratio of the values in I15:I16 is calculated in J15 at 0.6950. That ratio is an F-ratio and is tested in cell K15, which contains this formula:

    =F.DIST.RT(J15,H15,H16)

It returns the value 0.4049, which means that if the variances are equal in the population, we would observe an F-ratio as large as 0.6950 as much as 40% of the time.

The F.DIST.RT( ) function takes as its arguments the F-ratio itself (cell J15), the degrees of freedom for the numerator (cell H15) and the degrees of freedom for the denominator (cell H16). There is a different F distribution for every combination of degrees of freedom in an F-ratio's numerator and in its denominator.

Given these arguments, the F.DIST.RT( ) function returns the area in the F distribution that lies to the right of the value of the observed F-ratio. In this example, more than 40%

of the area lies to the right of the value 0.6950. Therefore, the calculated ratio is not unusually large at all, and we can continue to regard the ratio as typical of data sampled from a population where there's no difference in these two measures of variability.

In short, there's little empirical evidence that the incremental variance due to the interaction term is reliable. We can therefore remove the interaction term from the equation without losing any reliable predictive power.

There's a minor benefit to doing so. We can now put the degree of freedom associated with the interaction into the residual degrees of freedom. That marginally reduces the size of the residual denominator of the F-test, and in turn makes any remaining F-tests slightly more powerful.

But the principal benefit is the conclusion that there is no interaction between sex and education that expresses itself in income. If there were, it would be necessary to account for that interaction in any equations that we use to predict income on the basis of sex and education. More importantly, we would have to explain that interaction: Had an interaction been present, we might have had to explain, for example, the reason that women with less education earn more than men with more education. To explain that satisfactorily might well prove more difficult than can be managed.

You could run a couple of additional comparisons, one that tests the incremental variance explained by keeping Age in the regression equation, and one that runs the same sort of test on Education. But this section's rationale is principally to prepare the ground for doing models comparison in logistic regression, so we'll end the multiple regression example here and return to the example from Figure 8.9, repeated and extended in Figure 8.13.

Models Comparison in Logistic Regression

The statistical test of incremental variance that is explained by two different models using ordinary least squares—equivalently, using multiple regression—is the F-test. Logistic regression, because it relies on maximum likelihood estimates, uses chi-square instead of F ratios.

> **NOTE** The F-test and the chi-square test are actually close cousins. If you divide each of two independent chi-square variables by its degrees of freedom, their ratio forms an F distribution.

The model comparison is summarized in Figure 8.13. The comparison among the various models is shown in the range H6:L12. Here is what each of the columns in that range represents:

The LL Statistics

The LL figures appear in H6:H12. They are the sum of the individual log likelihoods in column E that result from different combinations of the coefficients.

Figure 8.13
Several columns in
Figure 8.9 have been
combined here to save
space.

	A	B	C	D	E	F	G	H	I	J	K	L
	G2				f_x	=SUM(E6:E41)						
1			Coefficients									
2	Intercept	Income	Age	Zip Code		Sum Log Likelihood:	-14.1601					
3	-20.0005	0.09112	0.12669	2.5843								
4												
5	Purchase	Income ($000)	Age	Zip Code	Log Likelihood			LL	D	Delta from intercept-only	df	P chi-square
6	0	79.015	50	1	-0.0204	Intercept only		-24.0569	48.1139	#N/A		#N/A
7	0	79.897	50	1	-0.0221							
8	0	82.818	47	1	-0.0197	Intercept & Income		-18.6020	37.2040	10.9099	1	0.0010
9	0	82.210	49	1	-0.0240							
10	0	87.656	42	1	-0.0163	Intercept, Income & Age		-18.0870	36.1740	11.9399	2	0.0026
11	0	86.013	47	1	-0.0263							
12	0	85.032	49	1	-0.0309	Intercept, Income, Age & Zip		-14.1601	28.3203	19.7936	3	0.0002

As I pointed out earlier, the closer that the total log likelihood comes to 0.0, the better. A total log likelihood of 0.0 would correspond to a total product of the individual probabilities of 1.0, and that can come about only when the probability of a correct prediction is 1.0 for each record: 1.0 * 1.0 * 1.0 . . . * 1.0 = 1.0. The log of 1.0 is 0.0, so the sum of the logs for a series of perfect predictions is 0.0.

Our predictions are not perfect, though, and in this example the individual log likelihoods total –14.16 for the full model, using the intercept and all three variables to predict purchasing behavior. You can find that value shown in cell G2 and also in cell H12.

Solver arrives at that value, the maximum of the total log likelihood, by varying the intercept and all three coefficients. This is demonstrated in the earlier section titled "Running Solver on the Logistic Regression Problem."

You can get the other values for the log likelihood in column H by running Solver three more times, each time changing which variables you leave in the equation. For example, to find the total log likelihood for a model that includes the intercept only, you would take these steps:

1. Set the intercept in A3 to 1, and each coefficient to 0.0. Setting a coefficient to 0.0 has the effect of removing the associated variable from the logistic regression equation.

2. Run Solver as described earlier in this chapter, but include the intercept only, in cell A3, in the By Changing Variable Cells box. So doing instructs Solver to ignore the three coefficients, leaving each of them at 0.0 and therefore omitting the three variables Income, Age, and Zip from the equation.

The result of predicting Purchase on the basis of the intercept only is a total log likelihood of –24.0569, shown in cell H6 of Figure 8.13.

The total log likelihood for the intercept only is larger than the total log likelihood of the full model, –14.160. But it's difficult to make any inferences on the basis of differences in log likelihood alone. Its magnitude depends on both the quality of the underlying predictions and on the number of records involved in the analysis. It's necessary first to turn the log likelihood into a form that follows a known distribution. It turns out that you can transform the log likelihood into a variable that follows a chi-square distribution.

The Deviance Statistic

The log likelihood figure, as we've seen, is by definition a negative number. The individual probabilities, column H in Figure 8.9, must each be between 0.0 and 1.0—by definition. The log of a positive number less than 1.0 is always negative, and therefore the sum of the log likelihoods must also be negative.

However, chi-square is always positive. Chi-square has many uses, but it is built on the sum of squared z-scores:

$$z = \frac{X - \mu}{\sigma}$$

The z-score is negative for each instance of a value X that is less than the mean μ. But chi-square is the sum of *squared* z-scores, and thus must always be a positive number. We can't sensibly ask where in the distribution of possible chi-squares for given degrees of freedom a negative log likelihood falls: The chi-square curve does not, *cannot* extend below a chi-square value of 0.0.

So, the log likelihood is normally multiplied by –2, which converts an inevitably negative log likelihood to an inevitably positive value that follows a chi-square distribution. We can then treat the result as a chi-square and make inferences about the probability of observing that value in a chi-square distribution.

Because the log likelihood is multiplied by –2, you'll sometimes see the result referred to as –2LL, in the output of computer programs and in theoretical discussions or empirical reports.

Unfortunately, there is little agreement among statisticians on how this quantity should be designated. While some refer to it as –2LL, others refer to it as the *deviance*, sometimes abbreviated as *D*. That is how I have chosen to designate it in Figure 8.13, column I. The term "deviance" alludes to the amount of the deviation between the predicted probabilities and the 0's and 1's that represent the actual outcome for a given record.

(Other writers refer to this quantity as G. You'll sometimes see G_M, referring to the deviance for the full, unrestricted model. Some sources claim that "G" refers to *goodness of fit*.)

Calculating the Log Likelihood and the Deviance Statistics

After you have a worksheet set up like those shown in Figure 8.5 (or even Figure 8.13, if you prefer not to see the intermediate values such as the logits or the odds), it's straightforward to calculate the results for different models and compare their results. For example, to get the base model that includes the intercept term only, you follow the two steps described in the section titled "The LL Statistics." To get the model that includes the intercept and the Income coefficient only, you could take these steps (cell addresses refer to Figure 8.13):

1. Set the intercept value in A3 to 1.0, and all the coefficients in B3:D3 to 0.0.

2. As described in the section titled "Running Solver on the Logistic Regression Problem," start Solver.

3. Leave the cell address in the Set Objective box at $G$2. In versions earlier than Excel 2010, the Set Objective box is labeled Set Target Cell. Make sure that the Max button is selected.

4. Click in the By Changing Variable Cells box. Click first in cell A3 and then cell B3, so that only their addresses are in the Variable Cells box.

5. Be sure that you have chosen GRG Nonlinear as the solution method and click Solve.

This sequence of steps should return a total log likelihood of –18.602, or something very close to that depending on the Solver settings you have in place for time, derivatives, and convergence. That's the value you see in cell H8 in Figure 8.13.

In general, to get the intercept, coefficients, and log likelihood for any given set of variables:

1. Set the intercept to 1.0 and all the coefficients to 0.0.

2. Start Solver and make sure that it's been instructed to maximize the value of the objective (a.k.a. target) cell.

3. Identify the cells containing the coefficients you want to use in the Changing Variable Cells box.

4. Use the GRG Nonlinear solution method and click Solve.

When Solver has completed its work for a given model, you should usually copy the resulting log likelihood value and paste it (as a value, not as a formula) into some other cell, as I've done with the range H6:H12 in Figure 8.13. Be sure to label that value with information about which variables were in the model that resulted in a given log likelihood.

Convert each log likelihood figure to a deviance by multiplying by –2, as shown in I6:I12 in Figure 8.13.

To determine the probability of getting a log likelihood as close to zero as you have done for a particular model, refer the log likelihood's deviance to the chi-square distribution for the associated degrees of freedom (df). The df will always be equal to the number of variable coefficients that were involved in calculating the logit for that model. So, for the intercept and Income model, the df is 1; for the intercept, Income and Zip model, the df is 2.

Calculate the probability associated with a given log likelihood using the chi-square test. In Figure 8.13, for example, the range H12:L12 contains the analysis for the full model: intercept as well as the Income, Age, and ZIP Code variables. For this model, H12 contains the log likelihood, I12 contains the deviance (–2 times the log likelihood).

When we test the full model, though, we are interested in testing how well it predicts, as compared to the model that uses the intercept only. This is directly analogous to the models comparison approach that is outlined earlier in this chapter, using ordinary least squares, in the section titled "Models Comparison in Multiple Regression."

Therefore, cell J12 calculates the difference between the deviance for the full model (cell I12) and for the intercept-only model (cell I6). Both these deviance values are the log likelihoods for their respective models, multiplied by –2, and are distributed as chi-square variables. The difference between them, 19.79 in cell J12, is also distributed as a chi-square variable. (In fact, at least one version of SPSS refers to that difference as "Chi-square" in its logistic regression output, and Stata's terminology is "LR Chi2.")

So we can test whether the reduction in the deviance due to the use of Income, Age, and ZIP Code is statistically improbable if, *in the population from which this sample has been taken*, knowledge of a person's income, age, and ZIP Code does not bring about a better prediction than the overall average alone. Bear in mind that if these variables do not make a meaningful contribution to the accuracy of the prediction, you might as well leave them out of the equation—and that's equivalent to setting their coefficients to 0.0.

Degrees of Freedom, Constraints, and Terminology

You might find that some sources state that the degrees of freedom to test one logistic regression model against another is equal to the "number of constraints." Although that's generally true, it's unnecessarily obtuse and counterintuitive.

In this context, "constraints" refers to the coefficients that are constrained to have the value 0.0, and a constrained model has at least one variable that is so constrained, as compared to some other, unconstrained model.

In the example that this section has been considering, the intercept-only model can be considered as "constrained." All three variables (income, age, and ZIP Code) are constrained to equal 0.0. In contrast, the full model contains all three variables, and each of the three coefficients is unconstrained: free to take on a value that improves the log likelihood.

So in that case, the number of constrained variables in the alternative model is three, and so is the value of the degrees of freedom for the test of the comparison. If you were comparing a Model A with three unconstrained variables to Model B with two unconstrained variables, the degrees of freedom would be 1: compared to Model A, one variable is constrained in Model B.

The reason that I regard the "number of constraints" approach as counterintuitive is that the very concept of "degrees of freedom" has to do with the number of items that are free to vary: that are unconstrained. Comparing a multiple regression equation that contains an interaction term with one that does not, you subtract the number of terms in the restricted equation from the number in the unrestricted equation, and the result is the degrees of freedom for the models comparison.

And in fact that's what happens in models comparison in logistic regression. You subtract the number of unconstrained variables in the restricted, constrained model from the number in the unrestricted, unconstrained model. In the present example, that's 3 – 0, or

3. If you were comparing a model with three unconstrained variables to one with two, the degrees of freedom would be 3 – 2 = 1.

It is said that the degrees of freedom for the test is equal to the number of constraints because subtracting the number of *unconstrained* variables in one model from the number of unconstrained variables in the other does work out to be the number of constraints. It's a shortcut, but like many shortcuts it's confusing if you don't have the rationale.

The Chi-Square Test

To test the full model against the intercept-only model, we use the chi-square test shown in column L of Figure 8.13. The test itself for the full model appears in cell L12, which shows the value 0.0002.

That value has the following meaning: Assume that in the full population from which we have taken a sample of 36 observations, the variables income, age, and ZIP Code do not improve our prediction of purchasing behavior beyond knowledge of the simple average, 39% purchasing.

In that case, we can calculate the probability of finding a deviance figure that we have obtained (cell I12, 28.32) that differs from the intercept-only value (48.11, cell I6) by as much as it does when income, age, and ZIP Code make no difference to purchasing behavior. In other words, how likely is it that the difference in deviance between the two models is just sampling error?

If that's very unlikely, then we have to revisit our original assumption—our null hypothesis—that the variables make no difference in the population that we took our sample from.

Cell L12 contains this formula:

=CHISQ.DIST.RT(J12,K12)

which tells us that only twice in ten thousand samples (0.02% of the time) would we get a difference in deviances as large as 19.79 (cell J12) with three degrees of freedom (cell K12) if there were no effect in the full population. That's good enough for most of us to reject the null hypothesis. Most of us would conclude that the variables make a difference to the predictive accuracy. To conclude otherwise would be equivalent to assuming that we have gotten our hands on one of the two samples in 10,000 that are really unusual.

But this finding doesn't tell us what variable or variables are responsible for the difference: income, age, or ZIP Code. To make that determination, we have to compare a model that has, say, both income and age with one that has income only. By comparing the two, we can often conclude whether or not the addition of age to the model makes a meaningful, reliable difference.

Other Model Comparisons

In a multiple regression analysis, you often use an *omnibus F-test* of the overall R^2 to determine whether there are any statistically reliable differences among any of the groups involved. For example, in an analysis that compares the effectiveness of a statin on men and women, your omnibus F-test of the R^2 value might tell you that there is a significant difference somewhere: between men and women, between the statin group and a comparison group, or in an interaction between sex and medication.

That F-test, however, would not tell you where the difference came from, because the R^2 is a measure of the effectiveness of the overall equation. You would not yet know whether a statistically significant R^2 was due to the sex of the subjects, the medication or its absence, or because men fared better with the statin and women fared better with the comparison medication. To investigate those more fine-grained differences, you would use a multiple comparison technique or, in a multiple regression, you might tend to use a models comparison approach. (The two techniques are often equivalent.)

It's similar in logistic regression. The comparison that this section has already discussed is between the full model and the intercept-only model. Figure 8.14 provides a look at income and age as they enter the equation.

Figure 8.14
Compared to Figure 8.13, this figure shows the coefficients that Solver used to maximize the likelihood (and thus minimize deviance) using the intercept and Income only.

	Coefficients				Sum Log Likelihood:	-18.6020					
Intercept	Income	Age	Zip Code								
-7.82552	0.07413	0	0								

Purchase	Income ($000)	Age	Zip Code	Log Likelihood			LL	D	Delta from intercept-only	df	P chi-square
0	79.015	50	1	-0.1308	Intercept only		-24.0569	48.1139	#N/A		#N/A
0	79.897	50	1	-0.1390							
0	82.818	47	1	-0.1699	Intercept & Income		-18.6020	37.2040	10.9099	1	0.0010
0	82.210	49	1	-0.1630							
0	87.656	42	1	-0.2352	Intercept, Income & Age		-18.0870	36.1740	11.9399	2	0.0026
0	86.013	47	1	-0.2108							
0	85.032	49	1	-0.1974	Intercept, Income, Age & Zip		-14.1601	28.3203	19.7936	3	0.0002
0	82.914	55	1	-0.1710			LL	D	Delta from intercept & Income	df	P chi-square
0	86.110	51	1	-0.2122	Intercept & Income		-18.6020	37.2040			
0	62.224	52	2	-0.0395							
0	86.864	52	1	-0.2231							
0	91.353	55	1	-0.2991	Intercept, Income & Age		-18.0870	36.1740	1.0300	1	0.3102

In Figure 8.14, row 8 contains the important information on the Income variable. The intercept was initialized to 1.0 and all the coefficients to 0.0, and Solver was instructed to maximize the log likelihood in cell G2 while allowing the intercept and the coefficient for Income to vary. Solver iterated through values for the intercept and the Income coefficient until it converged to the values shown in Figure 8.14, cells A3:B3. (Notice that the log likelihood in cell G2 equals that shown in cell H8; the range H8:L8 summarizes the information for the intercept-and-Income model.)

The result was a deviance of 37.20 (cell I8) for the "unconstrained" model. This value is 10.91 (cell J8) less than for the "constrained" model that contains the intercept only and whose deviance (cell I6) is 48.11.

As compared to the model with the intercept only, the intercept-and-Income model has one additional unconstrained variable, Income. The intercept-only model has the intercept and Income, but Income's coefficient is not allowed to vary and is constrained to zero. The other model has the intercept and Income, but Income's coefficient is unconstrained. There is one constraint in the more constrained model and no constraint in the less constrained model, so the model comparison has one degree of freedom. However you want to think of it, the proper degrees of freedom to test the comparison is 1, found in cell K8.

Lastly, here's the formula in cell L8:

=CHISQ.DIST.RT(J8,K8)

It returns 0.0010. Only one sample in one thousand would have a difference in deviances as large as 10.91 if Income had no effect on purchasing behavior. So we regard Income as a meaningful, reliable predictor of purchasing. What about Age?

Our purpose now is to determine whether Age has any meaningful and reliable effect on purchasing behavior, *over and above* what has already been accounted for by including Income. The appropriate model comparison is in the range H15:L17 in Figure 8.14.

The log likelihood and the deviance figures for intercept and Income are in H15:I15, and the log likelihood and deviance for intercept, Income and Age are in H17:I17. These figures are the same as those found in H8:I8 and in H10:I10. The only difference is that this comparison, which isolates Age, treats the Income-only model instead of the intercept-only model as the more constrained model.

The difference between the two deviances, 1.03, is in cell J17. The number of unconstrained variables in the model that includes Income and Age is 2; the number of unconstrained variables in the Income-only model is 1; 2 – 1 = 1, so the df for this comparison is 1. (If you prefer, the constrained model, Income-only, has one constrained variable, Age, when compared to the unconstrained model.) Either way that you think of it, the comparison has 1 df, as shown in cell K17.

The chi-square test itself is in cell L17:

=CHISQ.DIST.RT(J17,K17)

It returns 0.31. If in the population, Age did not improve the prediction of purchasing behavior over and above the accuracy of predictions based on Income alone, we would observe a difference in deviance as large as 1.03 as much as 31% of the time. That's quite a large percentage, and most people would take the position that Age fails to improve the prediction beyond that provided by the intercept and Income—and that Age can therefore be left out of the equation without losing any predictive accuracy.

The Wald Statistic

In multiple regression analysis, there's another way to judge whether a variable contributes reliably and meaningfully to the predictable variability in an outcome variable. For example, using Excel tools, both the LINEST() worksheet function and the Regression tool in the Data Analysis add-in report the regression coefficients and the standard error of each coefficient.

Instead of using the models comparison approach, you can divide each regression coefficient by its standard error, and the result is a t statistic: the distance of the coefficient from zero, measured in the number of standard errors. In other words, if a regression coefficient has a value of 4.5 and if its standard error is 1.5, the coefficient is 3 standard errors away from zero. The t statistic is 3.

With any reasonable sample size, that t statistic would be judged statistically significant. Using the appropriate Excel worksheet functions:

=T.DIST(-3,10,TRUE)

and

=T.DIST.RT(3,10)

you would find that a t statistic greater than 3 or less than –3, with as few as 10 degrees of freedom, would occur through sampling error only 1.3% of the time.

You could arrive at the same conclusion using the models comparison approach, contrasting the proportion of variance explained using the variable in the equation with the proportion explained when omitting the variable from the regression equation. (See this chapter's section titled "Models Comparison in Multiple Regression" for the details of carrying out this sort of analysis.)

It's largely a matter of personal preference, but I find that I like the richness of the information I get from evaluating variables via models comparison. When I run a complete multiple regression on two different models, the amount of information available is much greater than I get from simply examining a regression coefficient's t statistic.

Theorists have been seeking a fully satisfactory method of testing the coefficients used in logistic regression for decades. The Wald statistic appears to be the method of choice as of 2017 and has been for several years. The Wald statistic is analogous to the t statistic in multiple regression. The coefficient is divided by its standard error and the result is squared.

Most purely statistical applications such as SPSS and Stata report the statistical significance of the Wald ratio. (The standard error is available from the main diagonal of the variance-covariance matrix, which is also returned from these programs.)

It is generally thought that the Wald statistic is biased under some conditions, particularly relatively small sample sizes. The models comparison approach does not suffer from that difficulty, and therefore if you want to test the statistical significance associated with adding

8

a variable to the equation (or with dropping one from the equation), I urge you to use the models comparison approach and avoid making decisions based on the Wald statistic. However, with large samples, there may be very little practical difference between the results of the two approaches.

Pseudo R^2

As is the case for testing the statistical significance of the individual coefficients used in the logistic equations, attempts have been made to devise a logistic version of the R^2 used in least-squares regression analysis. There are many such versions and more than one are termed "pseudo R^2," so if you involve yourself with one of them be sure that you know which one it is.

One of the more popular versions is best termed McFadden R^2, but different sources refer to it as Pseudo R^2 and R^2_L. It is calculated using this formula:

$$1 - LL_M/LL_0$$

where LL_M refers to the likelihood ratio for the model that includes both the intercept and the variables you're interested in, and LL_0 refers to the likelihood ratio for the intercept-only model. However, even the mlogit contributed package for R uses a different approach to calculating what it labels as McFadden R^2.

The best move is to ignore these R^2 analogies and focus on the chi-square test of the comparison between the full model and the intercept-only model, described earlier in this chapter in the section titled "The Chi-Square Test."

Cross-Validation

The best test of a logistic regression model, though, comes through a process called *cross-validation*. This process has a long and honorable history, and it is satisfying both technically and intuitively.

To use cross-validation, you want a sizable sample—specifically, about twice the size of a sample that you might have thought adequate for a logistic regression analysis (or, for that matter, a least-squares analysis that involves multiple predictor variables).

The idea is to randomly select half the sample and run your logistic regression on it. Then use the coefficients that the analysis arrived at via the maximum likelihood approach described in this chapter, and apply them to the remaining sampled cases that were not used in the logistic regression.

Finish by comparing the log likelihoods (or the deviances if you want to use a chi-square test to compare the results) of the original analysis with the result of applying the coefficients to the remaining cases. You are, of course, hoping that the difference will be negligible. In that case, you have powerful evidence that the coefficients you arrived at are robust and will behave well with other samples that you might want to use.

Multinomial Logistic Regression

Chapter 7, "Logistic Regression: The Basics," and Chapter 8, "Logistic Regression: Further Issues," both discussed problems in binomial logistic regression. That is, the problems all involved outcome variables that take on just two values: for example, True and False, Buys and Doesn't Buy, Survives and Doesn't Survive. But you can extend logistic regression to situations that involve outcome variables that take on three or more values, usually but not necessarily strictly nominal values. This chapter discusses those situations.

Working with three or more values in an outcome variable complicates the situation somewhat, but not unreasonably so. In this chapter I'll discuss some of the problems that arise with three or more possible values in the outcome variable, and how logistic regression typically handles those problems. As in earlier chapters, I demonstrate the problem and its solution using Excel as the platform, and also show how you reach the same solution using the R statistical application.

The Multinomial Problem

When you are working with a binomial outcome variable, it's usually because your interest centers on only two outcomes: the patient survives or does not survive, the customer purchases the product or does not do so, the voter registers as a Republican or as a Democrat. You often have other alternatives available, such as survives but does not recover, purchases at a later time, and registers as an Independent. But your primary interest may lie in just two alternatives, and in that case you might well apply binomial logistic regression as discussed in the two preceding chapters.

Still, it frequently happens that when you have three or more alternatives available to you that are of real interest, the alternatives are a matter of choice. This is particularly so in the fields of economics and econometrics, where the antecedents of consumer choices in a free market are of particular interest. (The terminology applied in multinomial logistic regression is therefore often based on terms that connote choice—*alternative-specific*, for example, and *choice ID*.)

The literature on multinomial logistic regression includes several examples that have become quite well known through repetition, much like the Box–Jenkins series G in discussions of ARIMA analysis. I use two of those examples in this chapter.

Three Alternatives and Three Predictors

The study I describe in this section that was originally published in 1980 (Spector, L. and M. Mazzeo, "Probit Analysis and Economic Education," *Journal of Economic Education*, 11: 37–44). I've chosen their study in part because it uses a relatively small number of observations, but primarily because it is cited frequently in the literature as an example of logistic regression and related techniques. I have always found that the more sources I read about a particular technique, the easier it is for me to understand it. It helps if all those sources deal with the same set of observations.

Figure 9.1 shows the data layout of this study.

Figure 9.1
Rows 11 through 20 have been hidden in Figure 9.1 to save room.

	A	B	C	D
1	**GPA**	**TUCE**	**PSI**	**Letter Grade**
2	2.66	20	0	C
3	2.89	22	0	B
4	3.28	24	0	B
5	2.92	12	0	B
6	4.00	21	0	A
7	2.86	17	0	B
8	2.76	17	0	B
9	2.87	21	0	B
10	3.03	25	0	C
21	3.16	25	1	A
22	2.06	22	1	C
23	3.62	28	1	A
24	2.89	14	1	C
25	3.51	26	1	B
26	3.54	24	1	A
27	2.83	27	1	A
28	3.39	17	1	A
29	2.67	24	1	B
30	3.65	21	1	A
31	4.00	23	1	A
32	3.10	21	1	C
33	2.39	19	1	A

Columns A:C have background information on 32 cases, and column D contains the letter grades obtained by each of the 32 students. The idea in this study is to predict the letter grade earned by each student on the basis of the background information: each student's grade point average, score on a pretest named TUCE, and participation in a newly designed course of training designated as PSI.

Notice that three letter grades are to be predicted: A, B and C. There are, then, three possible outcomes in this dataset. Multinomial logistic regression derives two equations for its predictions in the three outcomes situation, in contrast to the binomial situation, which results in one equation only.

In general, logistic regression derives one equation fewer than the number of possible values in the outcome variable. For example, each of the analyses in Chapter 8 involved the binary outcome variable, and each resulted in a single equation. At the outset of the analysis, either you or the software select one of the outcomes to act as the base case (often termed the *reference level*), and each equation expresses the relationship between one of the outcomes and the base case. You'll see how the choice of the base case affects the interpretation of the analysis before the end of this section.

Figure 9.2 shows the layout of the same data as in Figure 9.1 in preparation for a logistic regression analysis.

Figure 9.2
The range B3:E5 is reserved for equation intercepts and coefficients.

	A	B	C	D	E	F	G	H	I	J	K	L	M	N
1			Coefficients											
2		Intercept	GPA	TUCE	PSI									
3	B	0.000	0.000	0.000	0.000									
4	A	0.000	0.000	0.000	0.000									
5	C	0.000	0.000	0.000	0.000						Sum Log Likelihood:			-35.156
6														
7	Letter Grade	C	A	GPA	TUCE	PSI		Logits			Probabilities			Log Likelihood
8	C	1	0	2.66	20	0	0.000	0.000	0.000	0.333	0.333	0.333		(1.099)
9	B	0	0	2.89	22	0	0.000	0.000	0.000	0.333	0.333	0.333		(1.099)
10	B	0	0	3.28	24	0	0.000	0.000	0.000	0.333	0.333	0.333		(1.099)
11	B	0	0	2.92	12	0	0.000	0.000	0.000	0.333	0.333	0.333		(1.099)
12	A	0	1	4.00	21	0	0.000	0.000	0.000	0.333	0.333	0.333		(1.099)
13	B	0	0	2.86	17	0	0.000	0.000	0.000	0.333	0.333	0.333		(1.099)
14	B	0	0	2.76	17	0	0.000	0.000	0.000	0.333	0.333	0.333		(1.099)
15	B	0	0	2.87	21	0	0.000	0.000	0.000	0.333	0.333	0.333		(1.099)
16	C	1	0	3.03	25	0	0.000	0.000	0.000	0.333	0.333	0.333		(1.099)
17	A	0	1	3.92	29	0	0.000	0.000	0.000	0.333	0.333	0.333		(1.099)
18	C	1	0	2.63	20	0	0.000	0.000	0.000	0.333	0.333	0.333		(1.099)
19	B	0	0	3.32	23	0	0.000	0.000	0.000	0.333	0.333	0.333		(1.099)
20	B	0	0	3.57	23	0	0.000	0.000	0.000	0.333	0.333	0.333		(1.099)
21	A	0	1	3.26	25	0	0.000	0.000	0.000	0.333	0.333	0.333		(1.099)
22	B	0	0	3.53	26	0	0.000	0.000	0.000	0.333	0.333	0.333		(1.099)
23	B	0	0	2.74	19	0	0.000	0.000	0.000	0.333	0.333	0.333		(1.099)

The differences between Figure 9.1 and Figure 9.2 consist of the ranges that you've seen in Chapter 8, adjusted for the fact that we now have three instead of only two outcomes. Here are the additions in Figure 9.2, spelled out.

Three Intercepts and Three Sets of Coefficients

The range B3:E5 contains the intercept and the coefficients for each of the three predictor variables, each in an equation for a different outcome value. As shown in Figure 9.2, all the intercepts and coefficients equal 0.0. After their values are optimized, the complete analysis will include:

- Values in the range B4:E5 that have been set to values that optimize the log likelihood. The range B4:E4 pertains to students who earn the letter grade A, and the range B5:E5 pertains to students who earn a C.

- Values in the range B3:E3 that remain with four 0.0 values. This range pertains to the base case, students who earn the letter grade B.

It is possible to eliminate the range B3:E3, leaving the values in the range B4:E5 to define the two equations that you get in a three-outcome logistic regression. But for convenience and clarity, this example works with the zeros in B3:E3.

Dummy Coding to Represent the Outcome Value

The next major difference between Figures 9.1 and 9.2 is in columns B and C, beginning in row 8. The values in that range represent dummy codes and identify two of the three letter grades that a student might receive. These dummy codes are used to calculate the log likelihood that is associated with each student.

As the data is set up, a student who receives a letter grade of C gets the number 1 in column B and a 0 in column C. A student who receives a letter grade of A gets a 1 in column C and a 0 in column B. A student who receives a B gets a 0 in both columns.

Setting up the dummy coding in this fashion, in the range B8:C39, defines the letter grade B as the base case—the case with a 0 in both column B and column C. There will be no equation for letter grade B, and the equations that define the outcomes for the grades of A and C establish the relationship between outcome grades A and B, and between outcome grades C and B.

Calculating the Logits

The logits for each of the three outcomes are given in the range G8:I39. The first of the three logits, in cell G8, pertains to the letter grade B. The formula to calculate its logit in cell G8 is as follows:

    =$B$3+$C$3*D8+$D$3*E8+$E$3*F8

That is, the equation sums the following four quantities:

- The intercept in cell B3
- The coefficient in cell C3 times the GPA in cell D8
- The coefficient in cell D3 times the TUCE in cell E8
- The coefficient in cell E3 times the PSI in cell F8

By using the dollar signs in the addresses for the intercept and coefficients in the formula just given, you make the references absolute and can copy the formula from row 8 through row 39 without altering the cell addresses of the intercept and coefficients.

The formulas for the logits in cells H8 and I8 are constructed in similar fashion:

Cell H8: =$B$4+$C$4*D8+$D$4*E8+$E$4*F8

Cell I8: =$B$5+$C$5*D8+$D$5*E8+$E$5*F8

So, the logits in columns G, H and I (and the probabilities in columns J, K and L) pertain to the letter grades B, A and C, respectively.

In each case, the cell references to the intercept and coefficients are shifted down by one row, from row 3 in cell G8 to row 4 in cell H8, and to row 5 in cell I8. Like the logit in cell G8, you can copy cells H8 and I8 down through row 39. The references to the students' TUCE and PSI values will adjust accordingly, and the references to the intercepts and coefficients will remain constant.

> **NOTE** After entering the formula in cell G8, you might find it convenient to make the references to cells D8, E8, and F8 mixed instead of relative. If you place a dollar sign before the D, the E, and the F, you will fix the references to their columns but not to their rows. A reference such as $D8 used in cell G8 can be copied to the right, into H8 and I8, without altering it, but when you copy it down into row 39 the reference will adjust from $D8 to $D39.

Converting the Logits to Probabilities

The range J8:L39 contains the probabilities calculated from the logits. If you refer to Figure 8.9 in Chapter 8, note that the predicted probability for a particular record is equal to the antilog of the logit divided by the quantity 1 plus the antilog of the logit. For example, if the logit is in cell E6, the predicted probability would be

=EXP(E6)/(1+EXP(E6))

A little later in this chapter, I explain the difference between calculating the predicted probabilities in the multinomial case and calculating them in the binomial case.

To continue with the analysis as Figure 9.2 plans it, the formula in cell J8 is as follows:

=EXP(G8)/(EXP($G8)+EXP($H8)+EXP($I8))

In words, this equation places the antilog of the logit in cell G8 in the numerator. The denominator consists of the sum of the antilogs of all three logits in cells G8, H8, and I8. The denominator remains the same in the calculation of all three probabilities in the range J8:L8. The numerator changes from the antilog of the value in cell G8, to that in H8, to that in I8, as you move from J8 to K8 to L8.

Notice the mixed referencing in the addresses of the cells that contain the logits. By fixing the columns to G, H, and I, but allowing the rows to vary, you make it possible to enter the previous formula in cell J8, copy it into K8 and L8, and then copy the range J8:L8 through J9:L39 without having to alter any of the cell addressing.

Here are the formulas in cells K8 and L8:

    =EXP(H8)/(EXP($G8)+EXP($H8)+EXP($I8))
    =EXP(I8)/(EXP($G8)+EXP($H8)+EXP($I8))

Calculating the Log Likelihoods

Finally, the log likelihood for each record is calculated in the range N8:N39 of Figure 9.3. The formula for the log likelihood in cell N8 is as follows:

    =(1–B8–C8)*LN(J8)+C8*LN(K8)+B8*LN(L8)

The formula works with the dummy codes in the range B8:C39 to determine which of the three probabilities should be used to calculate the log likelihood.

Suppose first that we are working with a student who received the letter grade B—that is, the base case in his example. Then that student would get a 0 in column B and a 0 in column C, and the second and third terms in the formula would therefore both result in 0.0. But in the first term, the quantity in parentheses, would evaluate to 1 – 0 – 0, and the result of the full formula would be the natural log of the probability in cell J8: that is the probability, as predicted by GPA, TUCE, and PSI, that the student would receive a B.

Now suppose that the student received a C as the letter grade, and therefore has a 1 in column B and a 0 in column C. In that case, the quantity in parentheses in the first term would evaluate to 1 – 1 – 0, and therefore the first term would equal 0.0. The formula's second term would also evaluate to zero because the student has a zero in column C. Because the student has a 1 in column B, the third term evaluates to the natural log of the probability that the student got a C—and because the first and the second terms evaluate to zero, that is the result of the full formula.

Finally, if the student got an A, the first term in the log likelihood formula evaluates to 0.0 because the quantity in parentheses returns 1 – 0 – 1. The student's 0 in column B causes the formula's third term to return 0.0, and the 1 in column C means that the second term returns the natural log of the predicted probability that the student got an A.

With the individual likelihoods in hand, we can total them to get the sum of the log likelihoods. And to convert that value to a chi square value, we multiply the sum of the log likelihoods by –2 just as was done in Chapter 8.

Understanding the Differences Between the Binomial and Multinomial Equations

Both this chapter and Chapter 8 have discussed logistic regression as you might perform it using Microsoft Excel. Chapter 8 analyzed a binary outcome variable, and this chapter has analyzed an outcome variable with three possible values. The differences in how the analyses are carried out probably seem radical. In fact, the differences are more apparent than real, and have to do with simplifications that are available in the binary situation. To explain why and how, let's revisit the binomial analysis shown in Figure 8.9 using the multinomial approach described in Figure 9.2.

See Figure 9.3, where the intercepts and the coefficients have been optimized by the use of Solver, just as they were in Figure 8.9.

Figure 9.3
The predicted probabilities are now in place in columns I:J.

H8			f_x		=$B$4+$C$4*D8+$D$4*E8+$E$4*F8						
	A	B	C	D	E	F	G	H	I	J	K
1		Intercept		Coefficients							
2			Income	Age	Zip Code						
3	No Purchase	0.000	0.000	0.000	0.000						
4	Purchase	-20.001	0.091	0.127	2.584						
5								Sum Log Likelihood:			-14.160
6											
7	Outcome	Purchase	Purchase Vector	Income ($000)	Age	Zip Code	Logits		Probabilities		Log Likelihood
8	No Purchase	0	0	79.015	50	1	0.000	-3.882	0.980	0.020	-0.020
9	No Purchase	0	0	79.897	50	1	0.000	-3.802	0.978	0.022	-0.022
10	No Purchase	0	0	82.818	47	1	0.000	-3.916	0.980	0.020	-0.020
11	No Purchase	0	0	82.210	49	1	0.000	-3.718	0.976	0.024	-0.024
12	No Purchase	0	0	87.656	42	1	0.000	-4.109	0.984	0.016	-0.016
13	No Purchase	0	0	86.013	47	1	0.000	-3.625	0.974	0.026	-0.026
14	No Purchase	0	0	85.032	49	1	0.000	-3.461	0.970	0.030	-0.031
15	No Purchase	0	0	82.914	55	1	0.000	-2.894	0.948	0.052	-0.054
16	No Purchase	0	0	86.110	51	1	0.000	-3.109	0.957	0.043	-0.044

Figure 9.3 shows the data analyzed in Figure 8.9, using the approach described so far in this chapter. For example, in Figure 8.9, the probability 0.020 in cell G6 was calculated by taking the antilog of the logit to get the odds into the cell F6, and then applying this formula in cell G6:

=F6/(1+F6)

In words, divide the odds in cell F6, the odds that this person *is* a buyer, by one plus those odds.

In contrast, in Figure 9.3, the same probability was calculated in cell J8 by means of this formula:

=EXP(H8)/(EXP($G8)+EXP($H8))

The numerator in this formula, EXP(H8), is the antilog of the logit that this person is a buyer: again, the predicted odds that this person is a buyer.

The denominator involves the antilog from the numerator, EXP(H8), just as you find in cell G6 of Figure 8.9. To that value, the formula adds the antilog of the logit in cell G8. That is the antilog for the base case, although we did not use that term in the binary situation. The logit for the base case is always zero, because its intercept and coefficients are always zero.

And the antilog of zero is always one. Therefore, although it's hidden behind the functions and the cell addresses, the formulas in cell J8 of Figure 9.3 and in cell G6 of Figure 8.9 are identical.

In Figure 8.9 we simply took the shortcut of using 1.0 in place of calculating the antilog of 0.0. In Figure 9.3, though, we can't take that shortcut because the denominator includes three terms: the antilog in the numerator, the base case (whose antilog is 1.0), *and* the antilog of the logit of the third possible outcome. Two of those terms have to be calculated explicitly for each record and so, in the interest of clarity, we make it always and calculate all three terms as antilogs.

Optimizing the Equations

With the worksheet set up as shown in Figure 9.2, it's time to optimize the equations by running Solver. See Figure 9.4.

Figure 9.4
The logistic regression after the sum of the log likelihoods has been maximized.

N8 =(1-B8-C8)*LN(J8)+C8*LN(K8)+B8*LN(L8)

	A	B	C	D	E	F	G	H	I	J	K	L	M	N
1			Coefficients								Sum Log Likelihood:			-24.786
2		Intercept	GPA	TUCE	PSI									
3	B	0.000	0.000	0.000	0.000								-2LL	49.572
4	A	-10.606	2.107	0.106	2.427									
5	C	6.778	-2.751	0.032	0.239									
6														
7	Letter Grade	C	A	GPA	TUCE	PSI		Logits			Probabilities			Log Likelihood
8	C	1	0	2.66	20	0	0.000	(2.882)	0.095	0.464	0.026	0.510		(0.673)
9	B	0	0	2.89	22	0	0.000	(2.186)	(0.474)	0.576	0.065	0.359		(0.551)
10	B	0	0	3.28	24	0	0.000	(1.152)	(1.484)	0.648	0.205	0.147		(0.434)
11	B	0	0	2.92	12	0	0.000	(3.182)	(0.874)	0.685	0.028	0.286		(0.378)
12	A	0	1	4.00	21	0	0.000	0.047	(3.559)	0.482	0.505	0.014		(0.684)
13	B	0	0	2.86	17	0	0.000	(2.779)	(0.550)	0.610	0.038	0.352		(0.494)
14	B	0	0	2.76	17	0	0.000	(2.989)	(0.275)	0.553	0.028	0.420		(0.593)
15	B	0	0	2.87	21	0	0.000	(2.334)	(0.451)	0.577	0.056	0.367		(0.550)
16	C	1	0	3.03	25	0	0.000	(1.573)	(0.764)	0.598	0.124	0.278		(1.279)
17	A	0	1	3.92	29	0	0.000	0.726	(3.086)	0.321	0.664	0.015		(0.409)
18	C	1	0	2.63	20	0	0.000	(2.946)	0.178	0.445	0.023	0.532		(0.632)
19	B	0	0	3.32	23	0	0.000	(1.174)	(1.625)	0.664	0.205	0.131		(0.409)
20	B	0	0	3.57	23	0	0.000	(0.647)	(2.313)	0.616	0.323	0.061		(0.484)

It's simple enough to optimize the equations using Solver, even in the multinomial situation. Starting with values as shown in Figure 9.2, take the steps to obtain the values shown in Figure 9.4:

1. Select cell N1.
2. Click the Ribbon's Data tab.
3. Click Solver in the Analyze group. (If you don't see Solver there, refer to Chapter 8 for instructions on locating and installing Solver.)
4. Make sure that cell N1 is specified in the Set Objective edit box, and click the Max radio button.

5. Enter the range address B4:E5 in the By Changing Variable Cells edit box. Be sure *not* to include B3:E3 in the variable cells' range.

6. Do not include any constraints. Unlike the constants used in exponential smoothing, there are no special constraints to place on coefficients and intercepts used in logistic regression.

7. Be sure to clear the checkbox labeled Make Unconstrained Variables Non-Negative.

8. Choose GRG Nonlinear in the Select a Solving Method drop-down box.

9. Click the Options button and click the GRG Nonlinear tab.

10. Be sure that the Use Multistart checkbox is cleared. (See the following Note.) Click OK.

11. Click Solve.

After a few seconds, Solver informs you that it has converged to a solution. The solution should be as is shown in Figure 9.4.

> **NOTE**
>
> I'd generally like to use Multistart with GRG solutions. But when I'm dealing with logarithms, as here, I tend to avoid that option. The reason is that I can easily end up with the logit greater than 706. That may cause the EXP( ) function to return an error value, which in turn would cause Solver to stop processing.
>
> The Multistart option causes Solver to try out various starting values in the variable cells, in order to reduce the chance of converging to a locally optimal value that is not also globally optimal. So, if you prefer to use Multistart in a logistic regression analysis, consider constraining the coefficients so that they will not return a result greater than 700 when multiplied by the observed values of the predictors.

Benchmarking the Excel Results Against R

There's no easy way—at least, none that I know of—to run a logistic regression analysis with an outcome variable that takes on more than two values. Regardless of whether you use Excel, R, or some other specifically statistical application, getting an accurate analysis requires great care.

Nevertheless, Excel is a good choice if you're still in the process of learning how logistic regression works. You can't learn to make the sausage without watching it happen. Subsequently, though, using one of R's logistic regression functions is probably safer, because there's liable to be less to go wrong.

That said, let's take a look at how you would use an R function to run the logistic regression analysis discussed so far this chapter. Chapter 8 discusses how to obtain and install the mlogit package in R. This chapter makes use of that function in the re-analysis of the data shown in Figures 9.1, 9.2 and 9.4.

The point is to establish that the `mlogit` function returns same results as does Excel. To that end, I suggest that you use either the `XLGetRange` function in the DescTools package or the `read.csv` function in R's base package. Either approach maximizes your chances of getting the data read accurately into an R data frame.

At this point I assume that you have read the data into R. If it has entered an R data frame accurately the results of using the `head` function should be as shown in Figure 9.5.

Figure 9.5
The data frame that contains the raw data is named `PSIData`.

```
> head(PSIData)
   GPA TUCE PSI Grade
1 2.66   20   0    C
2 2.89   22   0    B
3 3.28   24   0    B
4 2.92   12   0    B
5 4.00   21   0    A
6 2.86   17   0    B
> |
```

Converting the Raw Data Frame with `mlogit.data`

You can tell from Figure 9.5 that no alterations have as yet been made to the dataset. (The default for the `head` function is to display six records from the data frame.) It is usually helpful to do some prep work with the raw data to get it ready for the `mlogit` function. To take care of that we rely on the `mlogit.data` function. See Figure 9.6.

Figure 9.6
The Grade variable has been altered to contain TRUE/FALSE values.

```
> PSILong <- mlogit.data(PSIData,choice="Grade",shape="wide")
> head(PSILong)
     GPA TUCE PSI Grade chid alt
1.A 2.66   20   0 FALSE    1   A
1.B 2.66   20   0 FALSE    1   B
1.C 2.66   20   0  TRUE    1   C
2.A 2.89   22   0 FALSE    2   A
2.B 2.89   22   0  TRUE    2   B
2.C 2.89   22   0 FALSE    2   C
```

Figure 9.6 shows how the `mlogit.data` function is used to convert a data frame that's in the so-called "wide" format to the "long" format. For example, in Figure 9.5, one row of data is allocated to the first student, and all four of the observations for that student are shown in the same row. In contrast, in Figure 9.6, three rows are used to describe the first student, because the outcome variable, Grade, has three values.

The wide format, shown in Figure 9.5, names the grade specifically in the data frame's final column, where the first student receives a C grade. The long format, shown in Figure 9.6, names each possible grade, A, B, and C, in a separate row for each student. The fact that the first student received a C is shown by the value TRUE that has been assigned to the variable Grade in the data frame's long shape, in its third row.

Besides converting the Grade variable to Boolean TRUE/FALSE values, the `mlogit.data` function modifies the index that identifies the row. For example, in Figure 9.5, student number 1 is identified in the first column by the index 1. In Figure 9.6, it takes three rows to call out all the values that describe the first student. Therefore the index that identifies the first row is changed to 1.A, and to 1.B and 1.C for the second and third rows that identify the first student.

The `mlogit.data` function adds two more indexes to the long data frame in Figure 9.6. One index, *chid*, identifies the entire instance under which all the available choices are expressed. In this example that is a particular student.

The second, *alt* index simply shows the value of the outcome variable that applies to the row in question. You can see that the value of Grade is TRUE in the data frame's third row, and by looking to the third row's value for the alt index you can tell that the student received a grade of C. The principal intent of the alt index is to preserve the original values that have been replaced by Boolean values in the Grade variable (more generally, the variable that identifies the choice made in the wide format).

Notice the syntax used in the arguments to the `mlogit.data` function. There is a variety of arguments that the function can take, but the ones shown are a minimum if you expect to avoid warning or error messages. The argument represented by PSIData simply names the source of the data that is to be converted. The choice argument specifies which variable is to be treated as the outcome variable. And the shape argument specifies that the PSIData data frame conforms to the wide shape.

Applications such as R and its `mlogit` function allow for two broad classes of predictor variables. The `mlogit` function terms these variables as either *alternative-specific* or *individual-specific*. Individual-specific variables vary with the individual but not with the alternative. So, the first student has a GPA of 2.66 and that value does not change as the student's possible grade changes from A to B to C in the data frame's first three rows.

However, you often have predictor variables that do change along with the value of the outcome variable. I look at this a lot more closely later in the chapter, but for now consider that a car buyer might choose a Ford, a Toyota, or a GM. Those three brands will very likely have three different sticker prices, so if you want to use the cost of the car as a predictor, you need to account for all three prices. In that setup, the three predictors would be considered alternative-specific.

It's in the case of alternative-specific predictors that the distinction between the wide shape and the long shape becomes clearer. In the wide shape, with one row per record, you need to specify the sticker price of each car in the same row: the Ford price, the Toyota price, and the GM price. In the long shape, with one row per alternative per record, you need to specify only one alternative price per row. So the long shape is long because it includes a row for each alternative in each record. The wide shape is wide because it includes all the alternative-specific variables in the same row.

As it happens, the wide shape is cumbersome and difficult for the `mlogit` function to deal with. Although `mlogit` can deal with a wide shape, it's usually recommended that you convert a data frame with the wide shape to the long shape, via the `mlogit.data` function, before submitting the data to the `mlogit` function itself.

Calling the `mlogit` Function

Structuring the arguments to the `mlogit` function can be every bit as exacting as structuring an Excel worksheet to return the same results. But at least there's only one `mlogit` statement to worry about.

The statement to run the `mlogit` against the data first shown in Figure 9.1 is as follows:

```
PSIModel <- mlogit(Grade ~ 1 | GPA+TUCE+PSI, PSILong, shape="long",
alt.var="alt", reflevel="B")
```

You'll also find that statement at the top of Figure 9.7.

Figure 9.7
This `mlogit` statement is a simple example of a complicated function.

```
> PSIModel <- mlogit(Grade ~ 1 | GPA+TUCE+PSI,PSILong,shape="long",alt.var="alt",reflevel="B")
> summary(PSIModel)

Call:
mlogit(formula = Grade ~ 1 | GPA + TUCE + PSI, data = PSILong,
    reflevel = "B", shape = "long", alt.var = "alt", method = "nr",
    print.level = 0)

Frequencies of alternatives:
      B       A       C
0.40625 0.34375 0.25000

nr method
5 iterations, 0h:0m:0s
g'(-H)^-1g = 7.83E-07
gradient close to zero

Coefficients :
                 Estimate Std. Error t-value Pr(>|t|)
A:(intercept) -10.605706   5.123541 -2.0700  0.03845 *
C:(intercept)   6.778275   5.014041  1.3519  0.17642
A:GPA           2.107035   1.355412  1.5545  0.12006
C:GPA          -2.750675   1.704627 -1.6137  0.10660
A:TUCE          0.105934   0.145981  0.7257  0.46804
C:TUCE          0.031681   0.135456  0.2339  0.81508
A:PSI           2.426541   1.090474  2.2252  0.02607 *
C:PSI           0.239290   1.122025  0.2133  0.83112
---
Signif. codes:  0 '***' 0.001 '**' 0.01 '*' 0.05 '.' 0.1 ' ' 1

Log-Likelihood: -24.786
McFadden R^2:  0.28254
Likelihood ratio test : chisq = 19.521 (p.value = 0.0033679)
> |
```

The results of the `mlogit` function in this case are placed in an object named `PSIModel`. The name of the function itself, `mlogit`, follows the assignment operator in the statement. The function's arguments begin immediately following the opening parenthesis, and the arguments begin with a formula. That formula first specifies the name of the outcome variable: Here, that's Grade. The outcome variable is followed by the tilde(~), which separates the left side of the formula from the right side. On the right side is a specification that can have as many as three parts. If all three parts are given, the parts are separated by the piping symbol (|). You can specify all three parts if necessary, or only the first two (or conceivably only the first part). The three parts convey the information described in the following sections.

Part One: Alternative-Specific with Generic Coefficient

Part 1 contains the names of alternative-specific variables that are to have generic coefficients. The names are separated by plus signs (and that is true when you specify more than one variable in any of the three parts of the formula). Suppose that the subjects of an experiment can choose to travel either by train, plane, or automobile. You expect that the cost of going by train will differ from the cost of a plane ticket, and both will differ from the cost of going by a car.

So, the value of a cost variable will differ according to the type of travel chosen. But by putting the cost variable in the first part of the formula, you specify that you want it to have only one generic coefficient in the equation, which will not differ as a function of what mode of travel is actually chosen.

Part Two: Individual-Specific with Alternative-Specific Coefficients

Part 2 contains the names of variables that are individual-specific and that are to have alternative-specific coefficients. Continuing the example involving choice of mode of travel, suppose that the traveler's income is one of the variables. That's clearly an individual-specific variable because its value is the same whether the traveler chooses to go by train, plane or car.

However, by placing the variable in the second part of the formula specification—after the first piping symbol—you indicate to `mlogit` that the income coefficient should vary with the alternative. That is, in the travel example, the car, train, and plane alternatives should have different coefficients for the income variable.

Part Three: Alternative-Specific with Alternative-Specific Coefficients

In Part 3 of the formula, you specify (after the second piping symbol) variables that are alternative-specific, and thus are expected to have different values depending on the alternative, *and* that also are to have coefficients that vary with the alternatives.

For example, consider the length of time in transit for any journey of substantial length. Business travelers in particular may consider whether they can spend the transit time productively in their decision of whether to go by plane, train or automobile. They might conceivably decide that they can spend their time productively with access to broadband networks that are available on public transport but not necessarily in cars—certainly not if the traveler is the driver. In that case, it might be that the length of travel time is less important to their decision if they take the train or plane than if they decide to take a car. If that argument is plausible then it makes sense to allow for different coefficients for the different travel times that are associated with each travel mode.

In the PSI example, the full formula is given as

    Grade ~ 1 I GPA+TUCE+PSI

This specification omits any variables in Part 1 of the formula, and therefore there are no alternative-specific variables with generic coefficients. The 1 is included as a sort of placeholder so `mlogit` will treat the variable names that follow the piping symbol as individual-specific variables with alternative-specific coefficients. Notice that there's no second piping symbol here because, in this case, there is no third part to the formula.

Completing the `mlogit` Arguments

Compared to the formula specification, the remainder of the arguments to the `mlogit` function are very simple and straightforward. The full statement is repeated here for convenience:

```
PSIModel <- mlogit(Grade ~ 1 ¦ GPA+TUCE+PSI, PSILong, shape="long", alt.
var="alt", reflevel="B")
```

Following the formula, the next argument is `PSILong`, the name of the data frame that `mlogit` is to use. Its shape is specified as long (remember, it's not necessarily recommended but it is feasible to pass a data frame with a wide shape directly to the `mlogit` function), and the name of the index that contains the values of the alternatives is specified as `alt`.

Finally I specify the letter grade B as the reference level, which I have referred to earlier in this chapter as the base case.

When you submit that statement to R, the results of the `mlogit` analysis are stored in an object named `PSIModel`. You could then simply type the name `PSIModel` and press Enter, but you would get only the values of the intercepts and the coefficients. To get the fuller information provided in Figure 9.7, use the `summary` function with `PSIModel` as its sole argument.

At this point you're in a position to start making use of the coefficients and intercepts. You can use them, for example, to predict the grade that someone with a given GPA, TUCE, and PSI value would earn. (The prediction, of course, is more likely to be accurate when it applies to someone chosen from the same population as was the original sample.)

Furthermore, it's at this point that your choice of the reference level or base case takes on importance, because it plays a central role in the interpretation of the estimated coefficients. In this example we have set the base case to a grade of B, and the coefficient for GPA for those of a grade of C is –2.75 relative to a grade of B, the reference level. It would not be unreasonable, then, to say that a one unit increase in the GPA would lead to a 2.75 unit decrease in the likelihood of obtaining a C relative to the likelihood of obtaining a B. That makes intuitive sense: Someone with a higher GPA is less likely to obtain a C, and more likely to obtain a B, than otherwise.

Similarly, the coefficient for GPA, for those with a grade of A, is 2.107. Again, you could therefore take the position that an increase of one unit in GPA for those students would lead to an increase of 2.1 units in the likelihood of obtaining an A relative to the likelihood of receiving a B.

These inferences are not quite as strong as they would be in a simple linear regression context. Among other reasons, the inference depends on where you are in the range of values for the predictor variable in question. In linear regression, where we are working with straight regression lines, the fact of the coefficient is constant regardless of the value of the predictor. But, as you saw in Chapter 7, in logistic regression we expect the slope to change depending on its location in the range of the predictor value. So if you're making this sort of inference, it's wise to consider not just one predictor but also the simultaneous effect of the other predictor variables on the outcome.

Four Outcomes and One Predictor

Another example that's frequently cited in the literature on logistic regression concerns sport fishing. The study analyzes consumers' choice of whether to fish from a private boat, a charter boat, a pier, or the beach itself. Figure 9.8 shows how the data is laid out.

Figure 9.8

The dataset contains 1182 records, one predicted variable (Mode), and nine predictor variables.

	A	B	C	D	E	F	G	H	I	J
1	mode	price.beach	price.pier	price.boat	price.charter	catch.beach	catch.pier	catch.boat	catch.charter	income
2	charter	157.93	157.93	157.93	182.93	0.0678	0.0503	0.2601	0.5391	7083.3317
3	charter	15.114	15.114	10.534	34.534	0.1049	0.0451	0.1574	0.4671	1249.9998
4	boat	161.874	161.874	24.334	59.334	0.5333	0.4522	0.2413	1.0266	3749.9999
5	pier	15.134	15.134	55.93	84.93	0.0678	0.0789	0.1643	0.5391	2083.3332
6	boat	106.93	106.93	41.514	71.014	0.0678	0.0503	0.1082	0.324	4583.332
7	charter	192.474	192.474	28.934	63.934	0.5333	0.4522	0.1665	0.3975	4583.332

The variables are as follows:

- The choice variable, named *Mode*, in column A, indicates whether a person chose to fish from a charter boat, from a private boat, from the pier, or from the beach. Mode is the outcome variable.

- Columns B through E contain price information: for example, the first record, in row 2, shows that the price for this person to fish from the beach, from the pier, or from the boat is constant at 157.93. The cost for this person to fish from a charter boat is 182.93.

- Columns F through I contain catch rates: a rate that estimates the number or amount of fish that you could reasonably expect to catch from each of the four locales.

- Column J records the survey respondent's income.

Don't let the apparent inconsistencies in the prices throw you. The data is said to have been collected empirically during the 1990s, and perhaps it was, but it is odd that the price to fish from the beach is identical to the price to fish from a pier throughout the dataset. At any rate, the data's use in this chapter is illustrative only.

The predictor variables in columns B through J illustrate the two kinds of predictors often found in multinomial logistic regression. As discussed in the prior section, the price variables, in columns B through E, are usually termed *alternative-specific* variables. The expectation is that their value differs with the available choices: That is, the price of the beach alternative is expected to be different from the price of the charter alternative. Similarly, the value of the catch rate when fishing from the boat is expected to be different from the catch rate when fishing from the pier.

So the fact that this is a multinomial situation, rather than a binomial one, can result in as many different coefficients for a predictor as there are choices in the outcome variable. To recap: In this instance we have four choices, beach, pier, boat, and charter. It's normal to expect to have each of the four choices cost a different amount, and therefore we need to account for four different costs. Similarly, we expect there will be a different catch rate from each locale, and therefore we need to record four catch rates. Depending on our understanding of the situation in which the data was collected, we can decide to calculate a different price (and catch) coefficient for each venue, or to calculate a single generic coefficient for price (and catch).

Notice that each alternative-specific variable, such as `pier.price` or `boat.catch`, tends to differ from record to record. There's no particular reason to expect that the person recorded in row 2, who might be fishing in Oregon, must pay the same price to fish from a pier as the person fishing in Maine.

The variable in column J, Income, is an *individual-specific* variable, to contrast it with the alternative-specific variables in columns B through I. The values of an individual-specific variable vary across individuals, but are constant regardless of the choice of locale made by the individual. So, although the price and the catch rate may both differ according to where the individual wants to fish, the person's income does not. But the individual-specific variables' coefficients will often differ with the person's choice of value on the outcome variable: here, private boat, charter boat, pier, and beach.

There's another reason that dealing with a binary, two-valued outcome variable makes life easier than managing several possible outcomes. With a binary outcome variable there is only one alternative to compare an outcome to. If it's 70% that an item will sell, it's 30% that it won't. If it's 80% that a patient will recover, it's 20% that he won't. Not only is it clear what the alternative to an outcome is, there's no question about the probability to attach to that alternative.

But when you have to account for several possible outcomes, things get more complicated. Suppose, as in the prior section, that you are interested in what makes a traveler choose to travel by plane, train or automobile. Considerations such as speed and cost tend to affect the traveler's choice. How much does the travel time required affect the choice of a jet versus a train or the family car? At what point, if at all, does the shorter travel time on a plane cause the person to fly when she might otherwise drive? And to what degree does the shorter travel time mitigate the greater cost of flying? How does the availability of train travel impact that decision? (Questions such as these are particularly pertinent in the state where I live, which is preparing to spend upward of 60 billion dollars to construct high-speed rail access between Los Angeles and San Francisco.)

In order to address that sort of question, you have to account for multiple choices, not just two alternatives. And you have to account for variables whose values are specific to a particular choice. You may also need to account for variables whose values do not change depending on the choice of outcome, but that may exert a differential influence on the choice. For example, a person whose income is $30,000 per year might be unable to afford either a plane or train ticket, and therefore be forced to drive. But the person whose income is $100,000 per year might not have her choice limited by financial considerations. In that sort of case, the income variable does not change as a function of the choice of travel mode. But it does have an effect on the choice made.

Multinomial Analysis with an Individual-Specific Predictor

Let's take a look at how an analysis of the four fishing outcomes would go, using just one individual-specific predictor.

With almost 1,200 records and 10 variables, it's helpful that the fishing dataset is stored in the mlogit package. You can get the data set into R's workspace by means of this command:

```
data("Fishing",package="mlogit")
```

You can use R's XLView function to export the Fishing data frame directly into an Excel workbook. After the export is complete, you need to use Excel's text-to-columns capability to parse each row of data into 10 columns.

For this analysis I'm going to leave the price and catch variables out of the equation, and so I've deleted them from the worksheet. What remains appears in Figure 9.9.

Figure 9.9
It's much easier to construct the logistic regression analysis in Excel without extraneous variables.

	A	B
1	**mode**	**income**
2	charter	7083.3317
3	charter	1249.9998
4	boat	3749.9999
5	pier	2083.3332
6	boat	4583.332
7	charter	4583.332
8	beach	8750.001
9	charter	2083.3332
10	boat	3749.9999
11	boat	2916.6666
12	pier	3749.9999
13	boat	7083.3317
14	pier	1249.9998
15	pier	2083.3332

Figure 9.10 shows how to set up this data for analysis. I have included four vectors in columns B:E to indicate which outcome was chosen by each participant. Those vectors become useful when it's time to compute the log likelihood for each record.

Figure 9.10

The worksheet contains these values just prior to optimizing the intercept and coefficients.

▲	A	B	C	D	E	F	G	H	I	J	K	L	M	N	O
1			Coefficient								Sum Log Likelihood:	-1,638.600			
2		Intercepts	Income												
3	Beach	0.000	0.00000								-2LL	3277.200			
4	Boat	0.0000	0.0000												
5	Charter	0.0000	0.0000												
6	Pier	0.0000	0.0000												
7															
8															
9															
10		Boat	Charter	Pier	Beach				Logits			Probs			LL
11	mode	V1	V2	V3	V4	Income	Beach	Boat	Charter	Pier	Beach	Boat	Charter	Pier	
12	charter	0	1	0	0	7083.332	0 0.000	0.000	0.000	0.250	0.250	0.250	0.250	-1.39
13	charter	0	1	0	0	1250.000	0 0.000	0.000	0.000	0.250	0.250	0.250	0.250	-1.39
14	boat	1	0	0	0	3750.000	0 0.000	0.000	0.000	0.250	0.250	0.250	0.250	-1.39
15	pier	0	0	1	0	2083.333	0 0.000	0.000	0.000	0.250	0.250	0.250	0.250	-1.39
16	boat	1	0	0	0	4583.332	0 0.000	0.000	0.000	0.250	0.250	0.250	0.250	-1.39

The intercepts and the coefficients are calculated by Solver in the range B3:C7. The logits, starting in cell G12, are calculated as follows:

- For the beach, in cell G12, the formula is =$B$3+$C$3*F12.
- For the boat, in cell H12, the formula is =$B$4+$C$4*F12.
- For the charter, in cell I12, the formula is =$B$5+$C$5*F12.
- For the pier, in cell J12, the formula is =$B$6+$C$6*F12.

So the formulas for the logits simply run down the matrix in B3:C6 as you move across the predicted logits from G12 to J12. Each coefficient in C3:C6 multiplies the individual-specific variable income in column F and adds the result to each intercept in B3:B6.

The probabilities are calculated from the logits by means of the same formula used in the prior example of the PSI data frame. For example, the formula for the probability associated with the beach in cell K12 is

=EXP(G12)/(EXP($G$12)+EXP($H$12)+EXP($I$12)+EXP($J$12))

That is, the antilog of the logit for Beach, divided by the sum of the antilogs of all four logits.

Lastly, the log likelihoods are calculated in column O. The formulas in column O make use of the membership information in columns B through E to select the appropriate probability. For example, the formula in cell O12 is

=E12*LN(K12)+B12*LN(L12)+C12*LN(M12)+D12*LN(N12)

In this formula, only the Charter selection in cell C12 has the value 1. The remaining values in cells B12, D12, and E12 contain zeros and therefore only the probability for the charter enters the calculation of the log likelihood for that record.

The log likelihoods are summed in cell L1, and that cell is chosen as the target cell for Solver to optimize the values of the intercepts in the coefficients. As in the PSI example, Solver adjusts the values in the range B4:C6, leaving cells B3 and C3 with the value 0.0. The effect is to make Beach the reference level in this analysis.

Figure 9.11 shows the results of optimizing the intercepts and coefficients by means of Solver.

Figure 9.11
With this data in this model, the optimum value for the total log likelihood is –1,477.151.

	A	B	C	D	E	F	G	H	I	J	K	L	M	N	O
1			Coefficient						Sum Log Likelihood: -1,477.151						
2		Intercepts	Income												
3	Beach	0.000	0.0000000								-2LL	2954.301			
4	Boat	0.7389	0.0000919												
5	Charter	1.3413	-0.0000316												
6	Pier	0.8142	-0.0001434												
7															
8															
9															
10		Boat	Charter	Pier	Beach				Logits			Probs			LL
11	mode	V1	V2	V3	V4	Income	Beach	Boat	Charter	Pier	Beach	Boat	Charter	Pier	
12	charter	0	1	0	0	7083.332	0	1.390	1.117	-0.202	0.113	0.452	0.344	0.092	-1.07
13	charter	0	1	0	0	1250.000	0	0.854	1.302	0.635	0.112	0.264	0.412	0.212	-0.89
14	boat	1	0	0	0	3750.000	0	1.084	1.223	0.276	0.115	0.341	0.392	0.152	-1.08
15	pier	0	0	1	0	2083.333	0	0.930	1.275	0.515	0.114	0.288	0.407	0.190	-1.66
16	boat	1	0	0	0	4583.332	0	1.160	1.196	0.157	0.115	0.368	0.382	0.135	-1
17	charter	0	1	0	0	4583.332	0	1.160	1.196	0.157	0.115	0.368	0.382	0.135	-0.96

Let's compare the findings in Figure 9.11 with the results provided by R's `mlogit` function. See Figure 9.12.

Figure 9.12
The findings return by Excel and R are identical.

```
> data("Fishing",package="mlogit")
> FishModel <- mlogit(mode ~ 1 | income, Fishing, shape = "wide", varying=2:9)
> summary(FishModel)

Call:
mlogit(formula = mode ~ 1 | income, data = Fishing, shape = "wide",
    varying = 2:9, method = "nr", print.level = 0)

Frequencies of alternatives:
  beach     boat  charter     pier
0.11337 0.35364 0.38240 0.15059

nr method
4 iterations, 0h:0m:0s
g'(-H)^-1g = 8.32E-07
gradient close to zero

Coefficients :
                     Estimate  Std. Error t-value  Pr(>|t|)
boat:(intercept)    7.3892e-01  1.9673e-01  3.7560 0.0001727 ***
charter:(intercept) 1.3413e+00  1.9452e-01  6.8955 5.367e-12 ***
pier:(intercept)    8.1415e-01  2.2863e-01  3.5610 0.0003695 ***
boat:income         9.1906e-05  4.0664e-05  2.2602 0.0238116 *
charter:income     -3.1640e-05  4.1846e-05 -0.7561 0.4495908
pier:income        -1.4340e-04  5.3288e-05 -2.6911 0.0071223 **
---
Signif. codes:  0 '***' 0.001 '**' 0.01 '*' 0.05 '.' 0.1 ' ' 1

Log-Likelihood: -1477.2
McFadden R^2:  0.013736
Likelihood ratio test : chisq = 41.145 (p.value = 6.0931e-09)
> |
```

Notice in Figure 9.12 that I have skipped the step of converting the shape of the data frame from wide to long. By specifying the wide shape in the call to the `mlogit` function, you can avoid having to call the `mlogit.data` function to perform the conversion.

Multinomial Analysis with an Alternative-Specific Predictor

As a final example, let's take a look at the Fishing example using an alternative-specific variable, price, as the predictor. Recall that the Fishing dataset provides for a different price for each of the four modes: beach, boat, charter boat, and pier. The `mlogit` function employs a convenient naming convention that identifies each version of a given alternative-specific variable.

The Fishing dataset includes two such variables: *price* and *catch*. Because these variables are alternative-specific, it's necessary to distinguish the price of fishing from the beach from the price of fishing from a boat, from the price of fishing from a charter boat, and from the price of fishing from a pier. (The same is true of the *catch* variable, a measure of catch rate.) So, the fishing data set contains four price variables, named as follows:

- price.beach
- price.boat
- price.charter
- price.pier

However, the `mlogit` function recognizes the four instances of the *price* variable without making it necessary for you to specify each of them. For example, here is the call to `mlogit` as it's used in this section:

```
> FishModel <- mlogit(mode ~ 0 | 0 | price, Fishing, shape = "wide",
varying=2:9)
```

Notice that the `mlogit` function calls the *price* variable in the third part of the formula specification, following the second piping symbol. The four price variables in the dataset are not called out specifically, but are subsumed under the single use of the name *price*.

Excel has no such convenient naming shortcut. Each of the four price values must appear on the worksheet. Figure 9.13 shows one way to lay out the analysis for Excel.

Figure 9.13
The four price variables appear in columns B:E.

N9   × ✓ *fx*   {=EXP(J9)/SUM(EXP($J9:$M9))}

										Logits				Probabilities				
	A	B	C	D	E	F	G	H	I	J	K	L	M	N	O	P	Q	R
1	Mode	Coefficient																
2	beach	-0.0369														Sum Log Likelihood: -1224.7		
3	boat	-0.0210																
4	charter	-0.0143																
5	pier	-0.0348																
6																		
7																		
8	mode	price. beach	price. boat	price. charter	price. pier	Beach vector	Boat vector	Charter vector	Pier vector	beach	boat	charter	pier	beach	boat	charter	pier	Log Likeli-hood
9	charter	157.93	157.9	182.93	157.9	0	0	1	0	-5.825	-3.324	-2.623	-5.503	0.026	0.311	0.628	0.035	-0.465
10	charter	15.114	10.53	34.534	15.11	0	0	1	0	-0.557	-0.222	-0.495	-0.527	0.222	0.311	0.237	0.229	-1.440
11	boat	161.874	24.33	59.334	161.9	0	1	0	0	-5.971	-0.512	-0.851	-5.641	0.002	0.580	0.414	0.003	-0.544
12	pier	15.134	55.93	84.93	15.13	0	0	0	1	-0.558	-1.177	-1.218	-0.527	0.324	0.174	0.168	0.334	-1.096
13	boat	106.93	41.51	71.014	106.9	0	1	0	0	-3.944	-0.874	-1.018	-3.726	0.024	0.508	0.439	0.029	-0.678
14	charter	192.474	28.93	63.934	192.5	0	0	1	0	-7.100	-0.609	-0.917	-6.707	0.001	0.575	0.423	0.001	-0.861
15	beach	51.934	191.9	220.93	51.93	1	0	0	0	-1.916	-4.040	-3.167	-1.810	0.397	0.047	0.114	0.442	-0.923

The values for each of the four price variables appear in columns B:E, in rows 9 through 1190. The coefficient for each price variable appears in the range B2:B5. To simplify the example, I have called for no intercepts.

This example, with an alternative-specific variable, differs from the example shown in Figure 9.11 in the way that the logits are constructed. In Figure 9.11, the variable *income* is individual-specific. and therefore its value does not differ along with the choice of fishing mode. So the logits for each mode in the range G12:J12 are calculated with these formulas:

- G12: =$B$3+$C$3*F12
- H12: =$B$4+$C$4*F12
- I12: =$B$5+$C$5*F12
- J12: =$B$6+$C$6*F12

Notice that each formula specifies a different intercept (cells B3:B6), and a different coefficient (cells C3:C6) to multiply the *same* individual-specific variable, *income*, in cell F12.

But in Figure 9.13, the formulas for the logits in the range J9:M9 are

- J9: =$B$2*B9
- K9: =$B$3*C9
- L9: =$B$4*D9
- M9: =$B$5*E9

The latter four formulas omit the intercepts in order to keep things simple, as I mentioned earlier. But, as in Figure 9.11, they use four different coefficients with four different prices, in cells B9:E9. This is because *price*, unlike *income*, is an alternative-specific variable.

In Figure 9.13, the probabilities in columns N:Q could be calculated in the same way as in Figure 9.11. I have taken advantage of Excel's array formula capability to make the entry of the formulas a little easier and less error-prone. For example, in Figure 9.11, the formula in cell K12 for the probability that *beach* was chosen is

=EXP(G12)/(EXP($G12)+EXP($H12)+EXP($I12)+EXP($J12))

That is, the antilog of the logit in cell G12 divided by the sum of the antilogs in cells G12:J12. In contrast, the formula in cell N9 of Figure 9.13, again for the probability associated with the *beach* mode, is

{=EXP(J9)/SUM(EXP($J9:$M9))}

Notice the curly brackets surrounding the formula, indicating that it is an array-formula, entered by means of Ctrl+Shift+Enter instead of simply Enter. The array formula version has less to type and therefore less opportunity to make a typographical error. It returns exactly the same value as it would have had each of the logits in the range J9:M9 been called out specifically, as is done in the previous formula.

On the other hand, array formulas take a little bit more memory in Excel than do normal formulas. It's simply a matter of personal preference, it has nothing to do with the mathematics of logistic regression, and is offered here as only a suggestion.

In sum, that's what goes on in a multinomial regression analysis that uses an alternative-specific variable as a predictor rather than, as in Figure 9.11, an individual-specific variable. To demonstrate the equivalency, compare the coefficients and the sum of the log likelihoods in Figure 9.13 with the same values reported in Figure 9.14.

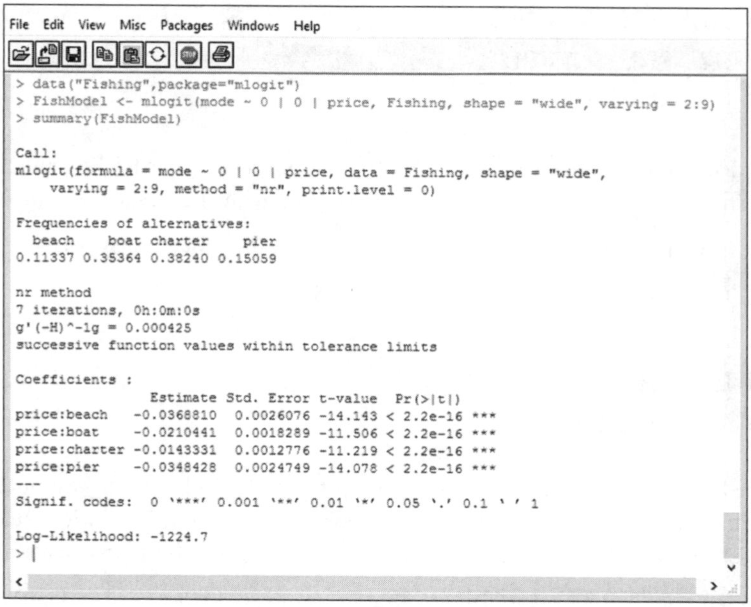

Figure 9.14
This `mlogit` analysis, which uses zeros to suppress intercepts, returns the same coefficients and log likelihood as does the Excel analysis in Figure 9.13.

```
File  Edit  View  Misc  Packages  Windows  Help

> data("Fishing",package="mlogit")
> FishModel <- mlogit(mode ~ 0 | 0 | price, Fishing, shape = "wide", varying = 2:9)
> summary(FishModel)

Call:
mlogit(formula = mode ~ 0 | 0 | price, data = Fishing, shape = "wide",
    varying = 2:9, method = "nr", print.level = 0)

Frequencies of alternatives:
  beach    boat charter    pier
0.11337 0.35364 0.38240 0.15059

nr method
7 iterations, 0h:0m:0s
g'(-H)^-1g = 0.000425
successive function values within tolerance limits

Coefficients :
               Estimate Std. Error t-value  Pr(>|t|)
price:beach   -0.0368810  0.0026076 -14.143 < 2.2e-16 ***
price:boat    -0.0210441  0.0018289 -11.506 < 2.2e-16 ***
price:charter -0.0143331  0.0012776 -11.219 < 2.2e-16 ***
price:pier    -0.0348428  0.0024749 -14.078 < 2.2e-16 ***
---
Signif. codes:  0 '***' 0.001 '**' 0.01 '*' 0.05 '.' 0.1 ' ' 1

Log-Likelihood: -1224.7
>
```

Principal Components Analysis

10

Having too many variables, and too many people or things, causes thorny problems in data analysis, and the issue is not simply the availability of sufficient computing power to handle all that data. It's extremely difficult to reach sensible conclusions—let alone communicate them—when you're awash in hundreds of distinct variables and tens of thousands of individual observations.

So, statisticians and theorists, beginning around 1900, started searching for methods of reducing all those variables to a smaller, more manageable set. Their aim was to reduce the information to meaningful combinations of variables without losing too much useful information in the process.

The family of methods that enabled the reduction of the number of variables became known as *principal components analysis* and its close cousin *factor analysis*. This chapter concerns the extraction of principal components from a set of variables, and discusses factor analysis primarily to help distinguish it from principal components analysis. You can regard principal components analysis as one type of factor analysis.

The Notion of a Principal Component

Suppose that you have a large set of measures on a large group of living beings, objects, or processes such as business transactions. For example:

- A medical researcher might have data from an array of lab tests on thousands of participants in a study of the effectiveness of a drug, probably including such measures as cholesterol levels, blood pressure, white cell counts, liver function indicators and so on.

■ If you deal with real estate transactions, you might maintain a database with the names of property owners, their estimated annual income, purchase cost of properties they own, age, ZIP Code, and so on.

■ A sales analyst for an online merchandising company might have available for each of several product lines a set of performance measures, such as quarterly revenues, profit margin, costs of advertising and distribution, cost of goods sold, and many others.

Regardless of the industry that you work in, it's very likely that you have an inventory of measures that at times becomes unwieldy. Despite the difficulty of dealing with, and interpreting, all those variables, each of them probably gives you a slightly different view of the people, objects, or lines of business that you're interested in. And in that case, it's very likely that each variable is uniquely and specifically valuable.

Nothing's free, though. To avail yourself of the richness in all that data, to evaluate the nuances that you could derive by examining the differential effects of advertising and distribution costs, you have to maintain and analyze too many variables. "Too many," that is, in a pragmatic sense. Your file server, database manager, and analysis engine can easily deal with them all simultaneously, but your brain probably can't. Bear in mind that I could easily have extended, into the hundreds or even thousands, the interesting variables listed in each of the foregoing bullet points.

Suppose, though, that there is an underlying structure to all those variables. A smaller set of variables, not directly accessible to the measuring instruments you have, might underlie the variables that you *are* able to measure. If that's the case, and if you can find a way to identify and quantify those underlying variables, you might solve some of the problems posed by the original, somewhat undifferentiated mass of data. And principal components analysis focuses on how *all* the observed variables contribute to each component. Each component is a linear composite of the full set of observed variables. Of course, different variables exert different weights on the value taken by the full composite.

A different take on the relationship between observed and underlying variables is to consider that the directly observed variables are best considered to be linear composites of one set of common components—or *factors*—and a set of unique components that each represents a specific variable. That's the viewpoint adopted by factor analysis.

In either case, you might be able to better understand the reality of the environment you're dealing with if you get a handle on how those underlying factors or components work.

Reducing Complexity

The quantitative psychologists (notably Charles Spearman) who developed this sort of analysis at the start of the twentieth century had various terms for the unseen, underlying traits that I've been discussing. One of those terms was *G factor*, which Spearman used to refer to a general intelligence factor thought to contribute to performance on a variety of tests. (The G factor was distinguished from a *specific factor*, one that was specific to particular abilities such as musical or verbal aptitude.)

Today we use terms such as *principal components*, *factors*, and *latent classes* to refer to the underlying variables that get expressed, in different ways, in the variables that we can observe and measure directly. Principal components analysis seeks to identify and quantify those components by analyzing the original, observable variables. In many cases, we can wind up working with just a few—on the order of, say, three to ten—principal components or factors instead of tens or hundreds of conventionally measured variables. When that happens, we have reduced complexity and perhaps arranged for a better view of how those underlying factors get expressed in the observable variables.

COMPONENTS AND FACTORS

Terminology presents something of a problem in this area of analytics. As I discuss in the final section of the chapter, principal components analysis and factor analysis differ in several important ways. However, both approaches seek to identify underlying structures. Principal components analysis refers to them as components and factor analysis refers to them as factors.

The two approaches borrow terminology from one another. Thus, even if you're reading about a principal components analysis, you're likely to find a table that displays the "factor structure." And because factor analyses often involve principal component analysis as an early step, you're likely to find write-ups of factor analysis using terminology that you might normally associate with principal components analysis.

I use the terms "component" and "factor" interchangeably in this chapter. This is partly because I want to avoid unfamiliar phrasing such as "component structure" and to stick with the more familiar "factor structure." And it's partly because, although there are subtle differences between factors and components, those differences have to do largely with how you view their roles.

10

Understanding Relationships Among Measurable Variables

We've all been confronted at one time or another by a correlation matrix of, say, ten variables. Making sense of the relationships between individual variables when you're gazing at 45 correlation coefficients is neither straightforward nor practical.

It's not sensible, either. If two of your variables were height and weight, you would surely observe a strong correlation between them. But particularly for people who are not yet 20 years old, age plays a part in both height and weight. You would have to ask yourself whether the relationship between height and weight would be as strong as it seems if the effect of age were controlled. And once you did that, you'd wonder about the effect of nutrition or exercise. You can see the potential for data paralysis.

But if you were able to identify underlying components, you might find that the relationships among the observable variables become much clearer. Suppose you identified an underlying component that itself has a strong correlation with both height and weight, and only a moderate correlation with age. You might, only a little arbitrarily, label that component "size." You could consider that size is a variable that describes beings that grow, and that helps to determine the strong relationship between height and weight—influenced to some lesser degree by age.

If you found four or five such components that underlie the ten variables that you have at hand, it becomes much easier to understand the various relationships among the variables. (It might even become more illuminating.)

And it becomes easier yet when you consider that you have arranged for those underlying components to be *independent of one another*. That is, the process you use to identify and quantify those components can cause them to be uncorrelated with one another—in statistical lingo, to be *mutually orthogonal*. When that's the case, you needn't wonder about the relationship between a "size" component and a "socio-economic" component; you know that the components have been derived in a way that makes them independent of one another.

Maximizing Variance

Variance, for lack of a better word, is good. Variance works. Variance clarifies.

If ten people have applied for a job and you give each one a test of their ability to do the job, you expect and want them to get different scores. If they all get the same score, you've wasted time and resources because you're no closer to distinguishing the best candidate than you were before.

In this sort of situation, you *want* the test to have variance, and that's true of all classification and selection situations. Variance enables you to tell one person or object from another, and one group of persons or objects from another. Only in a restricted set of situations—in particular, criterion-referenced testing, also termed pass-fail testing—are you unconcerned about variance. In those situations, if everybody passes the test, so much the better.

One of the characteristics of the way you go about identifying underlying components is that each component winds up accounting for as much variance as is available to it. There are a lot of issues packed into the prior sentence and the remainder of this chapter discusses them. Briefly, though...

The full set of observed, measured variables in your data set constitute the variance available to underlying components. If you have, say, ten variables to examine, there are ten "units" of variance. This isn't simply arbitrary. We frequently work with the standardized values of the observed variables, and a standardized variable is usually transformed so that it has a mean of 0 and a variance of 1. Therefore the total variance of 10 *uncorrelated* variables is 10.

The process of identifying underlying components is called *extraction*. The extraction process examines the size of the correlations among the available variables and uses them to create a new variable, a *principal component*, that comprises the existing variables. Each variable has a weight assigned to it, which depends on the strength of its correlations with the other existing variables and which expresses the variable's degree of association with the principal component.

So the newly extracted principal component—Size, perhaps—might look something like this:

Size = (Height coefficient) * Height + (Weight coefficient) * Weight

In practice, all the variables in the data set would be included in the equation that defines the newly extracted component. Normally, several of the variables would have relatively large correlations with the component. These variables are said to *load* heavily on the component. Other variables have little to do with the component. Political preference would not be expected to have much to do with a physical size component, and would not load heavily on it.

> **NOTE** The coefficients shown in the prior equation are *not* necessarily the same as loadings. You'll see in several different sections later in this chapter how coefficients and loadings differ.

Principal components are extracted sequentially from the original data set. When the extraction is complete for one component, all the variance in the full data set that can be attributed to that component is removed—*extracted*—from the collection of observed variables. The process then repeats on the reduced data set. The remaining variance is assigned to components as each is extracted.

All this has implications. One of the implications is that each component accounts for as much variance in the original variables as possible, given the correlations between those variables. The variance in each component is maximized, given that components extracted earlier have claimed the variance that's already been extracted. Therefore the differences between each person or object are also maximized. Everyone or everything has a score on the component, and the variance of those scores is maximized.

Another implication: The number of original variables in the analysis is equal to the number of components that can be extracted. If you are working with ten variables, you can extract ten components. You can't extract eleven. By the time you have extracted the tenth component, there's no variance left to extract.

In practice, though, you don't generally pay attention to all the components. It usually happens that after the first few components have been extracted, there's not much variance left in the data set to associate with the remaining possible components. You might find that of ten original variables, the first component accounts for 55% of the available variance, the second component accounts for another 20%, and the third component accounts for 15%.

This leaves 10% to be allocated among the remaining seven possible components. You would allow the analysis to continue to completion (it's usually a matter of microseconds), but both objective and subjective diagnostic tests would often tell you that the last few components aren't worth worrying about, and could well be due to nothing more than random error variation in the original variables.

Another implication is that the components are uncorrelated. The next section explores that issue in greater depth.

Components Are Mutually Orthogonal

One of the phenomena that you have to contend with in multiple regression is the presence of *shared variance*. Suppose you are investigating the relationship between cholesterol level as an outcome variable, and, as explanatory variables, both body weight and amount of red meat eaten weekly.

I'm making these numbers up, but suppose further that the correlation between cholesterol level and weight is 0.5. As discussed in Chapter 6, "Forecasting a Time Series: Regression," the square of the correlation between two variables, r^2 (or R^2 in the context of multiple regression) is the percent of variance the variables have in common. So if the simple correlation between weight and cholesterol level is 0.5, then 0.5^2 or 0.25, or 25% of the variance in weight is shared with cholesterol level. The percent of shared variance is a good (and standard) indicator of the strength of the relationship between two variables.

What of the amount of red meat consumed each week? I'm still making the numbers up, but suppose that the correlation between ounces of red meat eaten and cholesterol level is 0.6. In that case, red meat consumption and cholesterol share 0.6^2 or 36% of their variance.

Does that mean that weight and meat consumption together account for 25% + 36% = 61% of the variance in cholesterol levels? Probably not. The hitch is that weight and meat consumption are themselves correlated: there is a certain amount of variance that they share between them.

In that case, you can't simply add the two percentages together. If you do, you're counting some of the variance twice, and therefore overestimating the amount of variance in cholesterol levels that can be attributed to the combination of weight and meat consumption. First you have to remove the variance shared by the explanatory variables from one of them, so that you wind up adding together two *unique* variances. This is the process that multiple regression techniques such as forward inclusion, backward elimination, and stepwise regression are intended to carry out.

But when you're working with principal components, you avoid the ambiguity of the variance shared between explanatory variables. As I noted in the prior section, the first component extracts all the variance in the set of original, measured variables that can be attributed to that first component. When it's time to start extracting later components, there is no variance left that can be attributed to the components that have already been extracted.

Therefore, when you're working with the way that principal components combine to return an outcome, you can treat them as additive. There's no variance shared between them that could cause you to overstate their totals.

> **NOTE** Some analyses that are quite similar to principal components analysis—in particular, some types of factor analysis that use oblique rotation of factors—return factors that are not independent of one another, and that *are* correlated.

Using the Principal Components Add-In

Predictive Analytics with Excel has an add-in, named *Factor.xlsm*, available from the publisher's website at www.quepublishing.com/title/9780789758354, which you can use to extract principal components from a data matrix. The data can be in the form of raw data or a correlation matrix.

> **NOTE**
> The workbook is named *Factor.xlsm*. It is not formally an add-in, because its file extension is not *.xlsa*. Nevertheless, Excel treats it as an add-in: When you open the workbook, Excel puts the Principal Components link on the Ribbon's Add-Ins tab.

You get mostly the same results whether you choose to supply raw observations or a correlation matrix as the input data. The exception is component scores for each record. Without knowing the individual variable scores shown in a raw data list, Excel can't calculate individuals' component scores.

If you want to use raw data, it should be in the form of an Excel list or table. You can include the first row of the list or table so that the results will show the column headers as data labels.

If you use a correlation matrix, it must be rectangular. Therefore, if you use the Data Analysis add-in's Correlation tool, you have to fill in the upper triangle of the correlation matrix before submitting it to the principal components add-in. The Correlation tool creates a matrix that shows the main diagonal, consisting exclusively of 1.0 values, and the variable correlations below that diagonal. The upper triangle needs to be filled in before you can use the matrix as input to the principal components add-in.

Furthermore, using a correlation matrix, you need to specify the number of observations that the matrix is based on. This is so that a sphericity test (discussed later in this chapter) can take place.

In general, then, you'll probably find it easier to use a raw data list or table as input to the principal components add-in. If you do, you won't have to complete a triangular correlation matrix, and you won't have to specify the number of observations.

Figure 10.1 shows a sample of a data list which you could use as input, and also the correlation matrix for that data which you could use as input instead.

> **NOTE**
> In practice, you would surely have more variables to analyze and more individual observations at hand. Three variables do not make for an overwhelming amount of data to interpret. Twenty observations do not provide good, dependable indicators of the strength of the relationships between the variables. But such a small sample of variables and cases makes the example and its discussion much more crisp.

Figure 10.1
You can use either the list in A1:C21 or the correlation matrix in F2:H4 as input to the principal components add-in.

◢	A	B	C	D	E	F	G	H
1	Age	Income	Education			*Age*	*Income*	*Education*
2	7	4	3		Age	1		
3	4	1	8		Income	0.665126	1	
4	6	3	5		Education	-0.11561	-0.21227	1
5	8	6	1					
6	8	5	7					
7	7	2	9					
8	5	3	3					
9	9	5	8					
10	7	4	5					
11	8	2	2					
12	9	5	2					
13	8	4	2					
14	9	2	3					
15	8	4	7					
16	3	1	4					
17	3	1	3					
18	8	2	6					
19	1	2	5					
20	3	1	7					
21	6	3	3					

The correlation matrix in the range F2:H4 of Figure 10.1 was created using the Data Analysis add-in's correlation tool. You might have access to a triangular correlation matrix from some other application or even from a website or a print publication. If so, here's a quick way to convert it to a rectangular matrix:

1. Select the correlation matrix, including the blank cells but omitting any labels. In Figure 10.1, that's the range F2:H4.

2. On the Ribbon's Home tab, click the Copy button.

3. Select a cell a couple of rows below or to the right of the correlation matrix.

4. Click the drop-down on the Ribbon's Paste button and choose Paste Special. Fill the Transpose checkbox and click Paste.

5. Select the transposed matrix and click Copy.

6. Select the upper-left cell of the original matrix. In Figure 10.1, that's cell F2.

7. Click the Paste Button's drop-down and choose Paste Special. Fill the Skip Blanks checkbox and click Paste.

This sequence of steps fills in the empty cells in the correlation matrix. It might seem a little tedious but it's much less chancy—and much less tedious—than filling in the blank cells one by one with cell links.

When you're ready to run a principal components analysis, begin by opening the Factor. xlsm add-in. Then, with Factor.xlsm active, open the workbook that contains your data.

When you have the data available in one of the two layouts shown in Figure 10.1, click Principal Components in the Ribbon's Add-Ins tab. The dialog box shown in Figure 10.2 displays.

Figure 10.2
Use the Record IDs box only if you're supplying raw data.

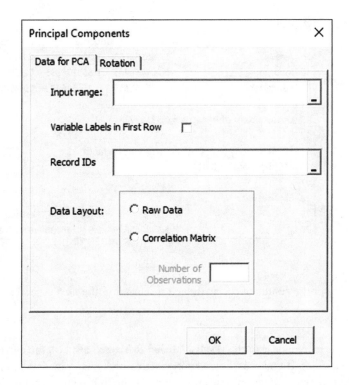

Assume first that you want to use the raw data in the range A1:C21 as your input. Follow these steps:

1. Click in the Input Range box and then drag through the range A1:C21.
2. Because you have column labels in A1:C1, select the Variable Labels in First Row checkbox.
3. Click the Raw Data option button.
4. Click OK to start the analysis.

The initial portion of the results appears in Figure 10.3.

Figure 10.3
The column headers from your input data are used to label the variables in the output.

◢	A	B	C	D
1	**R Matrix**			
2		Age	Income	Education
3	Age	1	0.665126158	-0.115614924
4	Income	0.665126158	1	-0.212274306
5	Education	-0.115614924	-0.212274306	1
6				
7	**R Inverse**			
8		Age	Income	Education
9	Age	1.795582653	-1.204496745	-0.048087558
10	Income	-1.204496745	1.855176395	0.254548482
11	Education	-0.048087558	0.254548482	1.048474463
12				
13	Determinant of R matrix = 0.531827			
14				
15	For sphericity test, Chi-square = 10.84, and df = 3			
16	P(Chi-square) = 0.013			
17				
18	**Eigenvalues**			
19		Factor 1	Factor 2	Factor 3
20		1.738265616	0.934246298	0.327486022

The meaning of the results of the analysis is discussed in the next several sections.

The R Matrix

The first matrix to appear in the results, labeled R Matrix, displays the correlations between the input variables. If you use a correlation matrix rather than raw data as input to the analysis, this matrix simply replicates the input. As the first section of this chapter suggests, the basis for a principal components analysis consists of the quantitative relationships between the variables, and they are shown in the correlation matrix.

The Inverse of the R Matrix

The inverse of the correlation matrix is both broadly useful and (at one time, at least) the most tedious and error-prone aspect of multivariate analysis. To get a basic understanding of the inverse of a matrix, we have to take a brief detour into matrix algebra.

Figure 10.4 shows the correlation matrix and its inverse from Figure 10.3. It also shows a matrix that consists of 1's and 0's, which is called an *identity matrix*.

Figure 10.4

A correlation matrix, its inverse, and an identity matrix are closely related to one another.

	A	B	C	D	E	F	G	H	I	J	K	L	M	N
1	R Matrix					R Inverse						Identity Matrix		
2		Age	Income	Educ			Age	Income	Educ					
3	Age	1	0.669	-0.101		Age	1.839	-1.282	-0.183			1	0	0
4	Income	0.669	1	-0.288		Income	-1.282	1.984	0.441			0	1	0
5	Educ	-0.101	-0.288	1		Educ	-0.183	0.441	1.109			0	0	1

An identity matrix is one with 1's in its main diagonal and 0s elsewhere. (An identity matrix is a special case of a *diagonal matrix*, which has non-zero values in its main diagonal and 0's in all other cells.)

A basic operation in matrix algebra is *matrix multiplication*. Intuitively, you might think that to multiply two matrices is simply a matter of multiplying together their corresponding elements, but it's a little more complicated than that. Figure 10.5 has a simple example of the procedure.

Figure 10.5

Matrix multiplication involves combining the rows of one matrix with the columns of another.

	A	B	C	D	E	F	G	H	I	J
1	Matrix A			Matrix B				Result Matrix		
2	4	2		5	2	5		32	22	26
3	6	2		6	7	3		42	26	36
4	3	5						45	41	30

To multiply Matrix A and Matrix B by hand, you would take these steps:

1. Multiply the first value in Matrix A's first *row* by the first value in Matrix B's first *column*.

2. Multiply the second value in Matrix A's first *row* by the second value in Matrix B's first *column*.

3. Add together the results of Steps 1 and 2 and place the result in the first row, first column of the result matrix.

You then repeat Steps 1 through 3 with the remaining rows of Matrix A and the remaining columns of Matrix B. You can find the individual formulas worked out in the result matrix if you download the workbook for this chapter from the publisher's website.

This procedure implies that of the two matrices involved, the number of columns in the first matrix must equal the number of rows in the second matrix. This restriction is often a matter for concern, but because correlation matrices are always square—and therefore have the same number of rows as columns—it's not an issue when you're dealing solely with correlation matrices, their inverses, and their transposes.

As you might expect, Excel provides a worksheet function that performs matrix multiplication. It's the MMULT( ) function, and to use it on Matrix A and Matrix B in Figure 10.5, you would take these three simple steps:

1. Select a range of cells with three columns and three rows.

2. Type the formula =MMULT(A2:B4,D2:F3).

3. Array-enter the formula with Ctrl+Shift+Enter rather than simply Enter.

There are a few points of interest about matrix multiplication that you should be aware of. One is that in general, matrix multiplication is not commutative. That is, in regular arithmetic, 9×7 returns the same result as 7×9 and in regular algebra, $xy = yx$. But in matrix algebra, *the following is not generally true* (using Excel function syntax for clarity):

   MMULT(MatrixA,MatrixB) = MMULT(MatrixB,MatrixA)

Order is important in matrix multiplication, so you often see the terms *premultiply* and *postmultiply*. For example, this array formula:

   = MMULT(MatrixB,MatrixA)

premultiplies MatrixA by MatrixB. Equivalently, MatrixA postmultiplies MatrixB.

> **NOTE** The noncommutative property of matrix multiplication had a fundamental role in the development of quantum physics in the 1920s and 1930s. Concepts such as eigenvalues and eigenvectors, which this chapter touches on in later sections, were also building blocks in the development of that branch of physics. This has nothing to do with principal components analysis. I just think it's a fun fact to know and tell.

This gets us back to the topic of an identity matrix. Although in general matrix multiplication is not commutative, this is nevertheless true:

   MMULT(I,MatrixA) = MMULT(MatrixA,I)

where I is an identity matrix and MatrixA is any square matrix. (More generally, MatrixA can be a matrix with any number of rows and columns, so long as the number of columns in the premultiplying matrix equals the number of rows in the postmultiplyng matrix.) Figure 10.6 illustrates this special property of identity matrices.

Figure 10.6
The array formulas used for the matrix multiplications are shown as text values starting in cells I1 and I6.

	A	B	C	D	E	F	G	H	I	J	K
1	Matrix A				Identity Matrix				{=MMULT(A2:C4,E2:G4)}		
2	4	2	8		1	0	0		4	2	8
3	6	2	9		0	1	0		6	2	9
4	3	5	10		0	0	1		3	5	10
5											
6	Identity Matrix				Matrix A				{=MMULT(A7:C9,E7:G9)}		
7	1	0	0		4	2	8		4	2	8
8	0	1	0		6	2	9		6	2	9
9	0	0	1		3	5	10		3	5	10

Matrices, Matrix Inverses, and Identity Matrices

After all that discussion about matrix multiplication, it's necessary to put it to work in the context of matrix inversion. In regular algebra, dividing one quantity by another might be designated in this way:

$$x\Big/y$$

You can accomplish the same thing if, instead of dividing, you multiply by the inverse of y:

$$\left(1\Big/y\right)x$$

And that's how division is accomplished in matrix algebra: Instead of dividing one matrix by another, you premultiply a matrix by the inverse of a matrix.

In matrix notation, a matrix is usually represented by a boldface and (usually) capital letter, such as **A**. You represent the inverse of **A** with a –1 as its exponent. So, the inverse of the matrix **A** is A^{-1}. And matrix "division" is shown in this fashion:

$$A^{-1}B$$

which indicates that **B** is "divided" by **A**.

There's one aspect of matrix "division" that's particularly important, even though it seldom arises in practice. That is the division of one square matrix by itself, or—more exactly—premultiplying a square matrix by another:

$$AB = I$$

If **B** is a square matrix and **I** is the identity matrix (1's in the diagonal and 0's everywhere else) then **A** is the inverse of **B**. That's one definition of the inverse of a square matrix: Premultiplying a square matrix by its inverse results in the identity matrix.

This aspect of matrix inverses is analogous to multiplying by an inverse in standard algebra:

$$\left(1\Big/x\right)x = 1$$

and in matrix algebra, you would write this:

$$X^{-1}X = I$$

where X is a square matrix and I is the identity matrix.

Figure 10.7 illustrates this relationship.

Features of the Correlation Matrix's Inverse

If the only use for the inverse of a correlation matrix were to provide a way to produce the identity matrix, it wouldn't be of much help. It turns out, though, that the inverse of the correlation matrix has some extremely useful properties.

Figure 10.7
When you multiply one matrix by its inverse, the order doesn't matter: You could use either $A^{-1}A$ or AA^{-1}.

	A	B	C	D	E	F	G	H	I	J	K
1	A^{-1}				A				{=MMULT(A2:C4,E2:G4)}		
2	-0.9615	0.7692	0.0769		4	2	8		1.00000	0.00000	0.00000
3	-1.2692	0.6154	0.4615		6	2	9		0.00000	1.00000	0.00000
4	0.9231	-0.5385	-0.1538		3	5	10		0.00000	0.00000	1.00000

One of the interesting characteristics of the relationships between variables is the amount of variance in each variable that's explained by the other variables. In the example that this chapter has been using, you might ask these questions:

- What percent of the variance in Age is associated with the variance in Income and Education?

- What percent of the variance in Income is associated with the variance in Age and Education?

- What percent of the variance in Education is associated with the variance in Income and Age?

You could answer those questions by running LINEST() three times, each time using a different variable as the predicted variable and the other two variables as the predictors (see Figure 10.8).

For example, to get the percent of variance in Age that is shared with the combination of Income and Age, you could use this formula on the data as laid out in Figure 10.8:

=INDEX(LINEST(A2:A21,B2:C21,,TRUE),3,1)

> **NOTE**
>
> Because the INDEX() function looks inside the LINEST() results for a single value, you need not array-enter the formula even though it uses the LINEST() function.

Figure 10.8
The values of R^2 are directly available from the inverse of the R matrix.

	A	B	C	D	E	F	G	H	I
1	Age	Income	Educ					From LINEST	From R^{-1}
2	7	4	3		Age by Income, Educ			0.443	0.443
3	4	1	8		Income by Age, Educ			0.461	0.461
4	6	3	5		Educ by Income, Age			0.046	0.046
5	8	6	1						
6	8	5	7						
7	7	2	9	R	Age	Income	Educ		
8	5	3	3	Age	1	0.665	-0.116		
9	9	5	8	Income	0.665	1	-0.212		
10	7	4	5	Educ	-0.116	-0.212	1		
11	8	2	2						
12	9	5	2						
13	8	4	2	R^{-1}	Age	Income	Educ		
14	9	2	3	Age	1.796	-1.204	-0.048		
15	8	4	7	Income	-1.204	1.855	0.255		
16	3	1	4	Educ	-0.048	0.255	1.048		
17	3	1	3						
18	8	2	6						
19	1	2	5						
20	3	1	7						
21	6	3	3						

That formula returns the full results of the LINEST() function as applied to the data in A2:C21. However, as used here, the INDEX() function returns the value in the third row, first column of those results, and the value of R^2 is always in that cell if you call for all the LINEST() statistics using TRUE as its fourth argument.

That R^2, the percent of variance in Age that is associated with variance in Income and Education, appears in cell H2 of Figure 10.8.

The identical value appears in cell I2. It is returned by this formula:

=1−1/F14

Notice that the correlation matrix for Age, Income, and Education appears in F8:H10. The inverse of that matrix, designated by R^{-1}, is found in F14:H16. You get that inverse by using Excel's MINVERSE() worksheet function. Take these steps:

1. Select a range of cells with the same dimensions as the existing matrix—here, that's three rows and three columns.

2. Type the formula =MINVERSE(F8:H10), adjusting the range argument according to where the existing matrix is found.

3. Finish with Ctrl+Shift+Enter. In this case, you must array-enter the formula.

> **NOTE**
>
> If you've ever calculated the inverse of a matrix by hand, you'll really appreciate the MINVERSE() function and how easy it is to use. Getting an inverse manually is torture, and it's so involved that you usually get it wrong.

Here's the formula that's in I2 once more:

=1–1/F14

In words, get the first element in the diagonal of the inverse matrix. Take the inverse of that value, by dividing it into 1, and subtract that ratio from 1. The result is the percent of the variance of one of the variables that it shares with the other variables in the original correlation matrix.

The formulas that are in I3 and I4 are as follows:

=1–1/G15

=1–1/H16

Notice that the basic pattern is the same in each formula. The only difference is that in each case, you use a different element from the main diagonal of the inverse of the original correlation matrix.

As I discussed earlier, these values are the percent of shared variance between one variable and the other variables in the correlation matrix. As such, they are also the R^2 values returned by LINEST(), shown in H3 and H4.

Another term for R^2 is *squared multiple correlation*, or *SMC*. SMCs are sometimes used in procedures that are similar to principal components analysis, and that are grouped under the general term *factor analysis*. Factor analysts often replace the 1.0 values in the diagonal of the original correlation matrix with the SMCs, for reasons that I touch on later in this chapter.

Matrix Inverses and Beta Coefficients

Don't get the idea that the only use there is for the inverse of a matrix is to calculate SMCs. The inverse of a matrix can also play a role in calculating the regression weights in a multiple regression equation. Figure 10.9 has an example.

I have added another variable, height (in inches), to the raw data matrix used in earlier figures in this chapter. You might use similar data if you want to test the notion that a person's height contributes, if only a little, to that person's income. Is it true that taller people are paid higher salaries?

You won't get the answer here because once again, I made the numbers up. Still, it's a good example of the range of roles that the inverses of matrices can play in multivariate analyses.

In Figure 10.9, cells F3:I3 show the first row of a LINEST() analysis of the raw data in cells A2:D21. Only the regression coefficients (cells F3:H3) and the intercept (cell I3) are shown.

The range G7:I9 contains a *covariance* (not a correlation) matrix for the independent variables Education, Age, and Height. The reason to use covariances instead of correlations is that we want to preserve the information about the variability of the individual variables. Recall that the definition of the correlation between variables X and Y is

$$r_{xy} = s_{xy} / s_x s_y$$

In words, the correlation is the covariance divided by the product of the standard deviations of the two variables. Dividing by the standard deviations forces the possible range of correlation coefficients into the range between −1.0 and +1.0. Doing so removes the effect of the variables' scales of measurement. That makes it possible to directly compare the correlation of, say, Age with Income to the correlation of Education with Height. All standard correlations fall within the range of −1.0 to +1.0 and are commensurate.

But the coefficients in a regression equation are intended to be used with variables in their original scale of measurement. Therefore, the analysis shown in Figure 10.9 must retain the effects of the scale of measurement on the variables, and so it uses covariances instead of correlations.

Figure 10.9
This analysis uses covariance matrices instead of correlation matrices.

	A	B	C	D	E	F	G	H	I
1	Income	Educ	Age	Height					
2	4	3	7	75		{=LINEST(A2:A21,B2:D21,,TRUE)}			
3	1	8	4	57		0.02740	0.43593	-0.07333	-1.29022
4	3	5	6	85					
5	6	1	8	75		Covariance matrix			
6	5	7	8	63			Education	Age	Height
7	2	9	7	61		Education	5.4275	-0.6275	-2.8644
8	3	3	5	57		Age	-0.6275	5.4275	-2.2646
9	5	8	9	59		Height	-2.864391	-2.2646	95
10	4	5	7	85					
11	2	2	8	56		Inverse of Covariance matrix			
12	5	2	9	59			Education	Age	Height
13	4	2	8	66		Education	0.19044	0.02466	0.00633
14	2	3	9	66		Age	0.02466	0.18929	0.00526
15	4	7	8	69		Height	0.00633	0.00526	0.01084
16	1	4	3	78					
17	1	3	3	59		Covariance, Income by Predictors			
18	2	6	8	78			Income		Betas
19	2	5	1	80		Educ	-0.75000		-0.07333
20	1	7	3	57		Age	2.35000		0.43593
21	3	3	6	75		Height	1.82556		0.02740

The range G13:I15 contains the inverse of the covariance matrix in G7:I9. The inversion process doesn't care whether it's applied to a correlation matrix or a covariance matrix, and here you have the inverse of a covariance matrix.

Cells G19:G21 contain the covariances of the dependent variable, Income, with the three independent variables: Education, Age, and Height.

Finally, cells I19:I21 contain this array formula:

=MMULT(G13:I15,G19:G21)

which postmultiplies the inverse of the covariance matrix of the independent variables by the covariance vector of the independent variables with the dependent variable.

> **NOTE** Technically, a *matrix* has more than one row and more than one column. A *vector* has one row and more than one column, or one column and more than one row. A *scalar* is a single number—in worksheet terms, a scalar would occupy a single cell.

Notice that the values returned by the matrix multiplication in I19:I21 are identical to the weights returned by LINEST() in F3:H3 (although LINEST()'s idiosyncrasy returns them in reverse of the order of the original variables on the worksheet).

Using matrix notation, the formula is

$$\mathbf{B} = \mathbf{C}^{-1}\mathbf{c}$$

where

- **B** is the matrix of beta weights.
- **C**$^{-1}$ is the inverse of the covariance matrix of the independent variables.
- **c** is a vector of covariances of the independent variables with the dependent variable.

Again, I do not recommend that you calculate the regression weights in this fashion. I have provided it to demonstrate that the inverse of a matrix that represents the strength of relationships between variables (whether correlation or covariance) plays an important role in the outcome of a multivariate analysis.

> **NOTE** You might have noticed that the intercept returned by LINEST() is not part of the results of the matrix algebra demonstrated in Figure 10.9. If you add a vector of 1's to the raw input data and a sum of squares and cross-products matrix instead of a covariance matrix, you can obtain the full regression equation. *Statistical Analysis: Microsoft Excel 2013* demonstrates the complete analysis using matrix algebra at the end of Chapter 4. But bear in mind that Excel no longer uses matrix algebra to calculate the results of LINEST(), but instead uses a method called *QR decomposition*, discussed briefly in the next section.

Singular Matrices

One problem that arises occasionally in the process of inverting a matrix is that of the *singular matrix*. A singular matrix cannot be inverted because it *has* no inverse.

This sort of thing can happen on rare occasions, particularly when someone has been a little careless in creating the raw data matrix. If two variables in the raw data matrix are perfectly correlated, the matrix is singular and has no inverse.

Singular matrices don't tend to show up on their own but usually require some human intervention. For example, one way to use multiple regression is to apply a coding scheme that assigns 1's and 0's (and sometimes –1's) to represent nominal variables such as make of car or political party. If that coding process is done carelessly, it's entirely possible to wind up with a couple of variables that are perfectly correlated.

On really rare occasions you might have a matrix that doesn't start life as a singular matrix, but the component extraction process leaves you with an intermediate matrix that *is* singular.

> **NOTE** One way to diagnose a singular matrix is by way of its *determinant*. Matrix determinants, like matrix inverses, have many uses but those are beyond the scope of a chapter on principal components analysis. Excel has a worksheet function, MDETERM(), that calculates a matrix determinant. A singular matrix has no inverse, but it does have a determinant, which is zero. If you suspect that you have a singular matrix, point MDETERM() at it. (MDETERM() does not require that it be array-entered.) If the function returns the value 0, your matrix is singular.

Unfortunately, there's not much that can be done immediately about a singular matrix, beyond checking that the data has been entered properly. Probably the best solution is to acquire more data and use it to generate another version of the matrix in the hope that it will be non-singular.

> **NOTE** Versions of Excel since 2003 have adopted a different method of getting to the regression equation's coefficients. The method, which is termed *QR decomposition*, replaces matrix inversion and therefore avoids the problem of determinants that equal 0 and the impossibility of inverting a singular matrix. The solution is not ideal—for example, it drops a predictor variable that is collinear with another predictor from the regression equation—but it does represent an improvement over the older matrix inversion method.

Testing for Uncorrelated Variables

One reason that you would like to have as many observations (people, objects, business transactions) as possible for your analysis is that the more observations, the more likely it is that the correlations you obtain are accurate estimators of the population correlations.

In small sample research (say, a few dozen observations through a very few hundred), it's entirely possible that sampling error might result in some correlations that are moderate (say, 0.5) or even fairly large (say, 0.7) when the correlation between the same variables in the full population is zero or near zero.

When two variables are uncorrelated because their relationship is random, you expect a scatterchart based on their values to look similar to the one in Figure 10.10.

The two variables, Street Address and Blogs Read Daily, are expected to be uncorrelated. In the two-dimensional space of an Excel scatterchart, they tend towards forming a circle.

Suppose you add a third variable such as Students in High School Graduating Class, or any other variable that you expect to be independent of the other two. If you were then able to create a scatterchart of the three variables on a three-dimensional computer screen, they would no longer form a circle but a sphere. The analogy continues through more variables and dimensions, but we aren't able to visualize four or more dimensions as easily as we can two or three.

With small samples it's all too easy to derive correlations of 0.2 to, say, 0.6 just because of sampling error, when the correlations in the population are 0.0. We would like to avoid being misled by the observed correlations. We can run a statistical test that tells us the likelihood that we would observe the correlations that we have from our sample, when the correlations in the population are actually 0.0.

Figure 10.10
Two variables that are statistically independent chart as a random spray of markers.

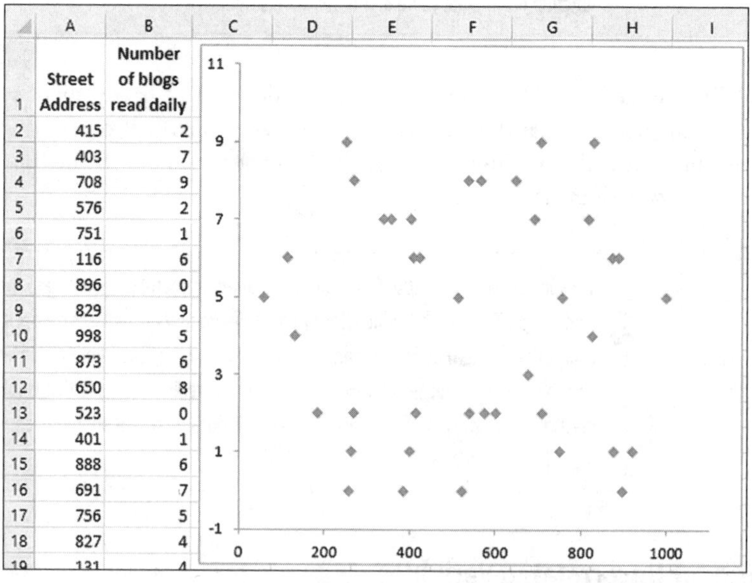

If the population correlations are 0.0, then the correlation matrix based on the full population is actually an identity matrix: one with 1's in the main diagonal and 0's elsewhere. If you had access to the full population, the correlation matrix might actually be an identity matrix. That would come about if the variables are statistically independent of one another (and thus the correlations are 0) but perfectly correlated with themselves (and therefore, the main diagonal contains 1's). At the same time, a small sample from that population might result in a correlation matrix such as the one that you see in cells B3:D5 in Figure 10.3.

In that case, a principal components analysis would be both pointless and inappropriate. Uncorrelated variables cannot mutually define an underlying component and each variable represents its own component.

Bartlett's test, shown in the range A15:A16 of Figure 10.3, assesses the likelihood that the correlation matrix based on the population is an identity matrix. If you get a significant result from Bartlett's test, you can conclude that there is at least one non-zero correlation in the population from which you got your data set, and that it makes sense to continue with the analysis. Bartlett's test calculates an (approximate) chi-square value.

The results of the principal components add-in that is available with this book calculates the appropriate degrees of freedom and the likelihood of an obtained sphericity value under a null hypothesis that the correlation matrix is an identity matrix. (Although the test is approximate, it has high statistical power.)

Using Eigenvalues

Like the inverse of the correlation matrix, eigenvalues have interpretations and uses throughout multivariate analysis in general and in principal components analysis in particular.

When principal components analysis extracts the first component from the data, that component accounts for the largest amount of variance possible in the set of measured variables.

It happens that as part of the extraction process, the component is positioned so that it has the highest correlation possible with each of the individual variables.

Visualize a box that contains a tiny universe. In that universe are galaxies of stars. The galaxies tend to be rather far from one another, but the individual stars in each galaxy are relatively close. Each galaxy represents a different variable and the stars in each galaxy represent individual observations of that variable.

Now you pick up a thin, straight rod and slide it into that tiny box-universe. There is a very large number of ways you could do so. You could start it out near one of the corners of the box or closer to the center of a side. You could orient the rod up and down, or left to right, or forward through the universe. (The rod does have to go through the center of the universe.) It can be vertical, horizontal, or on an angle.

The rules of principal components analysis position the rod for you: It must be positioned so that the overall distances between the centers of the galaxies and their nearest points on the rod are minimized. Notice that this is analogous to the least-squares principle.

That rod is the first principal component. The distances between the centers of the galaxies and the rod are actually correlations, but in a counterintuitive sort of way. A large correlation between a variable and a component means that the component is close to the variable—that the rod comes close to the center of that galaxy. (It's counterintuitive because we're used to thinking that a larger number of, say, miles indicates greater distance, whereas in our tiny universe, a large correlation indicates closer distance.)

Now take the square of each of those correlations. As this book has discussed in several chapters, the square of a correlation, or R^2, expresses the percent of shared variance between two variables—or, in this instance, between a variable and the combination of variables referred to as a component.

If you add together all those R^2 values, you get what's called an *eigenvalue*. It tells you how much of the total variance in all your observed variables is attributable to the component that you have extracted.

It is the continued product of the eigenvalues that results in the determinant of the original correlation matrix. That is, if you multiply all the eigenvalues together, the result is the correlation matrix's determinant.

Consider the implications of that fact. In the earlier section titled "Singular Matrices," I pointed out that a matrix whose determinant is zero is singular and therefore has no inverse. The only way that you can get zero as the value of the determinant is if at least one of the eigenvalues is zero: For example, $1.728 \times 1.272 \times 0$.

Because the eigenvalues are measures of the amount of the original variance attributable to each component, an eigenvalue of zero means that all the variance that could be attributed to that component has already been extracted and there's none left for it.

If all that variance is already accounted for, there must be another, earlier component that has extracted it. In that case, one (or more) of the variables in the correlation matrix is perfectly correlated with the variable whose variance has already been extracted. That's why a data matrix in which one variable is perfectly correlated with another, or with a combination of two or more other variables, has a zero determinant, is singular, and cannot be inverted.

> **NOTE**
> Recall that this chapter mentioned that the total amount of variance in the observed variables is equal to the number of variables: Each variable contributes one "unit" of variance. When you have extracted all the components, all the variance has been accounted for. When you add together the eigenvalues associated with all the components, therefore, you wind up with a sum that equals the number of variables that you started out with.

Using Component Eigenvectors

Figure 10.11 shows the continuation of the results of running the principal components add-in.

Figure 10.11
The eigenvectors have a
geometric interpretation.

	A	B	C	D	E
1	**Eigenvectors**				
2		Factor 1	Factor 2	Factor 3	
3	Age	0.663916	0.288961	0.689721	
4	Income	0.684634	0.136143	-0.71606	
5	Education	-0.30082	0.947611	-0.10744	
6					
7	**Factor Score Coefficients**				
8		Factor 1	Factor 2	Factor 3	
9	Age	0.503564	0.298957	1.20525	
10	Income	0.519279	0.140852	-1.25127	
11	Education	-0.22816	0.980391	-0.18775	
12					
13	**Factor Structure**				
14		Factor 1	Factor 2	Factor 3	
15	Age	0.875329	0.2793	0.394703	
16	Income	0.902644	0.131591	-0.40977	
17	Education	-0.39661	0.915927	-0.06149	
18					
19	**Variable**	**Communalities**			**SMCs**
20	Age	77%	8%	16%	0.443078
21	Income	81%	2%	17%	0.460968
22	Education	16%	84%	0%	0.046233
23					
24	**Factor Scores**				
25		Factor 1	Factor 2	Factor 3	
26		0.644496	-0.51807	-0.35582	
27		-1.52085	0.922444	0.164396	
28		-0.10993	0.102375	-0.20928	

10

Cells B3:D5 in Figure 10.11 contain what are called *eigenvectors*. Each component has
an eigenvector. Technically, the eigenvectors consist of direction cosines that rotate the
original data set to the principal components orientation in that little universe I asked you
to visualize. They tell Excel where to position the components so that:

- They are perpendicular to one another (and are therefore uncorrelated).
- They run through the center of the universe.
- They come as close as possible to each variable.

But the eigenvectors have more prosaic uses. One of them appears in Figure 10.12.

Figure 10.12
Combined with the eigenvalues, the eigenvectors give you the factor structure.

▲	A	B	C	D
1	**Eigenvectors**			
2		Factor 1	Factor 2	Factor 3
3	Age	0.663916	0.288961	0.689721
4	Income	0.684634	0.136143	-0.71606
5	Education	-0.30082	0.947611	-0.10744
6				
7	**Eigenvalues in a diagonal matrix**			
8		1.738266	0	0
9		0	0.934246	0
10		0	0	0.327486
11				
12	**Square roots of eigenvalues**			
13		1.318433	0	0
14		0	0.966564	0
15		0	0	0.572264
16				
17	**Factor structure matrix**			
18	Age	0.875329	0.2793	0.394703
19	Income	0.902644	0.131591	-0.40977
20	Education	-0.39661	0.915927	-0.06149

Figure 10.12 repeats in the range B3:D5 the eigenvectors shown in Figure 10.11. The eigenvalues are taken from Figure 10.3 and appear, recast in a diagonal matrix, in Figure 10.12, cells B8, C9 and D10. The square roots of the elements in that diagonal matrix are found in B13, C14, and D15.

Finally, cells B18:D20 contain this array formula:

=MMULT(B3:D5,B13:D15)

In matrix notation, this multiplication would be expressed as follows:

$$\mathbf{S} = \mathbf{VL}^{-1/2}$$

where $\mathbf{S}$ is the structure matrix, $\mathbf{V}$ is the eigenvector matrix, and $\mathbf{L}^{-1/2}$ is the diagonal matrix with the square roots of the eigenvalues.

The eigenvectors in B3:D5 are postmultiplied by the square roots of the eigenvalues, arrayed in a diagonal matrix. The result of this matrix multiplication is termed the *factor structure*, a fancy name for the correlations between the components and the observed variables. The role of the factor structure is discussed next.

Factor Loadings

The individual elements of the factor structure matrix are correlations, as I just noted, but they are more often referred to as *loadings*: for example, you might hear someone speak of the Age variable as loading high on Factor 1.

You often get your best sense for what a component represents when you examine the variables that have high loadings on the component. If only one variable carries a high load on a component, it's likely that the component represents whatever that variable measures. But you often find that more than one variable loads high on a given component, and then you need to figure out what that component represents for it to correlate strongly with those two variables.

In principal components analysis, it often happens that the first component extracted has high loadings with all or most of the variables. Subsequent components often have more moderate loadings, with some positive and some negative. In order to make sense of the loadings, it can be necessary to *rotate* the positions of the components in the universe so that the variable loadings make a more interpretable pattern. I'll go into that a little further at the end of this chapter.

Factor Score Coefficients

Another use for the eigenvectors is in deriving coefficients for the original variables that result in a factor score for each record. If you have started with a set of raw data, then you have access to the individuals' scores on each variable in the principal components analysis. In that case you can calculate each individual's value on a factor—or *factor score*—by means of an equation such as this one:

$$\text{Factor Score}_i = C_1 X_{1i} + C_2 X_{2i} + \ldots + C_n X_{ni}$$

where

- Factor Score$_i$ is the score on a factor for the i-th individual.
- C_1 is the coefficient for variable 1.
- X_{1i} is the i-th person's score for variable 1.

The equation is directly analogous to a multiple regression equation, in which regression coefficients for each variable are applied to individuals' scores on the associated variables.

Figure 10.13 shows how the eigenvalues and eigenvectors are used to derive the factor score coefficients.

The eigenvectors and the eigenvalues shown in Figure 10.13, cells B3:D5 and B8:D10, are identical to those shown in Figure 10.12. However, the diagonal matrix in B13:D15 contains not the square roots of the eigenvalues, as in Figure 10.12, but the reciprocals of the square roots. For example, the formula in cell B13 of Figure 10.13 is as follows:

=1/SQRT(B8)

Figure 10.13
The matrix algebra for the factor structure is just a short step from the algebra for the factor score coefficients.

	A	B	C	D
1	**Eigenvectors**			
2		Factor 1	Factor 2	Factor 3
3	Age	0.663916	0.288961	0.689721
4	Income	0.684634	0.136143	-0.71606
5	Education	-0.30082	0.947611	-0.10744
6				
7	**Eigenvalues in a diagonal matrix**			
8		1.738266	0	0
9		0	0.934246	0
10		0	0	0.327486
11				
12	**Inverses of square roots of eigenvalues**			
13		0.758476	0	0
14		0	1.034592	0
15		0	0	1.747445
16				
17	**Factor score coefficients**			
18	Age	0.503564	0.298957	1.20525
19	Income	0.519279	0.140852	-1.25127
20	Education	-0.22816	0.980391	-0.18775

The matrix multiplications in B18:D20 of both Figure 10.12 and 10.13 are identical, but because the reciprocals are used in B13:D15 of Figure 10.13, the results are different. Instead of factor loadings (the correlations between the factors and the variables), the result of the matrix multiplication in Figure 10.13 is the set of factor score coefficients.

You use them as sketched earlier in this section. Figure 10.14 shows how to obtain the full set of factor scores for all the individual observations. (If you submit a raw data list to the principal components add-in, instead of a correlation matrix, it automatically returns the factor scores.)

Figure 10.14 shows the original data list in columns A through C. This data set must be standardized before you can use it with the factor score coefficients, and that has been done in columns E through G. Each value in columns A through C has been converted to a z-score by subtracting the mean of the variable and dividing by the standard deviation. For example, the value in cell E2 is calculated with this formula:

=(A2-AVERAGE(A$2:A$21))/STDEV.P(A$2:A$21)

Figure 10.14
It's necessary first to standardize the original observations.

N2 {=MMULT(E2:G21,J2:L4)}

	A	B	C	D	E	F	G	H	I	J	K	L	M	N	O	P
1	Age	In-come	Educ		Age	In-come	Educ		Factor score coefficients					Factor 1	Factor 2	Factor 3
2	7	4	3		0.279	0.659	-0.708		Age	0.504	0.299	1.205		0.644	-0.518	-0.356
3	4	1	8		-1.009	-1.319	1.438		Inc.	0.519	0.141	-1.251		-1.521	0.922	0.164
4	6	3	5		-0.150	0.000	0.150		Educ.	-0.228	0.980	-0.188		-0.110	0.102	-0.209
5	8	6	1		0.708	1.978	-1.567							1.741	-1.046	-1.327
6	8	5	7		0.708	1.319	1.009							0.811	1.386	-0.986
7	7	2	9		0.279	-0.659	1.867		Age	Inc.	Educ	Fctr 1		-0.628	1.821	0.811
8	5	3	3		-0.579	0.000	-0.708		0.140	0.342	0.162	0.644		-0.130	-0.868	-0.565
9	9	5	8		1.137	1.319	1.438							0.930	1.936	-0.549
10	7	4	5		0.279	0.659	0.150							0.449	0.324	-0.517
11	8	2	2		0.708	-0.659	-1.137							0.274	-0.996	1.892
12	9	5	2		1.137	1.319	-1.137							1.517	-0.589	-0.066
13	8	4	2		0.708	0.659	-1.137							0.959	-0.811	0.242
14	9	2	3		1.137	-0.659	-0.708							0.392	-0.447	2.329
15	8	4	7		0.708	0.659	1.009							0.469	1.294	-0.161
16	3	1	4		-1.438	-1.319	-0.279							-1.345	-0.889	-0.031
17	3	1	3		-1.438	-1.319	-0.708							-1.247	-1.310	0.050
18	8	2	6		0.708	-0.659	0.579							-0.118	0.687	1.570
19	1	2	5		-2.296	-0.659	0.150							-1.533	-0.632	-1.971
20	3	1	7		-1.438	-1.319	1.009							-1.639	0.373	-0.272
21	6	3	3		-0.150	0.000	-0.708							0.086	-0.739	-0.048

Notice, by the way, that you use the population form of the standard deviation function in the denominator.

The range I7:L8 shows how you can painfully grind out the factor scores one by one, but I mean it to be illustrative only. The formulas used in I8:L8 are as follows:

I8: =E2*J2

J8: =F2*J3

K8: =G2*J4

L8: =I8+J8+K8

Cells I8:K8 each multiply an individual's z-score on a particular variable (E2:G2) by the factor score coefficient for that variable (J2:J4). Add up the results in cell L8 to get that individual's score on Factor 1. Compare the result to the one reported by the principal components add-in in Figure 10.15.

Before leaving Figure 10.14, though, notice the much easier method for obtaining all the factor scores for all the individual records shown in the range N2:P21. All that's necessary is to postmultiply the standardized individual variable scores in the range E2:G21 by the factor score coefficients in the range J2:L4. The Excel array formula in N2:P21 is as follows:

=MMULT(E2:G21,J2:L4)

Compare the result calculated manually in cell L8, 0.644, with the identical value returned by the MMULT() function in cell N2.

Figure 10.15 shows one important result of extracting factors from the original matrix of measured variables. That figure shows three scattercharts. Each chart plots one of the factors against one of the others, using the factor scores calculated in Figure 10.14. You can infer by eyeballing each chart that the factors are uncorrelated, but by adding a trendline to each chart, you can also display the R^2 value for the two plotted data series. R^2 is 0.000 in each case, because the two factors are uncorrelated in each case. (You can't see the trendline itself because the correlations are all 0.0. Therefore, the trendline is horizontal and lies directly on top of the horizontal value axis.)

Figure 10.15
Each factor is uncorrelated with each other factor.

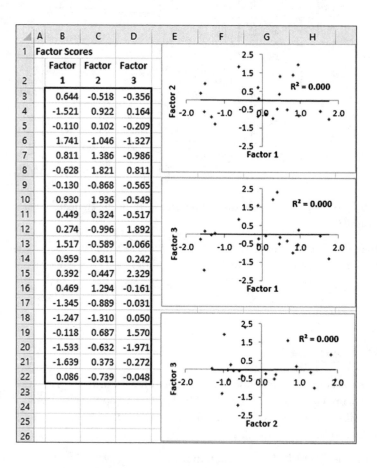

That the factors are uncorrelated is important for a variety of reasons. One is that they're *supposed* to be uncorrelated. If there were any correlation between the components, they would share variance. But the variance extraction process is intended to remove all the variance attributable to a particular component before moving on to the next component. That ensures that no two factors share any of the available variance and, therefore, that the factors (or, equivalently, the components) are uncorrelated, unique, and measure completely different underlying traits. (Again, though, this is the case only for orthogonal extraction and rotation. Oblique methods allow for correlated factors.)

Principal Components Distinguished from Factor Analysis

This chapter focuses primarily on principal components analysis, and you might be wondering where factor analysis fits into the discussion. A few meaningful differences distinguish factor analysis from principal components analysis, and this section provides an overview of how the approaches differ.

Distinguishing the Purposes

Principal components analysis is most often used to reduce a larger number of variables to a smaller number of components. Although principal components analysis extracts as many components as there are original variables, with real-world data you can usually ignore the components that are last to be extracted.

The general idea, as I've mentioned several times in this chapter, is to make a large inventory of variables more manageable. It usually proves more sensible to analyze the differences between groups when you do so on the basis of 3 or 4 important components rather than 20 or more measured, observed variables.

Given that point of view, principal components analysts generally view the components as arising from the measured variables.

In contrast, factor analysts are often engaged in the development of measures—of psychological or cognitive attributes, of batteries of health and medical tests, of variables such as market indexes that describe economic behavior, and so on. The viewpoint adopted is that certain factors, none of them directly measurable, underlie the variables that *can* be directly measured; those variables simply represent the different ways that the factors express themselves in everyday life.

Given that point of view, factor analysts generally view the variables as in some sense caused by the factors.

Those viewpoints—and I've oversimplified them terribly here—appear in the way that the data gets presented to the extraction process.

Distinguishing Unique from Shared Variance

As you've seen, principal components analysis seeks to assign all the variance in a set of variables to a set of principal components. At the end of the analysis, you might discard the final components if they don't account for a meaningful amount of the available variance. You might then use the factor score coefficients to convert measures on, say, twenty variables into measures on, say, four principal components without losing a significant amount of information. Then you're in a position to compare existing groups of people (or lines of business, or sets of medical diagnoses) on a manageable four components rather than on a potentially unmanageable 20 variables.

Because you want principal components analysis to account for *all* the available variance, the correlation matrix of the original variables has elements in its main diagonal that all equal 1.0. That's because each variable correlates perfectly with itself.

The off-diagonal elements of the correlation matrix—if you're working with real-world data—are all less than 1.0 and greater than –1.0. The variables are not perfectly correlated and therefore do not share all their variance.

The implication is that, of the total variance that exists in the data set, some of it is shared between variables: cholesterol levels and weight share variance; cost of goods sold and profit margin share variance; income and likelihood of purchasing share variance. But there is other variance that is unique to particular variables and is not shared. That unique variance is what keeps variables from being perfectly correlated with one another.

Factor analysis takes the view that the underlying factors express themselves only somewhat differently in the different measurable variables. Some of a variable's variance is shared with other variables that load high on the same factor. Equally, some of the variable's variance is unique to the variable: the variability that is not shared with the other variables.

In regression analysis, whether simple or multiple regression, the R^2 value quantifies the percent of variance in the dependent variable that is associated with the independent variables—say, 70%. The remaining 30% is either unique to the dependent variable or is simply error of some sort, such as sampling error, measurement error, one or more variables missing from the model, and so on.

The focus in factor analysis is on how the relationships between variables help to identify the underlying factors. Thus, factor analysis seeks to work only with the variance that variables share with one another. This is in contrast to principal components analysis, which focuses on attributing all the variance. Principal components analysis therefore admits all the available variance, whether shared or unique.

When the input correlation matrix has values of 1.0 in the main diagonal, all the variance for each variable is included. The only way to get to a correlation of 1.0 is if all the variables' variance is included. Else the R^2 cannot come to 100%, even when you're correlating a variable with itself.

But factor analysis (in particular the types that are termed *common factor analysis* and *image factor analysis*) does not put 1.0 in the correlation matrix's main diagonal; it puts the R^2 of each variable with the remaining variables in the diagonal. Those R^2 values are the SMCs—the squared multiple correlations—that I mentioned earlier in this chapter in the "Features of the Correlation Matrix's Inverse" section.

Because the SMCs are all larger than or equal to 0.0, and less than 1.0 (unless there's linear dependency in the input data, which means that the determinant is 0.0 and the matrix is singular), only the variance of each variable that is shared with other variables is included in the analysis.

> **NOTE**   You will sometimes see the SMCs referred to as a variable's *communality*, symbolized as h^2.

The thinking goes that one major purpose of factor analysis is to determine how variables covary and thus express the underlying factors in slightly different ways. In that case, it does not make sense to include variance that is specific or unique to a given variable in the analysis.

Rotating Axes

Recall that one of the rules that govern principal components analysis is that each additional component is uncorrelated with, or orthogonal to, existing components. This means that the components are independent of one another, and the geometric interpretation of the components is as axes that are perpendicular to one another. You can see this in three dimensions (in other words, three components) by visualizing an axis that's vertical, one that runs left to right, and one that runs straight ahead and parallel to your line of sight.

One result of this process is that principal components analysis often results in one general component on which most or even all the variables load strongly. Subsequent components tend to be bipolar, in the sense that some variables correlate positively and some negatively with the component.

This isn't always the ideal outcome because it doesn't necessarily produce clean factors that are easily defined by noting which variables load strongly on them. One way to achieve that result is to rotate the axes. Some methods rotate the components so that they are no longer orthogonal or perpendicular to one another.

There are various ways to manage that rotation. One of the best known and most frequently used is *Varimax*, which keeps the factors orthogonal to one another but rotates them as a full set. The effect is to leave the total amount of variance unchanged, but to allocate it differently across the factors. It can be possible to simplify and clarify the factor structure with this sort of rotation.

Other methods do not require the factors to remain orthogonal, but allow what's termed an *oblique* rotation. The idea behind oblique rotations is that the simple, clean structures that result from orthogonal factors might not describe the state of nature—that the underlying factors might not cooperate with our ideas of simple structure and instead insist on being correlated.

If you get the impression from all this that factor analysis is more art than science, you're right. And the current state of the art relies more on the analyst's experience and understanding of the nature of the original data set than on any algorithm or matrix operation.

10

Box-Jenkins ARIMA Models

Suppose you're fortunate enough to have at hand a nice long baseline of observations. You'd like to model how the data behaves over time, and if possible create a credible forecast. You have your choice of approaches for that task. As Chapter 4, "Forecasting a Time Series: Smoothing," and Chapter 6, "Forecasting a Time Series: Regression," showed, you could take a smoothing approach—that is, a variation on moving averages—or a regression approach, possibly one based on autoregression so that you're using the baseline to forecast itself.

How do you choose which approach, regression or some version of moving averages, to use? Or do you choose at all? Presumably you don't toss a coin, or take the easy out that I've seen some people opt for (they were comfortable with one approach and had the necessary software, and made their choice on that basis).

The Rationale for ARIMA

You might decide to try both smoothing and the autoregression approach and see which works better. Your criterion could be a least-squares test: You could sum the squared differences between the actual values and the associated forecast values, and choose the one that had the smaller sum.

That's not an entirely satisfactory approach, although it could work out well in the long run. Ideally you could forecast both ways for several time periods and decide which approach to put your faith in when you evaluated the outcomes. The problem there is that you don't usually have the luxury of waiting for several time periods. Furthermore, it's entirely possible that a couple of new observations might tip you from regression to smoothing or, of course, the other direction.

Deciding to Use ARIMA

Better would be some objective method based on the *structure* of your baseline, rather than a least-squares decision rule that might change with every time period that passes. That's where ARIMA (pronounced "Uh *Ree* Muh") comes into play.

ARIMA was developed and codified in the 1960s by two statistical theorists named Box and Jenkins (thus, you often read of "Box-Jenkins forecasting techniques"). The term *ARIMA* stands for:

- **AR: AutoRegressive.** The model and forecast can be based in part or completely on autoregression.

- **I: Integrated.** The baseline might need to be differenced (again, as discussed in Chapter 4) and the differenced series modeled. Then, when it comes time to make the forecasts, the differences are reversed by a simple process called *integrating*. In this context, integration reverses the process of differencing and puts the baseline back in its original scale of measurement.

- **MA: Moving Average.** Box and Jenkins gave this term a meaning that's a bit different from its usual definition. It refers not to an average of *values*, but an average of *errors*—differences between values and forecasts.

One major benefit of the ARIMA approach to forecasting a time series is that its procedures evaluate the *structure* of the baseline. It enables you to determine the degree of trend in the baseline, so that you can decide on an objective basis whether you should difference the series and make it stationary.

The ARIMA approach often provides you with the information you need to decide—again, on an objective basis—whether the baseline lends itself better to autoregressive or moving average techniques. It also tells you whether there is seasonality in the baseline and, if so, where it exists (that is, annual, quarterly, monthly, or even more frequent regularity in peaks and valleys).

I don't want to suggest that ARIMA solves all the problems you might encounter in predictive analytics. It is not as schematic and mechanistic as the prior few paragraphs might have made it seem. Much judgment is needed, the evidence can be contradictory, and the possibility of over-modeling the data is always there.

Nevertheless, the tools that the ARIMA approach offers can put you in a better position to make good forecasting decisions and to better understand why you made them.

ARIMA Notation

ARIMA notation expresses very compactly the sort of model that's being evaluated or used. The basic pattern is as follows:

$$\text{ARIMA}(p, d, q)$$

where these conventions are in use:

- ARIMA simply states that what follows describes an ARIMA model.
- p is the number of autoregressive parameters in the model.
- d is the number of times the series has been differenced to achieve stationarity, as discussed in Chapter 5.
- q is the number of moving average parameters in the model.

If the identification stage of ARIMA analysis suggests that the baseline is seasonal, the model calls the seasonality out with another three parameters, as follows:

ARIMA(p,d,q)(P,D,Q)

where the uppercase letters have the same meaning as the lowercase letters, but apply to seasonal parameters. So, if the preliminary analysis shows that there is annual seasonality in the data, the following model

ARIMA(1,0,0)(1,0,0)

indicates that there is one autoregressive parameter to be applied at the time-period level, and another autoregressive parameter to be applied at the seasonal level.

Therefore, if the baseline consists of weekly totals, the first autoregressive parameter (p) might be based on one week ago, and the first seasonal autoregressive parameter (P) might be based on one year ago. You'll see how these determinations are made when we take up what ARIMA calls the Identification stage in the next section.

It is entirely possible to encounter a model that has both an autoregressive and a moving average component:

ARIMA(1,0,1)

although you should be particularly careful of deciding that you have what's called a *mixed model* on your hands. The more parameters you stick into a model, the greater the danger of *overfitting*. You might be unwittingly taking advantage of peculiarities in the baseline that are not repeated in later observations. In forecasting, as in other sorts of analytics, the principle of parsimony is respected. You should use as small a number of parameters in the model you select as the data insist you use, and no more.

Some sources use AR, MA and ARMA to stress the nature of the model. For example:

- AR(2) to designate a purely autoregressive model such as ARIMA(2,0,0)
- MA(1) to designate a purely moving average model such as ARIMA(0,0,1)
- ARMA(1,1) to designate a mixed model such as ARIMA(1,0,1)

Those sources would specify that no differencing was needed for AR, MA, or ARMA. Differencing, and the subsequent integrating, would be indicated by the use of ARI, IMA, and ARIMA.

I will not follow that convention here. All ARIMA models are identified using the complete acronym. I mention the convention that uses AR, MA, ARMA, and so on only so that you'll recognize it when you run into it.

Stages in ARIMA Analysis

ARIMA analysis follows four sequential phases. You begin by examining the sorts of correlograms that Chapter 6 discusses. Their pattern usually enables you to identify the sort of time series that's represented in your baseline: for example, autoregressive, moving average or mixed.

After identifying the kind of time series you're dealing with, you estimate the values for the parameters. Just as with exponential smoothing or linear regression, you need to know the values of the coefficients you will use in conjunction with the observed data points.

When you have estimates of the ARIMA parameters, you get preliminary forecasts. These forecasts provide data that you can use to diagnose the model that the identification and estimation phases suggest. If the diagnosis indicates that you haven't identified enough reliable sources of variation, you should go back and re-identify or re-estimate. The diagnostic phase might also tell you that you have too many parameters: that you're over-modeling the baseline.

Finally, after your model has passed the diagnostic tests to your satisfaction, you can continue with the fourth phase, forecasting.

The four stages in ARIMA analysis are discussed in greater detail in the following sections.

The Identification Stage

During the identification stage, the nature of a baseline—autoregressive, moving average, or mixed; trended or stationary; seasonal or non-seasonal—is determined. The route to making the identification is via correlograms, which I introduced in Chapter 6.

The idea is that a time series—often termed a *process* by ARIMA analysts and other forecasters—that is best treated as a moving average process has a correlogram with a particular signature, as does an autoregressive process and mixed processes. Furthermore, a series that has substantial trend has an identifiable signature.

Identifying an AR Process

These signatures appear in the correlograms: the appearance of the ACF (autocorrelation function) correlogram, particularly in comparison with the appearance of the PACF (partial autocorrelation function) correlogram. The way these comparisons are defined is actually quite straightforward, although in practice interpreting them can be a challenge. Figure 11.1 has an example.

Figure 11.1
The ACF of an AR process dies out gradually and the PACF cuts off after a single spike.

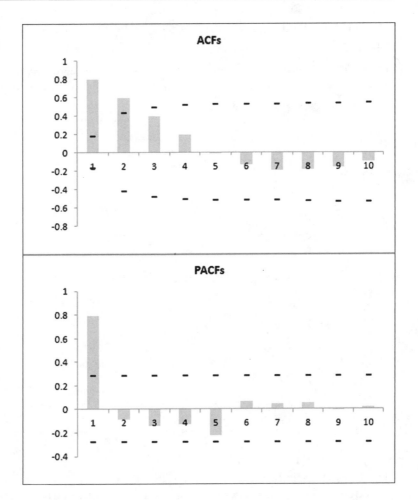

The ACFs and PACFs that are charted in Figure 11.1 belong to a classic ARIMA(1,0,0) process. It has one autoregressive component, requires no differencing, and has no moving average component. The ACFs gradually die out and the PACF cuts off after the first lag.

The fact that the PACF has only one spike indicates that there is only one autoregressive parameter. If there were two spikes, there would be two autoregressive parameters to estimate.

For example, suppose that the PACFs spiked at both lag 1 and lag 2, instead of simply at lag 1 as shown in Figure 11.1. That would tell you that to model the time series, you would base each time period's estimate on both one period and two periods back.

More frequently, if you find two spikes in a PACF correlogram, they indicate seasonality. If you have monthly data and find spikes at lag 1 and at lag 12, you would probably conclude that each new observation depends in part on the value of the series one period back (that is, last month) and 12 periods back (that is, last month one year earlier).

The time series itself that is the basis for the correlograms in Figure 11.1 appears in Figure 11.2.

You can't tell from the original time series whether it's autoregressive, moving average, mixed, or even just white noise. You need the ACF and PACF correlograms to identify the nature of the process.

Figure 11.2
The time series is already stationary and requires no differencing.

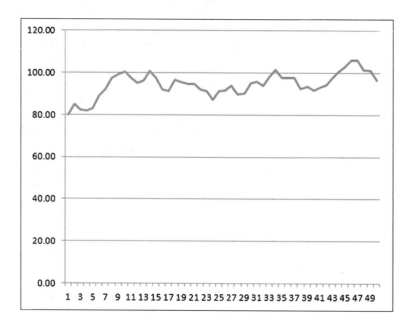

The ACFs shown in Figure 11.1 are all positive through lag 4 and nearly so at lag 5. This comes about when an AR process is driven by a positive correlation between one observation and the next. When it's a negative correlation, you get a jagged appearance in the chart of the raw data series, as shown in Figure 11.3.

For example, suppose that you have a baseline of values in the range K1:K50. In that case, you can get the correlation between the first 49 values and the second 49 values using a worksheet formula similar to this one:

=CORREL(K1:K49,K2:K50)

In the case of the data in Figure 11.3, the correlation between the first 49 values and the last 49 values is –0.43.

> **NOTE** Recall from Chapter 6 that the ACFs that form correlograms are calculated using a slightly different formula than the one used to calculate a Pearson correlation. In this case, the Pearson r is –0.43, whereas the lag 1 ACF is –0.42.

Figure 11.3
A negative correlation between one observation and the next causes an up-and-down, sawtooth pattern in the chart of the raw data.

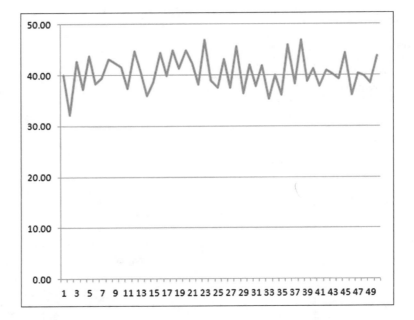

The negative correlation means that a relatively high value for a given time period is associated with a relatively low value for the preceding period and a relatively high value two periods back—thus the jagged appearance of a chart of the raw data. As you might expect, the effect shows up in the ACFs (see Figure 11.4).

Although the ACFs in Figure 11.4 alternate between positive and negative values, their absolute values die out. The accompanying PACF correlogram has a single negative spike at lag 1, so between them the ACFs and the PACFs indicate an ARIMA(1,0,0) process with a negative lag 1 ACF.

> **NOTE** The question of what constitutes a "spike" in a correlogram is one of the issues in ARIMA analysis that is best addressed through experience. Nevertheless, a good place to start is by considering that a spike has occurred in a correlogram when the ACF or the PACF exceeds the dashed line. In that case, the value is more than two standard errors from zero, and that's quite a distance.

The alternating negative and positive ACFs in Figure 11.4 reflect the negative lag 1 correlation. A high value is associated with another high value two periods back and with a low value one period back.

Identifying an MA Process

It's a fairly short step from identifying an AR process to identifying an MA process. In an AR process, the ACFs decline gradually as the lags increase, and the PACFs cut off abruptly, often after a single spike.

Figure 11.4
The ACF and PACF signature for an ARIMA(1,0,0) process where the correlation between time periods is negative.

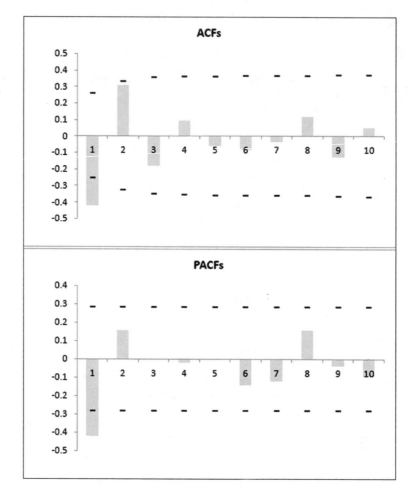

That pattern is reversed in MA processes. In an MA process, it's the ACFs that cut off abruptly and the PACFs that gradually decline. Figure 11.5 shows the ACFs and the PACFs for a moving average process, one in which the MA parameter is negative.

Notice in Figure 11.5 that there's a single spike in the ACFs, at lag 1, and that the PACFs—rather, their absolute values—gradually decline.

Figure 11.6 shows the same pattern, except that the PACFs decline gradually from roughly –0.3 to –0.1, from lag 1 through lag 6, and each PACF through lag 6 remains on the same side of zero. This is typical of MA processes with a positive MA parameter.

> **NOTE** A later section of this chapter, "The Estimation Stage," looks more deeply into the concepts of the AR parameter and the MA parameter.

Figure 11.5
The ACF and PACF signature for an ARIMA(0,0,1) process where the MA parameter is negative.

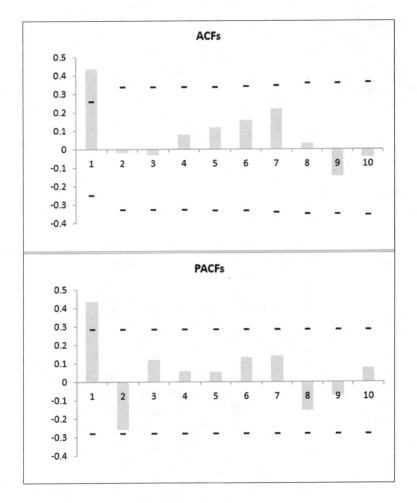

Differencing in ARIMA Analysis

The identification of an ARIMA process as autoregressive, moving average, or mixed depends heavily on the accurate calculation of the ACFs and PACFs at different lags in the time series. It is therefore critically important that the time series be stationary, not trended.

Recall from Chapter 6 that the time variable itself can induce a correlation between two variables that are not causally related. For example, you might find that over many years the amount of dollars that homeowners pay annually in property taxes correlates substantially with the amount of dollars that they pay in gasoline taxes. The two are not causally related: The market forces that set the price of housing and local services are different from those that set the price of gasoline and the services that its taxes pay for. But the correlation is a strong one because the passage of time, and the concomitant effect of inflation on purchasing power, induces a correlation between the two.

Figure 11.6
The pattern of the ACFs and PACFs in an ARIMA(0,0,1) process depends on whether the MA parameter is positive or negative.

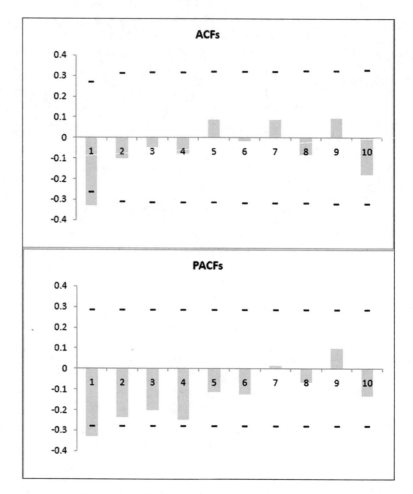

The concept is similar when you consider autocorrelation. There is often cause and effect between one time series and the same time series shifted forward by one period. For example, the median price of housing for the years 1970 through 2000 is strongly correlated with the price of housing for the years 1971 through 2001. Part of that correlation is causal: Homeowners try very hard, when selling a house, to obtain more than they paid for it. In consequence, over long periods of time there is persistent upward pressure on the price of housing and that pressure is causal.

At the same time, some of the rise in the cost of housing is due to the passage of time and therefore the erosion of purchasing power. That effect is largely independent of the pressure caused by homeowners' wish to turn a profit.

We want to isolate the effect of the time series upon itself and remove the influence of the (relatively uninteresting) passage of time from the analysis. Therefore, it's often necessary to make the time series stationary as an early part of the identification stage. There are several ways to do so, including converting the data to rates such as per capita dollars when population increases over time exert an effect on values. But it's often true that the most effective way to stationarize a trended time series is by means of *differencing*.

Chapter 6 touched on the topic of differencing to achieve stationarity, but a closer look is helpful here. Figure 11.7 shows a time series that is not stationary but trended.

Figure 11.7
The time series shows a pronounced upward trend.

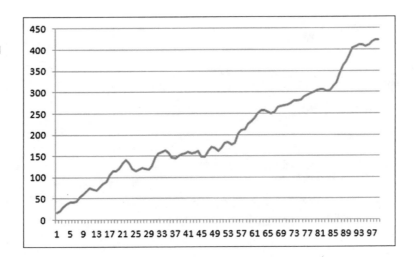

Before you can use ARIMA to model the time series in Figure 11.7 accurately, you must make it stationary. If you simply calculate the ACFs and PACFs of a trended series, you find that they're not meaningful. Figure 11.8 shows the correlograms for the data in Figure 11.7 before it is made stationary.

The pattern of the ACFs and the PACFs in Figure 11.8 suggest an AR process: The ACFs die out gradually and there's a single spike in the PACFs. This is an AR series, but the autoregression in the series is contaminated by the trend. Another way of putting this concept is to note that the autocorrelations beyond lag 1 are merely artifacts of the propagation of the lag 1 autocorrelation.

Furthermore, it's clear from eyeballing the original data in Figure 11.7 that the series is trended, not stationary. The difference between a stationary AR series and a trended AR series is reflected in the pattern of the ACFs in Figure 11.8, which do die out but do so only very gradually. Most AR(1,0,0) series have ACFs that drop close to zero after the third or fourth lag.

Figure 11.8
The ACFs die out very
slowly.

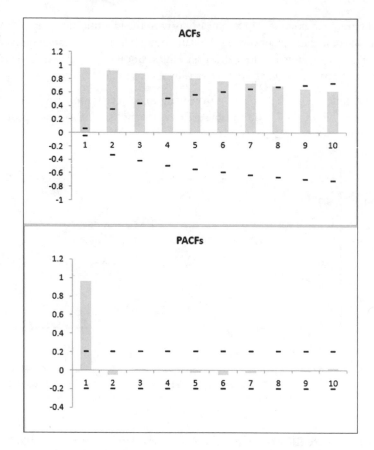

It's easy enough to difference a time series. If the original series is in, say, A1:A50, you could enter this formula in cell B2:

=A2–A1

Copy and paste that formula down into B3:B50 and you'll have a differenced series. If the differenced series is still trended, you can difference the differenced series, which leads to a model of, say, the ARIMA(1,2,0) or ARIMA(0,2,1) type. (Recall that the second parameter in the ARIMA notation is d, which stands for the number of differences that have been taken, and the need for subsequent integration.)

You lose one observation each time you difference a series, and over-differencing can create as many problems for ARIMA analysis as you can create by failing to difference a trended series. Be careful not to overdo it. Most time series are stationarized by first differencing and nearly all the rest require no more than second differencing.

Figure 11.9 shows the time series from Figure 11.7 after it's been stationarized.

The series now clearly has no trend. The correlograms for the differenced series appear in Figure 11.10.

After differencing, the time series turns out to look very much like an ARIMA(0,0,1) process. Taking first differences removes the autocorrelative nature of the series and clarifies its moving average nature. The ACF cuts off after lag 1, and the absolute values of the PACFs die out.

Figure 11.9
First differences of the data in Figure 11.7.

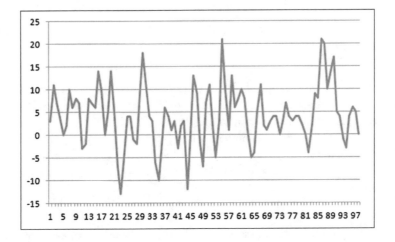

Figure 11.10
The PACFs die out much more rapidly than did the ACFs in Figure 11.8.

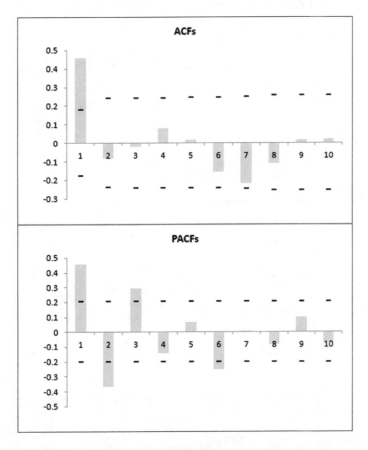

Using the ARIMA Workbook

Chapter 6 introduced the notion of ACFs, PACFs, and correlograms and mentioned the use of the software you need. There are many Excel add-ins and other utilities available for Internet download that calculate and display ACFs and PACFs. Some go further and calculate the autoregressive and moving average coefficients that apply to a time series.

I have made the ARIMA.xls add-in that creates the correlograms shown in this chapter's figures available for download from the publisher's website (www.quepublishing.com/title/9780789758354).

That file is not strictly an add-in, but a macro-enabled workbook. Because I have left the VBA project unprotected, if you're interested you can examine the code that calculates the ACFs, PACFs, and the error limits. Prior to Excel 2007 an add-in could not normally be opened to examine modules and forms in the VBA project. Now, however, the Ribbon includes standard .xlsm (macro-enabled workbooks) files in the Add-Ins tab's Menu Commands group. So, in a sense the ARIMA.xlsm workbook is an add-in, and in another sense it's not.

> **NOTE**
> If you do open the workbook's module to examine the code, please bear in mind that I am not by training a software engineer. I have done my fair share of coding, but the VBA you find in ARIMA.xlsm is not the work product of a professional.

As a reminder, to use the ARIMA.xlsm workbook you should open it first. Then open the workbook that contains your time series and click the Ribbon's Add-Ins tab. You'll find ARIMA in the Menu Commands group. Click ARIMA to get the dialog box shown in Figure 11.11.

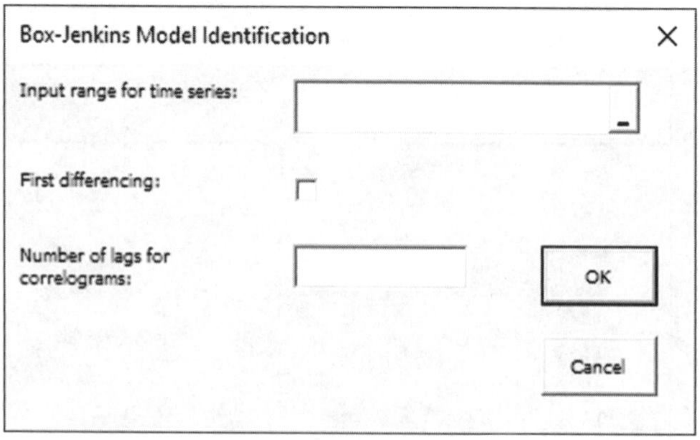

Figure 11.11
Only first differencing is available from the ARIMA.xlsm file.

Fill the checkbox if you want first differencing and indicate the number of lags you want for your correlograms.

It's unlikely, but if you find it necessary to difference the time series more than once, do that differencing directly on a worksheet as suggested in the prior section. Then submit the fully differenced time series to ARIMA.xlsm and do not fill the checkbox.

ARIMA.xlsm does not report the differenced series on a worksheet. Its main intent at the time that I coded it several years ago was to assist in ARIMA's identification stage, not the estimation and diagnostics stages when you would want access to an actual differenced series. As I pointed out, it's easy enough to use Excel worksheet formulas to do the differencing yourself.

Standard Errors in Correlograms

Bartlett developed an approximate test for the statistical significance of the difference of an ACF from zero. It is a sequential test in the sense that the ACFs are tested at all included lags. Following the conventions used by other ARIMA applications, I have included the results of Bartlett's test in the ARIMA.xlsm code by showing the standard errors of the ACFs and the PACFs on the charts.

Refer, for example, to Figure 11.10. Notice the dashes above and below the zero line for both correlograms. An ACF or a PACF that extends above or below the associated dash can be regarded as significantly non-zero—a *spike*. The dashes indicate the location of two standard errors above, or below, the zero line on the correlogram.

This information helps in a variety of ways. For example, I have referred several times in this chapter to a single spike in the PACFs of an AR process or in the ACFs of an MA process; put another way, the ACFs or the PACFs "cut off" after a particular lag. It's not necessarily the case that only a single spike exists. Two spikes in the ACF of an MA process or in the PACF of an AR process would indicate an ARIMA(0,0,2) or an ARIMA(2,0,0) model. In some borderline cases you want some criterion to help you decide if the ACFs or PACFs actually cut off or merely dipped closer to the zero line.

If an ACF or PACF falls below its upper dash and above its lower dash, you can regard that value as not significantly different from zero, and therefore equivalent to zero. Of course, as is the case with every sort of "statistical significance," whether you regard a probability as significant is a personal, subjective decision.

The standard errors for PACFs are constant and depend exclusively on the number of periods in the time series. If the number of time periods is k, then two standard errors above zero for PACFs is as follows:

$$2/\sqrt{k}$$

Two standard errors below the zero line on the PACF correlogram is simply the negative of the prior formula:

$$-2/\sqrt{k}$$

The standard errors for the ACFs are different, because the standard error at greater lags incorporates the ACFs at smaller lags. The idea is that, as noted earlier in this chapter, autocorrelations propagate as lags increase and therefore their standard errors must increase as well. But the very notion of a *partial* autocorrelation coefficient involves partialling out the effect of correlations at other lags, and therefore the standard errors do not take account of those correlations—and they can and do remain constant.

White Noise and Diagnostic Checking

One important sort of time series doesn't model on either an AR or MA basis. One of these time series appears in the correlograms in Figure 11.12.

Notice in Figure 11.12 that none of the ACFs and PACFs is significantly different from zero. This is bad news and good news. Which one it is depends on when you create the correlograms.

If the correlograms are based on your original time series, perhaps after you have differenced it, it's probably bad news. The process is random, white noise. You can't make any better forecast from your baseline than the mean of the existing observations. You might as well fold your tent and move on to some other, more interesting data set.

Figure 11.12
In a white noise process, there are no reliably non-zero autocorrelations or partial autocorrelations.

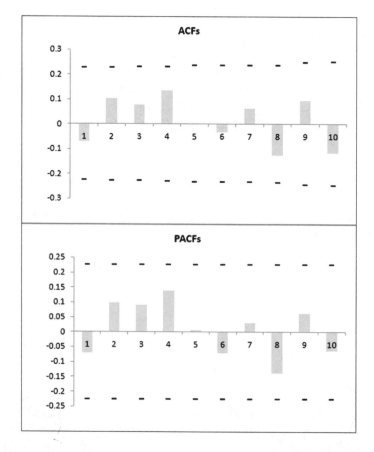

On the other hand, if the correlograms are based on *residuals*, it's good news. After you have estimated the parameters you'll use for your forecasts, your next step is to make tentative forecasts and subtract them from the actual values in your baseline. The result is *residuals*, and you want them to form a random series, with all genuine autocorrelation accounted for. This sort of check constitutes the *diagnostic* phase of ARIMA analysis.

You want this to occur as soon as possible, with the necessary differencing and complicated modeling held to a minimum. Ideally, you'd like your analysis to tell you that a simple model, such as ARIMA(1,0,0) or ARIMA(0,1,1), is necessary and sufficient for your data. A parsimonious model that accounts for the data well is always preferable to one that's complicated and that requires multiple AR and MA parameters.

Identifying Seasonal Models

Before we move on to the estimation stage of ARIMA analysis, let's take a quick glance at seasonal models. I don't propose to go into seasonal models in depth, but I want you to be able to recognize one when it crops up.

Figure 11.13 shows the correlograms for a process with a regular and a seasonal MA parameter.

The interpretation of the correlograms tends to get a little dicey when you start to move into even slightly more complicated models. The relatively large ACFs and PACFs at lags 1 and 12 in Figure 11.13 indicate that there's dependency from one period to the next and from one period to twelve periods later. This result is not unexpected from monthly consumer sales data.

The particular time series represented in Figure 11.13 is one that has been analyzed extensively. At least one very experienced analyst—not me, by the way—interprets the correlograms as an ARIMA(0,0,1)(0,0,1) model: one regular and one seasonal MA component. He reaches this conclusion because of the spikes in the ACF at lags 1 and 12; further, he interprets the PACF values at lags 1 and 12, which are –0.341 and –0.339 respectively, as showing gradual decline.

That pattern, spikes in the ACF and gradual decline in the PACF, indicates a moving average process, as I noted in earlier sections of this chapter. But it takes more chutzpah than I have to interpret a change in the lag 1 to lag 12 PACFs from –0.341 to –0.339 as evidence of gradual, *seasonal* decline.

That's why I said that things get dicey when the models get even slightly more complicated. And it provides more support for the principle of parsimony in building models. Over-differencing, for example, can suppress the effects of moving averages. Too complicated a model can become unstable and can return very different forecast results using different samples from the same process. (This phenomenon is sometimes termed *overfitting*.)

I don't want to frighten you away from considering a seasonal model if the correlograms suggest that you have one, or from a mixed model if the data supports that preferentially over one that's more straightforward. Just don't go looking for them when a simpler model fits the data.

Figure 11.13
Notice the spikes in the ACF at lags 1 and 12; the underlying time series is based on monthly data.

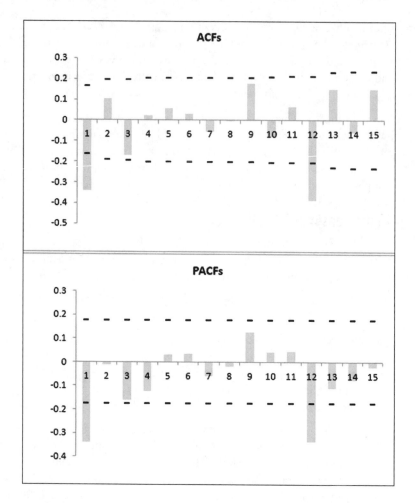

The Estimation Stage

You've identified a model for your time series baseline—very often, a simple ARIMA(1,0,0) or ARIMA(0,0,1) model, or if differencing is needed then it might be an ARIMA(1,1,0) or ARIMA(0,1,1). Your next step is estimation. You need to estimate the values of the parameters that you will use.

The reason is not solely that you need these parameters to make your forecast. You also need to step through a diagnostic stage, and the diagnostics depend on what your forecasts look like.

Estimating the Parameters for ARIMA(1,0,0)

We start with a simple ARIMA(1,0,0) process. You would take the same steps with an ARIMA(1,1,0) process, but in that case we'll assume that you have already differenced the series and are now ready to proceed with parameter estimation.

You can use the Excel worksheet functions LINEST() and TREND() to estimate the parameters for an AR process. If you have identified the process as ARIMA(1,0,0), you know that there's just one autoregressive parameter to account for. Apart from knowing the number of parameters, you need to know which lag that parameter involves.

In other words, you check the PACFs to verify where that parameter should point. Normally, the single spike in the PACF of an ARIMA(1,0,0) process is at lag 1 and you should therefore forecast the time series on the basis of the prior observation. For example, if your data set is in A1:A77, you can get the parameters by array-entering the LINEST() function as follows:

=LINEST(A2:A77,A1:A76,,TRUE)

In a range that has two columns and at least one row (to get all the results in this example, select a range with five rows and two columns before you array-enter that formula). The regression coefficient appears in the first row, first column and the intercept in the first row, second column. See Chapter 6 for full information on all the statistics that are returned by LINEST().

After you have entered the LINEST() function, you can use its results to prepare forecasts, either for diagnostic purposes or eventually for decision making. With your time series in A1:A77 and LINEST() entered in D1:E5, you could enter this formula in cell B2:

=$D$1*A1+$E$1

which multiplies the first observation in the time series by the regression coefficient in D1 and adds the intercept in E1. Then copy and paste that formula into B3:B78 to get your forecasts. Making the references to D1 and E1 absolute ensures that when you copy the formula down Column B, you are working with the same regression parameters.

Figure 11.14 shows how this works.

If you'd rather bypass LINEST() and get the forecasts directly, you could array-enter this formula in B2:B78:

=TREND(A2:A77,A1:A76,A77)

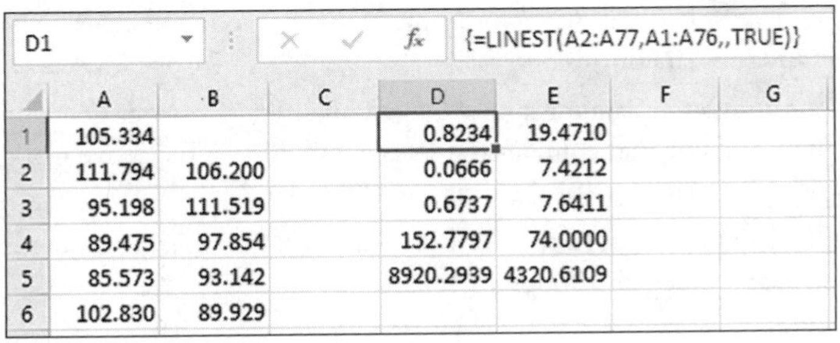

Figure 11.14
Using LINEST() instead of TREND() is a little more work but gives you much more information about the autoregression.

	A	B	C	D	E	F	G
D1				fx	{=LINEST(A2:A77,A1:A76,,TRUE)}		
1	105.334			0.8234	19.4710		
2	111.794	106.200		0.0666	7.4212		
3	95.198	111.519		0.6737	7.6411		
4	89.475	97.854		152.7797	74.0000		
5	85.573	93.142		8920.2939	4320.6109		
6	102.830	89.929					

The final reference to A77 in the arguments tells Excel to apply the regression equation, which is based on the relationship between A2:A77 and A1:A76, to the value in A77. This provides a final, one-step-ahead forecast.

Using TREND(), you can skip the step of obtaining the actual regression statistics with LINEST(). I much prefer to take that step even though it takes a few more seconds, because then I can get additional statistics such as the standard error of estimate, R^2, and so on.

> **N O T E** This outcome probably seems anticlimactic. If you've followed the material in this chapter through this point, it's fair to be asking yourself this: "Why did I go through all that, differencing the time series and getting correlograms, examining the ACFs and the PACFs, when all I had to do was enter something like =TREND(A2:A100,A1:A99)?"
>
> The answer is that when you're at square 1 you have a variety of choices for forecasts—for example, regression on some other variable, autoregression, weighted moving averages, and exponential smoothing.
>
> The exercise of getting the process signature in the ACFs and the PACFs is an important first step because it helps you select the forecasting method most appropriate for your data. As you'll see later in this chapter, it's also important because it helps you diagnose the adequacy of the model you selected.

Comparing Excel's Results to R's

R, the freeware statistical analysis application, has an ARIMA capability, in the form of several packages and functions that perform ARIMA analysis. It's useful to examine the results of R's ARIMA functions when applied to the time series in Figure 11.14, and to compare the results to those returned by LINEST().

There are a few preliminary steps that you need to take before you can start the analysis as I outline it here:

- You need to have installed R's contributed package *DescTools* on your computer. The DescTools package is needed to access the XLGetRange function, which I use here to import data from Excel into R. As I write this, that function is not available for Apple computers. If you're using an Apple, you need to use another method of pulling your time series data into R.

- Your time series data must be arranged in an Excel worksheet as shown in Figure 11.14. The workbook that contains the worksheet must be the active workbook, and the worksheet that contains the data must be active.

- The data must be selected: That is, you must have clicked in the first cell of the time series and dragged through its final cell.

With those preliminaries in place, you're set to run the analysis, as shown by the following set of R commands. Lines beginning with the > symbol are commands that you supply to R:

```
> library(DescTools)
> mydata <- XLGetRange(header=FALSE)
```

Read the data into R using the XLGetRange function. Note that you must first have loaded the *DescTools* package, by means of the library command, to access the XLGetRange function. The XLGetRange function coerces the data pulled from the Excel worksheet into an R data frame, here named mydata.

```
> mydatats <- ts(mydata)
```

Convert the mydata data frame to a time series object named mydatats, using R's ts function.

```
> arima(mydatats,order=c(1,0,0),method=("CSS"))
```

Pass the time series object to R's arima function. Notice that you specify the ARIMA model you want using the order keyword, followed by the p, d and q parameters enclosed in parentheses and preceded by the name of the function *c*. In this case, order calls for one autoregressive parameter, no differencing and no moving average parameter.

> **NOTE** R's *c* function combines its arguments into a vector.

You also specify the method that you want R to use as it estimates the parameters. The prior statement specified *CSS*, which stands for *conditional sum of squares*. Using this method, the parameters are optimized by minimizing the sum of the squared deviations between the actual and the forecast values. This is the standard, ordinary least-squares approach used by linear regression.

You can also specify *ML* as the method, in which case R estimates the parameters using maximum likelihood techniques instead of least squares. You can read more about maximum likelihood approaches in Chapter 8, "Logistic Regression: Further Issues," of this book.

The third and last method you can specify is *CSS-ML*. It is the default method, so it's the one that R uses if you don't specify a method. It uses conditional sums of squares to set the starting values for its search, and then uses maximum likelihood to iterate to the optimum estimates of the parameters.

You are unlikely to get the same results from R and Excel if you use either *ML* or *CSS-ML* as the method in R's *arima* function. Excel's LINEST() function employs a pure least-squares approach.

11

R responds to the statement that invokes *arima* as follows:

```
Call:
arima(x = mydatats, order = c(1, 0, 0), method = ("CSS"))

Coefficients:
                   ar1      intercept
                0.8233      110.2369
     s.e.       0.0653        4.8660
```

Notice that the coefficient labeled *ar1* is identical to the regression coefficient that LINEST() returns—see cell D1 in Figure 11.14.

The "intercept" is another matter. Although labeled *intercept* in the R output, it is more often termed phi-0, or Φ_0, in books and journal articles concerning ARIMA analysis. The Φ_0 parameter is related to the regression intercept (19.47, as shown in cell E1 of Figure 11.14) as follows:

$$\Phi_0 = \frac{Intercept}{1 - \Phi_1}$$

where Φ_1 is the coefficient. Using the actual values:

$$110.2369 = 19.471 / (1 - .8234)$$

You can use R to forecast from the model you have specified. Start by converting the mydatats time series object to an arima object:

```
> arimaobj <- arima(mydatats,order=c(1,0,0),method=("CSS"))
```

Then call R's predict function. Supply the name of the object you just created, which includes the parameter estimates as well as the original data. Specify the number of forecasts you want to make using the n.ahead keyword:

```
> predict(arimaobj,n.ahead=3)
```

R responds as follows:

```
$pred
Time Series:
Start = 78
End = 80
Frequency = 1
[1] 101.8721 103.3499 104.5665
```

The forecasts are identical to those you would make on the worksheet in Figure 11.14, as follows:

```
Cell B78: =$D$1*A77+$E$1
Cell B79: =$D$1*B78+$E$1
Cell B80: =$D$1*B79+$E$1
```

> **NOTE** You can verify that R and Excel return the same forecasts by opening the Excel workbook for Chapter 11, available from the publisher's website, and activating the worksheet named Fig 11-14.

In sum, using Excel you can easily get the same results that an application such as SAS, SPSS, or R would return if you're working with an ARIMA(1,0,0) process—quite a common one. Next, we look at a moving average process.

Exponential Smoothing and ARIMA(0,0,1)

Figure 11.15 shows the ACFs and PACFs for a moving average process.

Figure 11.15
No differencing was applied to the raw data series. The ACFs spike at lag 1 and the PACFs die out.

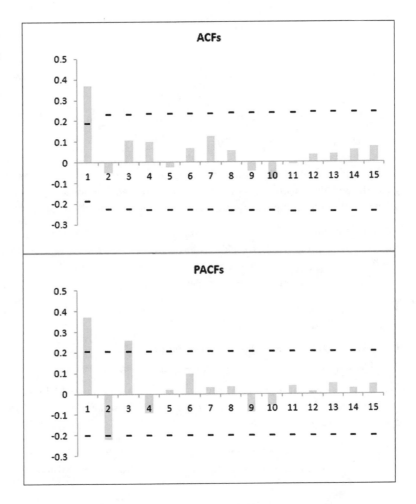

The correlograms point pretty clearly to an ARIMA(0,0,1) moving average process. An excerpt from the time series that gives rise to the correlograms appears in Figure 11.16.

Figure 11.16 uses the same sort of layout that you can find in Chapter 4. The original data series is in Column A. Because the forecasts are created using exponential smoothing, the smoothing constant and damping factor are found in E1 and E2.

Figure 11.16
The forecasts in
Column B are made using
exponential smoothing.

B5		▾	⋮	✕	✓	f_x	=$E$1*A4+$E$2*B4	

◢	A	B	C	D	E
1	Hits			Smoothing Constant	0.084399
2	107	#N/A		Damping Factor	0.915601
3	120	107			
4	116	108.0972		Sum of Squared Deviations	5604.859
5	112	108.7642			
6	113	109.0373			
7	109	109.3717			
8	95	109.3404			
9	106	108.13			
10	109	107.9503			

The smoothing constant is chosen by first putting this formula in cell E4:

=SUMXMY2(A3:A99,B3:B99)

The formula calculates the sum of the squared deviations of the forecasts in Column B from the actuals in Column A. Then Solver is invoked to minimize the value in cell E4 by changing the smoothing constant in E1. (This approach is discussed in detail in Chapter 4.)

What happens instead if you run the time series through R's *arima* function? With the range A2:A99 in Figure 11.16 selected in Excel, here are the R commands and results:

```
> library(DescTools)
> mydata <- XLGetRange(header=FALSE)
```

Read the data into R.

```
> mydatats <- ts(mydata)
```

Convert the data to a time series representation in R.

```
> arima(mydatats,order=c(0,1,1),method=("CSS"))
```

Call the arima function. Suppress the constant by specifying an ARIMA(0,1,1) model instead of ARIMA(0,0,1). Specify conditional sums of squares as the criterion for optimizing the moving average parameter.

> **NOTE** See the next section for an explanation of the use of the ARIMA(0,1,1) model.

Here are R's results:

```
Call:
arima(x=mydatats,order=c(0,1,1),method=("CSS"))
Coefficients:
          ma1
       -0.9156
s.e.    0.0520
sigma^2 estimated as 57.78:  log likelihood = -334.39,  aic = NA
```

Compare the ma1 parameter, –0.9156, with the damping factor reported in cell E2 of Figure 11.16, 0.9156. They are identical except for their signs. The sign of a moving average parameter is simply a matter of whether the forecast error is calculated by subtracting the forecast value from the associated actual value, or the actual value from the forecast value.

> **NOTE**
>
> For many years, Box-Jenkins ARIMA models have adopted the convention that a moving average parameter is subtracted in the model equation. That is:
>
> $$\hat{y}_{t+1} = y_t + \theta_0 + \varepsilon_{t+1} - \theta_1 \varepsilon_t$$
>
> Notice the minus sign prior to the θ_1 in the equation. If θ_1 the parameter is actually a negative number, then subtracting the final quantity in the equation results in adding its absolute value. This can sometimes result in confusion if the equation is "simplified" by conflating the two consecutive minus signs into one addition sign. It can also reverse the apparent directions of the ACFs and the PACFs in the correlograms.
>
> Of course there's nothing wrong with this convention. It's important, though, that you be aware of it so that you'll see what's going on if you're confronted by an apparent contradiction in the direction of the ACFs, the PACFs, or the moving average parameter.

Now convert the time series to an arima object:

```
> arimaobject <- arima(mydatats,order=c(0,1,1),method=("CSS"))
```

Call for a one-step-ahead forecast:

```
> predict(arimaobject,n.ahead=1)
```

R's forecast:

```
$pred
Time Series:
Start = 99
End = 99
Frequency = 1
[1] 99.85995
```

You can find the same forecast, 99.8599, at the bottom of the forecasts in Column B of the worksheet named Fig 11.16 in the Chapter 11 workbook.

Again, you get an accurate ARIMA analysis using native Excel formulas and functions (in the case of an MA process, in combination with Solver). In the AR process, you get identical results using LINEST().

Regardless of the nature of the time series, you need to begin by creating the correlograms so that you can evaluate the patterns of the ACFs and the PACFs. They will tell you if differencing is needed, and they will also tell you if you have a single parameter AR process—use LINEST()—a single parameter MA process (use exponential smoothing), a process with multiple parameters, or a white noise process.

As I noted earlier, if your original time series constitutes a white noise process, you need go no further. The time series will not predict itself reliably (but there might be some other variable that you can use for forecasting by means of traditional regression). If the white noise time series consists of residuals, actuals less forecasts, then you have probably constructed an appropriate model.

Using ARIMA(0,1,1) in Place of ARIMA(0,0,1)

When you specify an ARIMA(0,1,1) model to R's arima function, you are in effect telling R that it should not determine a constant term (you might see the phrase *constant term* referred to as the *trend parameter*) in the MA equation. That basic equation is

$$\hat{y}_{t+1} = y_t + \theta_0 + \varepsilon_{t+1} - \theta_1 \varepsilon_t$$

Figure 11.17
The forecasts in Column B are made using theta on the prior forecast error.

	A	B	C	D	E	F
	B4		× ✓	fx	=A3-($D$1*(A3-B3))	
1	Hits			θ_1 0.915601		
2	107					
3	120	107				
4	116	108.0972				
5	112	108.7642				
6	113	109.0373				
7	109	109.3717				
8	95	109.3404				

If you suppress the trend parameter θ_0 (which is equivalent to differencing the series) by setting it to zero, and set the error at time $t + 1$ to 0 (because it is not yet known as of time t), you get this equation:

$$\hat{y}_{t+1} = y_t - \theta_1 \varepsilon_t$$
$$\hat{y}_{t+1} = y_t - \theta_1 (y_t - \hat{y}_t)$$

You'll find the latter equation used in Figure 11.17, employing theta rather than a smoothing constant. Compare the forecasts in Figure 11.17 with those in Figure 11.16. You'll find that the results of exponential smoothing are identical to the results of the single parameter moving average equation.

One final adjustment to the moving average equation:

$$\hat{y}_{t+1} = (1 - \theta_1) y_t + \theta_1 \hat{y}_t$$

You might recognize the prior formula as the basic, simple exponential smoothing formula discussed in Chapter 4. In this representation, θ_1 is the damping factor and $1 - \theta_1$ is the smoothing constant.

Without the trend parameter, as implied by the ARIMA(0,1,1) designation, the moving average equation simplifies to the simple exponential smoothing equation. It would be a shock to find that the two returned results were not precisely equal to one another.

The Diagnostic and Forecasting Stages

The final two stages in the ARIMA process require little explanation by this point. The diagnostic stage consists of examining the residuals that you obtain from the model you have specified.

You obtain those residuals by obtaining forecasts from your model—you've seen examples of those forecasts in Figure 11.14, Column B, and Figure 11.16, also Column B. Subtract the forecasts from the associated actuals (for example, in Figure 11.16, the residual for the fifth time period is A6 – B6).

Then, push those residuals through a utility such as ARIMA.xlsm to generate ACFs and PACFs based on the residuals. You hope and expect to find random results, a white noise process such as that depicted in Figure 11.12, where none of the ACFs or PACFs exceeds two standard errors from zero.

Of course, if you get that pattern to the residuals, you're in good shape to move forward with the forecasts based on the model you have selected—that's the forecasting stage.

When you analyze the residuals, you might get ACFs or PACFs that are significantly different from zero. If you do, particularly if they are at the shorter lags such as 1 through 3, you should revisit the model you have fit. It's possible that you need to provide an additional parameter, changing, for example, an ARIMA(1,0,0) model to a two-parameter autoregressive ARIMA(2,0,0) model. It's at this point that experience dealing with ARIMA models becomes particularly important.

There are forecasting applications that are commercially available which take the position that forecasting in general, and ARIMA analysis in particular, are straightforward analytics procedures that can be completely automated. No decision-making on your part needed: Leave it to the code.

Don't you believe it. If you're going to create credible, useful quantitative forecasts, then you're going to have to get your hands dirty by digging into the data.

But if you do find or suspect that you need a more complicated ARIMA model than the basic versions discussed in this chapter, you should probably consider using an application that provides ARIMA analysis directly, such as R or SAS. Excel works wonderfully for the most frequently occurring, less-complicated models—and as I've mentioned in this chapter, it's best to go with the simpler model if it fits your data.

11

Varimax Factor Rotation in Excel

Chapter 10, "Principal Components Analysis," showed how principal components analysis (PCA) can be used to derive, or *extract*, underlying and unmeasured components that are expressed overtly in measured variables.

The analysis in Chapter 10 used a small data set, with only three variables and just a few records, to demonstrate the techniques and steps involved in PCA. Excel calculated a correlation matrix from that data set; the matrix was then run through a freeware add-in that identified three principal components.

With three original variables, you can't extract more than three components. If you do extract (and retain) as many components as you have variables, those components account for all the available variance in the original variables.

Usually, you want to retain fewer components than you have variables. The first two components extracted in Chapter 10's example accounted for most of the variance in the three original variables. Chapter 10's result is in line with the main goal of PCA and factor analysis: reducing the number of dimensions, and therefore simplifying the analysis without losing too much information. But you usually have many more than three original variables to deal with, and that means you're looking for a simpler structure.

Getting to a Simple Structure

In the middle of the twentieth century, a founder of the field of psychometrics, Louis Thurstone, proposed a list of criteria that a meaningful factor structure should meet. The list described what was to be termed a *simple structure*, because its intent was to simplify the pattern of variable loadings on the underlying components, or factors.

For example, an ideal simple structure would have factors that have either very large (say, .80 or more) or small (say, .20 or less) loadings on the available variables. In that case, it's fairly clear which variables are associated with the factor, and it's usually fairly clear what that factor represents.

Similarly, a simple factor structure would have variables that each load strongly on just a single factor. So, Variables 1, 2, and 5 might each load strongly on Factor 1 and weakly on Factor 2; Variables 3, 4, and 6 might each load strongly on Factor 2 and weakly on Factor 1.

As you'll see in this chapter, data on crime rates resolves to two factors: a personal crimes factor and a property crimes factor. But because real-world data often fails to conform to theoretical expectations, we find that the crime of rape has fairly high loadings on both factors. *A priori*, we would expect that crime to have a high loading on the personal crime factor only. Because it loads on both factors, the factor structure isn't as simple as we might wish, and the interpretation of the meaning of the factors is (slightly) weakened.

Nevertheless, simple structure is a goal that we can aim for and the closer we get, the more interpretable the results. Not all methods for dealing with components, or factors, follow the rules for simple structure, but if you know which rules you're following and which you're not, then you can understand your results more clearly.

Variables that load high on only one factor make it easier to understand the meaning of the unobserved factors. *Factors* that have either very strong or very weak loadings are more interpretable than those that don't. Given that an initial extraction of principal components might not (in fact, usually doesn't) result in a simple structure, how do we get from a relatively messy principal component structure to a relatively simple factor structure? The answer lies in *factor rotation*.

Rotating Factors: The Rationale

The idea behind factor rotation is that you leave the variables alone, plotted on their axes—which are the underlying components or factors that you have extracted by means of PCA. But you do rotate the axes around their origin: the point where the axes intersect.

The type of rotation described here, Varimax, rotates the axes so that they remain at right angles to one another (other types of rotation, termed *oblique rotations*, do not require axes to stay at right angles to one another). Recall from Chapter 10 that the principal components are extracted so that each component in sequence claims all the remaining variance that can be attributed to it. Therefore, subsequent components cannot share any variance with earlier components. If there is no shared variance, there can be no correlation. And if there's no correlation, the components are independent. That independence property of components, or orthogonality, is expressed geometrically as right angles: two orthogonal components are at right angles to one another.

The idea is that by rotating the axes, the way that the variables are projected onto them changes. And if the rotation is managed properly, the variables' projections are either close to the axes' origin (giving a small loading) or far from the origin (giving a large loading).

All this usually seems confusing at first read—or second or third—and a look at how it works in two dimensions can help to clarify matters.

In Figure 12.1, the vertical and horizontal axes represent two principal components that have been extracted from a data set. Because principal components are extracted in a way that ensures they are orthogonal, the components are at right angles to one another, just as you are accustomed to seeing in an Excel line or scatter chart.

Figure 12.1
The variable is located in the chart according to its projections on the two factors.

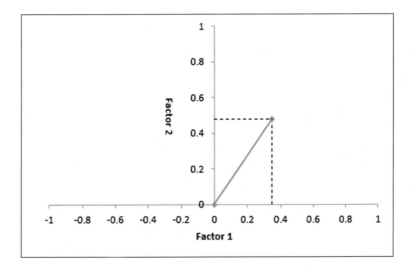

The variable that's charted in Figure 12.1 is represented by the diagonal vector—or more precisely, by the endpoint of that line. A vertical dashed line dropped from that endpoint to the horizontal axis represents the variable's projection on that axis. The point where the dashed line intersects the horizontal axis represents the variable's loading on the factor that the axis represents. In this case, the loading on that factor is 0.35. (Recall from Chapter 10 that the loading a variable has on a factor is the correlation of the variable with the factor; therefore, loadings can range from −1.0 to +1.0.)

Similarly, the variable loads at 0.48 on the other factor. That's where the horizontal dashed line intersects the vertical axis.

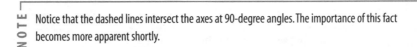

NOTE Notice that the dashed lines intersect the axes at 90-degree angles. The importance of this fact becomes more apparent shortly.

Neither of these loadings, 0.35 and 0.48, is especially useful. The variable doesn't bear a strong loading of, say, 0.80 or more on either component—that could make the variable helpful in identifying what the component represents. Neither loading is a weak one of, say,

0.20 or less, which would enable you to disregard the variable as you decide what the component is measuring.

In short, neither loading helps define the simple structure that we're aiming at, one in which a variable loads strongly on only one factor and in which the loadings on a given factor are either respectably strong or inconsequentially weak.

But what would happen if you rotated the axes, keeping the endpoint of the vector where it is in the plane that the original axes define? You might end up with something such as you see in Figure 12.2.

Figure 12.2
The variable's projections on the axes are very different from those in Figure 12.1.

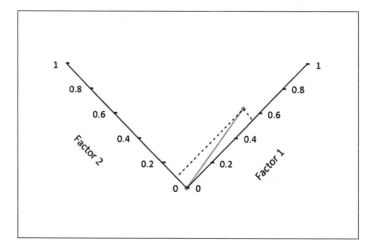

The dashed lines representing the projections, as well as the locations of the axes, have been redrawn in Figure 12.2. The axes have been rotated approximately 45 degrees from their original orientation, but the vector that represents the variable has not moved. The dashed lines still intersect the axes at 90-degree angles but because the axes have been rotated, the projections, *and therefore the loadings*, are different.

The projection on Factor 1 now intersects Factor 1's axis at about 0.55. The projection on Factor 2 intersects its axis at about 0.02. This is not an ideal outcome. You'd rather see a figure such as 0.85 instead of 0.55. But it's closer to the ideal simple structure than the one we had before rotating the axes, when the variable's loading on each factor was in the 0.3 to 0.5 range.

Why show the variable as a vector in the plane that's defined by the two axes? The variable's location is really a point, determined by the intersection of the two projections. When you draw a vector from the axes' origin to the intersection of the projections, the axis forms an angle with the vector: a fairly acute angle between the vector and the Factor 1 axis in Figure 12.2. And the logic that drives the rotation of the axes pays attention to the size of that angle.

The angle is sometimes referred to as *theta*. The cosine of theta times the length of the vector returns the point at which the projection intersects Factor 1: that is, the loading on the rotated Factor 1 axis. And the sine of theta times the length of the vector returns the loading on the rotated Factor 2 axis.

It's actually a good bit more complicated than the very simple situation I've depicted in Figures 12.1 and 12.2. But it's difficult to visualize what's going on when you add more axes and variables to the analysis, particularly in a two-dimensional medium such as a page in a book. And even an oversimplified diagram is helpful in visualizing what's going on with the arcane and mysterious sounding "Varimax factor rotation."

Why do you need to rotate the components/factors at all? Why not stick with the components as they are extracted by PCA? The reason is that the two tasks, component extraction and factor interpretation, are guided by different criteria. In PCA, which extracts the initial principal components, the idea is to assign as much variance in the entire data set as possible to each sequential component, and to keep those components orthogonal to one another. The location and direction of the components, in the space occupied by the variables, are guided by the goal of assigning as much variance as possible to the current component, subject to a few additional criteria that are mentioned in Chapter 10.

After those components are extracted, we want to simplify the way that the variables load on the components, subject (in the case of Varimax rotation) to the conditions that

- The factors remain orthogonal when they are rotated.
- The total assigned variance of each original variable is maintained. The pattern of the variance distribution across the variables that load on the factors can change—in fact, it must change if the rotation is to have any meaning at all. But the total assigned variance remains unchanged for each variable.

Extraction and Rotation: An Example

This section uses real-world data to illustrate how extracting principal components and then rotating them to a Varimax solution can uncover structure that may underlie observable variables. The example looks at how states in different regions of the United States exhibit similar crime patterns.

The data set comes from the 1972 edition of the *Statistical Abstract of the United States*, which reports crime rates (number of crimes per 100,000 population) in each of the 50 states for 1970 and 1971. The crimes are classified according to seven categories: murder, rape, robbery, assault, burglary, larceny, and auto theft. The report also classifies the states into several regions: New England, Middle Atlantic, East North Central, West North Central, South Atlantic, East South Central, West South Central, Mountain, and Pacific.

Figure 12.3 shows a portion of the data, just to give you an idea of what it looks like. The full data set is available in the Excel workbook for this chapter, which you can download from the publisher's website, www.quepublishing.com/title/9780789758354.

The process begins by putting the crime rates through a PCA routine that calculates principal components.

Figure 12.3
Number of crimes per
100,000 population, 1970.

	A	B	C	D	E	F	G	H	I
1	Murder	Rape	Robbery	Assault	Burglary	Larceny	Auto Theft	State	Region
2	1.5	7	12.6	62	562	1055	146	ME	NE
3	2	6	12.1	36	566	929	172	NH	NE
4	1.3	10.3	7.6	55	731	969	124	VT	NE
5	3.5	12	99.5	88	1134	1531	878	MA	NE
6	3.2	3.6	78.3	120	1019	2186	859	RI	NE
7	3.5	9.1	70.4	87	1084	1751	484	CT	NE
8	7.9	15.5	443.3	209	1414	2025	682	NY	MA
9	5.7	12.9	169.4	90	1041	1689	557	NJ	MA
10	5.3	11.3	106	90	594	1001	340	PA	MA
11	6.6	16	145.9	116	854	1944	493	OH	ENC
12	4.8	17.9	107.5	95	860	1791	429	IN	ENC
13	9.6	20.4	251.1	187	765	2028	518	IL	ENC
14	9.4	27.1	346.6	193	1571	2897	464	MI	ENC

As discussed in Chapter 10, PCA looks for components (also termed *factors* in factor analysis) that underlie the patterns of correlations among variables such as rates for different types of crimes. It can be more straightforward to examine two or three components than 7 to 10 original variables. Furthermore, the original variables might combine in ways that clarify what's going on in the data.

The data was processed using the Factor.xlsm workbook, also available from the publisher's website for this book. That workbook extracts principal components and rotates them using Varimax.

> **NOTE**   Alternatively, the user can choose Quartimax rotation. The Quartimax method is rarely used. It simplifies the rows of the factor structure matrix so that each variable has high loadings on as few factors as possible. (Varimax takes a different tack and simplifies the columns of the matrix so that each factor has some large loadings and some very small loadings.) The Factor.xlsm workbook supports Quartimax so you can compare the outcomes of the two rotation methods.

Figure 12.4 shows a portion of the results.

As I mentioned, one of your goals in PCA is to reduce the number of variables that you have to work with. Ideally, you'd like to gain more in simplicity by reducing the number of factors than you lose in information by ignoring some factors.

In PCA there are several different approaches to deciding how many components to retain, including significance tests, scree tests, cross-validation, and size of eigenvalues. (Eigenvalues are a measure of the amount of variability in the original data set that is attributable to each component that PCA extracts.)

In this case, I used Kaiser's recommendation that only components with eigenvalues greater than 1.0 should be retained—and here that criterion means that only Factor 1 and Factor 2 should be kept. Figure 12.4 shows that only Factor 1 and Factor 2 have eigenvalues greater than 1.0.

Figure 12.4
Two principal components emerged from the initial analysis.

⧄	A	B	C	D	E	F	G	H
1	**Eigenvalues**							
2		Factor 1	Factor 2	Factor 3	Factor 4	Factor 5	Factor 6	Factor 7
3		4.077	1.432	0.631	0.34	0.248	0.14	0.132
4								
5	**Factor Score Coefficients**							
6		Factor 1	Factor 2	Factor 3	Factor 4	Factor 5	Factor 6	Factor 7
7	Murder	0.137	0.539	0.012	0.564	0.407	0.268	1.625
8	Rape	0.209	0.097	0.453	-0.507	-1.523	-0.174	0.294
9	Robbery	0.192	-0.038	-0.76	-1.106	0.38	0.185	0.442
10	Assault	0.192	0.381	-0.014	0.115	0.273	0.269	-2.145
11	Burglary	0.216	-0.215	0.196	0.246	0.585	-2.095	0.074
12	Larceny	0.178	-0.335	0.64	-0.082	0.722	1.501	0.189
13	Auto Theft	0.175	-0.306	-0.594	1.03	-0.677	0.556	-0.033

CAUTION

Kaiser offers both technical and logical reasons for his recommendation. Among the logical reasons is this one: Because we are using PCA to allocate variance that variables have in common, a component should account for more variance than any single variable does. Because the total of the eigenvalues equals the number of variables, an eigenvalue of 1.0 or greater meets this criterion. It's a rule of thumb, not a sophisticated technical criterion (of which there are several). But it's sensible, and unlike some approaches, such as the scree test, it's objective.

Another approach to the problem of determining the number of components to retain is termed *parallel analysis*. Under this approach, which is a sort of Monte Carlo simulation, the eigenvalues derived from the actual sample are compared to (and sometimes adjusted for) eigenvalues derived from a sample of random numbers. These random numbers then constitute a sample with the same number of cases and uncorrelated variables as the actual data set.

R provides several functions that perform parallel analysis, such as the *paran* package.

The arguments adduced in favor of parallel analysis have persuaded plenty of theorists who specialize in multivariate analysis. Alas, I am not among them. Most statisticians regard Kaiser's criterion as a rule of thumb—one that can certainly be bent—and I'm among them, thanks be. I try to bear in mind that Kaiser was writing about principal components analysis, which places unities (rather than SMCs, as is usually done in common factor analysis) in the main diagonal of the correlation matrix, and that makes a difference. But I still prefer to rely on this advice from one of the most important books in the history of principal components analysis:

"[We] display the distribution of residual correlations following Kaiser's rule. If we feel that we want a tighter fit to the data we then specify a larger [number of components to retain] and recompute the residuals. The solution that makes us happiest usually has to be found by trial." (Cooley, W.W. and Lohnes, P.R. *Multivariate Data Analysis*. New York: Wiley, 1971.)

12

The Factor Score Coefficients in Figure 12.4 are used to convert records' values on the original variables to factor scores. There are actually a couple of steps (which are done on your behalf by Factor.xlsm):

1. Convert each record's values to z-scores. Subtract the variable's mean value from each record's actual value, and divide the result by the standard deviation for the variable. Treat the records as a population: that is, use STDEV.P( ) instead of STDEV.S( ) or, prior to Excel 2010, use STDEVP( ) instead of STDEV( ).

2. Multiply the z-scores by the factor score coefficients and total the results.

Here's how it works out for the state of Maine in 1970. Maine's original values on the seven crime rate variables are as follows:

1.5　　7　　12.6　　62　　562　　1055　　146

Maine's z-scores—the original values less the average for each variable, divided by the variable's standard deviation:

−1.4065　　−1.1844　　−0.9848　　−1.0879　　−1.0318　　−1.2646　　−1.1227

The factor score coefficients for the first factor, from Figure 12.4 (in Figure 12.4, they are shown in a column but have been transposed here to occupy a row):

0.137　　0.209　·　0.192　　0.192　　0.216　　0.178　　0.175

Now multiply the z-scores by the factor score coefficients and total the results:

0.137 * −1.4065 + 0.209 * −1.1844 +.....+ 0.175 * −1.1227 = −1.483

So Maine has a value of −1.483 on the first factor. I know this looks like a lot of work, but again, the workbook does it for you. It calculates the factor scores for each record, on each factor, if you give it individual records to work with. (You can supply a rectangular correlation matrix instead, but in that case you won't get individual factor scores.) I went through the arithmetic here just so you could see how it takes place.

Figure 12.5 shows the factor scores for each state on the first two factors: the ones that were kept because both their eigenvalues were greater than 1.0.

Again, Figure 12.5 shows just a partial list. The full set of state scores is in the workbook Chapter 12.xlsx.

Now you're in a position to chart these two "new" variables. (I put new in quote marks because these factors aren't really new. The theory behind PCA and factor analysis suggests that they were there all the time, not directly measurable, and simply got expressed as variables that can be counted or otherwise measured, such as the number of burglaries per 100,000 population.)

Figure 12.6 shows the chart.

Figure 12.5
You can treat the components, aka factors, just like variables. They are simply weighted combinations of the original variables.

	A	B	C	D
1	State	Region	Factor 1	Factor 2
2	ME	NE	-1.483	-0.261
3	NH	NE	-1.575	-0.333
4	VT	NE	-1.365	-0.309
5	MA	NE	0.107	-1.506
6	RI	NE	-0.019	-1.684
7	CT	NE	-0.365	-1.002
8	NY	MA	1.562	-0.4
9	NJ	MA	0.065	-0.723
10	PA	MA	-0.767	0.159
11	OH	ENC	0.105	-0.308
12	IN	ENC	-0.138	-0.471
13	IL	ENC	0.755	0.506
14	MI	ENC	1.82	-0.254

Figure 12.6
The way the components are derived means that they aren't correlated.

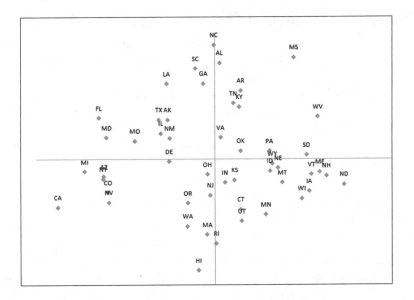

The chart has two dimensions, each corresponding to one of the factors that were extracted. The way that the states are distributed in the chart is tantalizing. Notice that states in the south and southeast regions of the United States *tend to* locate toward the top of the vertical axis (North and South Carolina, Alabama, Georgia, Louisiana, Mississippi, Tennessee, Texas, Arkansas). States in the western regions *tend to* locate toward the left, lower end of the horizontal axis (California, Arizona, Colorado, Nevada). There are two problems, though:

■ These are just tendencies. The definitely or moderately Eastern states—New York, Michigan, Maryland and Florida, for example—also show up to the left end of the horizontal axis.

■ We don't yet know what the dimensions—that is, the factors or components—represent. We should be able to figure that out from how the original variables load on the factors, but a little more manipulation is likely to help.

That manipulation comes in the form of what's called *rotation*. We want to take the two perpendicular axes in the figure and rotate them in a way that clarifies the loadings. In doing so, we want to keep the axes perpendicular to one another. We also want to leave the plots of the variables where they are now—that is, rotate the axes and leave the variables in place.

> **NOTE**   I discuss that rotation and its interpretation shortly. In addition to extracting the components as discussed in Chapter 10 and in this chapter, the Factor.xlsm workbook does the rotation for you.

Structure of Principal Components and Factors

In this case and many others, a problem remains after you've taken the initial step of extracting the principal components. If you look at how the individual variables are related to the two components, it's often unclear what those components represent. That's the case in this example, as shown in Figure 12.7. One characteristic of principal components analysis is that most of the variables tend to have moderate to strong loadings (which are in fact correlations) on the first factor. That's not surprising, because principal components analysis works by extracting as much variance from the measured variables as possible, assigning that variance to the first component. Only the leftover variance is available for the second, third, and subsequent components.

Figure 12.7 shows the sort of structure we obtain from the principal components extraction, in the range C5:D11.

Loadings is just another term for the correlations between the measured variables and the components or factors. Notice in Figure 12.7, cells C5:D11, that the first extracted component has strong loadings with six of the seven variables; only the Murder variable has a strong loading on the second factor. If we stopped here, we might well conclude that the two underlying factors are something like "Everything Except Murder" and "Murder." Not a very illuminating conclusion.

Figure 12.7
Original and rotated factor loadings for the U.S. crime rate data set.

A	B	C	D	E	F
2	**Original Components**				
3					**Sums of**
4		**Factor 1**	**Factor 2**		**Squares**
5	Murder	0.557478	0.771127		0.90542
6	Rape	0.850781	0.139177		0.74320
7	Robbery	0.782319	-0.05499		0.61505
8	Assault	0.78359	0.545901		0.91202
9	Burglary	0.881051	-0.30769		0.87092
10	Larceny	0.727605	-0.47966		0.75948
11	Auto Theft	0.71447	-0.43801		0.70232
12					
13	**Rotated Components**				
14					**Sums of**
15		**Factor 1**	**Factor 2**		**Squares**
16	Murder	-0.01467	0.951422		0.90542
17	Rape	0.598439	0.62054		0.74320
18	Robbery	0.659751	0.423999		0.61505
19	Assault	0.301258	0.906237		0.91202
20	Burglary	0.890052	0.28059		0.87092
21	Larceny	0.869991	0.050985		0.75948
22	Auto Theft	0.834549	0.076498		0.70232

> **NOTE**
> By the way, those original, unrotated factors are responsible for the chart in Figure 12.6—tantalizing but uncertain results.

Now notice the pattern of *rotated* loadings in the lower half of Figure 12.7, shown in the worksheet range C16:D22. Burglary, Larceny, and Auto Theft (and perhaps Robbery) load fairly strongly on Factor 1; Murder and Assault load strongly on Factor 2. Rape has a moderately strong loading on both Factor 1 and Factor 2. Despite the ambiguity of the loadings for Rape, it seems fairly clear that Factor 1 can be thought of as a Property Crimes factor, and Factor 2 can be thought of as a Personal Crimes factor. That structure is cleaner and clearer than the structure we get from the original principal components, in cells C5:D11.

Rotating Factors: The Results

How do we get from the original component loadings to the set of rotated factor loadings? The original components are derived in a way that prevents them from sharing variance. Remember that the first component gets all the variance that's available to it, the second component gets all the *remaining* variance that's available to it, and so on with subsequent components. This approach ensures that components have no shared variance, and therefore they are uncorrelated with one another.

A consequence of this approach is that the components are what factor analysts call orthogonal: Plotted on a two-dimensional chart, the components represent axes that are at right angles to each other, as shown in Figures 12.1 and 12.2.

Here's another way to think of this aspect of principal components. Suppose that you calculate scores on two (or more) factors for each record, as shown in this chapter's section titled "Extraction and Rotation: An Example." If you now correlate individuals' scores on Factor 1 with their scores on Factor 2, the correlation would be 0.0 (see Figure 12.8). The factors represent underlying concepts that, at least in the measured data sample, have nothing to do with one another.

> **NOTE** The Factor.xlsm workbook calculates and reports both the coefficients that you can use to obtain factor scores, and the resulting factor scores themselves. To assure yourself that the factors are uncorrelated, open the workbook and run its code on a sample data set. Then use Excel's CORREL( ) function as shown in Figure 12.8 to calculate the correlation between any two resulting sets of factor scores.

Figure 12.8
You get the same 0.0 correlation with both original and rotated components.

	A	B	C	D	E	F	G
					=CORREL(B2:B51,C2:C51)		
1	State	Property	Person		Correlation:		
2	ME	-1.03232	-1.09631		0.000000		
3	NH	-1.06329	-1.20923				
4	VT	-0.90915	-1.06444				
5	MA	0.986395	-1.14238				
6	RI	0.992521	-1.36068				
7	CT	0.307389	-1.02141				
8	NY	1.49036	0.614116				
9	NJ	0.484938	-0.54054				
10	PA	-0.70973	-0.33204				
11	OH	0.26859	-0.18348				
12	IN	0.17098	-0.4598				
13	IL	0.301862	0.857466				
14	MI	1.610667	0.885178				
15	WI	-0.51291	-1.36394				

Another consequence of the way in which the principal components are extracted is that each variable (here, Murder, Assault, and so on) has the highest correlation possible with each component. In fact, the loadings in Figure 12.7—as I've mentioned, they're actually correlations—are measures of the distance between the variables and the components. The higher the loading, the closer the component comes to the variable. The result is relatively high loadings for most or all of the variables on the first component, which in turn makes it difficult to interpret the meaning of that component and any components that are subsequently extracted.

After the component extraction is complete, the components are rotated around the measured variables, which remain in place. This often makes it possible to get a more interpretable pattern of loadings on the components. (At this point in the process, we tend to start referring to *factors* instead of *components*.) Some variables would be closer to the rotated factors, and some would be farther away, creating a clearer, less ambiguous pattern of loadings.

One rule of simple structure as implemented by the Varimax rotation is that the components must remain orthogonal to each other. They start out at right angles to one another, and using Varimax they maintain that orientation while rotating.

It's a real simplification, but you might think of two orthogonal factors as two spokes in a bicycle wheel, at right angles to one another. As you steer the bicycle, the wheel turns right and left, and it also tilts right and left as you lean one way or another, and of course the spokes rotate as the wheel spins. Those turns and tilts and spins rotate the wheel with respect to its stationary surroundings, but the spokes maintain their original orientation to one another. Similarly, the orthogonal rotation process in factor analysis maintains the relationships between the factors as it adjusts the factors' relationships to the stationary variables.

Another rule that governs the Varimax rotation of the factors is that the variables' total *communalities* must not change. A variable's communality with respect to a given factor is the square of the variable's loading on that factor. Because the loadings are correlations, the squares of the loadings are percentages of variance.

If you extract and rotate as many factors as there are variables, then a variable's total communality is 1.0, because the factors account collectively for 100% of a variable's variance. If you don't extract and rotate as many factors as there are variables, the extracted factors will account for only a portion of the available variance, but that portion is generally quite high.

Look again at the worksheet shown in Figure 12.7 and repeated here, with two additional rows, as Figure 12.9. The sum of the squared loadings for each variable appears in column F. The sum of the squared loadings for each factor appear in rows 12 and 24. (Keep in mind that the loadings are correlations, and therefore their squares represent percentages of shared variance.)

For example, 90.542% of the variance in the Murder variable is accounted for by Factors 1 and 2, regardless of whether the factors are original components (cell F5) or rotated factors (cell F16). What differs is the way that 90.542% is allocated across the two factors. The rotated loadings make possible a Property Crimes versus Personal Crimes interpretation, but the amount of explained variance in all seven variables remains the same as with the original, unrotated components.

12

Figure 12.9
Rotation adjusts the loadings and often clarifies the meanings of the factors.

| | | C24 | | ▼ | ⋮ | ✕ | ✓ | f_x | =SUMSQ(C17:C23) |

	A	B	C	D	E	F	G
2		Original Components					
3						Sums of	
4			Factor 1	Factor 2		Squares	
5		Murder	0.557478	0.771127		0.90542	
6		Rape	0.850781	0.139177		0.74320	
7		Robbery	0.782319	-0.05499		0.61505	
8		Assault	0.78359	0.545901		0.91202	
9		Burglary	0.881051	-0.30769		0.87092	
10		Larceny	0.727605	-0.47966		0.75948	
11		Auto Theft	0.71447	-0.43801		0.70232	
12		Sums of Squares	4.076776	1.431642		5.50842	
13							
14		Rotated Components					
15						Sums of	
16			Factor 1	Factor 2		Squares	
17		Murder	-0.01467	0.951422		0.90542	
18		Rape	0.598439	0.62054		0.74320	
19		Robbery	0.659751	0.423999		0.61505	
20		Assault	0.301258	0.906237		0.91202	
21		Burglary	0.890052	0.28059		0.87092	
22		Larceny	0.869991	0.050985		0.75948	
23		Auto Theft	0.834549	0.076498		0.70232	
24		Sums of Squares	3.129921	2.378496		5.50842	

Another way to view the same effect is to compare row 12 with row 24. These rows total the loadings of each variable on Factor 1 and Factor 2. The factor totals for the unrotated factors in cells C12:D12 differ from the totals for the rotated factors in C24:D24. Those differences are due to the Varimax rotation of the factors, and the resulting change in the loadings of the individual variables.

But the total variance explained by the two factors remains unchanged by the rotation: Compare the totals in cells F12 and F24.

In sum, the Varimax rotation doesn't alter the uncorrelated nature of the factors, the total amount of variance explained by the factors, or the individual variables' total communality. The rotation does alter the loadings of the individual variables on the factors, often with the result that the interpretation of the factors' meanings is made more straightforward.

Charting Records on Rotated Factors

What happens when you chart the states on the *rotated* components? The scatter chart in Figure 12.10 shows where each state falls on the Property Crimes factor and the Personal Crimes factor.

The chart in Figure 12.10 locates the states more clearly than does the chart of the unrotated components in Figure 12.6. In Figure 12.10, the states are better aligned regionally along the two factors identified as representing two different types of crimes: Property Crimes and Personal Crimes.

Figure 12.10
The directions of the axes have been reversed, to put higher x-axis scores on the left and higher y-axis scores at the bottom.

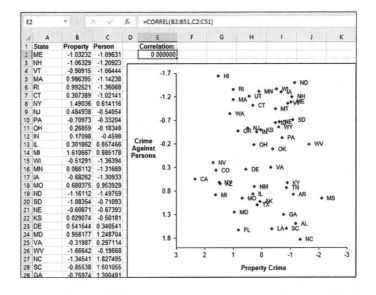

NOTE

Notice that the order of the values on the axes in Figure 12.10 has been reversed, vis-à-vis Figure 12.6. This change puts states with higher Property Crimes scores on the left and states with lower Personal Crimes scores at the top. The pattern of factor scores in the states therefore tends to put western states on the left and northern states at the top.

The tendencies I noted in the chart in Figure 12.6 are more pronounced in Figure 12.10 because the rotation of the axes altered the pattern of loadings on the factors.

These trends are now apparent:

■ Western states (CA, NV, AZ, CO, HI) have high scores on the Property Crimes factor.

■ Eastern states (WV, MS, NC, NH, ME) have low scores on the Property Crimes factor.

■ Southern states (TX, GA, FL, LA, SC, NC) have high scores on the Personal Crimes factor.

■ Northern states (ND, RI, MN, MA, VT) have low scores on the Personal Crimes factor.

NOTE

The designation of some states as, say, Eastern or Southern is somewhat arbitrary. A state such as North Carolina can legitimately be thought of as either an Eastern or a Southern state.

In sum, you probably suspected from the start that the raw crime rate data would define two factors: Property Crimes and Personal Crimes. But only by extracting the components and rotating them to clarify the loadings can you score the states on those factors—and find that the regions of the U.S. cluster accordingly.

Still in Figure 12.10, notice that the correlation of states' scores on the two factors confirms that the rotation leaves the factors uncorrelated: The CORREL( ) function in cell E2 returns a correlation of 0.0.

Using the Factor Workbook to Rotate Components

Chapter 10 discusses the use of the Factor workbook to extract principal components and to obtain data such as the factor structure and factor coefficients. I review that information briefly here and also discuss a couple of controls that pertain to starting with raw data (instead of with a correlation matrix) and rotating the initial component solution.

Begin by opening the workbook named Factor.xlsm, which is available for download from the publisher's website, www.quepublishing.com/title/9780789758354. Factor.xlsm works with Excel 2007 through 2016.

If you open Factor.xlsm with Excel 2007 or a more recent version, the Ribbon's Add-Ins tab gets a Principal Components item. It remains there even after you close Factor.xlsm, and will remain there until you delete the custom command (for example, right-click the command and choose Delete Custom Command from the shortcut menu). Factor.xlsm is not a true add-in: You can tell that because its extension is neither .xla nor .xlam. Nevertheless, Excel locates it in the Ribbon's Add-Ins tab.

To extract principal components from a raw data list or a correlation matrix, follow these steps *after* opening Factor.xlsm:

1. Open the workbook and activate the worksheet that contains your data.
2. Click the Principal Components command in the Ribbon's Add-Ins tab. The dialog box shown in Figure 12.11 appears.
3. As described in Chapter 10, use the Input Range box to specify the worksheet range that contains your data. If you have variable labels as headers at the top of each column and want them to be used in the output, include them in the range address.
4. Fill the Variable Labels in First Row checkbox if you included column headers in Step 3.
5. If you have record identifiers, such as people's names or state abbreviations, click in the Record IDs box and drag through the worksheet range that contains those IDs. If your worksheet contains a header row for the record IDs, omit it from the address in the Record IDs edit box.
6. Choose either Raw Data if you have a list that includes individual observations, or Correlation Matrix if you have a square correlation matrix to use as input.
7. If you're using a correlation matrix as input, enter the number of records on which the correlations are based.
8. Click the Rotation tab. The dialog box switches to the display shown in Figure 12.12.
9. Choose either Varimax or Quartimax rotation. For most real-world situations you're going to want to use Varimax.
10. Specify the number of factors to retain, and click OK to start processing.

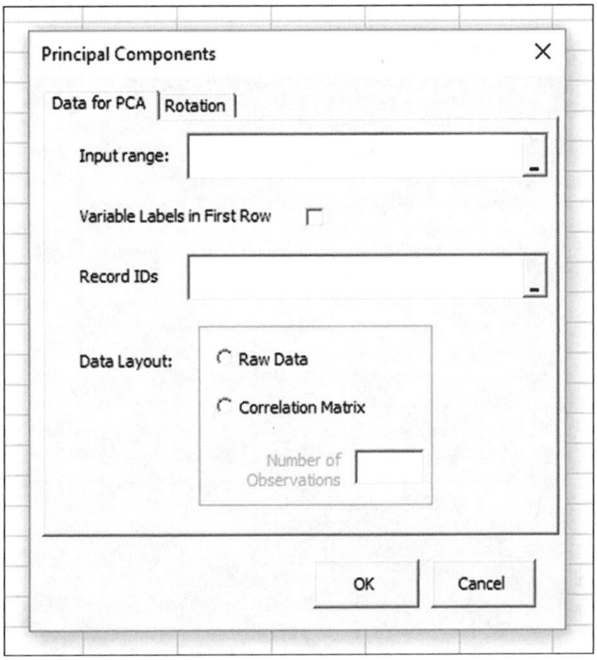

Figure 12.11
The Record IDs box is useful only if your data is in a list that includes unique record identifiers, such as names.

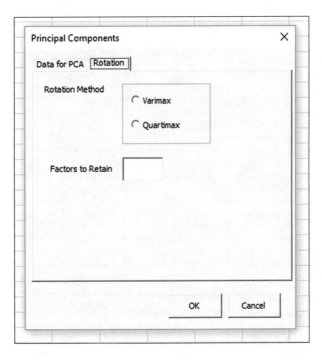

Figure 12.12
Quartimax is seldom used for factor analysis. It's provided here so that you can compare its results with those of Varimax.

12

To decide how many factors to retain in Step 10, you'll probably need to have seen the results of the principal components extraction already.

Index

A